CRIMINAL PRETRIAL ADVOCACY

CRIMINAL PRETRIAL ADVOCACY

TERRY ADAMSON

Distinguished Jurist in Residence
Trial Advocacy Team Coach
Pepperdine University School of Law
Malibu Superior Court Commissioner (retired)

H. MITCHELL CALDWELL

Professor of Law
Head Trial Advocacy Team Coach
Pepperdine University School of Law

VANDEPLAS PUBLISHING, LLC
UNITED STATES OF AMERICA

Criminal Pretrial Advocacy
First Edition 2013

Adamson, Terry and Caldwell, H. Mitchell

Published by:

Vandeplas Publishing, LLC – March 2013

801 International Parkway, 5th Floor
Lake Mary, FL. 32746
USA

www.vandeplaspublishing.com

ISBN 978-1-60042-188-4

Dedications

To my loving husband, Grant and my devoted daughters, Lauren and Megan.

- Terry Adamson

To my wonderful loving wife who is always there for me.

- H. Mitchell Caldwell

Acknowledgments

The authors gratefully acknowledge the generous support they have received from Pepperdine University School of Law in the production of this book and to the talented, dedicated students who worked enthusiastically as research assistants: Gor Arevian, Tiffany Bacon, Michael Boyd, Richard Rodriguez Campbell, Rebecca Charlesworth, Skye Daley, Kelly Everett, Anthony Greco, Brittany Henry, Adrienne Hewitt, Lukian Kobzeff, Rick Loesing, Shane Michael, Vincent Santos, Elizabeth Sutlian, Gabriella Tokatlian, Matthew Troncali, Brittany Vannoy, Sarah Wild, and Arsineh Zargarian. We thank Dean Deanell Tacha, Vice Dean Richard Cupp, and former Dean Kenneth Starr for their support and mentoring. A special thanks to the exceptionally dedicated RA Editor–In–Chief, Arsineh Zargarian and RA Managing Editor, Gor Arevian. These two research assistants went above and beyond our expectations as they diligently assisted in the research, editing, coordination, and graphic arts of the entire manuscript.

Special thanks to Los Angeles Deputy District Attorney Shane Michael for superb assistant editing. We gratefully appreciate the dedication and talent of RA Chief Cite Editor Lukian Kobzeff and Assistant Cite Editors Tiffany Bacon and Rick Loesing for their meticulous research and cite checking. We are indebted for the graphics to: Alison Rash, who illustrated all the comics in the book, Kelly Everett who illustrated all the symbols in the book, as well as Vincent Santos and Anthony Greco, who contributed significantly to the book's graphics, and especially to Gor Arevian, who is responsible for the vast majority of the book's graphics, for the book's cover art, and for formatting the entire manuscript.

We also thank Candace Warren, for tirelessly helping to prepare the manuscript, as well as RA and copy editor Lauren Adamson for dedicated proofreading. We are indebted to the following talented and highly respected criminal defense attorneys for their insights and editing: Steve Cron, Jon Bryant Artz, David Ogden, and Phillip Dunn. We thank Deputy District Attorney Mara McIlvain, Honorable Judge Laura Foland Priver, and Pepperdine Law Professor Naomi Goodno for their consulting and significant editing contributions. Thanks to Los Angeles District Attorney (Retired), Steve Cooley for his contributions, including the book's foreword. Finally, we thank our talented interns for diligent proofreading and editing: Ames Smith, Harry Glass, and Rosie Stutsman.

FOREWORD

There is no short cut to achievement. Life requires thorough preparation - veneer isn't worth anything.
—George Washington Carver

As the elected District Attorney of Los Angeles County for 12 years I have hired over 400 new prosecutors. Successful trial lawyers must possess qualities that are difficult to teach: presence, improvisation and the ability to communicate effectively with all audiences. Those abilities will not carry the day without education, training and **preparation**.

Criminal Pretrial Advocacy is a thorough, practical and accessible guide for criminal trial preparation. Terry Adamson and H. Mitchell Caldwell's career work has uniquely qualified them to write on this very important topic. Both began their careers as criminal prosecutors. Caldwell is now a highly regarded professor at Pepperdine University School of Law teaching core criminal procedure and advocacy courses. Professor Caldwell is also an active appellate lawyer and has been published extensively on numerous topics related to the practice of criminal law. Ms. Adamson left the Los Angeles County District Attorney's Office to become a Superior Court Commissioner and, later, esteemed law professor at Pepperdine. Professors Adamson and Caldwell bear down with great insight on the fundamentals of "real time" criminal justice. *Criminal Pretrial Advocacy* is a great resource for criminal law practitioners at all levels and those who aspire for a career in criminal trial advocacy.

Honorable Steve Cooley

Los Angeles County District Attorney 2000-2012

TABLE OF CONTENTS

PURPOSE AND COURSE OVERVIEW

"Opportunity is missed by most people because it comes dressed in overalls and looks like work."
–Thomas Edison

Over ninety percent of criminal cases reach a disposition before trial. Accordingly, criminal litigation largely consists of preparing cases for trial and settling them. *Criminal Pretrial Advocacy* provides students and beginning trial attorneys with the tools needed for trial preparation. Of course, should a case proceed to trial, the prepared advocate will be in a much better position to prevail. Preparation instills confidence and places litigators in a better position to achieve a positive settlement or trial result. As the legendary trial lawyer Gerry Spence puts it, "Ah, preparation! There is where the magic begins."[1]

Criminal Pretrial Advocacy provides the tools to enable lawyers to confidently and successfully prepare for criminal trials. This text explores the foundations of criminal pretrial advocacy: developing a persuasive case theory, filing criminal charges, arraignment and bail, interviewing witnesses and clients, proper discovery procedure, preliminary and grand jury hearings, pretrial motions, case settlements, and special pretrial considerations. This text also satisfies the need for a book that deals exclusively with criminal pretrial advocacy, especially one that emphasizes the practical rather than theoretical aspects of the law. As such, each chapter includes a discussion of strategy and ethics pertinent to its central topic.

This book can be used on its own for pretrial advocacy classes and as a reference for beginning trial lawyers. It will be most effective, however, when used in conjunction with the mock trial companion book, *Criminal Mock Trials*. The companion book presents a comprehensive set of case files with a variety of pretrial and trial issues for students to explore. Together these books present a series of criminal practice cases, strategies, hypothetical cases, examples from actual cases, checklists, and ethical considerations. The mock trial book will provide students and lawyers with the opportunity to prepare hypothetical cases, from filing charges through negotiating settlements. The stimulating pretrial advocacy and ethical issues will facilitate provocative discourse.

Criminal Mock Trials is designed for groups of four students per case file, consisting of two prosecutors and two defense counselors. From the facts presented in each mock trial, student prosecutors will choose what charges to file; students for the defense will decide how to respond to the charges against their client while developing their case theory. Subsequently, the students will engage in written and oral advocacy by conducting bail review hearings, arguing motions, and presenting their case for a preliminary hearing. The eight mock trials in *Criminal Mock Trials* present complex and realistic pretrial concerns. These mock trials provide a tangible opportunity to apply the lessons taught in this book.

While exploring this text and performing the oral exercises and mock hearings provided in these books, students and beginning litigators should begin to develop the skills to prepare for successful criminal advocacy. Although inherent talent is an element of effective litigation, much of the foundation for becoming a successful trial attorney comes from practice. *Criminal Pretrial Advocacy* will help law students and inexperienced criminal lawyers hone their skills, better enabling them to anticipate and

---

[1] GERRY SPENCE, HOW TO ARGUE AND WIN EVERY TIME 128 (1996).

resolve a wide range of criminal pretrial advocacy problems. With the analytical tools this text provides, students and beginning litigators should not only expect to firmly grasp pretrial procedures, but should also feel comfortable preparing a case for trial and litigating it each step of the way.

Pretrial advocacy is much more than submitting form motions. Effective pretrial preparation is the foundation to successful litigation and the key to obtaining favorable case settlements. It is crucial for attorneys to prepare their cases thoroughly and creatively before the first motion is ever submitted.

An advocate's triumphs in criminal law are the result of meticulous planning in the pretrial stages. Stellar pretrial advocacy requires strategic planning and diligent work. The ultimate goal is a favorable settlement or winning verdict. *Criminal Pretrial Advocacy* will provide students and beginning attorneys with the tools needed to achieve this goal.

The following are symbols that you will see throughout this text. The symbols are meant to assist you in identifying significant or helpful parts of the text that should supplement your learning.

TEXT SYMBOLS KEY

CHAPTER 1
WELCOME TO PRETRIAL ADVOCACY

"If I had eight hours to chop down a tree, I'd spend six sharpening my axe."
–Abraham Lincoln

The drama of a criminal trial plays out in the courtroom, where the opening statements, witnesses, and closing arguments are much like the scenes central to a stage play. But the reality is that few cases play out before a jury, and the vast majority of criminal cases are resolved without the benefit of trial. Consequently, the nuts and bolts of effective pretrial preparation will most often lead to a successful disposition or, should the case go to trial, to a strong foundation for trial. Developing a case theory, interviewing witnesses, completing the procedural requirements of discovery, filing motions with the court, conducting pretrial hearings, and complying with the court's procedural rules are the necessary elements of trial preparation and settlement.

Because any attorney's time is a limited commodity as well as a valuable resource, it is imperative to be efficient. To help lawyers work as efficiently as possible during the pretrial phase of a case, this text lays out a systematic process for trial preparation through clearly defined stages as well as detailing essential ethical and procedural requirements and strategy insights. Advocates following these steps will gain the confidence of a seasoned attorney whose axe is always sharpened and ready for trial.

THE ROLE OF THE ADVOCATE

The American criminal justice system is, first of all, an adversarial system, and furthermore, a system that considers factual guilt but requires *legal* guilt for conviction. Factual guilt addresses the question of whether the defendant actually committed the crime with which he is charged. Legal guilt addresses the question of whether the defendant is considered guilty under the law, a conclusion that requires the prosecution to prove each element of the crime beyond a reasonable doubt. Thus, acquittal does not necessarily signify innocence, but rather that the defendant is "not guilty" according to the law. According to case law and the ethical rules governing criminal trial practice, prosecutors and defense attorneys have distinct obligations and objectives when trying a criminal case.

A. ETHICAL OBLIGATIONS

Every attorney admitted to the bar is an officer of the court. As such, each has a duty to the justice system, to opposing counsel, and in the case of a defense attorney, to her client. Both prosecutors and defense attorneys alike are obligated to possess the legal knowledge and skill required for competent representation. Moreover, each must take care to be thoroughly prepared for every case. While preparation is a baseline requirement, different attorneys prepare to varying degrees, and it is the best prepared advocate who most often carries the day.

3

In addition to these requirements, the *Model Rules of Professional Conduct* impose stringent obligations on prosecutors and defense attorneys. Above all, the prosecutor's role is to seek justice on behalf of the people. Significantly, the authority of the prosecutor "does not arise from any right of the Government, but from power entrusted to the Government" by the people.[1] When a prosecutor "abuses this power and ignores ethical standards, he . . . not only undermines the public trust, but [also compromises the integrity of the justice system]. This alone compels the responsible and ethical exercise of [prosecutorial] power."[2] This great responsibility demands that a prosecutor file charges against an individual only if he believes that the defendant is both factually *and* legally guilty of the crime charged. The prosecutor has an ethical duty not to prosecute unless he believes it likely that a reasonable jury would convict the defendant of the charges against him. Specifically, the *Federal Rules of Criminal Procedure* provide a check on the power of the prosecutor to bring charges.[3]

Another component of the prosecutor's responsibility is to ensure a fair trial for the defendant. This includes turning over all exculpatory evidence to the defense during the discovery phase of the trial.[4] While the prosecutor should at all times be zealous and diligent in preparing and trying cases, he should never try to win at all costs. It is the duty of the prosecutor not to "persecute, but to prosecute, and . . . he should endeavor to protect the innocent as well as to prosecute the guilty."[5] As Supreme Court Justice George Sutherland wrote in 1935, a prosecutor should advocate with earnest vigor, "[b]ut, while he may strike hard blows, he is not at liberty to strike foul ones. It is as much his duty to refrain from improper methods calculated to produce a wrongful conviction as it is to use every legitimate means to bring about a just one."[6]

Conversely, the defense attorney's role is to advocate zealously for her client within the bounds of the ethical rules and the law. In light of this, a defense attorney's primary role is holding the government to its high burden to prove every element of its case beyond a reasonable doubt. This obligation is imposed on the defense by the Sixth Amendment to the U.S. Constitution, which affords every criminal defendant the right to effective assistance of counsel.[7] This assistance includes the duty of defense attorneys to investigate the circumstances of the case and to gather information.[8]

For many inexperienced defense attorneys, it may be difficult to embrace the idea of zealous advocacy when confronted with overwhelming evidence incriminating a defendant. Attorneys concerned with this ethical quandary might find consolation in Benjamin Franklin's oft-quoted maxim regarding the

---

[1] *In re* Doe, 801 F. Supp. 478, 480 (D.N.M. 1992) (emphasis omitted).

[2] *Id.*

[3] *See, e.g.,* FED. R. CRIM. P. 2.

[4] *See* MODEL RULES OF PROF'L CONDUCT R. 3.8 (2010); *see also* Brady v. Maryland, 373 U.S. 83 (1963).

[5] Bailey v. Commonwealth, 237 S.W. 415, 417 (Ky. 1922).

[6] Berger v. United States, 295 U.S. 78, 88 (1935).

[7] U.S. CONST. amend. VI.

[8] ABA STANDARDS FOR CRIMINAL JUSTICE PROSECUTION FUNCTION AND DEFENSE FUNCTION § 4-4.1(a) (3d ed. 1993).

criminal justice system: "it is better one hundred guilty Persons should escape than that one innocent Person should suffer."[9] As expected, defense cases are often not built upon a claim of innocence, but rather upon the government's failure to meet its burden of proof. Whether the defendant is factually guilty or innocent, a defense attorney's commitment to defend her client fervently should never waver. Since safeguards against unjust convictions are fundamental to our system of justice, defense attorneys are expected to serve as a check on the enormous power entrusted to the government.

It is not the defense attorney's role to judge whether her client committed the crime in question, and indeed, an attorney may never know whether her client is factually guilty. Sometimes a defendant will confess to a crime he did not commit, or he might insist on innocence in the face of clear evidence of guilt. Regardless, the defense attorney is not charged with the task of determining her client's culpability, but rather with the duty of providing competent, diligent representation as required under the *Model Rules of Professional Conduct* and guaranteed by the Constitution. In practice, much of a defense attorney's energy is expended trying to obtain a case settlement that is as favorable as possible for her client. Whether the case proceeds to trial or settles, the defense attorney must assign the highest priority to providing her client with competent representation.

By carrying out their ethical and professional obligations to their clients, defense lawyers also play an important role in protecting the integrity of democracy and the justice system. Attorneys who advocate for less savory clients, such as members of organizations with racist agendas or alleged serial murderers, still serve a necessary and vital role in the administration of justice as mandated by the Constitution. Every American is entitled to a fair trial before her individual rights may be compromised. Anything short of this would betray the Founders' enlightened vision of the American justice system.

On the other hand, while still zealously representing her client, a defense attorney must deal candidly with the court—and to that end, she may not call a witness, including the defendant, to testify if she has a reasonable certainty that the witness plans to commit perjury.[10] Attorneys must never, moreover, hide or destroy evidence. Ultimately, a criminal defense attorney "is under obligation to defend [his client] with all his skill and energy, but he also has moral and ethical obligations to the court[;] . . . [h]is obligation is to achieve a fair trial, not to see that his client is acquitted regardless of the merits."[11]

While prosecutors and defense attorneys fill dramatically different roles within the criminal justice system, together they aid the administration of justice. By strict obedience to the ethical standards of the *Model Rules*, advocates help create a just forum in which the drama of a criminal trial unfolds. Success comes not from manipulation of the jury, but from each advocate's careful preparation, effective presentation, and adherence to the ideals outlined in the Constitution. Truth and justice are not antiquated

---

[9] Benjamin Franklin, *Letter to Benjamin Vaughan, March 14, 1785*, *in* THE WRITINGS OF BENJAMIN FRANKLIN 291, 293 (Albert H. Smyth ed. 1992).

[10] MODEL RULES OF PROF'L CONDUCT R. 3.3 (2010).

[11] Mitchell v. United States, 259 F.2d 787, 792 (D.C. Cir. 1958).

notions of a bygone era; they are cornerstones of the American legal system, and both prosecution and defense counsel help ensure justice by espousing such ideals.

B. PRETRIAL PROCEDURE

Whether on the side of the prosecution or the defense, criminal attorneys can engage in competent representation only if they are well-versed in criminal procedure and the intricacies of the trial process. While this book focuses on criminal pretrial advocacy, rather than criminal procedure, a brief overview of the steps of pretrial procedure as a case moves through the criminal justice system is provided here. The aspects of criminal proceedings that involve advocacy, strategy, and ethics will be discussed in detail in the chapters that follow.

Most criminal trials typically begin with an arrest, which requires the arresting officer to have either a warrant or probable cause to believe the individual has committed a crime. After an arrest, a suspect is usually taken into custody and often interrogated; however, before any custodial interrogation, the defendant must be informed of his *Miranda* rights, including the right to remain silent and the right to counsel.[12] Once the right to counsel attaches, it is retained by the accused throughout the remainder of the adversarial process.

If the prosecutor files criminal charges, then he is ethically bound to file only those counts that he believes can be proved beyond a reasonable doubt. Even as early as this point, however, the criminal justice system provides a check on the prosecutor's power. The *Federal Rules of Criminal Procedure* require a defendant to be brought in front of a judge or magistrate without "unnecessary delay" after charges have been filed.[13] In most jurisdictions, the prohibition against "unnecessary delay" requires arraignment within forty-eight hours of arrest if the person is in custody, not including weekends or holidays.[14] After felony charges are filed, the defendant is usually arraigned on the basis of a complaint, but alternatively can be arraigned on an indictment from a grand jury proceeding. The defendant makes his first appearance in court during the arraignment. At such time, the charges are read; he is advised of his constitutional rights; and he enters a plea of guilty or not guilty. Defendants are entitled to an attorney from the arraignment stage throughout the completion of the case.

Usually at the arraignment, or within five days of it, a bail amount is determined or the defendant is released on his own recognizance.[15] At the conclusion of the arraignment, either a pretrial hearing (in the case of misdemeanor charges) or a preliminary hearing (in the case of felony charges) is scheduled. Alternatively, there may be a grand jury hearing instead of a preliminary hearing. In federal court, prosecutors typically choose to proceed by way of a grand jury hearing instead of a preliminary hearing. During the pretrial hearings, held after misdemeanor charges have been filed, the majority of evidentiary

---

[12] Miranda v. Arizona, 384 U.S. 436 (1966).

[13] FED. R. CRIM. P. 3(a)(1).

[14] *See, e.g.,* CAL. PENAL CODE § 825 (Deering 2012).

[15] Releasing a person on his own recognizance means the judge trusts the defendant to return to court for his preliminary hearing and the remainder of the case. Thus, the defendant is released without posting bail.

motions are submitted and most cases reach a disposition. If no disposition is reached, a trial date must be scheduled within the time mandated by the applicable jurisdiction. In California, for instance, the trial must be scheduled within thirty days of the arraignment date if the defendant is in custody or within forty-five days if he is not in custody for a misdemeanor or infraction case or sixty days for a felony charge.[16] Trial can be either by judge or by jury; however, both the prosecution and the defense have a right to a jury trial. Unless both sides waive this right, the case will be tried in front of a jury. In a bench trial, a judge will be the sole finder of fact. If the defendant is found guilty, he is entitled to a sentencing hearing within twenty days of his conviction.

In felony cases, unless there is a grand jury indictment, the defendant is entitled to a preliminary hearing. During preliminary hearings, the prosecutor must present evidence to convince a judge that a strong suspicion exists that the defendant committed the crime. This burden is analogous to a finding of probable cause. If this burden is met, then the defendant is "held to answer" and will be arraigned again on a document referred to as an information. This document is the post-preliminary hearing equivalent of a complaint. Defendants may also be arraigned on an indictment received from a grand jury, which is the preferred method in federal court. A grand jury proceeding is a hearing at which the prosecutor presents evidence to show probable cause that the defendant has committed a crime. Notably, the defendant and defense attorney do not necessarily have a right to be present at a grand jury proceeding.

The preliminary hearing, also sometimes referred to as a probable cause hearing, should not be confused with a judicial determination of probable cause (sometimes referred to as a forty-eight hour hearing) in which anyone arrested without a warrant is entitled to have a judicial officer determine that probable cause exists before the defendant can remain incarcerated. This *ex parte* hearing is known as a "*Gerstein* hearing."[17] The Fourth Amendment requires that a defendant is entitled to a "prompt" determination of probable cause.[18] The U.S. Supreme Court determined that this *ex parte* proceeding generally must be held within forty-eight hours of the defendant's arrest to meet the requirements of the Fourth Amendment.[19] The defendant does not have the right to an attorney at a *Gerstein* hearing. In fact, the defendant does not even have a right to be present at this probable cause determination. Typically, the proceeding simply consists of a magistrate reviewing an affidavit of the police officer that arrested the defendant (without a warrant) and deciding whether there is probable cause to believe that the defendant committed the crime. The probable cause determination is not an adversarial hearing, and the magistrate's determination may be based on an oral or written representation of the arresting officer. The forty-eight hour rule is also not rigid. If the *ex parte* probable cause hearing does not occur within forty-eight hours of a warrantless arrest, then the burden shifts to the government to show that there was an emergency or other extraordinary occurrence.[20] The forty-eight hours do not exclude weekends or court

---

[16] CAL. PENAL CODE § 1382 (Deering 2012).

[17] Gerstein v. Pugh, 420 U.S. 103 (1975).

[18] U.S. CONST. amend. IV.

[19] County of Riverside v. McLaughlin, 500 U.S. 44, 56 (1991).

[20] *Id.* at 57.

holidays; thus, magistrates must make probable cause determinations on the weekends and court holidays. If the magistrate determines that the arresting officer's affidavit does not show probable cause to find that the defendant committed a crime, then the defendant is released from custody. The Supreme Court allows probable cause hearings to be combined with other pretrial proceedings, such as arraignments and bail hearings, as long as the hearing is prompt.[21]

Typically, in felony cases, a pretrial conference date will be set at the second arraignment (the arraignment on the information), or in federal court or jurisdictions that rely on grand jury indictments, it will be set after the arraignment on the indictment. This pretrial proceeding is not an evidentiary hearing; it is a status conference where a number of topics may be discussed, including: settlement, discovery matters, evidentiary issues, and key trial timelines. Many felony cases reach a disposition at this stage. If, however, no agreement can be reached, a trial date is set within the jurisdiction's statutory mandated time, unless the defendant "waives time," meaning that he agrees to schedule a preliminary hearing or trial beyond the deadline in order to give his attorney more time to prepare for trial. In California, for example, a felony trial must be set within sixty days of the arraignment on the information, unless there is a time waiver.[22]

In federal court, the preliminary hearing (which is held if there is not an indictment) must be within fourteen days of the arraignment if the defendant is in custody and twenty-one days if he is out of custody.[23] The Speedy Trial Act of 1974 dictates that the information or indictment must be filed within thirty days from the date of arrest, and in the case of felony offenses where the grand jury is not in session, there are an additional thirty days for filing. Trial must start within seventy days of either the filing date or the date the defendant appeared before the court for the offense, whichever date occurred later.[24] Furthermore, if the government detains a defendant solely to await trial or designates a person awaiting trial as a high risk, then the trial must generally begin within ninety days.[25] In other words, the Speedy Trial Act dictates that the time between the indictment and the commencement of the trial must typically be within seventy days, however, federal courts allow the time to be tolled if there is good cause. While the federal courts generally require the trial to be within seventy days of the indictment, state courts have differing time requirements, although all jurisdictions generally require the trial to commence within one year of the indictment (unless the time is tolled for good cause). It is important to understand that there is not a bright line test to determine if a defendant's right to a speedy trial has been violated. The Sixth Amendment right to a speedy trial does not apply to indictment delays. There is no right to a speedy indictment because the Sixth Amendment right only applies after formal charges of a crime have been initiated.[26] There is an exception, however, if the pre-indictment delay was due to bad faith wherein

---

[21] *Id.* at 58.

[22] CAL. PENAL CODE § 1382 (Deering 2012).

[23] FED. R. CRIM. P. 5.1(c).

[24] Speedy Trial Act of 1974, 18 U.S.C. § 3161 (2006).

[25] *Id.* § 3164.

[26] United States v. Marion, 404 U.S. 307, 313 (1971).

the prosecution purposely delayed filing an indictment in order to prejudice the defendant, this would be unconstitutional because it would be a due process violation, even though it would not be a speedy trial violation.[27] Further, the Supreme Court has held that since the Sixth Amendment applies to criminal proceedings, which do not begin until after the grand jury completes its hearing, there is no Sixth Amendment right to a timely indictment.[28]

The Supreme Court has devised a balancing test to determine whether delays in bringing a defendant to trial are constitutional. The Court in *Barker v. Wingo* came up with a balancing test which focuses on four factors: the length of the delay, the reasons for the delay, the defendant's assertion of his rights, and the prejudice to the defendant.[29] The Court has also held that excessive delay between the indictment and the trial raises a presumption of prejudice to the defendant if the delay was caused by the prosecution's negligence and such post indictment delay may constitute a Sixth Amendment speedy trial violation.[30]

State courts, however, vary regarding time limitations for preliminary hearings. In California, for example, in-custody defendants charged with felonies are entitled to a preliminary hearing within ten court days of the arraignment (not including weekends and holidays) and a trial within sixty calendar days of the arraignment on the information. Defendants charged with misdemeanors in California are entitled to a trial within thirty days of arraignment if in custody and within forty-five days if out-of-custody.[31] In all jurisdictions, a defendant has the option to waive time, thereby permitting a delay. Out-of-custody defendants—those who have been arrested but are not detained—typically waive time, allowing for case preparation and settlement conferences. Proceedings cannot, however, be delayed indefinitely by the defense because the prosecution has a "public interest in the prompt disposition of criminal cases."[32] During the time between court appearances, effective defense attorneys will often encourage their clients to pursue acts of contrition—perhaps through counseling sessions, the performance of community service, or payment of restitution—in order to strengthen their positions when later negotiating a case settlement.

Case settlements, resulting from plea bargaining, are the rule and not the exception. Nonetheless some critics of plea bargaining have suggested that innocent people might be persuaded to plead guilty in order to avoid the risks associated with trial and, indeed, in some cases that is a legitimate concern. Yet, this practice is highly efficient and allows the court to focus its resources on those cases that are unable to be resolved. Case settlements allow both the prosecution and the defense the opportunity to negotiate an outcome that is satisfactory to both sides and to avoid the risk, time, and expense of litigation. Given the

---

[27] United States v. Mays, 549 F.2d 670 (9th Cir. 1977).

[28] United States v. Mandujano, 425 U.S. 564, 581 (1976).

[29] Barker v. Wingo, 407 U.S. 514, 530 (1972).

[30] Doggett v. United States, 505 U.S. 647, 657–58 (1992).

[31] *See* CAL. PENAL CODE § 859b (Deering 2012); CAL. PENAL CODE § 1382 (Deering 2012).

[32] FED. R. CRIM. P. 5.1(c)–(d). Some jurisdictions require that good cause be shown. *See* CAL. PENAL CODE § 859b (Deering 2012).

likelihood of an early disposition, successful attorneys must be skilled negotiators. Strategically speaking, maintaining an ethical approach to the law and a good reputation is the best preparation defense counsel can have, as the decision to reduce charges or recommend leniency is contingent on the prosecutor's approval. Thus, the ability to settle cases successfully is not dependent on the attorney's conduct and preparation in any single case, but is affected by how she conducts herself regularly and consistently.

Since this discussion of pretrial procedure is not exhaustive, this cursory introduction should not be taken as a substitute for a comprehensive understanding of the *Federal Rules of Criminal Procedure* and the rules specific to distinct state jurisdictions. Rather, it is meant to serve only as an overview of the chapters in this book, which discuss these procedural elements in greater detail and lay out methods for being successful at all aspects of pretrial litigation, such as drafting motions and interviewing clients. As with all aspects of criminal pretrial preparation, a thorough understanding of an attorney's obligations and the procedural elements that serve as the framework for the criminal justice system will make for more effective advocacy.

CHAPTER 2
DEVELOPING A CASE THEORY

"Now the general who wins a battle makes many calculations in his temple ere the battle is fought. The general who loses a battle makes but few calculations beforehand. Thus do many calculations lead to victory, and few calculations to defeat . . . ."

–Sun Tzu

Many experienced attorneys are fond of referring to trial as war. While the metaphor is grandiose and often drastically overstated, the two share one important aspect: the key to victory in each is preparation and planning. Essential to that preparation and planning for both pretrial and trial is the development of a case theory. While the benefits of a case theory in trial are obvious, they are perhaps not as obvious in the pretrial process. Nonetheless, any successful trial lawyer will attest to the essential role of a sound case theory during the pretrial phase. As will become evident throughout this chapter, the case theory dictates all pretrial strategy from motions to settlement conferences. An effective and persuasive case theory will have two components: a legal theory, explaining why the client prevails based on the law; and a factual theory, explaining why the client prevails based on the facts. The legal and factual theories must be consistent and complementary, and together they should answer three critical questions: 1) What happened? 2) Why did it happen? 3) How do these facts make for a persuasive case theory?

A successful case theory is the product of time and effort. Together, these nourish an advocate's ideas and allow the seed of a case theory to grow. With proper care, an effective plan, and focused cultivation, a case theory yields a solid foundation upon which to build a case. But the evolution from a case theory to a well-grounded foundation does not happen rapidly. Work must begin when charges are first brought, sometimes many months before trial, and must continue as the case theory is grown and refined throughout trial preparation. Development of a winning case theory begins long before any appearance in front of the judge takes place, and this development can continue through all stages of litigation up until a favorable result. The following summary maps out the development of a successful case theory:

A. CONSULT THE JURY INSTRUCTIONS

Following a thorough review of the case file, including the police reports and any supplemental information, it is time to identify the legal elements of the charged offenses. The case theory is born from the jury instructions. Each criminal charge has accompanying instructions that list the legal elements that must be established for conviction.[1] Trial preparation begins here, and these elements should be focal points throughout the entire process.

---

[1] All jurisdictions have standardized jury instructions that can be consulted in preparation for trial. Jury instructions, which are given to jurors prior to deliberation, list the elements or factors that must be satisfied for each criminal charge in order to convict.

B. IDENTIFY AND NARROW A FACTUAL THEORY

After having become familiar with the legal elements, counsel must then narrow the focus of the case theory to match the evidence and the law as set forth in the jury instructions. This process of refinement assists in identifying and organizing ideas while relating them to the law and the evidence at hand. Refinement may lead to recognition that some ideas are not as significant or relevant as originally imagined. For example, certain witness statements may point towards a critical omission that hurts or helps the case. Weighing the significance of the ideas that evolve during the narrowing process helps to formulate the case theory.

C. DEVELOP A THEME

While developing a case theory, counsel must develop a theme that will help the trier of fact appreciate and understand the case theory. A case's theme is not the same as a case theory, but rather, a well-crafted theme works to breathe life into a case theory. For example, in the O.J. Simpson murder trial, the defense theorized that someone other than Simpson committed the crime. A catchy buzz phrase relating to a bloody glove offered into evidence encapsulated their theme: "If it doesn't fit, you must acquit." Defense counsel successfully communicated this theme to persuade the jurors of their case theory.

D. BOLSTER THE THEME AND CASE THEORY WITH BUZZWORDS

While paying particular attention to the jury instructions and the emerging themes, counsel should identify recurring words and phrases that encapsulate and reinforce the theme. Ultimately, these carefully crafted words and phrases will serve as signposts that remind jurors of key arguments, significant witness testimony, and critical evidence. Together, these signposts form the theme of the case and, when effectively presented, the buzzwords should permeate the jurors' minds as they evaluate the case.

E. CONSIDER THE OPPOSITION'S APPROACH TO ITS CASE

It does not suffice, by the same token, simply to present a theory to the jury and hope for the best. The crafting of a case theory must necessarily take account of the opposition. Anticipating an opponent's case theory is the fifth step of case theory development. Of course, opposing counsel are engaged in their own preparation as well. If the opponent has done her job, she will also have considered the arguments she might encounter and will have developed her own case theory by taking these possibilities into account.

F. EXAMINE THE EVIDENCE FOR ADMISSIBILITY AND CREDIBILITY ISSUES

The sixth step in the process of developing a case theory is evaluating the admissibility and credibility of both physical evidence and witnesses. Advocates should not assume that just because someone said something, a defendant did something, or a detective found something at the scene of the crime, that that piece of evidence will be admissible. It is not enough to be familiar with the rules of evidence; an advocate must intimately understand the rules and how they relate to the specific evidence in the case. Further, counsel needs to consider the credibility of witness testimony and other evidence. However strong an argument may at first appear, a single assertion from a witness or a single piece of contrary evidence can destroy a case theory. Ultimately, the credibility of the evidence and the witnesses presented will reflect counsel's degree of preparation coming to trial.

G. MAINTAIN THE APPROPRIATE PRESENCE IN FRONT OF THE JURY

The final step in the evaluation of a case theory must be to take into account the role of the jury. It is a core concern to anticipate how jurors will view the case: how they might react to certain evidence, how the theme as developed through buzzwords will affect them, or how they will value a witness's credibility. A misplaced idea or a word open to misinterpretation can make the difference between a conviction and an acquittal. By keeping this in mind, an advocate will help protect the delicate relationship developed with the jury, starting with *voir dire*, and developed throughout trial.

The following sections of this chapter discuss the methodologies used to develop each of the seven suggested steps.

CONSULT THE JURY INSTRUCTIONS

Jury instructions contain every element of an offense that the prosecution must prove, as well as the standard of proof needed to obtain a guilty verdict. Prosecutors must know exactly what must be demonstrated in order to secure convictions, as well as what preparations are necessary to present the most persuasive case. Likewise, defense counsel must know what the prosecution needs to prove, and what preparations she must make to prevent the prosecution from meeting its burden of proof.

A. BREAKING DOWN THE ELEMENTS

Most jurisdictions have standardized jury instructions for each crime in the penal code, defining for the jury exactly what must be proven before the defendant can be convicted. This can be exemplified in practice using a basic, hypothetical criminal case, *Oceana v. King*, which will be examined throughout this chapter.

HYPO: *Oceana v. King*

Just over a year ago, Regina Queen and Rex King finalized a bitter divorce in which she claimed her former husband routinely beat her. She provided medical records of hospital visits documenting bruises and broken bones. Each time she had gone to the hospital, however, she had explained the injuries away as the result of her own clumsiness, telling the doctors things such as, "I fell down the stairs again."

Since their divorce, Queen and King had no contact until a few weeks ago when they ran into each other during the late-night happy hour at the En Passant Lounge. The two had a few drinks together, and at the end of the evening, King drove his ex-wife back to her apartment. Queen has now accused King of raping her shortly after they arrived.

Armed with Queen's testimony, photographs cataloguing bruises on her body, and a DNA analysis of semen recovered in the course of a rape kit exam that matched the defendant, the State of Oceana has charged King. Under the Oceana Penal Code, rape is defined as "nonconsensual sexual intercourse against the accuser's will or under threat or force." A look at the Oceana Criminal Jury Instructions reveals the following:

- If you find that the defendant had sexual intercourse against the will of the complaining witness, you must vote guilty.
- "Sexual intercourse" is defined as penetration of one person's vagina or anus with the sexual organ of another.
- "Against the complaining witness's will" is defined as lacking the complaining witness's consent or occurring under threat or force.

Counsel should consider jury instructions from a neutral perspective and evaluate each point one at a time. The jury instructions offer a specific definition of sexual intercourse. Thus, it is crucial to ask whether sexual intercourse between Queen and King took place according to this definition. Since DNA analysis of the semen clearly suggests an affirmative answer, it is likely that the parties will stipulate to this first element, meaning that there is agreement between both sides that certain facts are uncontested. As to the second element, counsel must ask whether the sexual intercourse between Queen and King took place against Queen's will. This answer is not as clear. The evidence shows that the former couple had a few drinks together before King drove Queen home; Queen claims that King then beat and raped her. Conversely, King is most likely to refute the rape allegation by arguing that the sex was consensual. Thus, consent—the central part of this jury instruction—will be the major point of contention at trial and, consequently, the foundation of the prosecutor's and defense attorney's respective legal theories.

Both sides have stipulated that sexual intercourse took place, but it is disputed whether it occurred against Queen's will. The jury instructions state that to be unlawfully against the complaining witness's will, sexual intercourse must occur without consent or under threat or force. It is the prosecutor's burden to prove this, so his most promising course of action may be to build a case theory around King's history of abusing Queen. Queen maintains that King abused her throughout their marriage. The hospital records verify her injuries; however, Queen repeatedly told hospital staff that the bruises and broken bones were a result of her own clumsiness, rather than any abuse by King, so this presents a challenge for the prosecution.

After carefully considering all the available evidence, the prosecutor would likely decide to use the allegedly documented abuse of Queen by King, as well as the bruises she suffered the night of the alleged attack, to show that King forced her to have intercourse. Thus, an effective prosecution case theory would focus on establishing nonconsensual intercourse. This case theory will demonstrate to the jury that King's routine beatings of Queen instilled fear in Queen, and that Queen's fear of King vitiated her consent.

Defense counsel will likely view the jury instructions differently. The jury instructions state that, for sexual intercourse to be against a victim's will, it must either lack consent or be under threat or force. The prosecution is proceeding on a case theory of fear and violence, stemming from the "threat or force" clause. A defense attorney should anticipate this approach and focus, in developing her case theory, on the issue of consent in order to refute the prosecution's claims. The prosecution's theory centers on King's alleged history of abuse of Queen, as purportedly verified by hospital records. The records, however, state that Queen attributed her injuries to her own clumsiness. Furthermore, Queen has admitted that both she and King met at a bar and both consumed alcoholic beverages on the night of the incident. These two factors may cast doubt on the prosecution's theory that the intercourse occurred under threat or force. Thus, the defense will base part of its case theory on the assertion that Queen changed her story about the cause of her injuries during her marriage only after the couple decided to divorce. Therefore, the defense might argue that it is plausible the intercourse was consensual and that Queen is now fabricating a story in order to explain away her behavior or in an attempt to once more damage King's reputation.

It is important to recognize that, whether the case is viewed from the perspective of the prosecutor or defense counsel, the theory is grounded, from the outset, in the law. Ultimately, the jury will reach a verdict on the basis of the law and the corresponding jury instructions, so it is crucial to develop a case theory with this critical relationship in mind.

B. Understanding the Unfamiliar

In the course of an advocate's career, there will undoubtedly be occasions when he is unfamiliar with a particular charge or criminal statute. Not all crimes are as readily understandable as murder, rape, or driving under the influence. In these instances, it may be difficult to grasp what must be proven to ensure conviction. Section A above illustrates how examining elements of the jury instructions and pairing them with critical facts can guide advocates towards a basic legal theory in a relatively simple rape case. The following example, based on a controversial prosecution in 2008 concerning the crime of patient abuse, demonstrates how even an unfamiliar criminal charge should be handled by following the same steps.[2]

HYPO: *Oceana v. Erickson*

John Tobias suffered cardiac arrest and was rushed to a nearby hospital. When he arrived, he was stabilized by the hospital staff but fell into a deep coma and had to be placed on a respirator to survive. His attending physician determined that John had sustained severe brain damage and was unlikely to survive more than a few days if removed from the respirator. Faced with this diagnosis, John's family consented to have him removed from life support. At this point, Dr. Alex Erickson, an organ harvester and transplant surgeon, was called to the hospital so that he might collect any viable organs once John died. The longer John remained alive, however, the longer his organs were deprived of oxygen, and the less suitable they became for transplantation.

---

[2] Prosecutors from San Luis Obispo, California made national headlines when they decided to charge medical prodigy Dr. Hootan Roozrokh with a crime for potentially over-medicating a terminal, comatose patient. Jesse McKinley, *Surgeon Accused of Speeding a Death to Get Organs*, N.Y. TIMES (Feb. 27, 2008), http://www.nytimes.com/2008/02/27/us/27transplant.html?pagewanted=all. The case was used for the 2009 CACJ National Trial Advocacy Invitational Tournament, with the problem authored by attorney David Diamond. (Used with permission of David Diamond).

> Just before Tobias was removed from the respirator, Dr. Erickson had his team administer painkillers that carried the risk of a particular side effect—they could restrict respiratory function and thus accelerate the death of someone being removed from a respirator. John died several hours later, in a significantly shorter amount of time than his attending physician anticipated.

The state of Oceana decided to charge Dr. Erickson with "patient abuse" under a new statute that, until then, had only been used in the prosecution of doctors and medical staff who abused the elderly in places like nursing homes. A sample of the jury instructions in the case reads as follows:

To prove the defendant is guilty of *patient abuse*, the People must prove:

1. John Tobias was placed in a situation where his person or health was endangered.

2. The defendant was *criminally negligent* when he caused or permitted John Tobias to suffer *great bodily injury* or be endangered.

3. *Great bodily injury* means substantial or significant injury. It is an injury that is greater than minor or moderate harm.

4. *Criminal negligence* involves more than ordinary carelessness, inattention, or mistake in judgment. A person acts with criminal negligence when he or she acts in a reckless way that causes a high risk of death or great bodily harm.

For a criminal attorney, this is where the development of the case theory originates. In reviewing these instructions, the following questions should be considered to help guide case theory development:

1. Given the facts and the jury instructions, what elements must the prosecution prove?

2. From the defense's perspective, what facts attack the People's weakest point in the case such that reasonable doubt might arise?

3. What is the basic case theory on either side?

Jury instructions provide jurors with the tools needed to determine how to apply the evidence. As obvious as it might seem, jurors—and sometimes lawyers too—can get carried away with focusing on the facts and lose sight of the legal requirements. With the case of Dr. Erickson, the facts can easily mislead one into believing that the prosecution needs to prove that the drugs his team administered caused John Tobias's death. In fact, patient abuse as outlined in the jury instructions does not require that at all. The instructions should be reviewed again while identifying the bare minimum that must be proved in order for the prosecution to earn a conviction.

In criminal trials, the defendant is always accused of *acting* criminally in some way. For that reason, to understand an unfamiliar charge—a charge like patient abuse—the key words will be verbs or verb phrases. Two of the verbs in Point 1 of these instructions—"was placed" and "was endangered"— are crucial. If the defendant did not *place* the victim in the situation where his or her life *was endangered*, then the defendant is not guilty. Just as in *Oceana v. King*, by identifying the components of the patient abuse crime from a neutral perspective, it becomes clear that the prosecution's burden is actually much lower than establishing that the defendant caused John Tobias's death. At a minimum, the prosecution needs to prove that Dr. Erickson *acted in a reckless way* by placing John Tobias in a situation that *permitted* him to be endangered.

When those elements of the jury instructions are broken down and aligned with the facts, a case theory should begin to crystallize. Since John Tobias was in a coma and was diagnosed as being in a terminal condition before he died, whether or not his health was "endangered" is unlikely to be a point of contention. The issue is whether *Dr. Erickson* is responsible for that endangerment: did Dr. Erickson place John Tobias in the situation that led to his death, and did he act recklessly in doing so? To demonstrate those elements, it will be important to examine whether or not the type of drugs and dosage could be considered to have been recklessly administered under the circumstances. Did Dr. Erickson cause John Tobias to be placed in a situation any more dangerous than the one in which he already existed as a terminally ill, comatose patient? The prosecution must focus their case theory on making the jury see how Dr. Erickson's actions reach the threshold of these elements, while consistently reminding the jury that that is the sole burden of proof the prosecution must meet—and nothing more.

Conversely, by identifying what actually needs to be proved in this case, the necessary features of a strong defense theory also begin to emerge. The defense attorney must urge the jurors to consider whether or not Dr. Erickson acted recklessly by giving painkillers to a patient who was about to be removed from life support. Defense counsel will also want to focus on the patient's medical history, and the particular events of that day, including the circumstances that originally brought him under Dr. Erickson's care: John Tobias had gone into cardiac arrest, was diagnosed as having severe brain damage, and his family asked for him to be removed from life support. All of this happened before Dr. Erickson was ever called in as a physician on John Tobias's case. The defense will want the jurors to ask themselves why this man is even on trial, since Tobias had been put on life support well before Dr. Erickson's involvement.

In both the *King* and *Erickson* cases, the jury instructions help identify the critical elements that need to be proven for either side to prevail. Examining them early on allows advocates to understand precisely what the case is about, and helps narrow down the possible theories to the one most likely to succeed. Whether from the perspective of a prosecutor or a defense attorney, understanding the jury instructions is integral to drafting the case theory that each respective side will advance during the various stages of litigation.

IDENTIFY AND NARROW A WINNING THEORY

As counsel for each side reviews the jury instructions and decides upon the critical elements and facts involved in an alleged crime, the legal portion of the case theory should begin to emerge. Even with an effective theory, however, explaining why a defendant is or is not legally guilty of a particular crime, there will likely be a number of possible explanations that can be argued to prove or disprove the defendant's guilt. Consequently, after recognizing the pertinent legal issues and assessing how they relate to the case, counsel must narrow these possibilities in order to present a logical, factual theory to the jury.

"Ladies and gentlemen, Exhibit A is a copy of the $400 bar tab my client ran up at The California Pub the night of the robbery. But if you don't believe that, Exhibit B is his theater ticket to a movie he saw at the Atlanta Cineplex that same night."

Effective litigators must present a concise explanation of the case theory. Often, early in case development, various versions or accounts may surface; thus, counsel must work through a variety of possible factual theories and decide upon the strongest trial option. Counsel should consider all the possibilities and be wary of hastily rejecting theories early on; one theory that might initially be dismissed as too implausible may actually be the most persuasive once both sides present their evidence. After developing all reasonable variations, counsel should determine which theory makes the most sense. Is it logical? Is it realistic? Is it believable? Can it be proven? Can the other side disprove it?

While it is always possible to use a different theory later, it should go without saying that it is ill-advised to change the theory mid-trial. On the other hand, a defense attorney may find it practical or even necessary to adjust her case theory after the prosecution has presented its case-in-chief in order to ensure her case is both responsive *and* persuasive. One way or the other, a case should be coherent and consistent from beginning to end. In order to achieve this, the case theory should be woven into every phase of the trial.

Without a single, coherent theory, an advocate runs the risk of appearing as if she does not sufficiently know her case, the facts, or even her client. Thus, she risks losing credibility with the jury. Picture a defense attorney who represents to the jury that her client, on trial for burglary, was either out of town *or* was mentally unable to form the requisite intent because he was intoxicated. By asserting multiple-choice defenses, the attorney significantly dilutes the persuasiveness of *both* theories. What juror would believe the defendant was out of town if the defendant's own attorney has claimed the defendant *was* there but simply did not mean to commit the crime?

For similar reasons, it is equally dangerous for a prosecutor to present such multiple-choice theories, since an advocate's credibility undergirds his entire case. Without credibility, he relinquishes the persuasive power of his perspective of the case. Worse yet, when a prosecutor presents various possible scenarios, it is more difficult to prove beyond a reasonable doubt that the defendant committed the charged offense. If the prosecutor permits jurors to believe the crime could have occurred in any one of five ways, what is to stop the jurors from believing the crime could also have occurred in the way the defense proposed? A far more persuasive and far less confusing approach is to present a single explanation for what the prosecution is asserting *actually* happened.

In order to narrow down the available theories, the attorney must first consider what she thinks the evidence shows. If an advocate believes the crime occurred in a specific way, she will be much more capable of convincing twelve other individuals the crime happened that way as well. Next, the attorney should consider *why* she believes that this is what happened. Which pieces of evidence are convincing, and which are not? Do corroborating witnesses and documentary evidence support that the client was in another location at the time of the crime, for example? Those same pieces of evidence that lead the advocate to believe the crime occurred in a certain way are more likely to convince a jury. Based on those facts, what is the strongest factual scenario that supports the theory? Defense attorneys should consider which element the prosecution will have difficulty proving. This element will be the battlefield. Even if the prosecution can prove every other element beyond a reasonable doubt, a lack of proof on just one element means the prosecution will not have met its burden.

Attorneys for each side should avoid neglecting facts that contradict their version of events and should be sure to reconcile any apparently inconsistent facts with those that are clearly established or undisputed. Trial counsel should be able to explain the case in a logical and compelling way. Jurors are real people who possess ordinary human instincts, desires, values, and beliefs. Counsel should consider what the jurors will believe and how to encourage them to *want* to believe their portrayal of the facts.

DEVELOP A THEME

Your honor, he keeps repeating that theme! It's killing my case!

After building the body of a case by developing and narrowing both legal and factual theories, the next step is forging the theme. The theme should capture the essence of the case by taking the form of a one-or two-sentence sound bite with high-impact buzzwords that emphasize critical points in the case theory. Buzzwords can be garnered from a number of different sources: an image, an idea, a literary reference, a well-known saying, or even a biblical passage. An advocate's creativity is the only limit. If the jury remembers only one thing, it should be the lawyer's theme.

Excellent case themes transcend the facts of a particular case and resonate with a jury because they connect with the jurors' life experiences and values. Case themes ought to command universal appeal. The theme acts as a short and powerful message that can be repeated throughout the presentation of the case, from *voir dire* up through the closing argument. The theme must be consistent with the case theory and appropriate to the composition and geographical location of the jurors. For instance, how would a biblical reference impact a particular jury compared to utilizing a pop culture reference? It would be unusual to find a group of people for whom both would be equally appropriate. Understanding the jury's demographic is important.

A. ILLUSTRATION OF A THEME: DEFENSE

The theme invoked by defense counsel in the O.J. Simpson murder trial was integral to the defense victory. In 1994, Simpson, a popular former football star and actor, was charged with the brutal murder of his ex-wife, Nicole Brown Simpson, and her friend, Ronald Goldman. Simpson hired a high-profile defense team, dubbed the "Dream Team" in the press, comprised of some of the best trial  attorneys in the country, including Robert Shapiro, F. Lee Bailey, and Johnnie Cochran. The case was widely reported on across the country. Long after the lengthy stream of testimony, evidence, and analysis had ended, in a trial that lasted over nine months, there was one phrase that almost anyone who lived through the case can probably recite verbatim: "If [the glove] doesn't fit, you must acquit."[3] The defense argued that the glove in question, supposedly worn by Simpson during the murder, had been planted, along with other evidence, by police officers at the scene.

This theme, introduced by Cochran, is direct, powerful, and catchy. It sums up, in a one-sentence, rhyming sound bite, the Simpson team's overall theory that police and prosecutors were careless in reviewing the evidence before they "rushed to judgment." Simpson's defense counsel took it one step further, matching an image to the phrase, when, in a theatrical display, Simpson struggled to pull the glove on his hand. Nine months after the trial began, Simpson was found not guilty.

B. ILLUSTRATION OF A THEME: PROSECUTION

While a catchy sound bite can be one way to ensure that a jury remembers the essence of a case, it is not always a necessity. At times, a catchy sound bite may even be inappropriate for the subject matter of a trial, or as it might relate to  the jurors deliberating the case. In such instances, it is important to remember that a theme is not a rhyme structure, but represents the focus of a case.

There are few things imaginable that could be of such grave import and incredible magnitude that they would entice an associate justice of the United States Supreme Court to take a leave of absence from the Court, but the atrocities committed in Nazi Germany by the German High Command were exactly that. When the war crimes trials began in Nuremberg in 1945, Justice Robert Houghwout Jackson was tasked with proving the conspiracy charge levied against the upper echelon of the Nazi party—the charge that would tie all of their acts together, making them jointly guilty of one vast criminal enterprise. From the opening statement to his closing argument, Jackson peppered his case with a variation of this simple reminder to the jury of his case theme: "[I]t is their overt acts which we charge to be crimes," acts which are supported "by documents of their own making, the authenticity of which has not been challenged."[4]

---

[3] *See* David Margolick, *Simpson's Lawyer Tells Jury that Evidence 'Doesn't Fit,'* N.Y. TIMES (Sept. 28, 1995), http://www.nytimes.com/1995/09/28/us/simpson-s-lawyer-tells-jury-that-evidence-doesn-t-fit.html?pagewanted=all&src=pm.

[4] MICHAEL S. LIEF ET AL., LADIES AND GENTLEMEN OF THE JURY: GREATEST CLOSING ARGUMENTS IN MODERN LAW 22, 26 (2000).

While it is easy to fall into the trap of trying to make a case theme something epic or larger-than-life, an attorney should always remember that at the end of the day, she needs to win on the basis of the law. A simple phrase that the jurors take with them, reminding them of why one side should win, is oftentimes the best theme. Jackson's convictions attained at Nuremberg are a testament to that. Consider the *Oceana v. King* hypothetical from earlier in this chapter. What theme might be developed for the prosecution? For the defense?

BOLSTER THE CASE THEORY AND THEME WITH BUZZWORDS

After an attorney has examined the jury instructions and narrowed the focus, the overall case theory and theme should begin to form. As they crystallize, it is important to start developing phrases or buzzwords that will convey the message to the jury. The words should capture the essence of the case theory and theme that will resonate in the minds of the jury.

A well-placed word or phrase can be significant: adding one word to a sentence can make the difference between clarity or confusion, conviction or acquittal. Actually choosing that perfect word, however, is not nearly as easy as simply recognizing that a single word or creative turn-of-phrase can make a critical difference in a trial's outcome. Certainly, finding the right buzzwords—words that ignite a fire in jurors' minds that continues to burn long after the sound of the word has passed—is not an exact science. Even when counsel finds the right words, variables such as pace of delivery and vocal inflection can impact the desired effect. While there is no single way to pick buzzwords, there are steps that can help ensure the greatest likelihood of success.

A. THE GOAL OF BUZZWORDS

Before selecting buzzwords or phrases, it is important to recognize the goal to be accomplished with the words themselves. Certainly, buzzwords should convey a message. When examining the jury instructions, begin to develop the case theory that provides the basis of the message that the buzzwords will focus upon. The chosen words or phrases should clearly relate back to the case theory and, at the same time, advance it.

In the case of *Oceana v. King*, the critical issue in the case is whether the sexual act between King and Queen was consensual. The battle that will ensue between the prosecution and defense will certainly focus on that issue. Thus, the issue of consent should provide a source of buzzwords that will evoke in the jurors an idea that clearly relates to the advocate's argument. Consider the word "consent" and a list of other words or phrases that might be useful for each side. Often, the best place to start is a thesaurus. In this case, there are synonyms for the word "consent" for the defense and antonyms for the prosecution's use of the same term.

CHART 2.1

Defense	Prosecution
agreement, allowance, approval, compliance, permission, understanding, willingness, history of passion, understanding of acceptance	denial, disapproval, objection, protest, refusal, history of abuse, pattern of violence, lack of compassion, rejection of values

The two lists above might serve as a starting point from which buzzwords for each side might be selected. Each word or phrase has a distinct connotation. For the defense, the words are clearly suggestive: a understanding regarding consensual sex existed, and Queen was a willing partner. For the prosecution, the suggestions lean in a different direction: Queen did not consent to sex, and King was a violent person who disregarded her autonomy.

The way in which these ideas relate to a case theory should be simple and clear. The simplicity of these words serves several functions. First, jurors are not inclined to draw conclusions on their own. For that reason, buzzwords that do not overcomplicate the issue or require the jury to make too much effort to connect the chosen words or phrases into a coherent idea are best. Choosing words outside the general lexicon might not be wise, just as phrases that are too long could alienate the jury. Furthermore, legalese should be avoided. By keeping the buzzwords and phrases relatively simple, an advocate eases the burden placed on jurors to make sense of the case.

B. LOUD AND CLEAR

The clarity of the message is, of course, a primary consideration. The more elaborate and convoluted the buzzwords, the less likely it becomes that the jury will relate them to the case theory in the way the speaker intends. Although clarity goes hand in hand with simplicity, clarity extends beyond the mere selection of simple words. Clarity depends just as much upon the logical and coherent presentation of buzzwords within a well-ordered argument. After carefully considering the case's details, advocates should decide upon the order in which to present the chosen words and ideas in the most persuasive fashion.

There are different approaches to laying out an argument, and each has its own value. No single way is necessarily better than another, so advocates should choose an organizational structure appropriate to the details of their particular case. Indeed, depending on the case, a creative synthesis may be the best option. The following chart offers some examples:

CHART 2.2

Type of Argument	Organizational Structure
Chronological	Present the events of the case in the order in which they occurred.
By Element	Evaluate the legal elements of the crime and present evidence systematically consistent with each element.

Strength of Argument: *Primacy and Recency*	Consider the strength of evidence (and related buzzwords) and organize accordingly. Most attorneys like to begin strong and end strong, since people tend to remember the first and last things they hear. Attorneys will differ, however, as to whether the strongest argument should go at the beginning or end of their presentation.
Persuasive Language	Similar to the strength of the argument, some facts and related buzzwords may have a more persuasive and effective tone.
Personalize or Depersonalize	Constructing and emphasizing buzzwords that characterize the defendant differently will subconsciously affect the jury.
Vivid Language	An emphasis on action verbs and personification will provide your jury with an image to accompany your argument.

Repetition is also an effective method for ensuring the clarity of the message. Numerous studies show that repeated themes tend to resonate longer in jurors' minds. The more a juror hears the same words and ideas, the more likely she will remember them and connect them to the evidence presented. From the outset of the case-in-chief, the case theory and theme should be readily apparent to the jurors and the buzzwords or phrases chosen to promote the theory and theme should be closely and clearly linked to both. This clear connection should begin with the opening statement, be developed through witness examinations, and summarized in the closing argument. The constant return to the case theory and theme through the use of buzzwords will provide an advocate's case with unity and cohesion, which should encourage the jurors to find for his side.

C. Choosing Buzzwords

Just as the jury instructions are the best place to start when developing a case theory, it is also wise to begin with the jury instructions when choosing a theme and the most persuasive way to advance that theme is through buzzwords. Returning to one of the jury instructions from the *Erickson* patient abuse case and focusing on the words of the critical elements:

John Tobias *was placed* in a situation where his person or health *was endangered*.

As mentioned previously, looking at the verbs of the instruction is a simple way of understanding the charge and helps focus the legal component of the case theory. In this instance, we looked at "was placed" and "was endangered." Since verbs also express the action of the crime, these action words can often have the most impact on a jury. Thus, focusing on them can create the kind of buzzwords that will establish and reinforce the theme, tie the case theory together, and leave the jurors with something memorable as they enter their deliberations. Moreover, stressing the critical words in one way or another will help to simplify the argument. Working from these instructions, an advocate might decide to focus on the word "place." The ultimate evolution of identifying this buzzword might appear in this way in the defense's closing argument:

Erickson Closing Argument

"The first question you must ask is this: did Alex Erickson place John Tobias in a position where his health was endangered?

"I want to emphasize the word 'place,' because the prosecution is asserting that Dr. Erickson 'placed' John Tobias in that position. But that's not true. John Tobias had suffered cardiac arrest and irreversible brain damage; he was in a profound coma; and his parents decided to withdraw life support. All of this occurred before Dr. Erickson ever arrived at Angels Regional Medical Center. Therefore, he could not have possibly 'placed' him in the position in which his life was endangered."

By drawing attention to the word "place," the defense has highlighted for the jury a significant element of the case. Ideally, this emphasis was already clear to the jurors, since it would have been introduced in the opening statement and developed through key testimony. By the time jurors hear the closing argument, it should be clear to them that the doctor did not "place" his patient in that position.

This example also illustrates an additional focus for the advocate as she seeks to introduce buzzwords to the jury. Before she ever delivers her closing argument, she has the luxury of knowing exactly what she will say. Because she knows the conclusion she wants the jury to draw, she can provide hints and clues along the way that will gently suggest to the jury their ultimate destination. In *Oceana v. Erickson*, the defense counsel understands that the prosecution intends to prove that the defendant is an "overzealous" and "reckless" person, maybe even a "killer." To combat this tone, counsel can personalize the defendant. To do so, the human elements of his character should be drawn out. He has a name, "Alex Erickson." He has a profession—that of a "doctor" who works to "save lives." He is "compassionate" and "responsible." While the meaning of a word is significant, it is often the connotation that can be more persuasive. The list of words below contrasts words that can be used by opposing sides.

CHART 2.3

Defendant	Alex Erickson
Overzealous	Compassionate
Reckless	Responsible
Killer	Doctor
Organ Harvester	Life-Saver

These buzzwords are not simple synonyms of key words taken from the jury instructions, but are words that will be repeated throughout the trial, during *voir dire,* the opening statement, direct and cross examinations, and the closing argument. With each subtle use of the term "defendant," the prosecution works to depersonalize the accused. With each use of the term "doctor," the defense attorney counters with a word evoking respect and reverence for her client.

As mentioned at the beginning of this chapter, criminal trial attorneys often compare the litigation process to going to war—and with good reason. Criminal trials are hotly contested battles where a person's future is in jeopardy. They are battles for the real estate of each juror's conscience, and zealous advocates must take advantage of every opportunity to claim that territory as their own. Tone, connotation, and the words that counsel use can have varying effects on a jury.

CHART 2.4

Prosecution's Labels	Defense's Buzzwords
Defendant	Alex Erickson, Dr. Erickson, doctor
Overzealous	Compassionate
Reckless	Responsible
Organ Harvester	Transplant Surgeon
Death	Passing
Victim	Patient

As demonstrated by the chart above, while the prosecution's labels all have negative connotations, the defense's buzzwords are positive. Counsel rely on these subtle suggestions, in addition to overt expressions, to vie for the minds of the jurors in order to convince them of a given point of view. While the jurors may not always consciously recognize a lawyer's methods, they will absorb the differences in tone and connotation between the lawyers' presentation.

The prosecutor may attempt to demonize and vilify the defendant. Astute defense attorneys anticipate the ways in which the State casts the client in a negative light, and stand ready to rebuff the accusations against their client. The inverse is true for prosecutors. Sterile buzzwords will depersonalize the accused, and will keep the jury from sympathizing with him. The effective use of buzzwords that are calculated to enhance the theme will aid in the battle for the minds of the jury.

D. STICKINESS

As discussed, the main ideas developed as part of the case theory must join together to form a theme. It is this theme that must be seared into the minds of the jurors before they deliberate. The premise is simple, but figuring out how to create an idea that sticks in a juror's mind is the tricky part. Often, a single word or a phrase will simplify an entire case and, if conveyed correctly, can turn a verdict.

To harken back to the Simpson trial, the theme that stuck was: "If [the glove] doesn't fit, you must acquit."[5] After a very lengthy trial, Johnnie Cochran, lead attorney for the defense, focused the message of long hours of testimony and a "mountain of evidence" by reciting a basic rhyme in his closing argument. It almost seems too simple, but that one sentence made a difference. It reminded the jury of a compelling, key moment in the trial: when the defendant stood in front of the jury box and unsuccessfully tried to pull on a bloody glove—one of the prosecution's proposed key pieces of damaging evidence—onto his hand. With his by-now-familiar catchphrase during the closing argument, Cochran also conveyed to the jury

---

[5] Margolick, *supra* note 3.

exactly what he sought from them: an acquittal. This combination of elements—a vivid moment from the trial, a crucial piece of evidence, mention of the verdict he desired, and a simple, easy-to-remember rhyme—created an idea that persisted in the minds of jurors and those watching the trial, and ultimately led to Simpson's acquittal.

E. TYING IT ALL TOGETHER

The first goal of buzzwords is to convey a message to the jury in a simple and clear way. As explained, there are a number of ways to do this. In order to discover these buzzwords, counsel can look to the case theory that has developed from the jury instructions. This will allow an advocate to formulate ideas that will evolve into simple words and phrases. Each word and phrase should impact the jurors' minds in a way that helps them easily understand the case theory and corresponding theme, and makes the theory and theme linger with them throughout the trial and during their deliberations. These words and phrases should become the foundation for everything that follows, from the opening statement up through the closing argument. Ultimately, buzzwords can be the key to victory.

ANTICIPATE YOUR OPPONENT

Just as the success of a case hinges on the case theory and theme developed, it is important to be ever-conscious of the efforts of opposing counsel. However committed a successful advocate may be to preparing her case, the opponent is gearing up for trial in an equally committed manner, and failure to recognize this can have disastrous results. An opponent's ability to develop a strong, strategic case theory should never be underestimated. Just as trials may be likened to battles, trial preparation can be viewed as a game of chess. Setting up the case theory before stepping into the courtroom is similar to positioning chess pieces that threaten and defend before putting the opponent in "check" and, ultimately, "checkmate." Trial itself is much like the calculated decision to start capturing an opponent's chess pieces.

By contemplating the prosecution's perspective in *Oceana v. King*, the importance of tactical thinking in prosecuting criminal trials is revealed as well as the types of strategies a prosecutor must consider when presenting the case to a jury. In *King*, the defendant's ex-wife has accused him of raping her after they shared drinks at the En Passant Lounge. (*The Queen moves forward and threatens the King.*) The prosecutor, cognizant of the jury instructions, matches the elements of the crime to the facts and is confident about the evidence:

1. Queen is a credible and sympathetic victim.

2. The DNA matches that of the defendant.

3. Queen's injuries are indicative of resistance.

The prosecutor has painstakingly developed his overall case theory, selected the theme that will be reinforced with buzzwords, and, at first blush, everything seems cut and dry: there is an alleged history of abuse; King and Queen ended on bad terms; they had a relatively pleasant encounter at a bar; King tried to make it into more than it was; and when Queen rejected him, he beat and raped her. What appears one way from the prosecutor's perspective can, however, be interpreted very differently by a defense attorney. In order to convict King, the prosecutor will need to think like a defense attorney and anticipate the moves that defense counsel will make to reframe the evidence in the defendant's favor.

> 1. Reflect back on the King fact pattern and think about the basic case theories you formed when looking at the jury instructions. What strengths and weaknesses do you see in the prosecution's case?

> 2. Now put yourself in the defense's shoes. What kind of evidence would you want to present to counteract the strengths and exploit those weaknesses?

> 3. Based on what you anticipate as either a prosecutor or defense attorney, how will you respond?

Now, let us look at one way the case might unfold: with the realization that he is facing serious criminal charges, King hires White & Knight LLP to represent him as he desperately professes his innocence. Defense counsel, recognizing that the presence of the semen makes it nearly impossible to claim that sex never occurred, will undoubtedly focus on arguing that the sex was consensual. No matter what reason the defense gives for Queen's making a false accusation, a consent defense will necessarily attempt to present her as a liar to the jury. (*White & Knight swoop in to protect King with his consent defense.*)

To attack this defense, the prosecutor will need to give support to Queen's credibility and make her eventual testimony more believable while simultaneously undermining King. The prosecutor may want to enter the hospital records to demonstrate that Queen left King because he physically abused her during their marriage. The prosecutor will argue that the photographs of the injuries she suffered the night of the attack are a clear continuation of that pattern of violence. (*From the castle walls, troops take their position and prepare to bury White & Knight's consent defense in a*

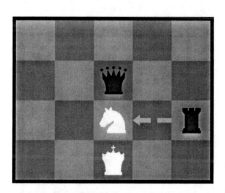

barrage of documentary evidence and photographs.)

In turn, however, White & Knight react. Just as the prosecutor is prepared to refute the defense's evidence, the defense is ready to refute the prosecution's evidence. Perhaps the prosecutor should expect another explanation for the bruises Queen suffered that night. At trial, King may take the stand in his own defense and testify that Queen made a habit of drinking heavily during their marriage and would, upon occasion, accidentally injure herself while intoxicated. He might further explain that, on the night of the

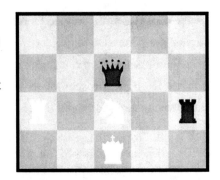

purported crime, Queen was too drunk to drive, so he gave her a lift home. Because she had so much to drink, she slipped and fell down the stairs as they walked up her apartment steps together. (*The King's castle tower directly opposes your own.*)

An attorney should be careful not to presume a lack of preparation on the part of opposing counsel. It may be that they have considered every prosecution move, and they might be able to counter each argument persuasively. For this reason, it is crucial to be diligent in exploring every possible theory and ready to rebuff an opponent's attacks. In developing the case theory, the prosecution anticipated the defense's attempt to explain away the bruising. This may be achieved by calling Dr. Bishop, a medical expert and forensic pathologist, who can testify that these kinds of injuries are only explained by directed

force resulting from striking or punching—not a tumble down a flight of stairs. (*Because the prosecution expected the unexpected in devising his case theory, he had reinforcements ready to save the day and the bishop moves into position.*)

By anticipating the moves of the defense correctly, the endgame might play out in the prosecution's favor: during the trial, the past history of abuse undermines the consent defense and helps support Queen's accusation. (*Rook takes Knight.*)

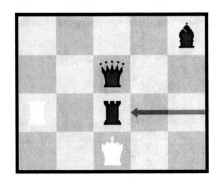

The defense, however, then brings evidence that King and Queen left En Passant together because Queen was too drunk to drive, and that Queen fell down

the stairs—explaining the source of her bruises. (*Rook takes Rook.*)

The testimony of the prosecution's expert, however, bolsters Queen's claims that the bruises were caused by directed physical blows. This helps confirm her testimony while simultaneously damaging King. Checkmate. (*Queen takes Rook.*)

This abridged game of chess may seem unrealistic because it fails to consider other possible moves or strategies; however, just like an unabridged game of chess, actual case theory and trial planning are infinitely more complex. In the real world, this case may be far from over. The unexpected in the courtroom can bring about the downfall of even the best attorney. That is why it is absolutely essential to have a detailed understanding of the facts in the case and work out a game plan that anticipates an opponent's moves to the best of an advocate's ability.

1. Look back to the hypothetical Erickson case and place yourself in the role of the prosecution or the defense. When considering the case theory and examining the jury instructions, what weaknesses did you notice on both sides?

2. How would you exploit them? What other explanations can you think of that might turn those weaknesses into strengths?

3. Based on the limited facts, what would be your ideal evidence? Do you think you could find it? Would it be admissible?

CONSIDER ADMISSIBILITY AND CREDIBILITY ISSUES

Once an attorney has developed the legal and factual theories, selected a compelling theme, chosen suitable buzzwords, and anticipated defenses for the case's weakest points, it is important to remember that cases are not won or lost based on *all* of the evidence—but on the *admissible* evidence. An essential component of all trial preparation is the determination of what evidence will be admitted during trial and what evidence will be excluded. In addition to determining admissibility, it is also crucial to consider the credibility of various pieces of evidence.

A. ADMISSIBILITY

A case theory can be founded only on facts and evidence that are admissible. While the evidentiary rules in each jurisdiction will vary, there are certain basic principles that apply in all jurisdictions. Common admissibility issues are relevance, hearsay, prior convictions or bad acts, character evidence, and potential *Miranda* or search and seizure issues.

If an initial theory is found to rely on facts that are determined to be inadmissible, the theory must be modified or abandoned. For example, in the *Oceana v. King* hypothetical, what if Queen and King were never married, but instead, the facts presented a case of rape where the only issue was identity? The prosecutor's case will then rest heavily on DNA evidence connecting King to the crime. Supposing, however, that there is a possibility that this evidence was collected in violation of King's constitutional rights, then the prosecutor would have to consider a scenario in which the evidence might be ruled inadmissible.

Even if the judge rules the DNA evidence inadmissible, the prosecutor can still offer evidence of Queen's injuries and testimony. While this evidence may indicate that a crime has been committed, it may not connect King to the crime. King's attorney might assert what criminal trial lawyers like to call the "Some Other Dude Did It" defense. In this case, the prosecutor should search for additional evidence to support the theory that King is the perpetrator. Perhaps an additional witness can corroborate the claim that King was at the scene of the crime, or maybe Queen can identify physical features unique to King, such as a distinct tattoo.

Even if the prosecutor is fairly certain that the DNA evidence will be admitted, he must be flexible and prepared for the worst. Judges, while intimately familiar with the law, are only human and may rule incorrectly on admissibility. Just as it is crucial to take into account an opponent's strategy, it is equally important to consider that judicial rulings may not go as desired. Counsel should prepare for a fight and be open to changing or adjusting their case theory as necessary at any point during the proceedings based upon a favorable or unfavorable ruling. Additionally, counsel should work to exclude evidence that is damaging. Each trial is an intellectual battle, and much like a game of chess, every move must be carefully considered.

In *King*, the defense attorney should seek to admit evidence of Queen's sexual history, especially if it suggests promiscuity or otherwise supports a consent defense. On the other hand, the prosecutor should vigorously try to exclude such evidence. Whether this evidence will be admitted could be a close call within the judge's discretion.[6]

B. CREDIBILITY

Returning to *King*, what if the DNA evidence was ruled inadmissible and the defense has asserted the "Some Other Dude Did It" theory, and King has a seemingly airtight alibi? According to King's girlfriend, Penelope Pawn, King was home during the alleged rape—but Pawn has some credibility issues. First, since some evidence suggests that King is Pawn's sole financial provider, Pawn may be testifying to maintain her financial support—an obvious bias. Second, evidence also shows that Pawn has previously lied on her tax returns. Evidence of previous instances of dishonesty, if admissible at trial, may cause the jury to doubt her testimony. As a result, the defense attorney may want to reconsider her case theory. It may not have to be abandoned if other witnesses come forward to testify that King was home, or if other physical evidence can support the theory. If, however, this evidence does not materialize, defense counsel should consider switching to a consent theory.

C. BRINGING IT INTO FOCUS

Throughout pretrial and trial, it is important to stay organized. The following charts provide examples of how evidence might be tracked when considering its admissibility and its credibility. First, jury instructions should be read to determine the elements of the case. Then, evidence should be assessed

---

[6] For more information on the admission of a victim's sexual history, consult Federal Rule of Evidence 413 and corresponding state statutes within your jurisdiction.

to determine which facts support or undermine each element. Lastly, the evidence should be reviewed to ascertain whether there are credibility or admissibility issues.

CHART 2.5
PROSECUTION CASE-IN-CHIEF: *Oceana v. King*

Elements of the Case	Evidence	Admissibility Issues	Credibility Issues
Sexual intercourse with the victim	Victim's testimony	N/A	Past sexual history?
	DNA evidence	Violation of constitutional rights in collection?	N/A
Against the victim's will, *i.e.*, lacking consent or under threat or force	Victim's testimony	N/A	Past sexual history?
	Scratch marks, bruises, signs of physical harm	N/A	Alternate source of marks?

CHART 2.6
DEFENSE CONSENT THEORY: *Oceana v. King*

Elements of the Case	Evidence	Admissibility Issues	Credibility Issues
Sexual intercourse with the victim	Not disputed with consent defense.		
Against the victim's will, *i.e.*, lacking consent or under threat or force	Defendant's testimony	N/A	Defendant's demeanor and believability?
	Scratch marks, bruises, etc.	N/A	Alternate source of marks?
	Instances of victim's past consent	Consult rules of evidence.	N/A

By considering these issues and organizing the evidence while developing the case theory, advocates are more likely to avoid setbacks as the case proceeds. The jury may only consider admissible evidence and, once presented, credible evidence will help the advocate's case. In the words of one of the great American trial lawyers, Gerry Spence: "Credibility comes out of the bone—deeper yet, out of the marrow. . . . Great pretenses win nothing. . . . To win, we must be believed."[7]

REMEMBER THE JURY

It is paramount to remember to whom the case is being presented: the jury. As intuitive as it sounds, it is something that is sometimes overlooked. In the struggle to develop a case theory, scrutinize evidence, study official reports, and argue motions in preparation for trial, an attorney sometimes forgets what it is he must really do during trial: convince the jury that he is right and his opponent is wrong.

A. YOU ARE ALWAYS ON STAGE

The reality is that jurors begin to formulate their opinions about a case long before they ever hear opening statements or a word of testimony. From the first moment prospective jurors see counsel during the jury selection process, they will make judgments about the advocates, and those judgments, no matter how unfair or unfounded, will influence their opinions of the advocates from that point forward. In *The Seven Habits of Highly Effective People*, author Stephen R. Covey says communications experts estimate "that only 10 percent of our communication is represented by the words we say. Another 30 percent is represented by our sounds, and 60 percent by our body language."[8] This means that the way an advocate sits at counsel's table, the way he listens to the judge, and even the way he clears his throat may impact a juror who will eventually decide the outcome of the case.

1. Manage the Impressions Made on the Jury

It is not only the client who is being scrutinized. The jury will be judging advocates just as they are judging the advocate's client and the case presented. Successful attorneys are likeable. Gaining favor with the jury can go a long way in making them more receptive to the case theory.

The prosecutor's diamond ring is gaudy. I'm voting for the defense.

Successful attorneys avoid distracting the jurors by, among other things, managing their appearance so that it reflects a professional image. An attorney should be well-dressed, but not flashy or inappropriate. An attorney who wears a short skirt might upset the sensibilities of a conservative juror. Bright or poorly fitting suits may suggest to a juror that an advocate is arrogant or slovenly. Gaudy watches or jewelry may suggest an extravagance that

---

[7] GERRY SPENCE, HOW TO ARGUE AND WIN EVERY TIME 47–48 (1995).

[8] STEPHEN R. COVEY, SEVEN HABITS OF HIGHLY EFFECTIVE PEOPLE: RESTORING THE CHARACTER ETHIC 241 (1990).

offends jurors. Too much makeup, perfume, or cologne might also put jurors off. Although there may be no rational foundation for any of these judgments, and an ideal, objective juror would not make them, human nature is such that a person's unconscious or instinctive responses can significantly impact her opinions and beliefs.

2. The Jury Wants to Hear About a Motive

While motive is not an element of any offense (with the exception of hate crimes), juries are always curious about the motive. Presenting the jury with a motive helps the prosecutor meet his burden of proving his case beyond a reasonable doubt; at the same time, if the defense can establish a lack of motive, a jury is far more likely to return a not guilty verdict. In the *King* and *Erickson* hypothetical cases, motive is not an element of the crime, and yet an advocate should recognize that the average person seeks an explanation for the defendant's actions.

Why would a doctor want to overdose a terminally ill patient?

How should one examine Dr. Erickson's motive from opposing perspectives? For the prosecution, Dr. Erickson's desire to make sure he collected organs still viable for transplant could be one motive to accelerate his patient's death. Conversely, the defense could explain that the defendant administered painkillers in order to bring comfort to his dying patient. The same is true in the *King* case:

Why would King rape his ex-wife? If he didn't, why would she lie about it?

It is simply human nature to want to know the answers to these sorts of questions. Motives are important because they help the jury make sense of the case theory. Even though it is legally unnecessary, an effective advocate plans and prepares to establish motive as a part of her overall message to a jury.

B. BE CLEAR AND LOGICAL

In addition to keeping the jury in mind when developing a case theory, it is just as important for an advocate to think about what he is trying to convey and how the jury will interpret the information put forth. The audience is not a roomful of lawyers; juries are comprised of postal workers, teachers, retirees, business executives, among other workers, and unemployed individuals. Most jurors are not particularly familiar with legal terminology, and they will not always make inferences that might seem obvious to lawyers. These facts should be accounted for when developing a case theory.

For instance, a possible defense theory might present a particular scenario as a horrible set of circumstances set in motion by a husband walking in on his wife having sex with another man. If the result was the unfortunate and unintentional killing of the victim, an effective defense theory could focus on how emotionally traumatic it was to witness this event and how the defendant's actions were actually involuntary, unintentional *re*actions, which he could not control.

A possible prosecution case theory might focus on the time disparity between the moment that the husband walked in on his wife and the time of the murder, and how this gap in time supports the contention that the defendant intended to commit the murder. For instance, the defendant might have witnessed the affair, but then left the bedroom to retrieve and load a revolver from the opposite side of the house. The prosecution's case theory might be that, during this time, the defendant had time to deliberate the consequences of his actions, and did so, in fact. Therefore, what resulted was a conscious and deliberate decision to murder the victim.

The case theory should be clear and concise enough to be easily understood by a layperson. A confusing case theory will distract the jury from the story being told, and distracted juries are unlikely to continue listening to something they do not understand. The more alienated the jury, the less likely it is to return a favorable verdict.

C. CAPTIVATE THE AUDIENCE

Attorneys should not be afraid to introduce a little drama into the case theory. Today's juries demand more than a dry presentation of the facts and a recitation of the law. Television crime dramas have changed what juries expect from attorneys. They expect attorneys to be charismatic, entertaining, and intelligent, but they also are wary of the lawyer who fulfills the negative stereotypes often associated with attorneys. Needless to say, managing the expectations of the jury often requires a delicate balancing act.

Because jurors might expect the high drama of film or television, they will undoubtedly find the tedious testimony of expert witnesses who speak in scientific terms to be dry and boring. Juries may struggle to stay awake during seemingly trivial procedural matters they may not understand—matters, in fact, crucial to the attorney's case. Presenting a creative, or even unconventional, case theory will keep the jury tuned into a litigator's argument and, in turn, make them more likely to return a winning verdict.

D. SELL THE CASE

Effective attorneys believe their cas e theory. For a defense attorney, believing in the case should not be confused with believing the client is not guilty; instead, it means believing the prosecution will not be able to prove the elements of their case beyond a reasonable doubt. Juries will sense when an attorney does not believe her case. If the attorney does not believe in her case, neither will the jury. Advocates must have confidence and conviction in their cases and communicate that confidence and conviction to the jurors.

If you don't think outside the box, you will look ridiculous.

THINKING OUTSIDE THE BOX

Sometimes advocates are blessed with a clear-cut case; the case theory is obvious, and the pretrial preparation can proceed with comfort, confidence, and ease. Unfortunately, these cases are rare. Instead, it is more likely that an advocate will find herself with a case that, on its surface, may not present a clear case theory. Effective advocates prove themselves in such cases. When confronted with a problematic case, be creative: think outside the traditional box.

HYPO: *The Vengeful Husband*

You are a defense attorney and your client is desperate for help. Through an anonymous letter, he learned his wife was having an affair with one of his best friends. The client confirms his fears from neighbors who saw the two together and becomes distraught. This results in what a friend of your client's called "exhibitions of grief" so "violent" that it took the friend a considerable amount of time just to calm your client down. Your client could not sleep or eat, and when he confronted his wife and she confessed to the affair, he spent that night sobbing until finally succumbing to exhaustion.

The next day, his wife's lover was standing on the street outside their house attempting to signal her for another rendezvous. Your client, in broad daylight, with his neighbors and passersby watching, emerged from his home holding a gun. He shot at his former friend five times, with three of the bullets striking the target. Your client continued firing even as the man attempted to crawl away, begging him to stop.

You take notes from the interview and you analyze the facts. In your jurisdiction, your client will face the death penalty if convicted of murder. Since the victim was defenseless and begging for mercy, a self-defense theory will not work. Attempting to reduce the charge to manslaughter is equally futile because too much time elapsed between when he learned of the affair and when the killing occurred. There is no evidence your client suffered from any kind of long-term psychosis that would have made him unable to understand the criminality of his actions. What do you do?

A. CREATING A NOVEL THEORY

When considering the answer to that last question in the "Vengeful Husband" hypothetical, one thought might be to proceed under a theory of temporary insanity: the news of the affair caused the defendant to lose himself for a day or two, and over that time period, he was no longer able to determine right from wrong. The only trouble is that this particular case took place in 1859 and no attorney had ever yet advanced such a defense theory in the United States.

The facts above are those of *United States v. Sickles*,[9] a case that is considered by some to be "The Trial of the Nineteenth Century," in which Sickles, a U.S. Congressman, shot and killed District Attorney Phillip Barton Key, the son of Francis Scott Key, in Lafayette Square, Washington, D.C.[10] Sickles's defense  attorneys chose to go to trial with a case theory no one had ever heard in an American court before. Sickles, he argued, was not responsible for his actions because he had momentarily lost his ability to understand the consequences of his actions.[11] In his closing argument, defense counsel, James Brady, emphasized that Sickles needed only to be insane at the moment he committed the crime, stating:

> Suppose that the great, big, full, bursting heart of one oppressed by a terrible wrong could not find in sobs or tears any relief, what would have become of his brain? . . .
> The question is whether he was laboring under the species of insanity which satisfies you that he was quite unaware of the nature, character, and consequences of the

---

[9] 2 Hay. & Haz. 319 (D.C. Cir. 1859); *See* MICHAEL S. LIEF & H. MITCHELL CALDWELL, THE DEVIL'S ADVOCATES: GREATEST CLOSING ARGUMENTS IN CRIMINAL LAW 313–29 (2006) (discussing *Sickles*).

[10] *See* LIEF & CALDWELL, *supra* note 9, at 313–29.

[11] *Id.*

act he was committing, or in other words, whether he was under the influence of a diseased mind and was really unconscious *at the time he was committing the act* that was a crime.[12]

At the end of the day, the jurors were left questioning whether or not Sickles was sane when he killed Phillip Key. They ultimately acquitted him. While creating reasonable doubt as to whether their client had the mental capacity to commit a murder, Sickles's attorneys also created a new affirmative defense for criminal defendants. Though the burden of proving insanity has changed over the 150 years since the *Sickles* case, temporary insanity remains a defense to this day.

B. MODERN NOVEL THEORIES

1. Defense

Novel case theories are not a thing of the past. Criminal law continues to be redefined by practicing attorneys, particularly as our understanding of psychology continues to grow. Today, the term "battered woman's syndrome" is commonly used by even the general public, but just a little over thirty years ago one would have been hard-pressed to find anyone who had heard of it. That is, until Michigan defense lawyer Aryon Greydanus branched off from the foundation laid by Sickles's attorneys long before he was even born. Greydanus constructed a temporary insanity defense based on the traumatic effects of violent, long-term spousal abuse in 1978.[13] His client, a woman named Francine Hughes, was accused of killing her husband by burning down their house while he was asleep inside.[14] Using psychological and medical testimony, Greydanus effectively demonstrated to the jury how years of constant mistreatment and battery had driven her to commit the crime, and she was found not guilty.[15] The story of the case was so sensational when it occurred that it became a non-fiction book, as well as a made-for-TV movie, both entitled *The Burning Bed*.[16]

REAL CASE

The case, the book, and the movie all helped to spur interest and research into the effects of spousal abuse. While spousal abuse no longer provides grounds for a determination of temporary insanity, all fifty states (in varying degrees) allow evidence of abuse as part of a self-defense theory. Even though it may not be present in the same form today as Greydanus used it in 1977, his case theory, which began with his thinking outside the box, has significantly impacted the American legal world for decades.

---

[12] *Id.* at 354–56 (emphasis added).

[13] Sarah M. Buel, *Effective Assistance of Counsel for Battered Women Defendants: A Normative Construct*, 26 HARV. WOMEN'S L.J. 217, 316 (2003).

[14] *Id.* at 302.

[15] *Id.* at 316.

[16] *Id.*; FAITH MCNULTY, THE BURNING BED (1980).

2. Prosecution

Being creative and thinking of evidence to support a novel case theory is not the sole province of defense attorneys. As noted earlier during the *Oceana v. King* hypothetical, rape cases can be particularly difficult for prosecutors, depending on the kind of evidence they have available. Rape cases do not usually have witnesses, other than the victim, who are able to offer direct evidence. Typically, these cases involve circumstantial evidence, when it is available, and often turn on the credibility of the alleged victim and the defendant. This was true in *Kansas v. Marks*, a case that reached the Kansas State Supreme Court in 1982.[17]

While at a bar, a young female college student was approached by a man claiming to be a physician and Ph.D. who was working on an analytical book about people.[18] He told her his work consisted of collecting a series of interviews with individuals with varied backgrounds and experiences. According to her testimony, the man eventually convinced her to come back to his apartment, where he drugged her and then proceeded to engage in non-consensual sex. There was little physical harm detected, aside from some laceration of vaginal tissue, and the defendant argued that the sex had been consensual. The case became one of "he said, she said."

At the time, post-traumatic stress disorder had already become a recognized psychological condition, but its application to rape victims was a new and burgeoning field. Needing to bolster the credibility of their witness to gain a conviction, the prosecution put an expert on the stand to discuss the psychological symptoms that a person suffers long after a rape has taken place. The prosecution further established that the alleged victim had been experiencing many of these symptoms. Even though defense counsel argued that the expert's testimony was unduly prejudicial, the trial court ruled it sufficiently probative in value to be evaluated by the jury.[19] The State Supreme Court, affirming the conviction, upheld the ruling.

As with temporary insanity and battered woman's syndrome, evidence regarding rape trauma syndrome continues to be found admissible in courts throughout the United States in relevant circumstances. This is particularly true when prosecutors are faced with a consent defense, or are in need of explaining the behavior of victims who have suffered a severe psychological impact from the assault, such as a victim who, frozen from fright, does not attempt to flee her unarmed attacker.

C. BE CREATIVE

When developing their case theories, advocates need to be open to new possibilities. In many ways, this is a creative process. No matter which side an advocate is representing in a particular case, while in the courtroom she is at the forefront of the ever-changing legal landscape and has the power to shape that landscape's future. Finally, just because a defense or prosecutorial theory has not been asserted before, this does not mean that it cannot be presented or even that it should not be attempted.

---

[17] 647 P.2d 1292 (Kan. 1982).

[18] *Id.* at 1294–96.

[19] *Id.* at 1300.

OCEANA V. ERICKSON:
PROSECUTION'S OPENING STATEMENT

A. INTRODUCING CASE THEORY AND BUZZWORDS

Johnny "JT" Tobias should have died lying comfortably in a bed. He should have died with his doctor at his side as his heart stopped beating. But instead, he died lying stripped naked and comatose, on a cold, steel operating table. He died with his body covered in surgical prep solution, with an **organ harvester** hovering over him. A **harvester** so anxious to pick over his body parts that he pumped Johnny full of drugs he did not need, to treat symptoms he never had.	Personalize victim **Buzzwords** Depersonalize defendant
Ladies and gentlemen, when we are dealing with end of life issues, we should not have to worry about the real motivations of the people we trust to take care of us. **Every day, every hour, every minute of life is precious**, and a conscientious doctor's focus and attention should be solely on our well-being— nowhere else.	**Theme: victim's life mattered**
In the State of Oceana, we have made it a crime to **endanger** members of our society who are made helpless by virtue of handicap or disease—people like Johnny Tobias—because they cannot protect themselves. That crime is patient abuse, and, to be convicted of that crime according to the law, we must prove that the defendant **created a situation** that **placed** an especially vulnerable person in harm's way.	**Jury instructions** **Jury instructions** **Jury instructions**
Over the course of this trial, we will show that the defendant **put Johnny at risk** when he took over his care with the **intention of harvesting his organs.** He then **endangered** Johnny's life by ordering painkillers and anti-anxiety medications that had the potential to accelerate his death and served no valid medical purpose.	**Jury instructions** **Motivation** **Jury instructions** **Case theory**
It is my responsibility to obtain some degree of justice for the victim and his family because no one should ever have the right to determine on behalf of Johnny Tobias whether or not certain **moments of his life were not worth living.** But in this case, the evidence will show you that was exactly the kind of power the defendant decided he had.	**Theme: victim's life mattered** **Stir jurors' emotions**

B. PRESENTATION OF FAVORABLE FACTS

As an **organ-harvesting surgeon**, the defendant works for a corporation that procures and distributes people's organs. It is what he does; that is his job. And it is a job he had done admirably hundreds of times before, with donors that were already dead. But the problem was that this time it was not a dead donor, **but a living patient. Johnny Tobias was still alive. His heart was still beating and his lungs still continued to breathe.**	**Buzzwords** Deflect unfavorable facts **Theme: victim's life mattered** **Evoke emotions**

C. ANTICIPATING YOUR OPPONENT

Now, during this trial, you will hear testimony that there is a conflict of interest for organ harvesters when they are also the doctors treating a living patient—and with someone like Johnny, the longer he lived, the less chance there was that his organs could be successfully transplanted. **But what the defense's expert will want you to believe is that, because there was no governing universal protocol or national standard in place, the defendant couldn't have known the right course of action.** The trouble with that is that there *was* an ethical protocol in place on that day. **Our ethical protocol—the law created to protect people like Johnny Tobias—and the facts of this case will show you that patient abuse laws were broken.** The only explanation the facts and the law will support is that the defendant put Johnny at risk because his primary focus was on harvesting his viable organs, and not on prolonging what remained of his life.	**Anticipating defense arguments** **Theme: victim's life mattered** **Motive**

OCEANA V. ERICKSON:
DEFENSE'S CLOSING ARGUMENT

A. INTRODUCTION OF CASE THEORY

The State does not know the amount of medication administered to John Tobias. The State does not know what ethical standard was appropriate. The State does not even know the cause of death. But we do know that **John Tobias was going to die, and there was nothing more that could be done to save him.** Motivated by their son's desire to be an organ donor and knowing that his condition would not improve, his parents made the decision to withdraw life support and let their son die peacefully. Dr. Alex Erickson worked to fulfill their	**Summarizing case theory**

wishes—**to ease John Tobias's passing and to permit him to die with dignity.** And for that, Alex Erickson has been accused of a crime. The prosecution, in its misguided quest to blame John Tobias's death on someone, has charged Alex Erickson with patient abuse, but there is no evidence to support this charge.	**Summarizing case theory**
	Innocent motive
The prosecution's case is based on pure speculation. It is based on murky assertions and unfounded conclusions. It is based on arguments the evidence simply does not support. But you, as a jury, will have the opportunity to show the prosecution that Alex Erickson did nothing wrong.	**Theme: Speculation and considering the opposition**

B. EXPLANATION OF JURY INSTRUCTIONS AND BUZZWORDS

Now, in a short while, the judge will read you the final jury instructions, but I want to focus on two important questions. If the answer to either of them is "no," then you must return a not guilty verdict.	**Emphasizing jury instruction**
(1) The first question is this: Did Alex Erickson **place John Tobias in a position where his health was endangered**?	**Buzzword from jury instructions**
I want to emphasize the word "**place**," because the prosecution is asserting that Dr. Erickson put John Tobias in that position. But that's not true. John Tobias had suffered cardiac arrest and irreversible brain damage; he was in a profound coma. His doctor had prescribed end of life care but his parents had decided to withdraw life support. All of this occurred before Dr. Erickson arrived at Angels Regional Medical Center on May 1, 2007.	**Emphasize prosecution's burden**
Yet the prosecution claims Dr. Erickson *placed* him in this *endangered* position. But that is not true. It is a tragedy that a young man was taken from his family, but we cannot ignore the fact that John Tobias was going to die. His presiding physician determined there was nothing more that could be done.	**Language from jury instructions**
(2) The second question is whether or not Dr. Erickson **created a high risk of death or great bodily harm** for John Tobias.	**Buzzword taken from jury instruction**
If the prosecution has not proved beyond a reasonable doubt that Dr. Erickson **created** that high risk—that great bodily harm—then he is not guilty. Here I want to focus on the word "**create**." We know what that means. It means to make something from nothing. The prosecution is saying that Dr. Erickson **created** that risk of death, but you cannot **create** a risk of something when that something is already a certainty.	**Buzzwords**
Dr. Erickson did not **place** John Tobias in that position where his health was endangered. Dr. Erickson did not **create** a high risk of death.	**Negating elements of offense**

C. Credibility/Developing a Factual Theory and Theme

The Angel State Donor Network called Dr. Erickson and his team. He was called because he is one of the most qualified surgeons in the world. **Remember that Dr. Erickson was educated at the best schools and hospitals in the world. And he sat in that witness chair and testified that he had taken an oath to keep his patients from harm, and that is exactly what he did for John Tobias.**	**Enforcing client credibility** **Personalizing defendant**
We also heard the testimony of Dr. Jon Colton. Dr. Colton, recognized by the court as an expert, testified that Dr. Erickson did not violate any protocol and that there is no evidence that, at any time, Dr. Erickson did anything to endanger John Tobias.	
These are things we know. But there are many things the prosecution does not know. Their case is based on **pure speculation.** And pure speculation cannot satisfy their burden of proof beyond a reasonable doubt.	**Theme: Speculation**
You heard Dr. Mahoney. He was unable to testify with certainty about critical elements of the prosecution's case. **They do not know how much medicine was administered and cannot be certain how many doses were administered. They do not have a protocol to point to. They do not have a coroner's report to corroborate their position and they do not know the official cause of death.**	**Theme: Speculation**

D. Tying It All Together

The prosecution says Dr. Erickson was anxious to get those organs, but that is not true. Dr. Erickson stayed with his patient for ten hours, long after he knew those organs were no longer viable. But he did so because he had a duty, and he saw it through.	
They say Dr. Alex Erickson **placed** John Tobias's health in danger and he **created** a high risk of death. But the truth is that, by accusing him of a crime, the prosecution has **placed** Alex Erickson in danger, and they have **created** a risk for all of us. The prosecution does not see that, because they are **blindly grasping at straws of guilt that are not there.** But as a jury, by returning a not guilty verdict, you can open their eyes by showing them that Dr. Erickson did nothing wrong, that he upheld his oath, that Dr. Alex Erickson did his job.	**Highlighting buzzwords** **Theme: Speculation**

LABELS TO IDENTIFY THE PLAYERS

For the Prosecution	For the Defense
The Defendant	Mr. Smith, the accused
The Defendant	Doctor Everett, Father O'Malley
Child molester/registered sex offender	Mr. Jones
The People	The Prosecution, the government, the State
The surviving victim	The alleged victim, complaining witness
The perpetrator/murderer/killer/assailant	The wrongly accused
Officer of the peace, law enforcement	Cop
Mary Jones	The decedent or the accuser
Unemployed	Between jobs, looking for a job
Drug user/addict	In treatment
Drunk	Recovering alcoholic, rehabilitated
Transient	Mr. Smith
The witness is a man of faith	The witness is a religious zealot
Cheater, womanizer, philanderer	Imperfect human being, sociable
Transvestite	Alternative lifestyle
D has an extensive criminal history	D does not have a perfect past
Overzealous	Compassionate
Reckless	Responsible
Organ Harvester	Transplant Surgeon
Victim	Patient
Rapist	Date

LABELS FOR THE INCIDENT

For the Prosecution	For the Defense
Mary June's terrible ordeal	Ms. June's story
The Defendant's story	What really happened
The Defendant's girlfriend's story	Bill's solid alibi
The tragic event, the crime	The event in question, the occurrence
The brutal attack	The incident
The beating/stabbing/shooting	The alleged altercation
The vicious crime spree	Alleged incidents
The crime scene	The site of the incident
Ripped off his/her clothes	His/her clothes came off
Pried the money from his hands	Took the money from him
Bashed, smacked, walloped, knocked, smashed	Nudged, contacted, hit
Bludgeoned, pistol whipped	Hit, contacted, tapped
Came unglued, lost temper, went ballistic	Became emotional
Grabbed his arm	Took or held his arm
Lied, fabricated, falsified	Misspoke, was mistaken
Arrested	Was held in confinement or against his will
Got into a fight	Had an argument
The police restrained him	The police pinned him against the concrete
Questioning	Interrogation
The police subdued	The police beat, bludgeoned
Defendant stormed out of the room	Bill left the room
Blood gushed from her wound	The injury
The jagged knife slashed her throat	The unfortunate crime
Crash	Accident
Defendant's threat	Alleged remark
Brutal rape	Consensual sex
Murder/killing	Homicide
Death	Passing
Blindfolded	Unable to see
Threat of force	Fraudulent consent
Money	Property

LABELS TO IDENTIFY EVIDENCE

For the Prosecution	For the Defense
AK 47, rifle	Registered firearm for home protection
9mm semiautomatic	The alleged firearm
Jagged edged knife	Hunting knife
Club	Baseball bat
Irrefutable DNA evidence	Circumstantial Evidence
Uncontested evidence	The State's version
The defense's pure speculation	Reasonable Doubt
Solid case	Full of doubt
Credible, trustworthy evidence	Fabricated, unreliable evidence
Positive, definite, or certain ID, definitive	Tainted, questionable ID, weak, false

LEGAL PHRASES

For the Prosecution	For the Defense
The people will prove Justice for the People The crime with which the Defendant has been charged	You won't hear . . . Justice for the wrongly accused The unfounded accusation
Legalese	**Plain Language**
Activated my siren I detected the odor of alcohol Subsequent Prior Exited my patrol vehicle	I turned on my siren It smelled like alcohol After Before Got out of my car

SUMMARY

Developing the case theory is, perhaps, the most important of all strategic elements essential to pretrial preparation and successful advocacy. Effectively developed and persuasive case theories are comprised of both legal theory and factual theory. As such, these two elements must come together to convey *what* happened and *why* it happened, while simultaneously persuading the judge, opposing counsel, or perhaps a jury, of counsel's targeted outcome. It must be emphasized, however, that the development of a winning case theory takes time and careful consideration, ultimately serving as the foundation upon which counsel builds its case.

To recap what was noted in this chapter, there are seven steps that can assist the attorney in his development of a case theory, and they are as follows: consulting the jury instructions; identifying and narrowing a factual theory; developing a clear theme; incorporating buzzwords; anticipating opposing counsel's strategy; considering evidentiary issues, and, finally, anticipating juror response to the case as presented. Each of these steps takes time to craft if they are to be successful, and the attorney must, accordingly, approach the task of developing his case with thoughtful and deliberate preparation.

Whether representing the prosecution or defense, counsel must look to the jury instructions in order to precisely identify exactly what needs to be proven, and how the attorney will set about providing that proof. Whatever case theory counsel chooses to adopt, they should first consider how the jury instructions might benefit their case. For example, defense counsel might consider whether one element in particular will be especially challenging for the prosecution to prove, and if she identifies such an element, then that is where her focus should lie. Meanwhile, the prosecution should also consider whether there are aspects of the crime charged that are *not* actually elements, and thereby do *not* need proving. For example, motive is not an element of murder and, as a result, the prosecution may look to the jury instructions to fully identify what, correspondingly, they do not have to prove. Counsel should identify what works to their advantage and utilize it in the client's case. The jury instructions provide a focused point of reference from which a successful case theory might be developed.

Once a legal theory has been pinned down, counsel must then apply the facts of their particular case, as a clear theory will convey the legal significance of such facts. After adopting a theory that relates the facts to the law, counsel should select a theme for the case. Themes are most effective when they are focused, memorable, and at the same time effectively serve to communicate counsel's argument. A theory, however, should also be bolstered with buzzwords. Buzzwords should be chosen carefully because when they are effectively incorporated into the case theory, they assist in not only maintaining the theme, but also in commanding the listener's attention. Careful and appropriate word choice can make a case theory more attractive, and therefore more believable. While focusing on one's own work product is important, counsel should also anticipate the opposition's ongoing preparation. Counsel can react to their opponent's case theory and discredit it well before it is ever presented in the courtroom.

Counsel, however, must at all times remember that developing a case theory ultimately depends on what admissible evidence is at their disposal, and the theory should be tailored to revolve around what can actually be brought in at trial. And, finally, in order for any case theory to be compelling, the jury has to be generally receptive to the attorney from the outset. The reality is that jurors might not be receptive to even the most skillfully crafted case theory if they perceive counsel in a negative light. In order to really "sell the case," counsel should put forth an image that is at once professional, personable, and articulate. Creativity in constructing and presenting the case theory can, of course, go a long way towards achieving a successful outcome for the client. In sum, it will be the most prepared counsel who will come to court with a case theory that aids them in effectively persuading *any* jury.

CHECKLIST

✓ Consult the jury instructions: the jury instructions lay out the legal elements that must be proven to establish a conviction. Carefully break down the instructions to identify key terms and match them up with the facts and evidence of the case.

✓ Narrow and identify a winning theory: a case theory concisely explains to the jury why the defendant is innocent or guilty. Whereas a prosecutor must explain the defendant's actual involvement in the crime, a defense attorney must explain either why the defendant could not have been involved, or why the defendant was not legally culpable for his conduct. Decide on a single, coherent explanation that is supported by the evidence and that addresses the legal requirements for conviction detailed in the jury instructions.

✓ Develop a theme: a case theme sums up the overall theory in a brief, easily understood message that resonates in jurors' minds. Formulate a theme that will stay with them as they deliberate their verdict.

✓ Bolster the case theory and theme with buzzwords: develop a list of buzzwords that communicate to jurors in a straightforward manner your version of the case. Incorporate your chosen buzzwords into your presentation, using an organizational structure that will logically and persuasively convey your message to the jury.

✓ Anticipate your opponent's approach: always think through the points that your opponent will likely make, bearing in mind how these points might undermine your position. Be prepared to defend every element of your case and, when developing your argument, be certain to have identified any weaknesses in your case that might easily be attacked.

✓ Examine the evidence for admissibility and credibility issues: since a case theory can be founded only on facts and evidence that are admitted, be certain to consider the pieces of evidence that might potentially be excluded from the jury's consideration. Develop a back-up plan if a piece of evidence cannot be used as you planned, or if its credibility is called into question.

✓ Remember the jury: do everything you can to ensure that the jurors receive a positive impression from the very first time you meet them. Work to convince them of your case theory both by appealing to logic and by working to captivate their interest throughout the trial. Finally, remember that the jury always wants to hear about motive, even when it might not be legally relevant.

✓ And lastly: always think outside the box. Both prosecutors and defense attorneys are constantly redefining the practice of law by presenting novel case theories. As you develop your own case theories, remember to be creative.

CHAPTER 3
CHARGING

"A wise man, therefore, proportions his belief to the evidence."
–David Hume

"Charging," also known as "filing," occurs when the government exercises its discretion to bring charges against the accused and is the formal initiation of criminal proceedings against a defendant. The formal charging document, which lists the charges filed against a defendant, is called the complaint, and enumerates all of the charges against the accused. Although drafting a complaint might seem like a relatively easy task, its significance should not be underestimated. Jurisdictions have different standards for what constitutes a proper complaint. In nearly each jurisdiction, if the complaint is defective, the State cannot continue with the prosecution of the accused. In some instances, a flawed complaint can even result in an overturned conviction. In short, hyper-accuracy cannot be overemphasized.

A complaint serves three main purposes. First, the complaint informs the defendant of the exact criminal charges and allegations that he is facing. Second, the complaint also informs the judge and prosecutor who will be assigned to the case of the exact charges that the State will need to prove in order to obtain a conviction. Third, the complaint establishes a formal record of the charges while also serving as a defense against future prosecutions for the same offense.

Although jurisdictions have various standards for criminal complaints, there are some fundamental components. *Hamling v. United States* laid out the most basic components that a complaint should include.[1] A proper complaint must contain:

1. Identification of the accused;
2. Applicable law(s) and date(s) of violation(s);
3. Existence of probable cause supporting the arrest and charge;
4. Signed affidavit by the prosecutor;
5. Provision of bail to be determined by a judge or magistrate.

Not all defendants, notably, are charged via a complaint. In instances where a grand jury is convened to determine if probable cause exists to bring charges, the accused will be charged via a grand jury indictment. Typically, in federal court, defendants are charged via a grand jury indictment, rather than through the process of a prosecutor filing a complaint. The grand jury, like a petit jury, consists of citizens from the community. The grand jury process is discussed in detail in Chapter 9.

---

[1] Hamling v. United States, 418 U.S. 87, 118 (1974) ("[A]n indictment is sufficient if it, first, contains the elements of the offense charged and fairly informs a defendant of the charge against which he must defend, and, second, enables him to plead an acquittal or conviction in bar of future prosecutions for the same offense.").

THE DECISION TO PROSECUTE

Charging begins with the prosecution's decision to file charges. By the time a prosecutor has to decide whether to file charges, law enforcement has investigated the alleged crime and gathered evidence. At this juncture, the prosecuting agency must decide whether to file charges, and if so, what charges to file. Typically, a police officer submits a police report to a filing prosecutor and requests charges to be filed against a suspect. Sometimes the police officer will drop off a stack of police reports to the prosecutor (often called the "filing deputy"), and in some instances the police officer will explain the evidence and attempt to persuade the prosecutor to file criminal charges. Criminal charges should only be filed if the following four requirements have been satisfied: there is sufficient admissible evidence to prove all elements of each charge; there is sufficient admissible evidence of the identity of the charged individual as the perpetrator; the filing deputy is satisfied that the evidence proves the accused is guilty; and the admissible evidence is strong enough that the defendant will probably be convicted, even taking into account the most plausible defense. While the standard for filing charges is usually only probable cause, most prosecutorial agencies apply a more stringent standard because the case will ultimately need to be proved beyond a reasonable doubt. Jurisdictions vary as to the extent of prosecutorial discretion. In California, for instance, the prosecutor is given statutory discretion to initiate and conduct prosecutions for public offenses.[2]

Once the decision is made whether or not to file charges, there is little review by the courts.[3] Prosecuting agencies have very broad discretion to file or decline to file charges, and no higher authority has the power to review a filing decision.[4] This broad grant of discretion, however, is conditioned on the

ethical duty not to abuse it.[5] The American Bar Association provides *Standards of Criminal Justice* that guide prosecutors in exercising their discretion to bring charges.[6] Unless the prosecutor believes that the defendant has committed the charged crime and there is a reasonable probability that he can prove the case to a jury beyond a reasonable doubt, for example, he should not file charges because the prosecutor's job is to seek justice and not to obtain a conviction at any cost.[7] A prosecutor should consider the probability of conviction after reviewing all the admissible evidence balanced against the most plausible defense

---

[2] CAL. GOV'T CODE § 26500 (Deering 2012). *See* 4 B.E. WITKIN ET AL., CALIFORNIA CRIMINAL LAW § 18 (3d ed. 2000).

[3] *See* United States v. Giannattasio, 979 F.2d 98, 100 (7th Cir. 1992) ("A judge in our system does not have the authority to tell prosecutors which crimes to prosecute or when to prosecute them. Prosecutorial discretion resides in the executive, . . . and that discretion, . . . is not reviewable for simple abuse of discretion.").

[4] *E.g.*, Town of Newton v. Rumery, 480 U.S. 386, 396 (1987) (broad discretion afforded prosecutors is appropriate because prosecutors, not courts, must evaluate strength of case, allocation of resources, and enforcement priorities).

[5] *See, e.g.*, Berger v. United States, 295 U.S. 78, 88 (1935) (the prosecutor is in a "peculiar and very definite sense the servant of the law, the twofold aim of which guilt shall not escape or innocence suffer").

[6] ABA STANDARDS FOR CRIMINAL JUSTICE PROSECUTION FUNCTION AND DEFENSE FUNCTION (3d ed. 1993) (hereinafter "STANDARDS").

[7] *Id.* 3-1.2(c). *But see* Bruce A. Green & Fred C. Zacharias, *Prosecutorial Neutrality*, 2004 WIS. L. REV. 837, 903 (2004) (noting that while prosecutors should be "fair" and should remain "neutral" and be engaged in "seek[ing]

inherent in the evidence.[8] While there are multiple factors that can influence the decision to prosecute, there are certain factors that are improper grounds for charging and should not be considered when deciding whether to file charges against a defendant. These include: political pressure, public opinion, improper bias (such as race, religion, nationality, gender or other personal bias), or other personal motivations such as publicity or promotion.[9] Other improper factors include personal animosity or some other association with the suspect, victim, or witnesses.

CHART 3.1

Improper Bases for Filing Charges

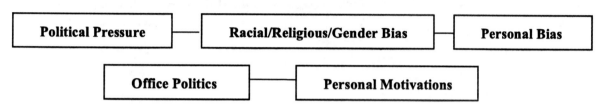

| Political Pressure | — | Racial/Religious/Gender Bias | — | Personal Bias |

| Office Politics | — | Personal Motivations |

For example, in the recent high-publicity case mentioned below, three young college athletes' reputations were left irreparably harmed largely because a District Attorney blindly pursued convictions in spite of the available evidence.[10] In 2006, Duke University made national headlines when three lacrosse players were accused of raping an exotic dancer at a party. The scandal garnered national attention for being a hate crime because all three players were white and the accuser was African-American. The Durham County District Attorney drew attention for his overly zealous prosecution of the case despite the discovery of exculpatory evidence, including inconsistencies in the accuser's testimony, solid alibis, and DNA evidence vindicating the players. In 2007, the State Bar of North Carolina's disciplinary panel found the District Attorney guilty of fraud, dishonesty, deceit, and misrepresentation. He was subsequently disbarred and went on to face criminal contempt charges for making false statements before a judge and disciplinary panel.

An important lesson from the Duke Lacrosse Scandal is that the stigma associated with criminal charges is severe. Although the law presumes a person is innocent until proven guilty, society is oftentimes not so forgiving. People who have been exonerated or acquitted can face the consequences of a wrongful prosecution for an indefinite period after the proceedings against them have concluded.

As for the victims of crimes, under the Crime Victims' Rights Statute they are allowed to give prosecutors input about their perspective on the offense, although this does not give victims the right to

---

justice," that such words really have no "fixed meaning" and are only "proxies for a constellation of other, sometimes equally vague, normative expectations about how prosecutors should make decisions").

[8] *See* STANDARDS § 3-3.9(a), (f). *See also id.* § 3-3.6(c); CAL. R. PROF'L CONDUCT 5-110 (2012).

[9] STANDARDS § 3-3.1(b).

[10] Duke University, *Looking Back at the Duke Lacrosse Case*, DUKE OFFICE OF NEWS & COMMC'N, http://today.duke.edu/showcase/lacrosseincident/ (last visited Jan. 25, 2013).

influence the charging decision.[11] Approximately half of the states have provisions that allow similar victim input. The prosecutor's charging discretion is broad; however, there is a mechanism to ensure that there is probable cause that the accused committed a crime. Before being bound over to face a trial, there must either be a probable cause determination by a grand jury, or by a magistrate at a preliminary hearing. A thorough review of preliminary hearings and grand jury hearings is contained in Chapters 8 and 9 respectively.

Furthermore, when considering juries and potential jury panels, a prosecutor should not allow local political or social attitudes to discourage him from filing charges even if he thinks a local jury may unreasonably refuse to convict. If, for example, an instance of battery against a police officer occurs in a community hostile towards law enforcement, the prosecutor should still not be swayed from charging and seeking justice. Regardless of local sensibilities, the prosecutor's duty is to enforce the law on behalf of the People.

A. PROSECUTORIAL DISCRETION

There are myriad reasons why prosecutors are given such wide discretion regarding whether and what charges to file. Prosecutors should have the ability to make decisions based on what is fair and just in each circumstance. Sometimes there are circumstances that mitigate the accused's conduct such that justice will be best served if no charges are filed. In some instances, there are antiquated laws still in existence, for example, statutes that criminalize some types of consensual sexual acts between adults. Additionally, since taxpayer money and law enforcement resources are finite, it is sometimes more practical not to prosecute minor violations. Likewise, some cases are just too weak to meet the burden of proof required for a conviction. Prosecutors are also given the discretion to reject filing charges and then upon further investigation or further reflection to change their decision and choose to file charges. As long as the charging decision is made in good faith, the initial decision to decline to file charges does not bind the prosecution. The court does not presume that pretrial prosecutorial decisions are vindictive.[12] As long as the charging decision is properly motivated, with the intent to seek justice, prosecutors are given wide filing latitude. However, there are some checks designed to prevent prosecuting agencies from abusing their power.

Most jurisdictions allow grand juries to initiate criminal charges by indicting a defendant even if a prosecuting agency declines to file charges; however, this rarely occurs. It is also possible, albeit unusual, that a prosecutor could be impeached for being incompetent, corrupt, or for having been convicted of a serious offense. In extraordinary circumstances involving allegations of government corruption or conflicts of interest, a special prosecutor may be appointed to replace the prosecutor. Additionally, a prosecutor's discretion can be limited if a defendant can prove that his equal protection rights were violated, and that charges against him

---

[11] 18 U.S.C. § 3771 (2006).

[12] United States v. Goodwin, 457 U.S. 368, 372–73 (1982).

were the result of discriminating against a protected class (such as race, religion, or sexual orientation).[13] These challenges to prosecutorial discretion rarely prevail. Finally, the defense can have charges dismissed if they are able to prove that the prosecution was vindictive. For example, if a defendant has been convicted of a misdemeanor, and granted a re-trial, it would be an abuse of discretion for the prosecution to file a felony charge for conduct that arose from the same offense.[14] Importantly, in federal court and the vast majority of state courts, prosecutors are immune from being sued for malicious prosecution. Since the checks on prosecutors' filing decisions are so few, it is imperative that prosecutors wisely and fairly exercise their discretion and do not abuse their charging power. Such an abuse would undermine the public's confidence in the criminal justice system, and would constitute a serious breach of ethics. After considering the evidence, the prosecutor generally has five options:

1. File the charges requested by the presenting detective;
2. Decline to file charges;
3. File charges of a more/less serious degree;
4. Request further investigation; or
5. Diversion.

If the prosecutor finds that the evidence uncovered by the presenting detective rises to the level of probable cause for the proposed charge, then he can proceed by filing a complaint. Of course, if the prosecutor finds that there is not enough evidence, or if there are other problems of proof, then he can decline to file charges altogether. Alternatively, the prosecutor may determine that the evidence warrants filing more serious charges, enhancements, or allegations. Accordingly, the filing prosecutor has the discretion to file charges that are more serious or less serious than what was requested by the presenting detective. Notably, the prosecutor has the option of requesting further investigation before deciding whether to file charges. Lastly, a prosecutor may also elect to divert a case.

If the prosecutor elects to divert the case, then there is a disposition of the case without a conviction; typically, the defendant will agree to certain conditions, such as obeying all criminal laws and completing counseling or substance abuse rehabilitation. If the defendant abides by the terms of the diversion for an agreed upon period of time, then the charges are dismissed. If the defendant does not abide by the terms of the diversion, then he faces criminal prosecution. Diversion is most often granted in cases in which the defendant has no significant criminal record and the charges involve minor offenses, such as being under the influence of narcotics, possession of narcotics, or minor battery and alcohol offenses.

It is entirely appropriate for the filing deputy to request the investigating detective to complete further investigation before making a charging decision. For instance, all material witnesses should be interviewed if possible; all scientific evidence, leads such as DNA,

---

[13] Oyler v. Boles, 368 U.S. 448 (1962).

[14] Blackledge v. Perry, 417 U.S. 21, 27–28 (1974).

fingerprints, chemical analysis and ballistics evidence, should be exhausted; and the law enforcement crime lab should be requested to conduct appropriate examinations. If feasible, the accused should be given his *Miranda* rights and questioned. Preferably, statements by the accused and other witnesses should be in writing and signed or audio or video recorded. It may be beneficial, moreover, for the prosecutor to request that the detective conduct further investigation such as visiting the crime scene, conducting simulations, or gathering further evidence. If necessary, the prosecutor can request a search warrant from a magistrate if it is believed that certain evidence, such as files or computer records, or items such as blood or fibers, could be obtained from the accused's home, office, vehicle, or person. Generally, the police will be more cooperative regarding conducting further investigations before charges are filed, as they have a greater incentive to investigate a case thoroughly at the stage when they are trying to convince the prosecutor to file charges.

B. HORIZONTAL V. VERTICAL PROSECUTION

Should charges be filed, the procedural path that a case follows depends on the jurisdiction. A prosecuting agency can be structured in many different ways; the two most common forms are vertical and horizontal prosecution. Horizontal prosecution of a case can be illustrated by imagining the life of a case on a spectrum with charging at the beginning, sentencing at the end, and other stages in between with each stage of the prosecution potentially handled by a different prosecutor.

CHART 3.2
Horizontal Prosecution

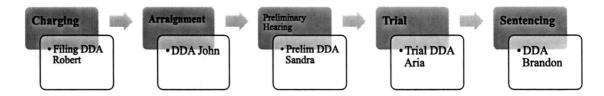

Typically, horizontally structured prosecuting agencies have a group of prosecutors who exclusively handle one stage of the process, whether it is charging, preliminary hearings, or trials. Conversely, vertical prosecution can be imagined on a vertical line with one prosecutor handling the case from top to bottom. Vertical prosecution is most commonly used by specially assigned units, such as those investigating major narcotics crimes, sex crimes, child abuse, gang crimes, or crimes against peace officers. Given the specialized nature of those types of prosecutions, it is more practical to have one experienced, trained prosecutor handling the case the entire way through. Oftentimes, these crimes are more serious and require a certain degree of experience and training. Moreover, certain offenses, such as sex crimes and child abuse, involve criminal acts of a personal nature such that it takes time to cultivate trust among victims and witnesses. Chapters 5 and 6 explore how the interviewing of witnesses, including victims, can be a delicate process. Once the prosecutor has gained the victim's trust and put her at ease, it would be counterproductive to pass the case to another deputy and begin the process anew.

CHART 3.2
Vertical Prosecution

HYPO: *Oceana v. Lenient*

Charges have been brought against a man, Howard Lenient, for beating and raping his girlfriend, Tyra Banker. The victim has two young children, one of whom witnessed the alleged beating. It is clear that, in order to secure a conviction, Banker and at least one of her children will have to testify. The preparation of the case will likely take as much as a year, and there will need to be consistent contact between the district attorney's office and the woman and her children.

Consider the problems that horizontal prosecution might present in such a situation. How might the victim react to meeting with two or three different attorneys in the first few months after charges are filed? How might the presence of different attorneys affect the children who are entirely unfamiliar with the criminal process, and are already fearful of the man who allegedly beat and raped their mother? How uncomfortable might it be for the victim and her children to have to relate the traumatic events to a series of different prosecutors?

GETTING DOWN TO BUSINESS

A. CASE EVALUATION

Not every case presented to a prosecutor will be filed.[15] A shrewd prosecutor will conduct a thorough evaluation of a case before he decides to bring charges, and the most important aspect of this evaluation is weighing the evidence.[16] Only admissible evidence can support filing a criminal charge. Thus, even if a prosecutor has what seems like a mountain of evidence, he might find that the case will likely result in a dismissal or acquittal after weeding out the inadmissible evidence, the weak evidence,

---

[15] For instance, less than two percent of drug arrests lead to federal prosecutions. Sara Sun Beale, *The Many Faces of Overcriminalization: From Morals and Mattress Tags to Overfederalization*, 54 AM. U. L. REV. 747, 764 (2005). It is estimated by several commentators that from fifty to eighty percent of felony cases initiated by the police do not go past the prosecutor's office or a preliminary hearing. Donald McIntyre & David Lippman, *Prosecutors and Early Disposition of Felony Cases*, 56 A.B.A. J. 1154, 1154 (1970).

[16] *See* STANDARDS § 3-3.9(a) ("A prosecutor [shall] not . . . permit the continued pendency of criminal charges in the absence of sufficient admissible evidence to support a conviction.").

and the evidence that will not survive a motion to suppress. Just as police officers cannot legally detain a suspect based on a hunch, prosecutors cannot ethically or legally file criminal charges against a suspect unless the available evidence supports the probability of obtaining a conviction. Further, prosecutors should remember that they represent the citizens of their state (or nation in the case of U.S. Attorneys), and they should not be pressured into filing or rejecting charges based on the wishes of individuals, including victims, detectives, political groups, or the public consensus. It is particularly important when dealing with high profile cases that prosecutors act with integrity and resist making decisions based on public pressure.

Prosecutors must also be mindful of the difference between actual guilt and legal guilt. In other words, before using his discretion to file charges, the prosecutor must believe not only that a suspect committed a crime, but also that there will be sufficient evidence to prove that the suspect committed the crime. Additionally, prosecutors must follow the law; their discretion does not afford them the power to pick and choose which laws to uphold. The legislature makes the laws; law enforcement officers arrest those whom they believe have violated the laws; and prosecutors use their discretion to determine whom to charge with crimes. Although prosecutors are given wide latitude when filing charges, they must adhere to ethical and legal standards in order to maintain the public's confidence. Prosecutors would be wise to remember that their duty is not only to protect victims, but to also uphold the presumption of innocence and to make sure that the suspect's rights are not violated. If the police have clearly violated a suspect's constitutional rights by illegally obtaining evidence (such as by searching a suspect's home without probable cause, in violation of the Fourth Amendment), the prosecutor should not file the charges unless there is independent evidence that does not stem from the illegal search.

During the initial investigation, if the accused makes a statement negating criminal liability, then that statement should be investigated regardless of how implausible it might sound. In a similar vein, initial scientific examinations should be completed as expeditiously as possible. This is especially true when there is doubt as to the outcome of the examination. If significant deficiencies in the initial investigation remain, then the prosecutor should insist upon further investigation before filing in order to clear up the unresolved issues, even if it means allowing the accused to be released and rearrested at a later date. Prosecutors also need to resist pressure from police officers to file charges if the prosecutor is not convinced that the charges can be proved in a court of law. A key point to remember is that if the investigators do not try to obtain all probative evidence, such as by lifting fingerprints at the crime scene, the defense will surely point out this failure at trial. Such arguments are debilitating to the prosecution because of the difficulty of rebutting such comments. Therefore, it is critical that prosecutors make every effort to encourage thorough investigations.

When evaluating a case, a prosecutor should ask himself two important questions. First, did a crime in fact occur? And second, is there sufficient admissible evidence to prove that the suspect committed the crime? In the eyes of the law, no chargeable offense can be proven if there is insufficient evidence to support it. If there is no violation of the jurisdiction's law, then there is no use wasting the jurisdiction's resources to prosecute the act. Second, even if a crime has occurred, the evidence must further show that the defendant is likely the person who committed it. Because a trial is a determination of a specific individual's guilt or innocence, identifying the defendant as the perpetrator is absolutely crucial and failure to do so constitutes irreversible error. The prosecution will never meet its burden of proof unless the evidence satisfies both of these elements.

B. EVIDENTIARY ANALYSIS

Evidence can be direct or circumstantial.[17] Both types of evidence are of equal weight if determined to be reliable. Direct evidence occurs when a witness testifies through personal knowledge that the defendant is culpable, while circumstantial evidence does not expressly prove that the defendant committed the crime. Instead, circumstantial evidence allows the triers of fact to infer from a set of facts that the defendant is guilty. A standard example of direct evidence is eyewitness testimony, whereas a typical example of circumstantial evidence is fingerprint or DNA evidence. In closing arguments before a jury, prosecutors often explain circumstantial evidence by presenting an analogy. An example would be the following:

TAKE NOTE

Direct evidence would be if a witness testified that he went outside and saw it was raining. Circumstantial evidence would be if someone inside a windowless room concluded that it was raining because someone entered the room carrying a wet umbrella and wearing a raincoat, dripping with water.

HYPO: *Oceana v. Spasely*

A witness, Judy Elroy, hears gunshots and opens her front door to see a man fleeing from her neighbor's apartment. She calls the police, who then respond to the scene. When they arrive, officers find a murdered woman and a gun in the apartment adjacent to Elroy's. A ballistics expert performs analysis on the bullet lodged in the victim's chest, and it turns out to match the gun that officers found. A fingerprint lifted from the gun handle is entered into the police fingerprint database, and it returns a match to the suspect, George Spasely.

The suspect, Spasely, is arrested and placed in a lineup with five other, similar-looking people. Elroy picks out Spasely as the person she saw running away from the apartment. She also testifies at trial about hearing the gunshots, seeing Spasely flee, and picking him out of the lineup.

Which aspects of the evidence in this hypothetical are direct evidence and which are circumstantial evidence? Is the direct or circumstantial evidence more convincing in this hypothetical, or are they equally persuasive? In general, which type of evidence do you think is more reliable? Have the increasingly sophisticated scientific techniques employed in the analysis of circumstantial evidence, such as DNA, had an impact on the reliability of this type if evidence?

---

[17] Direct evidence "is based on personal knowledge or observation and that, if true, proves a fact without inference or presumption." BLACK'S LAW DICTIONARY 636 (9th ed. 2009). Circumstantial evidence is "based on inference and not on personal knowledge or observation." *Id.* Circumstantial evidence has also been defined as "[e]vidence of some collateral fact, from which the existence or non-existence of some fact in question may be inferred as a probable consequence . . . ." William P. Richardson, *The Law of Evidence* § 111, at 68 (3d ed. 1928) *in* BLACK'S LAW DICTIONARY 636 (9th ed. 2009).

When assessing the strengths and weaknesses of the evidence, the prosecutor should first determine what kind of evidence he is dealing with. Everything the witness testifies that she saw or heard is direct evidence. The ballistics conclusion and the fingerprint results are circumstantial evidence. If the evidence is direct, the prosecutor should consider such factors as a witness's mistake in identification, bias or motive to lie, substance abuse issues, and ability to accurately recollect the events she witnessed. In cases resting on direct evidence to establish identity, and when only one independent witness can prove the identity of the accused, a prosecutor should generally file charges only if the witness knows the accused, the identification permits no reasonable possibility of a mistake, or the accused has unique physical characteristics (e.g., a unique tattoo, a scar, piercings, or a conspicuous mole). In some cases, it is advisable for the filing prosecutor to interview the victim or other witnesses personally before deciding whether to file charges. This is particularly helpful in sex crime cases in which the credibility of the victim is especially crucial. Another example would be a case that hinges on the testimony of an informant witness. Informant witnesses, also disparagingly called "snitch witnesses," are often untrustworthy, and a prosecutor might want to assess such a witness's credibility personally before making a filing decision. During a personal interview, the prosecutor can evaluate the witness's credibility and demeanor as well as the probability that the witness will cooperate with the prosecution. Chapter 5 provides an extensive discussion of witness interviews.

For circumstantial evidence, the prosecution should consider any defense or alternate explanation that can be offered and the plausibility of that defense or alternate explanation. Even inadmissible evidence, such as the results of a polygraph test, may be considered by the prosecution in determining whether to file charges.

1. Affirmative Defenses

A prosecutor needs to be aware of possible affirmative defenses, but should not decline to charge merely because of a possible affirmative defense. If an affirmative defense is plausible, however, and if such a defense would completely exonerate the accused, then the prosecutor should not bring charges. Examples of affirmative defenses are insanity,[18] double jeopardy,[19] and entrapment.[20] Because the facts necessary to establish these defenses are generally not available at the time of the filing, and because the burden rests on the accused to raise them at trial, affirmative defenses pose their own challenges. Two other technical affirmative defenses that a prosecutor needs to evaluate carefully at charging are self-defense and defense of others. The prosecutor should avoid filing charges if a successful affirmative defense (which the prosecutor could not refute) would completely exonerate the accused. If it is unclear whether the affirmative defense can be proved, then the matter should proceed, and the trier of fact can make a determination after hearing the evidence.

---

[18] *E.g.*, S.D. CODIFIED LAWS § 22-1-2 (2012) ("at the time of committing the act, the person was incapable of knowing its wrongfulness").

[19] *E.g.*, WASH. CONST. art. 1, § 9 ("no person shall be . . . twice put in jeopardy for the same offense").

[20] Entrapment generally focuses on the conduct of the law enforcement officials that induced or encouraged the individual to engage in the prohibited conduct. *See, e.g.*, State v. Powell, 726 P.2d 266, 267 (Haw. 1986).

HYPO: *Oceana v. Thompson*

Assume that there is a fight in a bar and the accused, Brad Thompson, is alleged to have stabbed the victim, Curtis Brown, four times, including once in the back. Brown was unarmed and was of much smaller stature than Thompson. Brown was drunk and started the fight by screaming at Thompson and then punching him once in the face. Two eyewitnesses at the bar saw the fight and agree that Brown punched Thompson, then Thompson pulled out a knife and stabbed Brown four times. Although Brown lived, he sustained brain damage, including some memory loss, and does not recall the altercation.

Are there triable issues in this hypothetical case? Should the case be filed so that a judge or jury will ultimately decide whether there is enough evidence to convict? Would the filing decision be different if Brown was armed with a knife and tried to stab Thompson first? What if Brown succeeded in stabbing Thompson first, but the result was a superficial wound, and Thompson responded with stabbings that resulted in critical wounds? How does the fact that Brown was drunk affect the strength or weakness of the prosecution's case?

C. OVERCHARGING

ETHICS

Since a case is only as good as the evidence that supports it, a prosecutor must charge realistically and practically. A prosecutor should charge to the fullest extent that the evidence permits if, and only if, he is convinced of a reasonable probability of conviction at trial. After all, one of the biggest mistakes a prosecutor can make is overcharging a case.

Many prosecutors have made the mistake of inflating the charges against a defendant with the intent of intimidating the defendant into accepting a plea bargain. The tendered plea bargain might appear more favorable than the sentence the defendant could potentially receive at trial. While this may seem like a foolproof strategy, it could prove disastrous for the prosecutor. The defense attorney could easily spot the deficiencies in the evidence and advise his client not to take the offer. Overcharging may also affect the prosecutor's credibility. In almost any jurisdiction, the criminal bar is a small world and most prosecutors and defense attorneys frequently work together. A prosecutor who gains a reputation for overcharging will find it difficult to have his offers taken seriously at the plea bargaining stage. Finally, and most importantly, overcharging is unethical.[21] It cannot be over-emphasized that prosecutors are entrusted with enormous power when making the charging decision. In order to keep this power in check, prosecutors must remember that their professional duty is to seek justice. A more detailed discussion of overcharging and how it relates to plea bargaining is available in Chapter 12.

---

[21] The prosecutor in a criminal case shall "refrain from prosecuting a charge that the prosecutor knows is not supported by probable cause." MODEL RULES OF PROF'L CONDUCT R. 3.8(a) (2006). "In other words, if the case proceeds to trial, then the evidence must reasonably support the number and degree of the filed charges. This fundamental prosecutorial obligation is rooted in the underlying goal of the criminal justice system—to convict and punish only the guilty and to avoid a wrongful conviction or punishment of the innocent." *See* H. Mitchell Caldwell, *Coercive Plea Bargaining: The Unrecognized Scourge of the Justice System*, 61 CATH. U. L. REV. 63, 67 (2011).

D. EVIDENTIARY STANDARDS

Depending on the stage of the proceedings, the standard of evidence the prosecution must meet varies. Standards of evidence can be imagined on a spectrum, ranging from most to least demanding. The most stringent, and consequently, most common standard of evidence used in criminal prosecutions, is proof beyond a reasonable doubt. Although people frequently hear this phrase in films and television shows, few have carefully considered its meaning. In fact, there is no universal definition for the standard of proof beyond a reasonable doubt. The U.S. Supreme Court has stated that "[a]lthough this standard is an ancient and honored aspect of our criminal justice system, it defies easy explication."[22] The only jury instruction invalidated by the Court was in *Cage v. Louisiana*, in which the justices invalidated a jury instruction that defined reasonable doubt as "*actual, substantial*" doubt that would "*give rise to a grave uncertainty.*"[23] The jury instruction required is "not an absolute or mathematical certainty, but a moral certainty."[24] The Court reasoned that the words "substantial" and "grave" connote a higher degree of doubt than is required under the reasonable doubt standard. The Court then reasoned that the phrase "moral certainty," as opposed to evidentiary certainty, could lead the jury to find the defendant guilty based on a lesser standard than the reasonable doubt standard required by the Due Process Clause of the Fifth Amendment.[25] To understand the standard of "beyond a reasonable doubt," it is also helpful to consider what it is not. California Jury Instructions, for example, remind a juror that "beyond a reasonable doubt" does not mean free from all doubt "because everything relating to human affairs is open to some possible or imaginary doubt."[26] Florida instructs the jury that reasonable doubt is not mere possible doubt, nor a speculative, imaginary, or forced doubt.[27] Texas takes it further by warning jurors that the "beyond a reasonable doubt" standard is "not an excuse to avoid the performance of an unpleasant duty."[28] "Beyond a reasonable doubt" also does not mean a "grave uncertainty" or "actual substantial doubt."[29] Basically, "beyond a reasonable doubt" means that any doubt left in the juror's mind is not a reasonable one: that the prosecutor has proved that his case theory is the only reasonable explanation and that the defense case theory is not reasonable.[30]

Next on the spectrum of evidentiary standards is preponderance of the evidence. Mathematically speaking, this means more than half, so as little as 50.00001%. To put it even more simply,

---

[22] Victor v. Nebraska, 511 U.S. 1, 1 (1994).

[23] Cage v. Louisiana, 498 U.S. 39, 40 (1990) (quoting State v. Cage, 554 So. 2d 39, 41 (La. 1989)).

[24] *Id.*

[25] *Id.* at 41.

[26] CAL. PENAL CODE § 1096 (Deering 2012).

[27] FLA. STAT. ANN. STANDARD CRIM. JURY INSTRUCTIONS § 3.7 (West 2012).

[28] 1 LEONARD B. SAND ET AL., MODERN FEDERAL JURY INSTRUCTIONS § 4.01 (1987).

[29] Cage v. Louisiana, 498 U.S. 39, 41 (1990); *see also* MATTHEW BENDER ET AL., MODERN FEDERAL JURY INSTRUCTIONS—CRIMINAL ¶ 4.01, at 4-2 (2012).

[30] *See* JUDICIAL COUNCIL OF CALIFORNIA CRIMINAL JURY INSTRUCTION 220 (2006).

"preponderance of the evidence" means "more likely than not," or a slight tipping of the scales of justice. Although more commonly used in civil law, this standard applies to motions in criminal cases.

Below that is the standard of "probable cause." This standard is met when the preliminary hearing produces sufficient evidence to have the defendant held to answer. This concept is fully explored in Chapter 8. The distinctions between enough evidence to bring charges and enough evidence to convict are important. In spite of the fact that there might be enough evidence for the prosecution to survive a preliminary hearing, this does not mean that a case is strong enough to result in a conviction.

CHART 3.2
Steps of Proof

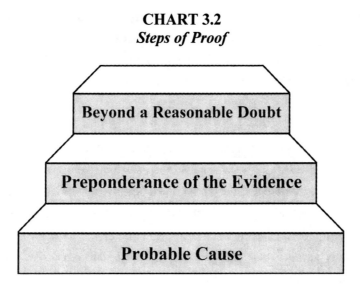

1. Challenging Cases

Certain crimes are by their nature more difficult to prove. These include sexual allegations, claims of police brutality, corruption, white-collar crimes, domestic violence, and minor offenses, such as possession of marijuana for personal use. Such offenses may be difficult to prove or may involve charges that jurors think should not be crimes.

HYPO: *Oceana v. Mac*

In a rape case, assume the victim, Sally Mae testifies that she met the defendant, Freddy Mac on a blind date and afterward the two of them went back to her apartment, where she claims they began to "fool around." She admits the "fooling around" began as a consensual act, but a few minutes into it she did not want it to go further, and told Mac to stop, but he refused and pinned her down when she resisted. If the Oceana penal code defines rape as an act of sexual intercourse by means of force, violence, or duress, then Mae's testimony is enough to satisfy the elements. The trial deputy assigned to this case, however, would find it difficult to prove this case beyond a reasonable doubt at trial because the defense attorney could easily shatter the prosecutor's case with a well-argued consent defense. This type of "he said, she said" case is extremely difficult to prove, unless there are bruises, vaginal tears, or other signs of force. The bottom line is that the prosecutor must bring charges only when he believes he can convince the jury beyond a reasonable doubt to convict. A one-on-one, "he said, she said" case that is not supported by physical evidence, such as injuries, is not likely to result in a conviction.

If the trier of fact believes that the victim was emotionally coerced or physically forced to have sex, then this would be sufficient to warrant a rape conviction. What type of evidence would be persuasive to show coercion or physical force? What if the suspect threatened to harm or kill the victim or her family if she did not submit? What if the defendant choked her, but the marks on her neck faded by the time she alerted police, so there was no visible sign of injury? What if other victims in previous uncharged incidents told the police that the suspect had attacked them in the past? What types of factors should be taken into account when deciding when to file rape charges in a "he said, she said" date rape case?

If the prosecutor decides to reject filing charges for reasons other than a lack of sufficient evidence, it should be only when such an action would clearly serve society.[31] Whether proceeding with charges or declining to charge, the prosecutor should always bear in mind that crimes are prosecuted on behalf of all the citizens of the state, and that crimes are committed primarily against society and only secondarily against individuals. The prosecutor also needs to remember that the victim is neither a party to the prosecution nor a client of the prosecutor. Therefore, declining to charge based on the victim's request for no prosecution should be limited to very narrow situations. While a prosecutor should not decline to charge because of the victim's lack of cooperation, the prosecutor should still assess the victim's willingness to testify truthfully when determining whether the case can be successfully prosecuted. If a prosecutor ultimately decides to decline charging, he should sign a statement to that effect, explaining the reason for the rejection. It should be noted that in cases in which the victim is a minor (under age eighteen), then the victim's parents might decide not to allow their child to testify. Sometimes, especially in cases such as sexual assaults, psychologists, child advocates, or the child's parents will determine that it would be too traumatic for the child to be involved in the prosecution. In such circumstances, the prosecution will have no option but to decline to prosecute, unless they can prove the case without the testimony of the child witness.

---

[31] *See* STANDARDS § 3-3.9(b)(i)–(vii) (1993). *See also* § 3-3.9 cmt. at 73–74 (1993).

E. OTHER CONSIDERATIONS

1. Criminal History of the Accused

One of the first things a prudent district attorney will look into is the criminal history of the accused.[32] The fastest way to determine a defendant's criminal history is his record of arrests and convictions, commonly referred to as a "rap sheet" (formally, a "record of arrest and prosecution"). A rap sheet can tell a prosecutor a great deal about a defendant, especially if it is particularly lengthy or if the crimes are of escalating seriousness. Prior convictions, especially those that involve felonies or charges similar to the current arrest, are aggravating factors. On the other hand, if the case before the prosecutor is the defendant's first interaction with the criminal justice system, this will be a mitigating factor in the decision whether to charge, and if so, what number and what types of charges to file.

2. Law Enforcement Priorities

If certain crimes are more of a nuisance in a jurisdiction than in others, or if a jurisdiction is disproportionately affected by an epidemic of a specific crime, then law enforcement may prioritize prosecution of that crime over others.[33] For instance, if there is a drastic increase in drug dealing in a community, it likely follows that drug-related street crimes and citizen complaints of drug dealing will increase. Consequently, law enforcement might choose to crack down on drug trafficking and focus their efforts on drug-related crimes. The result would be that the local prosecuting agency would see an increase in narcotics cases brought to filing deputies for charging.

3. Community Priorities

Like law enforcement priorities, community priorities could also influence charging. Some communities might take a certain crime more seriously than others. Crime is a universal concern because it affects everyone living in the community.[34] Law enforcement agencies, however, do not have infinite resources and cannot prosecute every crime.[35] Naturally, offenders who commit crimes that constitute a greater nuisance or that are more prevalent in the community will have charges filed against them more often than offenders who commit non-priority crimes. For example, some cities strictly prosecute offenses such as graffiti, which are seen as de-moralizing to a community, whereas other cities may not have the resources or citizens' complaints to prosecute these types of misdemeanors.

4. Corpus Delicti

Before charging a crime, the prosecutor must be convinced that there is a *corpus delicti,* which is Latin for "body of crime." In other words, the prosecutor must be convinced that there is proof that a

---

[32] NDAA NAT'L PROSECUTION STANDARDS 4-2.4(c) (2009).

[33] *Id.* 4.24(e), (l).

[34] *See* R. MICHAEL CASSIDY, PROSECUTORIAL ETHICS 14 (2005) ("the prosecutor must engage in a delicate calculus, having in mind the public's interest in effective law enforcement, the costs and benefits of the prosecution").

[35] NDAA NAT'L PROSECUTION STANDARDS 4.24 (j). *See also* STANDARDS § 3-3.9 cmt. at 73 (1993) ("A prosecutor should adopt a 'first things first' policy, giving greatest attention to those areas of criminal activity that pose the most serious threat to the security and order of the community.").

crime has been committed. The most common examples of *corpora delicti* include evidence of a body for a homicide, burned property for arson, or stolen property in order to prove larceny. A confession without proof of a crime is not a proper basis for bringing criminal charges,[36] although only slight proof that a crime has been committed is necessary when there is a confession. A reasonable possibility is the standard of proof required for a judge to find that there is a *corpus delicti*. For example, if the suspect confesses in detail to a murder but the victim's body is never found, then the fact that the victim disappeared coupled with the confession will be sufficient to satisfy this requirement. Conversely, if the suspect confesses to theft but nothing is reported stolen that matches his confession, then this would not be sufficient to file charges. Sometimes corroboration or enough circumstantial evidence can satisfy the *corpus delicti* requirement. In the rare case in which the suspect makes a judicial confession, the requirement of *corpus delicti* has been met.[37]

5. Victims

When charging sex crimes, a prosecutor needs to be aware that the number of touches or sex acts committed will determine the number of charges fileable; therefore, a thorough interview with the victim should be conducted before making a charging decision. Every separate sexual act that violates the penal code is a separate charge that carries potential prison time, even if the acts were committed against the same victim on the same day.

As already discussed, in most jurisdictions, it is not the victim's choice to "press" or "drop" charges; rather, the prosecutor has sole discretion in that decision. In many communities, there are victim services coordinators to help victims deal with the trauma of the judicial process and encourage them to cooperate with the prosecution. Domestic violence should not be treated less seriously than crimes of violence committed by strangers; domestic violence is often repetitive in nature and frequently escalates in seriousness. The victim's reluctance to cooperate should not be a reason for dismissal, as her reluctance is commonly caused by factors independent of the specific case itself. The prosecutor should make an objective assessment of the defendant's culpability and propensity for violence to determine whether to charge. Issues dealing with the credibility and reluctance of victims and other witnesses will be fully addressed in Chapter 5.

F. FELONIES AND SPECIAL ALLEGATIONS

Crimes are broken down into three categories: felonies, misdemeanors, and infractions. Felonies, generally, are those crimes with the potential for state prison, and misdemeanors are offenses where jail time is a possibility. On the other hand, infractions are offenses where jail time is not a possibility. By and large, there is no right to an attorney or a jury trial for infractions.[38] Some offenses are "wobblers"

---

[36] State v. Aten, 927 P.2d 210, 218 (Wash. 1996) (en banc).

[37] People v. Hill, 37 P.2d 849, 855 (Cal. Ct. App. 1934). *See also* People v. Redd, 78 Cal. Rptr. 368, 372 (Cal. Ct. App. 1969).

[38] For the right to counsel, see Argersinger v. Hamlin, 407 U.S. 25, 37–38 (1972) (holding that the defendant cannot be imprisoned without the right to counsel in any petty, misdemeanor, or felony case "absent a knowing and intelligent waiver . . . [t]his holding is applicable to all criminal prosecutions"); Scott v. Illinois, 440 U.S. 367, 373

meaning that they could be charged as a felony or misdemeanor (such as drug possession). Other offenses are "wobblets" meaning that they could be filed as a misdemeanor or infraction (such as disturbing the peace).

Additional factors that may be weighed in considering a felony prosecution include recidivism, the severity of the crime, the probability of continued criminal conduct, criminal intent, and whether there is eligibility for probation. Recidivism might include a conviction for the same type of criminal conduct, or any serious offense. Severity of the crime includes the use of a deadly weapon or instrument, conduct that caused permanent injuries, possession of a loaded firearm, or conduct that caused considerable property damage. When deciding whether to charge a felony or a misdemeanor, a prosecutor should not consider the attitude of the victim, witnesses, or law enforcement, and should also not consider the accused's family, economic, immigration, or professional status. On the other hand, a prosecutor may consider the defendant's cooperation or perhaps the defendant's youth when evaluating whether to file felony or misdemeanor charges.[39] Forms of cooperation can include a voluntary confession, genuine remorse, assistance in the recovery of property, and voluntary restitution. If the defendant has a substance abuse problem and is in the process of rehabilitation, or willing to undergo rehabilitation, this is also a factor in the defendant's favor.

In the case of a "wobbler," or when the penal code allows the prosecutor discretion between charging a felony or a misdemeanor, prosecutors typically choose to file a felony because they have discretion to reduce it later to a misdemeanor.[40] It is generally the consensus of prosecutorial agencies that domestic violence cases should be vigorously prosecuted at both the misdemeanor and felony levels, even if the victim refuses to cooperate, so long as there is sufficient evidence to support a conviction. Victims of domestic abuse often feel intimidated by their batterers, and also sometimes feel pressured for financial reasons not to pursue cases when the primary income earner of the household is a batterer, so leaving the charging decision in the hands of the victim would often perpetuate the cycle of violence. Since crimes are offenses against society, and not just against an individual, the prosecutor must make a filing decision independently of a victim's request.

(1979) (affirming the holding in *Argersinger* by stating that "actual imprisonment" is the "line defining the constitutional right to appointment of counsel"). For the right to a jury trial, see Duncan v. Louisiana, 391 U.S. 145, 159 (1968) (holding that "[c]rimes carrying possible penalties up to six months do not require a jury trial if they otherwise qualify as petty offenses") (citing Cheff v. Schnackenberg, 384 U.S. 373 (1966))); Baldwin v. New York, 399 U.S. 66, 69 (1970) (holding that "no offense can be deemed 'petty' for purposes of the right to trial by jury where imprisonment for more than six months is authorized").

[39] General factors that may be considered include defendant's general background, prior record, age, and many other particular factors. *See generally* JOHN WESLEY HALL, JR., PROFESSIONAL RESPONSIBILITY OF THE CRIMINAL LAWYER § 11:12 (2d ed. 1996).

[40] *E.g.*, CAL. PENAL CODE § 17 (Deering 2012); People v. Walker, 76 Cal. Rptr. 924 (Cal. Ct. App. 1969). For further discussion on the mechanics, application, and constitutionality of wobblers, see Loren Gordon, Comment, *Where to Commit a Crime if You Can Only Spare a Few Days to Serve the Time: The Constitutionality of California's Wobbler Statutes as Applied in the State Today*, 33 SW. U. L. REV. 497 (2004).

If there are special allegations that would enhance the penalty, such as prior violent felony convictions or possession of weapons, then a prosecutor should generally charge all applicable allegations when there is sufficient evidence. A special allegation may apply, for example, if there is great bodily injury, or if the injury is serious enough to require hospitalization, or involves incapacitation for a significant period of time. Since each county prosecutor's office will most likely have its own charging manual, prosecutors should be familiar with their office's charging manual and refer to it when filing criminal charges. Inexperienced prosecutors, moreover, should consult with their supervisors when they are unsure about charging decisions.

THE CHARGING DOCUMENT

An initial charging document can take two forms: a complaint or an indictment. As mentioned earlier, a complaint is a document prepared by a prosecutor that formally articulates the charges against the accused. An indictment, on the other hand, is a decision handed down by a grand jury that holds the defendant to answer to the charges. The contents of the charging document vary by jurisdiction, just as jurisdictions will differ as to whether a complaint or an indictment is normally issued. Grand jury proceedings are discussed in further detail in Chapter 9.

A. SIMPLICITY AND SUCCINCTNESS

The complaint needs to enumerate, in plain language, the charges against the accused. Because the complaint serves as formal notice to the defendant that he is being charged, it must be easily understood. The complaint cannot be bogged down by legal jargon since most criminal defendants are laypersons, who do not have the background or education to understand technical legal language. In the interests of simplicity, it is equally important for the complaint to be brief and to-the-point.

B. ENUMERATION OF THE CHARGES

The complaint needs to thoroughly catalog—in terms of charges and counts—every single offense of which the prosecutor intends to accuse the defendant. A charge corresponds to the specific section of the penal code that the defendant is accused of violating; a count is one occurrence of a charge. Thus, if a defendant is on trial for three counts of robbery, he is accused of violating the penal code section against robbery three times. The separate counts can result from committing a crime against different victims or on different days. Except where statutes limit multiple punishments, a prosecutor should charge all appropriate charges relating to a single course of conduct. This should be done when there is evidentiary sufficiency for each count, when the policies relating to the appropriate charge level have been satisfied, and when the charge does, in fact, describe separate criminal conduct, and is not just a technical difference. The complaint must also give all the appropriate notice requirements, such as registration as a particular type of offender.

C. OBJECTING TO A DEFICIENT COMPLAINT

If a complaint is defective, the defendant may file an opposition, called a "demurrer." Law students may recall demurrers from their first-year civil procedure class. Criminal and civil demurrers are similar: both are motions by the defense to end proceedings because of a failure to state a claim. It is important to remember, however, that a defendant cannot use a demurrer to challenge the insufficiency of the evidence against him, but rather, only defects that appear on the face of the accusatory instrument. There are four grounds upon which a defendant can base a demurrer.[41]

1. Failure to Allege Essential Elements

The prosecution must allege that the defendant committed each element of a crime in order to charge the defendant with that crime.[42] This is arguably the most severe complaint deficiency, and it will probably fail to survive a demurrer.

2. Failure to Allege Sufficient Specific Facts

In addition to alleging every element of the case, the complaint must also allege sufficiently specific facts to support the elements.[43] It must also show that the defendant is the specific person who committed that specific crime. Because filing charges is a relatively early stage of the proceedings, complete precision is not expected. A complaint that is overbroad or limited to vagaries, however, is defective on its face.

3. Multiplicity of Charges

Another major flaw that could sustain a demurrer is multiplicity.[44] Although multiplicity is often confused with duplicity, the two are quite different. Duplicity is when two or more distinct offenses are joined into a single count. Generally, duplicity is not fatal to a complaint. Multiplicity occurs when a single offense is charged in several counts, such as more than one count of robbery alleged against the defendant, involving the same victim on the same date. Unlike duplicity, multiplicity will most likely render a complaint defective.

4. Barred Prosecution

Sometimes a complaint alleges charges that cannot legally be prosecuted. The most common reason is that the statute of limitations has run.[45] Almost all crimes, other than murder, have a statute of limitations, the rationale being that people should not live indefinitely in fear that charges might be brought against them. Moreover, with the passage of time, witnesses or physical evidence may become unavailable and memories can fade, thus a suspect's ability to mount a defense could well diminish.

---

[41] *See* CAL. CIV. PROC. CODE § 430.10 (Deering 2012).

[42] Rakestraw v. Cal. Physicians' Serv., 96 Cal. Rptr. 2d 354, 356 (Cal. Ct. App. 2000).

[43] Lee Newman, M.D., Inc. v. Wells Fargo Bank, 104 Cal. Rptr. 2d 310, 314 (Cal. Ct. App. 2001).

[44] CAL. CIV. PROC. CODE § 430.10(c) (Deering 2012).

[45] Friends of Shingle Springs Interchange, Inc. v. County of El Dorado, 133 Cal. Rptr. 3d 626, 636 (Cal. Ct. App. 2011).

Another reason for which an individual cannot be charged with a crime is immunity, which applies to diplomats or government officials acting in their official capacities. If the law prohibits prosecution of an offense, any complaint attempting to charge a defendant will not survive a demurrer.

D. AMENDING THE COMPLAINT

A complaint can generally be amended at any time before the defendant pleads or before a demurrer is sustained. If the prosecutor wishes to amend the complaint after either of those events, he may need to seek permission from the court. Courts usually have broad discretion in granting the prosecution leave to amend the complaint. Typically, a complaint is amended if new information comes to light or if circumstances change. For example, if a defendant is charged with attempted murder and the victim dies, then the complaint is amended to charge the defendant with murder. All amendments, however, must be supported by evidence that meets the same standard as the evidence required to prove the original complaint. While the prosecution is allowed to amend the complaint to *correct* substantial defects, all added counts must be supported by the evidence. Different state jurisdictions have their own rules regarding the limitations on charging offenses. For example, under the *Kellett* doctrine, the prosecution must join and prosecute all offenses that originate from the same conduct.[46] Prosecuting closely related individual offenses at separate trials may violate the defendant's constitutional right to due process. If all the offenses stemming from the same conduct are not prosecuted in a single proceeding, none of the omitted offenses may be charged at any subsequent proceeding if the initial proceeding has resulted in acquittal or conviction.[47] The Supreme Court has also "clearly warned that prosecution of closely related individual offenses at separate trials may constitute an impermissible denial of that fundamental fairness required by the due process clause of the Fourteenth Amendment."[48] The logic behind the *Kellett* doctrine is similar to that of double jeopardy: once a defendant has been either acquitted or convicted of charges, it is unfair to face criminal charges arising from the same course of conduct. Of course, the accused might still face a civil lawsuit, such as a wrongful death case arising from a homicide. A civil lawsuit would generally be filed by a victim or the family of a decedent victim, such as the one filed by Ron Goldman's family after O.J. Simpson was acquitted of murder. Alternatively, the government can file a violation of civil liberties lawsuit, such as the one brought against the police officers who were acquitted of beating Rodney King in the famous videotaped police brutality incident that sparked the 1992 Los Angeles riots.[49]

---

[46] Kellett v. Superior Court, 409 P.2d 206 (Cal. 1966) (en banc).

[47] *Id.*

[48] *Id.* at 209 (citing Ciucci v. Illinois, 356 U.S. 571, 575 (1958)). *See also* Abbate v. United States, 359 U.S. 187, 196 (1959) (Brennan, J., concurring); Hoag v. New Jersey, 356 U.S. 464, 467 (1958); Blockburger v. United States, 284 U.S. 299, 304 (1932) (Supreme Court held that a defendant is exempt from subsequent punishment or prosecution only if the act he committed violates more than one statutory provision and "each provision requires proof of a fact which the other does not").

[49] United States v. Koon, 34 F.3d 1416 (9th Cir. 1994).

Because any amended complaint supersedes the original, any amendments to the complaint should be in written form; however, a complaint can also be constructively amended. A constructive amendment occurs when the prosecutor broadens the possible grounds for conviction beyond those specified in the complaint. This commonly occurs during the prosecution's presentation of evidence or oral argument during the preliminary hearing stage. While the effect of constructive amendments at the state level varies by jurisdiction, they are fatal to a conviction at the federal level. Constructive amendments allow the elements of the offense to be altered in such a way that the defendant is held to answer for a crime other than the one in the original complaint. Nevertheless, not every deviation from the terms of the complaint will be considered a constructive amendment. A variance occurs when the charges in the original complaint are unchanged but the proof offered at the preliminary hearing supports an entirely different charge. While constructive amendments are considered errors *per se,* the Supreme Court has found that variances do not necessarily invalidate a conviction if they add nothing new to the indictment and do not have the effect of broadening the crimes for which the defendant can be charged.[50] It is important to note that preliminary hearing judges have the power to amend complaints on their own to conform to the proof that they heard at the preliminary hearing. Preliminary hearings are discussed in further detail in Chapter 8.

THE ROLE OF THE DEFENSE

As stated, the prosecution has wide latitude in filing charges. Although this chapter has been devoted to prosecutorial discretion and responsibilities when filing charges, the defense still has a role to play at the charging stage. Some defense attorneys find it beneficial to meet with the prosecutor to offer input before charges are filed against their client. The prosecuting agency is not under any obligation to confer with the defense before filing charges, but many prosecutors will meet with a defense attorney, even at the filing stage, and listen to the defense's position. Defense attorneys who have earned a good reputation for integrity are more likely to have a chance to persuade the prosecutor to make a decision that is beneficial to the defense. For example, a defense lawyer who presents the prosecutor with a packet of information that includes reference letters on behalf of the accused, a rap sheet showing a lack of prior convictions, proof that the client has paid restitution, or has made arrangements to pay it, or proof that the defendant is in rehabilitation for substance abuse, is in a better position to influence the filing decision positively. Additionally, defense attorneys at this stage sometimes bring witnesses, such as the alleged victim (especially in domestic violence cases) or character witnesses to explain why the charges should not be filed, or why less serious charges should be considered. Furthermore, if the defense has specific legal or factual grounds for believing that a motion to suppress evidence or some other significant motion will be granted, this could be a beneficial time to explain this to the prosecutor. A detailed discussion of the impact of motions can be found in Chapters 10 and 11.

---

[50] United States v. Miller, 471 U.S. 130, 144 (1985).

Sometimes the defense can enlighten the prosecution as to the legal reasons why charges should not be filed, such as an expired statute of limitations or diplomatic immunity. Perhaps the defense will be able to work out an immunity deal for her client in exchange for information or testimony about a more culpable criminal. Alternatively, the defense lawyer might be able to present a complete defense to the potential charge by providing information or documents. For example, in a possession of marijuana case, a valid prescription for medical marijuana could persuade the prosecutor not to bring charges against the client. Likewise, if the client is accused of stealing an item from an individual, proof that the accused was, in fact, the owner of the item (such as a title certificate (pink slip) for a vehicle) could provide the necessary proof to dissuade the state from bringing criminal charges. Proof that the complaining witness or other potential prosecution witnesses have significant criminal records or are otherwise not credible, could also dissuade the state from bringing charges against the accused. Perhaps the defense attorney can bring tangible evidence, such as a tape recording or text messages, showing that the alleged victim was actually threatening the defendant. Because the prosecutor's duty is to seek justice and to refrain from filing charges unless it is probable that a conviction will be attained, the prosecutor should meet with the defense attorney if the defense lawyer has information that may exonerate the defendant. Finally, meeting with the prosecutor can be beneficial at the filing stage for the purpose of having the State agree not to oppose a release on the defendant's own recognizance with a promise to make court appearances or to a bail reduction. Bail issues and strategy are fully discussed in Chapter 4.

SAMPLE COMPLAINTS

SUPERIOR COURT OF THE STATE OF OCEANA
FOR THE COUNTY OF MALIWOOD

THE PEOPLE OF THE STATE OF OCEANA,	CASE NO. OC032188
Plaintiff,	
v.	
Eric Daniels (08/17/1977)	FELONY COMPLAINT
Defendant(s).	

The undersigned is informed and believes that:

COUNT 1

On or about April 28, CY-1, in the County of Maliwood, the crime of POSSESSION OF A CONTROLLED SUBSTANCE, in violation of HEALTH & SAFETY CODE SECTION 11377(a), a Felony, was committed by ERIC DANIELS, who did unlawfully possess a controlled substance, to wit, methamphetamine.

"NOTICE: Conviction of this offense will require you to register pursuant to Health and Safety Code section 11590. Failure to do so is a crime pursuant to Health and Safety Code section 11594."

* * * * *

It is further alleged as to count(s) 1 pursuant to Penal Code section 667.5(b) that the defendant(s), ERIC DANIELS, has suffered the following prior conviction(s):

Case No.	Charge Code/Statue	Conv. Date	County of Court	State	Court Type
OC032188	HS 11368	11/10/ C.Y.-2	Maliwood	OC	SUPERIOR

and that a term was served as described in Penal Code section 667.5 for said offense(s), and that the defendant did not remain free of prison custody for, and did commit an offense resulting in a felony conviction during, a period of five years subsequent to the conclusion of said term.

NOTICE: Conviction of this offense will require the defendant to provide DNA samples and print impressions pursuant to Penal Code sections 296 and 296.1. Willful refusal to provide the samples and impressions is a crime.

NOTICE: The People of the State of Oceana intend to present evidence and seek jury findings regarding all applicable circumstances in aggravation, pursuant to Penal Code section 1170(b) and *Cunningham v. Oceana* (2007) 549 U.S. 270.

I DECLARE UNDER PENALTY OF PERJURY THAT THE FOREGOING IS TRUE AND CORRECT AND THAT THIS COMPLAINT, CASE NUMBER OC032188, CONSISTS OF 1 COUNT(S).

Executed at Maliwood, County of Oceana, on May 18, C.Y.-1

Dillon Rogers
DILLON ROGERS
DECLARANT AND COMPLAINANT

Nick Zollinger, District Attorney

BY: *Brittany King*
BRITTANY KING, DEPUTY

AGENCY: LASD – MALIWOOD PATROL I/O: DILLON ID NO.: 223379 PHONE: (401) 387-1644
DR NO: 911024511231185 OPERATOR: RH PRELIM. TIME EST.: 2 HOURS

DEFENDANT	CII NO.	DOB	BOOKING NO.	BAIL RECOM'D	CUSTODY R'TN
DANIELS, ERIC	011873522	8/17/1977	2721538	$30,000	06/28/C.Y.-1

Pursuant to Penal Code Section 1054.5(b), the People are hereby informally requesting that defense counsel provide discovery to the People as required by Penal Code Section 1054.3.

SUPERIOR COURT OF THE STATE OF OCEANA
FOR THE COUNTY OF MALIWOOD

THE PEOPLE OF THE STATE OF OCEANA, Plaintiff, v. **Brett Downey (08/17/1986)** Defendant(s).	**CASE NO. OC058702** *MISDEMEANOR COMPLAINT*

The undersigned is informed and believes that:

COUNT 1

On or about May 7, CY-1, in the County of Maliwood, the crime of D.U.I. CAUSING INJURY, in violation of VEHICLE CODE SECTION 23153(a), a Misdemeanor, was committed by BRETT DOWNEY, who did unlawfully, while under the influence of an alcoholic beverage and a drug and under their combined influence, drive a vehicle and in so driving, concurrently did an act forbidden by law and neglected a duty imposed by law which proximately caused bodily injury to Casey Hague.

* * * * *

COUNT 2

On or about May 7, CY-1, in the County of Maliwood, the crime of DRIVING with A .08% BLOOD ALCOHOL CAUSING INJURY, in violation of VEHICLE CODE SECTION 23153(b), a Misdemeanor, was committed by BRETT DOWNEY, who did unlawfully while having .08 percent and more, by weight, of alcohol in his blood, drive a vehicle and in so driving did an act forbidden by law and neglected a duty imposed by law which proximately caused bodily injury to Casey Hague.

It is further alleged as to count(s) 1 and 2 that the defendant's concentration of blood alcohol was .15 percent by weight or more, within the meaning of Vehicle Code section 23578.

* * * * *

COUNT 3

On or about May 7, CY-1 in the County of Maliwood, the crime of UNLICENSED DRIVER, in violation of VEHICLE CODE SECTION 12500(a), a Misdemeanor, was committed by BRETT DOWNEY, who did unlawfully drive a motor vehicle upon a highway without holding a valid driver's license issued under the Vehicle Code of the State of Oceana.

* * * * *

NOTICE: The People of the State of Oceana intend to present evidence and seek jury findings regarding all applicable circumstances in aggravation, pursuant to Penal Code section 1170(b) and *Cunningham v. Oceana* **(2007) 549 U.S. 270.**

Further, attached hereto and incorporated herein are official reports and documents of a law enforcement agency which the undersigned believes establish probable cause for the arrest of defendant(s) BRETT DOWNEY for the above-listed crimes.

I DECLARE UNDER PENALTY OF PERJURY THAT THE FOREGOING IS TRUE AND CORRECT AND THAT THIS COMPLAINT, CASE NUMBER OC032188, CONSISTS OF 3 COUNT(S).

Executed at Maliwood, County of Oceana, on May 18, CY-1

Richard Johnson
RICHARD JOHNSON
DECLARANT AND COMPLAINANT

....
Nick Zollinger, District Attorney

BY: *Brittany King*
BRITTANY KING, DEPUTY

AGENCY: LASD – MALIWOOD PATROL   I/O: DILLON   ID NO.: 223379   PHONE: (401) 265-3490

DR NO: OPERATOR: RH

| DEFENDANT CII NO. | DOB | BOOKING NO, | BAIL RECOM'D |
CUSTODY R'TN DATE			
Downey, Brett 096583241 8/17/1977 7231866		$45,000	07/07/CY-1

Pursuant to Penal Code Section 1054.5(b), the People are hereby informally requesting that defense counsel provide discovery to the People as required by Penal Code Section 1054.3.

SUMMARY

Charging, or filing, formally initiates criminal proceedings against a defendant. The government, or prosecution, has broad discretion in terms of deciding when to bring charges against the accused, such charges being described within the formal document known as the complaint. This document must conform to local rules and cannot be defective or an overturned conviction may result.

When charging, the prosecution has several options. First, the filing deputy can file the charges requested by the police, or alternatively, it might file charges that are more or less serious than those law enforcement requested. Another choice might be that the prosecution requests further investigation prior to making a filing decision. Finally, the prosecutor may elect to reject filing of charges altogether. If the case is a "wobbler," then the prosecutor has the choice of whether to file it as a felony or as a misdemeanor. When appropriate, the prosecutor also may file allegations, such as use of a firearm. The most significant factors to consider in making charging decisions are the strength of the evidence, the severity of the offense, and the defendant's prior record.

In certain circumstances the prosecutor can instead elect to divert the case, which places certain conditions on the accused that, once fulfilled, will result in a dismissal of the charges levied against him. In making charging decisions, prosecutors may also take into account what is in the best interests of the community, including keeping its citizens safe. If a particular type of conduct is causing a problem in the community, or alternatively, if the conduct represents only a mild infraction that is generally tolerated within the community, then this is something that prosecutors may take into account. It is also worth mentioning that while the prosecution is given broad discretion in filing charges, it is unethical to overcharge. Indeed, while the prosecutor has wide discretion in deciding to file charges, there are some limitations. In federal cases and in some state jurisdictions, a grand jury may be summoned to hear evidence and decide whether to issue an indictment.

Lastly, if the defense objects to the charges, then they may file a demurrer, thereby asking the court to dismiss the charges for failure to state a claim; however, complaints can generally be amended any time before a demurrer is sustained. Otherwise, the prosecutor will need the court's permission to amend the complaint as filed. Moreover, the defense, if they are retained before charges are filed, should advocate for their client at this stage in the proceedings. Persuasive defense attorneys can present the prosecutor with information that, in some instances, might sway the prosecution either to file less serious charges, or perhaps not file charges at all.

CHECKLIST

✓ Charging is the formal initiation of criminal proceedings against the defendant. The complaint contains the charges leveled against the defendant and creates a formal record.

✓ Prosecutors have broad discretion in determining whether to charge or to decline to charge a defendant. A prosecutor's behavior, however, should fall within certain ethical boundaries; the role of a prosecutor is to seek justice, not to seek conviction at any cost.

✓ After careful consideration and review of the evidence, a prosecutor generally has five options: file the charges, decline to file the charges, file a more or less serious charge, request further investigation, or diversion.

✓ The most important inquiry in the charging decision is determining the weight of the evidence. There must be sufficient admissible evidence to prove legal guilt.

✓ When conducting evidentiary analysis, keep in mind that direct and circumstantial evidence carry equal weight if determined to be reliable. Direct evidence directly shows via witness testimony that the defendant is culpable; circumstantial evidence does not expressly prove the defendant committed the crime, but implies the defendant is guilty. Circumstantial evidence, such as DNA, fingerprint evidence, and ballistics evidence, can be highly persuasive.

✓ A prosecutor should be aware of possible affirmative defenses that the defendant may plead, but the prosecutor should not decline to charge due to a possible affirmative defense. Affirmative defenses include insanity, entrapment, and double jeopardy, among others.

✓ A crucial mistake that prosecutors sometimes make is to overcharge. While inflating a charge to force a plea bargain might be tempting, an able defense attorney will see through the evidence and will advise his client to not take the plea. Further, overcharging damages the prosecutor's credibility, and is unethical.

✓ When determining whether to charge, the prosecutor can take into account other considerations such as the past criminal history of the accused, law enforcement priorities, and community priorities.

✓ The charging document should be simple and succinct, and should enumerate the charges and counts for all offenses. The defense can object to a deficient complaint for one of four reasons: failure to allege essential elements, failure to allege sufficient specific facts, multiplicity of charges, or barred prosecution for reasons such as immunity or an expired statute of limitations.

✓ Defense attorneys should actively represent their clients, even at the filing stage, if possible. The defense attorney should present any mitigating information to the prosecution.

CHAPTER 4
ARRAIGNMENT AND BAIL REVIEW

"You never get a second chance to make a first impression."
–Attributed to Will Rogers

During the early, pretrial phase of a case, there are proceedings that take place in the courtroom—before a judge and on the record. The first of these procedural steps for both the prosecution and defense is the arraignment.

Since the arraignment is often the first time an attorney appears before the court for a specific case, this appearance is important for setting a professional tone. For a prosecutor, this is the first opportunity to come across as a thoroughly prepared and competent professional in the eyes of both the court and defense counsel. For a defense attorney, it is an opportunity to generate an initial positive impression on the court and opposing counsel, and perhaps more importantly, on her client.

Even before attorneys have the opportunity to make a good impression on the jury during *voir dire*, the arraignment provides them with a chance to shine in court. This entails appearing confident without seeming arrogant. As the advocate works to set the appropriate tone for the case, she is also being evaluated both professionally and, to some extent, personally. Whether a prosecutor, public defender, or private defense attorney, a criminal advocate will interact with many of the same people on a regular basis. Because prosecutors, public defenders, judges, clerks, and court personnel will quickly become familiar with any attorney making court appearances, they will form opinions based on an advocate's conduct both inside and outside the courtroom. It is beneficial throughout an attorney's career to establish a reputation as an advocate who is knowledgeable and persuasive as well as trustworthy and respectful.

ARRAIGNMENT OVERVIEW

The Sixth Amendment to the U.S. Constitution guarantees that in "all criminal prosecutions, the accused shall enjoy the right to a speedy and public trial."[1] The first procedural step on the path to trial—and indeed, the first time the defendant sets foot in a courtroom—is the arraignment, a right reserved for every criminal defendant. It is an integral part of the justice system that criminal proceedings are public events and that the accused has the right to appear before a magistrate in a timely manner to hear the charges brought against him. In the words of the Arraignment Clause of the Sixth Amendment, a defendant facing criminal prosecution will "be informed of the nature and cause of the accusation."[2] This guarantee manifests itself in the form of arraignment proceedings, and is statutorily enunciated in the *Federal Rules of Criminal Procedure*. Rule 10, titled "Arraignment," states that "[a]n arraignment must be conducted in open court and must consist of: (1) ensuring that the defendant has a copy of the

---

[1] U.S. CONST. amend. VI.

[2] *Id.*

indictment or information; (2) reading the indictment or information to the defendant or stating to the defendant the substance of the charge; and then (3) asking the defendant to plead to the indictment or information."[3] The U.S. Supreme Court also reaffirmed the importance of the arraignment when it stated in *Hamilton v. Alabama*: "Under federal law an arraignment is a *sine qua non*[4] to the trial itself—the preliminary stage where the accused is informed of the indictment and pleads to it, thereby formulating the issue to be tried."[5] Although state jurisdictions' arraignment norms may differ slightly from the federal statutory requirements, the general procedure and requirements of the arraignment are well established in all jurisdictions.

A. TIMING

A fundamental principle of the criminal justice system assures defendants that the procedural process will begin shortly after an arrest. Federal courts require that defendants must be brought before a judicial officer "without unnecessary delay."[6] State courts have similar requirements. The Supreme Court has imposed a forty-eight hour time period following the filing of a complaint, during which a defendant is entitled to be brought before a magistrate and arraigned, although some exceptions do exist.[7] It is important to note that the forty-eight hour time period refers to *court* days and not calendar days; this distinction is crucial for an attorney's understanding of the procedural timing. For example, if a defendant is arrested on a Friday, he is entitled to an arraignment by Monday, not over the weekend. If that Monday falls on a court holiday, the arraignment then takes place on Tuesday. The forty-eight-hour rule is not inflexible, however. If, for example, the defendant could not be brought to court on time because he had a medical complication, this would constitute good cause for a short delay of the proceedings.

The forty-eight hour arraignment rule should not be confused with a probable cause proceeding known as a *Gerstein* hearing, which must occur within forty-eight hours of a warrantless arrest. Anyone arrested without a warrant is entitled to have a judicial officer determine that probable cause exists before the defendant can remain incarcerated.[8] In this non-adversarial, *ex parte* proceeding, a magistrate reviews an oral or written representation by the arresting police officer and determines whether there is probable cause that the defendant committed a crime. While the forty-eight hour *Gerstein* rule is not rigid, it does not exclude weekends and holidays.[9]

---

[3] FED. R. CRIM. P. 10(a).

[4] *See* OXFORD ENGLISH DICTIONARY Vol. IX 74 (1933) (Latin phrase for "[i]ndispensable, absolutely necessary or essential").

[5] Hamilton v. Alabama, 368 U.S. 52, 54 n.4 (1961).

[6] FED. R. CRIM. P. 5(a)(1)(A).

[7] *See* County of Riverside v. McLaughlin, 500 U.S. 44 (1991).

[8] Gerstein v. Pugh, 420 U.S. 103 (1975).

[9] *McLaughlin*, 500 U.S. at 44.

B. READING OF CHARGES

The formal reading of the charges by a magistrate provides the accused with his first opportunity to appear before the court and serves as notice of the charges against him; the charges are listed on the "complaint." This is true regardless of whether the charges allege felonies or misdemeanors. In practice, however, it is typical for the defense attorney to waive the formality of having the charges read in court. Often, the judge will turn to defense counsel and inquire, "counsel, do you waive formal reading of the complaint and statement of rights and enter a plea of not guilty?" If the prosecutor has filed felony charges, then the defendant is entitled to a preliminary hearing following this initial arraignment, unless there has been a grand jury indictment. The intricacies of preliminary hearings will be explained in Chapter 8, but for now, it is sufficient to understand that a preliminary hearing is a kind of "mini-trial" where the prosecution must establish the elements of each alleged charge. The burden of proof for such hearings, which are conducted without a jury, is much lower than at trial. If the presiding judge or magistrate determines that the defendant should be "held to answer" after the preliminary hearing, then an "information" is filed and the defendant will be re-arraigned on the information, which is the post-preliminary hearing version of a complaint. In the event that the prosecution has initiated the case through a grand jury and the grand jury issues an indictment, then the arraignment takes place on the basis of the indictment, rather than the information. If a grand jury proceeding is held, as is typically the case in federal court, this proceeding eliminates the need for a preliminary hearing.[10] Grand jury proceedings will be examined in Chapter 9.

The reading of the charge or charges makes known to the defendant the specific crimes the prosecution believes have been committed. This provides the defendant and defense counsel with the sections of the criminal codes that the defendant allegedly violated, as the Supreme Court put it, "thereby formulating the issue to be tried."[11] The charging document, whether it is a complaint, information, or indictment, is essentially an instrument of notice; it makes the defendant aware of the specific crimes for which he is being charged.

The court must provide the defendant with a copy of the arraigning document (complaint, information, or indictment) and ensure that it is not defective. First, to determine the accuracy of the arraigning document, the court will confirm that the defendant appearing before the court is the same person named in the complaint. In addition to attempting to resolve any discrepancies relating to identity, the court will also establish proper jurisdiction for the case since, typically, a crime can only be tried in the county or parish in which it occurred, unless, of course, a motion to change venue is granted.[12] There may arise other situations that could render the charging document defective: for instance, a defendant who is eighteen at the time of the arraignment, but was seventeen at the time of the alleged crime, must be tried as a juvenile in most cases. A criminal court does not have proper standing to hear such a case, unless, after a hearing, the defendant is found unfit to be tried as a minor, or unless the relevant

---

[10] A comprehensive discussion of grand juries is located in Chapter 9.

[11] Hamilton v. Alabama, 368 U.S. 52, 54 n.4 (1961).

[12] Skilling v. United States, 130 S. Ct. 2896, 2912–13 (2010).

jurisdiction allows defendants who are at least sixteen years old and charged with particularly serious offenses to be tried in adult criminal court.[13]

September						
S	M	T	W	TH	F	S
				1	2 *Defendant Arrested*	3
4	5 **Labor Day**	6 Defendant's Arraignment	7	8	9	10

C. ADVISEMENT OF RIGHTS

Perhaps the most important phase of the arraignment proceeding for the defendant is the advisement of his constitutional rights. The rights preserved by the Bill of Rights and articulated by the court during the arraignment include: the right to a speedy trial, the right not to make self-incriminating statements, the right to confront and cross-examine witnesses against the defendant, the right to be tried before a jury of peers, and the right to counsel.

At this stage of the procedural process, perhaps the most valuable right for any defendant is the Sixth Amendment right to counsel. In *Rothgery v. Gillespie County*, the Supreme Court held that the right to counsel "attaches" at the defendant's first appearance before a judicial officer after a formal charge is made because this initiates adversarial proceedings and the defendant's liberty is already subject to restriction at that point.[14] This first appearance is generally the arraignment.[15]

Whereas it is a federal prosecutor or district attorney who represents the government, the defendant is most likely in an unfamiliar position and without the requisite knowledge to adequately represent himself. For this reason, if the defendant has not already retained private counsel, the reading of rights by the court informs the defendant that he has the right to legal representation at all critical stages of trial, including the arraignment.[16] In a criminal case involving any possibility of incarceration, the

---

[13] The legal age of a minor can vary among jurisdictions, however. In California, for example, defendants sixteen years or older may be tried as adults in certain circumstances. CAL. WELF. & INST. CODE § 707 (Deering 2012).

[14] Rothgery v. Gillespie County, 554 U.S. 191, 213 (2008).

[15] The Court, in its plurality opinion in *Kirby v. Illinois*, 406 U.S. 682, 689 (1972), listed other "adversar[ial] judicial criminal proceedings" that can trigger the right to counsel. The Court makes clear that the "first formal proceeding" is the point of attachment. *Rothgery*, 554 U.S. at 203. In addition to arraignment, the first formal proceeding might be the formal charge, preliminary hearing, indictment, or reading of information. *Id.* at 198.

[16] The Supreme Court of the United States defined different "critical stages" of trial. These stages include, but are not limited to: interrogations, arraignment, preliminary hearings, trial, and sentencing. *See generally* Brewer v.

court must inform an indigent defendant that he is entitled to a court-appointed attorney; however, if he is charged only with an infraction or a misdemeanor for which no custody is possible, then he need not be so informed.[17]

D. DEFENDANT'S DECISION REGARDING REPRESENTATION

At the arraignment stage, it is possible that a defendant has not yet retained private counsel, and it may be that he has not spoken with an attorney at all. During the arraignment, he can indicate to the court whether he would like to be represented by a public defender, to retain private counsel, or to represent himself (*pro per* representation). If the defendant has not yet met with an attorney, the court may, on its own or at the request of the defendant, postpone the arraignment hearing until such time as the defendant will have received the assistance of counsel. This postponement is known as a "continuance." If, however, the defendant does not agree to a time waiver, then the court must enter a "not guilty plea" on the defendant's behalf and continue the case as a pretrial hearing during which the defendant has the right to assistance of counsel.

The defendant's decision to opt for a public defender or private counsel at this phase is not binding. The defendant can choose the public defender (if he is indigent) and, at some later point, hire private counsel if he is able. Similarly, a defendant can retain private counsel for the preliminary procedural stages, and then, if he is unable to continue paying the legal fees he incurs, request a public defender. Although the defendant may switch counsel, he does not have the right to choose from among different public defenders. A *pro per* defendant is entitled to change his mind up to the point of trial or case settlement and request the assistance of counsel. By the same token, the court has discretion to determine whether the defendant's motion either to represent himself, or to switch to attorney representation, is timely. The judge can deny a motion that is untimely because, for instance, it will unfairly delay the trial.

A public defender will generally be appointed by the judge to represent indigent defendants. Defendants who are brought into court in custody are often represented by a public defender, at least until they have the opportunity to retain private counsel. If a defendant asks to have a public defender appointed, then he will need to establish that he is indigent and unable to afford a private attorney.[18] If a public defender is in fact appointed, she will often interview the defendant prior to arraignment. If defense counsel deems it necessary, she can move to continue the arraignment in order to review the case more thoroughly with her client, to investigate the case, or to consider any mental or medical defenses. In order to continue the arraignment (or any other proceeding), the defendant must provide explicit approval;

Williams, 430 U.S. 387, 401 (1977) (interrogations); Coleman v. Alabama, 399 U.S. 1, 10 (1970) (preliminary hearing); *Hamilton*, 368 U.S. at 53 (arraignment).

[17] Argersinger v. Hamlin, 407 U.S. 25, 40 (1972).

[18] To establish indigency, a defendant will likely have to list assets; the public defender will then examine the financial form and determine if the defendant qualifies to be represented by the public defender. This form is confidential and may not be reviewed by anyone other than the public defender. Local rules or statutes typically establish the elements of indigency.

both the defendant and his attorney must, on the record, waive the right to speedy proceedings.[19]

As discussed in Chapter 10, a motion to continue is a standard tool used by both prosecution and defense. A continuance might be requested for a number of reasons: often further discovery is required, a chemist's laboratory report may not be complete, or an expert witness may be unavailable to testify on certain dates. In complicated cases, the defense attorney may simply need more time to prepare the defense case. It should be noted that this non-exhaustive list only scratches the surface of potential motions, and that continuances, as well as other motions, can be effective tools throughout the proceedings, not merely at the arraignment.

Although the Supreme Court has upheld every defendant's constitutional right to counsel, defendants also have the right to represent themselves *pro per*. In *Faretta v. California*, the Supreme Court held that a defendant has a constitutional right to proceed without counsel when he voluntarily and intelligently elects to do so, and that the state may not force a lawyer upon him when he insists that he wants to conduct his own defense.[20] The standards for a "voluntary" and "intelligent" decision are quite low. The Court, when deciding *Faretta*, held that "a defendant need not himself have the skill and experience of a lawyer in order competently and intelligently choose self-representation."[21] In fact, the accused has the right to represent himself if he "knows what he is doing and his choice is made with eyes open."[22] As a protection against frivolous self-representation, however, the court, at its initiative and discretion, may appoint standby or advisory counsel in order to ensure a fair trial for the defendant. Some jurisdictions, such as California, have determined that defendants do not have the right to standby counsel; rather, it is a matter left up to the judge's discretion.

Pro per representation can introduce special challenges, distinct from those associated with a defendant represented by an attorney. Often, a *pro per* defendant—particularly one in custody—has lots of time on his hands. This will afford him the opportunity to generate motions that may or may not be legally appropriate. These motions might unduly consume the judge's time or may simply be without merit. As a prosecutor, it is important to remain aware of these concerns, all the while bearing in mind that it is the prosecutor's duty to help protect the defendant's rights, even when the *pro per* defendant may himself be ignorant of such rights.

---

[19] For most misdemeanors, some states will allow attorneys to appear on the defendant's behalf, without the defendant being present. *See, e.g.*, CAL. PENAL CODE § 977 (Deering 2012).

[20] Faretta v. California, 422 U.S. 806 (1975).

[21] *Id.* at 835.

[22] *Id.* (quoting Adams v. United States *ex rel.* McCann, 317 U.S. 269, 279 (1942)).

E. ENTERING A PLEA

After the presiding magistrate reads the charges to the defendant, the defendant must enter his plea. He has three options: not guilty, guilty, or no contest (*nolo contendere*).[23] In some circumstances, there is a fourth option of pleading not guilty by reason of insanity. At this initial reading of the rights, most defendants will plead not guilty. In cases involving minor charges, when the evidence favors the prosecution, the defendant will sometimes choose to settle the case at the arraignment stage to get the ordeal behind him. Even in such minor cases, however, a defense attorney must keep in mind the potential harm to a client who faces criminal charges. In addition to the physical and emotional stress that such charges may present, a defendant may also suffer loss of good reputation, financial loss, or even loss of privileges (such as possession of a driver's license) or rights (such as possession of a firearm). For these reasons, it is appropriate to consult with the client and frankly discuss the realities of trial and likelihood of and consequences that might result from a conviction.

Sometimes the prosecutor will offer the defendant a case settlement at the arraignment, although this is unusual in a felony case. Typically, at some point before the preliminary hearing (or pretrial hearing, if the charge is a misdemeanor), the prosecution will offer the defendant a case settlement or sentence recommendation. The defendant is under no obligation to accept any plea, and the defendant retains sole discretion whether to accept or deny a plea offer.[24] An experienced defense attorney may present to the prosecutor problems of proof and equities, in an effort to secure a satisfactory outcome. The process of plea bargaining is discussed in detail in Chapter 12.

Every defense attorney must advocate on behalf of her client in plea negotiations. As explained in Chapter 12, being an effective negotiator is one of the most important roles a defense attorney must play. Understanding the prosecutor's plea offer and informing the defendant are issues that must be attended to with close attention. This requires careful calculation on the part of the defense attorney, who must weigh the defendant's interests and the details of the plea deal against the likelihood of conviction on the basis of the available evidence and applicable law. Although the decision to accept a plea agreement ultimately rests with the defendant, it is the defense attorney's obligation to provide her client with as much relevant information as possible on which to base his decision.

F. WITHDRAWING A PLEA

While withdrawing a plea is difficult, and discussed more thoroughly in Chapter 12, if the record reveals certain deficiencies, such as a failure to advise the defendant of the *Boykin-Tahl* rights, then defense counsel should consider a motion to withdraw the plea. *Boykin-Tahl* rights are rights that are read and waived when a defendant enters a guilty plea. To ensure that the waiver of rights and entry of a

---

[23] A "no contest" plea means that the defendant does not contest the charges, and for the purposes of conviction and sentencing, it is effectively the same as a "guilty" plea. A critical difference, however, is that a "no contest" plea cannot be used against the defendant to establish liability in a civil trial.

[24] MODEL RULES OF PROF'L CONDUCT R. 1.2 (2010). In addition to accepting or refusing a plea offer, the defendant retains exclusive discretion to determine whether he wants a jury trial, whether he wants to waive his right to a speedy trial, and whether he will testify on his own behalf.

guilty or no contest plea will survive appellate court review, prosecutors and judges should demonstrate that the defendant was made aware of all of the pertinent constitutional rights, and knowingly, voluntarily, and intelligently waived and gave them up. Pleas that are uninformed or coerced are unconstitutional. The *Boykin-Tahl* waivers delineate the specific rights, such as the right to confront and cross-examine witnesses, the right to a jury trial, and the right against self-incrimination. Generally, for serious or priorable offenses the court will have defendants initial, sign, and date a written form that explains the basic rights that a defendant is giving up if he pleads guilty. Additionally, the waivers are taken orally in open court and memorialized by a court reporter. This provides a double check that the defendant was made aware of his rights before entering into a guilty or no contest plea. The court clerk in most instances will also record her notes in the court file to show that the defendant was made aware of and waived his basic constitutional rights. This procedure is particularly important for priorable offenses, wherein subsequent offenses or probation violations will result in more serious consequences, such as more time in custody. The prosecution will also make sure that the defendant and his lawyer agree that there is a finding of fact before the defendant enters a guilty plea. This means that the defendant and his attorney acknowledge that there is reason to believe that the defendant committed the alleged crime(s).

HYPO: *Oceana v. Watson*

Immediately following his arraignment, Arthur Watson retained Mycroft Doyle, a private defense attorney. Watson was charged with possession of methamphetamine. At his arraignment and prior to discovery, Moriarty, his public defender, advised him to plead guilty after reviewing the police report. Watson agreed, and he pled guilty to the charge.

Watson then told Doyle that he wanted to change his plea to not guilty. After reviewing the record, Doyle saw a potential deficiency in the court's reading of Watson's *Boykin-Tahl* rights.

If you were Doyle, what would you look for in the record to see if Watson's rights were violated? Is there a basis to withdraw the plea?

BAIL OVERVIEW

Whether or not a defendant remains in custody is, of course, of utmost importance to the defendant. Indeed, the resolution of bail proceedings is a critical step in the procedural process, since a defense attorney will find it much easier to meet with the defendant and prepare for trial if her client is not in custody. Having immediate access to the client, rather than working through the limitations of custody, can facilitate defense trial preparation. For this reason, understanding the bail process is essential for all criminal attorneys. Moreover, defendants who remain in custody are more likely to accept a plea deal as a way to be released from jail. Defense counsel should ensure that the state is not using high bail as leverage to pressure a defendant into entering a guilty plea.

A. RELEASE ON BAIL OR ON OWN RECOGNIZANCE

The Eighth Amendment to the U.S. Constitution stipulates that "[e]xcessive bail shall not be required," but there is no guarantee that bail will be available to each criminal defendant.[25] The Supreme Court in *Stack v. Boyle* reiterated this principle by holding that the Eighth Amendment provides that bail cannot be excessive when it is in fact available.[26] The Court has further implied that for certain crimes, like murder, there is no constitutional right to bail, although it has never explicitly ruled that the Constitution actually ever guarantees bail.[27] More than forty states do not offer bail for capital crimes like murder, but a small number of states permit bail for capital offenses.[28]

Conversely, some states preclude bail for non-capital offenses, although this restriction is applied to specific crimes and on a case-by-case basis.[29] The Arizona Court of Appeals, for example, held that, in cases in which the defendant is accused of sexual conduct with a minor younger than fifteen years of age, bail may be denied.[30] Meanwhile, the Supreme Court of Utah has held that, when a person is charged with committing a felony while on probation for a previous felony conviction, bail may also be denied.[31]

HYPO: *Oceana v. Collins*

Bill Collins had been arrested for beating his wife, Charlotte. A violent husband, he had punched her on a previous occasion while out on bail and awaiting trial on a separate domestic violence charge. To further complicate matters, Bill and Charlotte have two daughters together. Teachers at the girls' elementary school have expressed their concerns to Charlotte because on several occasions the girls have come to school with bruises on their arms and legs. In addition, Bill has left Charlotte several times in the past. He has moved out and disappeared for months at a time. Charlotte is never sure of where he goes or whom he stays with.

If you were the judge, would you grant Mr. Collins bail? Would you deny bail for the non-capital offense he committed here? What justification would a judge have for precluding bail? What factors should the judge consider for determining bail? Would you consider bail with certain added conditions designed to ensure the safety of all parties?

---

[25] U.S. CONST. amend. VIII.

[26] Stack v. Boyle, 342 U.S. 1 (1951).

[27] The Supreme Court has never held that the "no excessive bail" clause in the Eighth Amendment applies to state prosecutions. State jurisdictions regulate bail at their discretion, but generally, the current standard directs most state courts to consider the defendant's flight risk and the defendant's danger to the community when contemplating bail.

[28] *See* RICHARD G. SINGER, CRIMINAL PROCEDURE II: FROM BAIL TO JAIL 16 (2d ed. 2008) ("[W]here the proof is evident or the presumption great," bail can be precluded in most states). Whether the defendant has the burden to show that the proof of his guilt is not evident varies from state to state. *Id.*

[29] *Id.* at 17. Bail is commonly precluded for non-capital offenses such as stalking or domestic violence. *Id.*

[30] Simpson v. Owens, 85 P.3d 478, 481 (Ariz. Ct. App. 2004).

[31] Scott v. Ryan, 548 P.2d 235, 236 (Utah 1976).

Different crimes will, of course, carry different bail amounts, and these will vary from one jurisdiction to another. Sometimes, it is not even a judge who makes the bail decision. While a judge or magistrate will typically set bail for all felonies, judges in some states do not determine bail for all crimes. In Maine, for example, a bail commissioner—whose position requires no legal training—can set bail.[32] In other states, a police officer may set the amount of bail. Such procedural exceptions to the standard rule that judges set bail can have the benefit of conserving judicial resources and maximizing efficiency. Regardless of who sets bail, however, the factors considered when determining bail remain constant.

At every arraignment hearing, the question of custody is at issue, and whoever determines bail must consider many factors. The impartial judicial officer must determine whether the defendant will remain in or be remanded into custody, permitted to post bail, or released on his own recognizance (an "O.R. release," or "O.R."). The court will weigh aggravating and mitigating circumstances when making this decision. Pursuant to the Supreme Court's holding in *United States v. Salerno*, courts may consider, among other factors, the danger that the defendant poses to the community and the likelihood that the defendant will fail to appear.[33] The Court, in upholding the Bail Reform Act of 1984, clarified that governments have a regulatory interest in preventing danger to the community. The Court recognized that individuals have a fundamental interest in liberty, but held that this right may sometimes be subordinate to the greater needs of society to be protected from danger. The Court determined that it is the prosecution's burden to prove by clear and convincing evidence that the arrestee poses an "identified and articulable threat to an individual or the community . . . ."[34] Some states have adopted preventive detention laws. As discussed earlier, some states will interpret the danger of the defendant to the community more strictly than other states. In Arizona, the threat posed by a defendant who commits sexual crimes against minors makes the defendant ineligible for bail in some instances. Meanwhile, the Supreme Court of Alabama has held that all non-capital offenses are bailable, whatever the nature of the crime.[35] Critics argue that predicting future dangerousness is inherently unreliable and it is thus unfair to incarcerate defendants who have not yet been convicted of crimes for future offenses that they might commit.[36] The nature of the crime, however, is not the only consideration for a court in setting bail.

For instance, in a political scandal that rocked Los Angeles County in 2010, elected officials of a small, incorporated city were accused of misappropriating public funds during the economic recession.[37]

---

[32] ME. REV. STAT. ANN. tit. 15, § 1023 (2006).

[33] United States v. Salerno, 481 U.S. 739, 742–43 (1987). The Court also noted that an arrestee may be "incarcerated until trial if he presents a risk of flight." *Id.* at 749.

[34] *Id.* at 751.

[35] *Ex parte* Colbert, 805 So. 2d 687, 689 (Ala. 2001).

[36] *See* John Monahan, *Prediction of Crime and Recidivism, in* 3 ENCYCLOPEDIA OF CRIME AND JUSTICE 1125, 1129 (Joshua Dressler et al. eds., 2002).

[37] On September 21, 2010, Los Angeles District Attorney Steve Cooley announced that he would be arresting and filing charges against eight current and former City of Bell officials, including Bell's former city manager Robert Rizzo, for misappropriating $5.5 million in public funds; the week prior on September 15, 2010, the California Attorney General filed a civil enforcement action against these defendants. *See generally* Memorandum of Points

Several public officials were arrested and taken into custody after they allegedly bolstered their salaries by hundreds of thousands of dollars, or millions in the case of the city manager, for essentially part-time city council positions. When the city manager was arraigned, the court faced a critical decision that illustrates the nature of bail review and the myriad of aggravating and mitigating factors a court must consider before making a determination whether to permit release on bail or to keep the defendant in the government's custody. Because the city manager had access to significant amounts of money, the judge, concerned that he presented a flight risk, accordingly set a high bail amount of $3.2 million (the judge subsequently reduced the bail to $2 million).

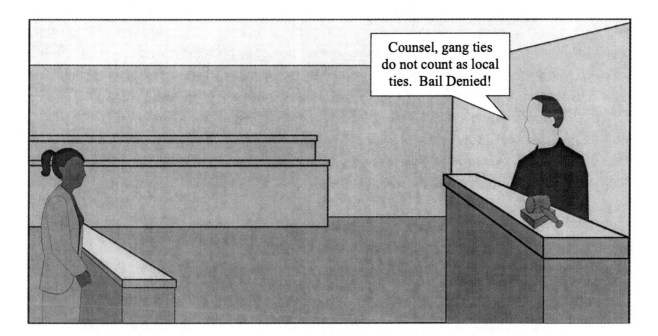

A court can take other measures to ensure that a defendant who might be released on bail will not flee. For example, the court has the right to require a defendant to surrender his passport or to wear an electronic monitoring device. These actions have the dual effect of allowing a defendant to remain free of custody, while also providing assurances that the defendant will not flee and that the public will be protected. All criminal attorneys, particularly defense lawyers, must fully understand the conditions of bail, which can be highly specific. In order to protect her client, it is vital for the defense attorney to ensure both that her request to the court is entirely clear and that she thoroughly grasps the details of the judge's ruling.

B. CONDITIONS OF RELEASE

Bail motions, unlike many of the other procedural elements of the criminal process, are flexible

and Authorities in Support of the Attorney General's Motion for Appointment of a Monitor for the City of Bell, California v. Rizzo (No. BC445497) (Cal. Superior, Oct. 21, 2010), 2010 WL 4970185.

and can be submitted to the court at any time by either side. When considering a bail motion, a judge will presume, for the purposes of the motion only, that the charges are true. The purpose of a bail determination, however, is not to punish the defendant. Therefore, after having evaluated the aggravating and mitigating factors, a court can tailor the conditions of bail to the particularities of the case. As an attorney, it is important to keep this in mind because bail motions present an opportunity to develop creative solutions that effectively balance the opposing sides' interests.

All defense attorneys should acknowledge their clients' desire to be out of custody. This desire will generally be countered by the prosecution's desire to keep the defendants in custody. Because of these opposing interests, an effective defense attorney should cast the defendant's situation in a light that will encourage the court to release a defendant. On the other hand, an effective prosecutor will typically seek to persuade a judge that the defendant should not be released on his own recognizance (O.R.). It is important that prosecutors remember their role should be to seek justice. Thus, if the offense before the court is not serious and the defendant does not have a prior criminal record or present a flight risk, the prosecution should not oppose an O.R. release. The ingenuity of these opposing arguments can be decisive in persuading a judge.

For example, when the city manager charged with corruption was released after he met bail, the judge required that he wear an electric monitoring device and that he surrender his passport.[38]

CHART 4.1
Available Bail Conditions

- Obey all criminal laws.

- Obey all orders of the Court.

- Do not drive with any alcohol or intoxicating substances in the blood system.

- Do not contact or threaten the alleged victim or witnesses (including through third parties) whether orally, in writing, or through any technological means.

- Stay gainfully employed.

- Stay in school.

- Surrender passport until completion of case.

- Stay away from the location of the arrest.

- Do not travel outside of the United States without permission of the Court.

- Do not use or possess dangerous weapons.

- Attend weekly AA (Alcoholics Anonymous) or NA (Narcotics Anonymous) meetings.

- Attend anger management or other counseling sessions.

- Wear an electronic monitoring device.

- Do not use or possess controlled substances without a valid prescription.

- Obey all protective orders and/or restraining orders.

Some crimes will require a court to consider more specific bail conditions. For example, the following lists of bail conditions may be implemented when the defendant has been accused of a sex crime or the defendant is a minor.

---

[38] Richard Winton, *Bell's Robert Rizzo cleared to be released on $2-million bail*, L.A. TIMES (Oct. 7, 2010), http://articles.latimes.com/2010/oct/07/local/la-me-1007-rizzo-bail-20101007.

1. Bail Conditions for Sex Crimes or Child Abuse Cases

- Stay away from parks and schools.

- Stay away from children under the age of sixteen unless in the company of a person authorized by the court.

- Agree to supervised custody visits of the defendant's children.

- Provide DNA samples.

- Provide HIV test results.

2. Bail Conditions for Young Defendants[39]

- Abide by all household rules of the parent(s) or guardian(s).

- Stay away from individuals whom the parent(s) or guardian(s) believe are a bad influence on defendant.

- Do not wear gang colors, use gang signs, or affiliate with known gang members.

- Abide by a court-imposed curfew.

Importantly, a violation of bail conditions can lead to revocation of bail, even though the conditions of bail can sometimes seem cumbersome or overly complex. A common condition of bail release is known as a "protective order"; it often has a greater specificity than a general condition of release.

C. PROTECTIVE ORDERS

When a judge makes the decision to release a defendant on his own recognizance, oftentimes a condition of the release is a protective order, particularly when the alleged crime is of a violent nature. Protective orders are initiated by a prosecutor's request through a bail motion or on the court's own initiative. Like a restraining order, a protective order limits a defendant's actions upon his release from custody. A protective order typically restricts a defendant from contacting a victim, witness, or other party associated with a case, and from approaching within a certain distance of the victim or place of arrest. These orders are not only applicable to out-of-custody defendants; even if a defendant remains in custody, he will be subject to a protective order prohibiting him from any form of contact with the victim or a third party. For example, a judge may order a defendant who is in jail pending trial, not to call, text, e-mail, or write to the alleged victim, either personally or through a third party.

In a domestic violence case in which the defendant has been charged with assaulting his partner, a prosecutor may seek a protective order that shelters the victim and any children from the defendant. These orders can forbid a defendant from, for instance, coming, within 100 yards of a witness, in order to ensure the witness's safety. These orders can also seek to preserve the integrity of the justice system by preventing threats against participants in the proceedings or any other actions that would compromise the participants' honest and open cooperation. If a known associate of an organized gang is charged with racketeering, for example, a protective order may bar the defendant from contacting known associates of the gang and thereby potentially contaminating witnesses' testimony.

---

[39] "Young" defendants are usually in their teens or early twenties and living with parent(s).

D. DETERMINING BAIL USING A BAIL SCHEDULE

After a court determines that a defendant must post bail, the judge will consult a bail schedule. Jurisdictions have predetermined bail schedules that provide the magistrate with guidelines for setting the bail amount. While bail schedules may vary from jurisdiction to jurisdiction, the schedule typically considers the nature of the crime and any enhancements, as well as any of the defendant's prior convictions. As mentioned earlier, the court will also consider the aggravating and mitigating circumstances that might call for justifiable deviations from the general guideline ("presumptive bail") in the bail schedule.

CHART 4.2
BAIL SCHEDULE: *Oceana Penal Code*

PENAL CODE SECTION	OFFENSE	PRESUMPTIVE BAIL
187	Murder – (w/special circumstances)	NOT BAILABLE
187	Murder – (all other murders)	$1,000,000
192(a)	Manslaughter – voluntary	$100,000
211	Robbery – First Degree	$100,000
211	Robbery – Second Degree	$50,000
243	Battery	$50,000
261	Rape	$250,000
273.5	Corporal Injury of Spouse	$50,000
459	Burglary – residential	$50,000
459	Burglary – all others	$20,000

E. PAYING BAIL

After the court sets bail, a defendant cannot be released until he posts the bail. In instances where a defendant cannot afford bail, he might hire a bail bonds company that will then post the bail on his behalf. This typically costs the defendant ten percent of the total bail, a fee that the bail bond company will keep even if the defendant makes all court appearances.[40] But many bail bondsmen will reduce that percentage depending on the defendant or the lawyer with whom they might have an established working relationship. If the defendant fails to appear in court or to comply with any other condition of bail, the entire bail is forfeited and the bail bondsman will then try to have the defendant arrested so as to set aside the bail forfeiture.

---

[40] "The court must declare the bail forfeited if a condition of the bond is breached." FED. R. CRIM. P. 46(f)(1).

When the defendant can post bail, the money he uses must satisfy certain requirements before the court will accept it. For instance, when the city manager's bail in the City of Bell case referred to earlier was set at $2 million, questions arose about the legality of the money he intended to use to post bail. To determine whether the source of bail funds is legitimate, a court may conduct a *Nebbia* hearing before accepting bond payment.[41] Once the court was satisfied that the city manager had not illegally acquired the money he offered in payment of the bond, he was released. As the defendant, the city manager bore the burden of proof and had to establish by probable cause that the bail money was procured by legal means and not as the fruit of criminal, or otherwise unlawful, conduct. If a defendant fails to carry his burden, the court can reject the funds and the defendant will remain in custody.

Before setting the city manager's bail, the court considered proposals from both the district attorney and the city manager's attorney. The prosecutor requested a $3.2 million bail while the defense sought a $100,000 bail.[42] A $2 million total was ultimately set; however, had the city manager been unable to procure that amount of money, his attorney would have been free to raise the bail issue again. As stated above, bail is unlike many other procedural issues that might arise during the course of trial, and either the prosecutor or defense attorney can raise the issue of bail at any time by making a bail review motion.

F. MOTIONS

In most jurisdictions, if the prosecution seeks bail higher than the amount articulated by the bail schedule, the prosecutor's office must file a written bail deviation motion.[43] A bail deviation motion must be supported by an affidavit written by the investigating officer in the case, together with witness testimony or some other proof, such as any record of the defendant's prior offenses ("rap sheet"). The defense will be given an opportunity to counter this motion, and the judge retains wide latitude in setting bail.

1. Possible Reasons for Bail Deviation Hearings

- In an attempted murder case, the victim died after proceedings had been initiated.

- In a stalking case, the defendant continued to harass the victim by way of jail phone or third parties.

- In a criminal threats case, the defendant continued to send threatening messages.

- Further investigation shows that the defendant is a gang member.

- Further investigation shows that the defendant has been convicted in prior criminal cases.

- Further investigation shows that the defendant has committed other crimes using an alias.

---

[41] *See* United States v. Nebbia, 357 F.2d 303 (2d Cir. 1966). States have hearings that are analogous to the federal *Nebbia* hearing. In California, for example, this is a "1275 Bail Motion" hearing. CAL. PENAL CODE § 1275.1 (Deering 2012).

[42] *Audit Finds Calif. City Officials Mismanaged $50M*, FOXNEWS.COM (Sept. 22, 2010) http://www.foxnews.com/politics/2010/09/22/audit-finds-calif-city-officials-mismanaged-m/.

[43] The prosecutor may seek a higher bail for any number of reasons, such as new information.

In state court, a bail motion is usually a quick oral motion brought by the defense. Typically, it is not necessary to provide opposing counsel with notice or to put the motion in writing, although the formality of this process can vary by jurisdiction. The defense attorney will briefly state the reasons that a lower bail amount or release on the defendant's own recognizance should be granted, and the prosecution will respond. A defense attorney might seek to lower bail because the defendant's incarceration is keeping him from working and paying his family's bills. Although less likely, a prosecutor might want to increase bail once new evidence of a defendant's likelihood of fleeing comes to light. Additionally, the prosecution may move to alter the terms of bail if the victim's circumstances have changed; for example, if the alleged victim in an attempted murder case later dies, the prosecutor will move to amend the charge, seeking to increase bail, or even to eliminate the possibility of release on bail altogether. Ongoing mindfulness of a defendant's situation is a necessary concern for all criminal attorneys.

HYPO: *Oceana v. Dent*

On the 25th of May, officers in Oceana arrested Douglas Dent suspected of trafficking drugs into the state. Narcotics agents recovered nearly 200 pounds of marijuana and another 50 kilograms of cocaine during the arrest. The police believe the drugs are linked to a major drug cartel.

At arraignment on the day following the arrest, Judge Marvin set bail at $500,000. In the five days since the initial bail determination, a flurry of events and new evidence have led both the prosecutor and defense counsel to consider the appropriateness of the $500,000 bail.

Dent is a single parent, widowed just six months ago, and the sole provider for his two children, who have been living with a state-appointed guardian since the defendant's arrest. A local computer engineering company employs the defendant as an administrative assistant; his employers have been supportive but they cannot continue to employ him if he cannot come to work.

The defendant's attorney has compiled a packet in support of her client. The packet includes information about the defendant's active role in his church, the different local organizations in which he participates, and the fact that he has no prior criminal charges against him.

The prosecutor, for his part, has uncovered information since the arrest linking the defendant to other drug crimes. There is also evidence that, while in custody, the defendant has orchestrated threats against a potential witness in the case. Other evidence suggests that contrary to the defendant's insistence that he is a "pawn" in a larger drug ring, the defendant may actually be the head of the cartel's operation in Oceana.

Using the information above as a guide, how would you draft a motion to review bail if you were the prosecutor? How would you draft the bail motion if you were the defense attorney? What aggravating and mitigating circumstances might affect the court's review of your motion? What bail amount would you request if you were representing Dent? Do you think you could obtain an O.R. release? As the prosecutor, how would you respond to a bail or O.R. motion?

An attorney's ability to persuade the court at a bail hearing may also be helpful in achieving a satisfactory case settlement. If the case involves a monetary loss and money is owed to an alleged victim, it might be wise for the defense to come to court with proof that the defendant has made restitution to the victim or is in the process of doing so. Such efforts are not an admission of guilt; rather, they demonstrate to the judge that the defendant and defense counsel are taking the case seriously and are prepared to take the appropriate steps to resolve the case.

USING ARRAIGNMENT AND BAIL REVIEW TO YOUR ADVANTAGE

The hallmark of effective advocacy is the ability to take any aspect of a case and turn it to an advantage. Although the arraignment of a defendant might seem a trivial element of a criminal case, it is a key procedural phase that affords a criminal attorney the opportunity to distinguish herself in the eyes of the court and opposing counsel. It can also provide opportunities to set the tone for a case, to cultivate trust between a defense lawyer and her client, or to establish a positive rapport between a prosecutor and a victim. Underestimating the significance of arraignment and bail or failing to appreciate the critical rights associated with this stage can negatively impact the outcome of a trial and can even damage the attorney's reputation. At this phase of a case, no less than any other, a criminal attorney must therefore act with integrity as a zealous advocate for her side.

A. ETHICAL CONSIDERATIONS

When determining how to approach bail hearings, a lawyer has an ethical duty to take many factors into consideration. Such considerations might include the defendant's job, family situation, and socio-economic status. Because every person's situation is unique, bail hearings and procedures should be evaluated on a case-by-case basis. The defense should not always argue for lower bail, and conversely, the prosecution should not always object to O.R. or a bail reduction. By treating each case individually and fairly, the lawyers maintain integrity and credibility with the judge, which is a favorable advantage for future cases.

Judges, of course, must also ethically consider all the factors when determining how to handle bail. Likelihood of fleeing and posing a threat to the community are not the only factors that courts consider. When setting bail, a judge must also examine the seriousness of the charges and the defendant's prior criminal convictions or failures to appear in court (even on traffic matters). Judges should not allow defense counsel to argue the merits of the case, but should instead presume the charges to be true for bail purposes. Even though the judge will be guided by the bail schedule, she should view each case individually when determining bail.

Judges are presented with a dilemma when counsel argues that a defendant's wealth or poverty is a factor that should be considered when determining bail or O.R. For example, a public defender may argue that a defendant will be unable to keep his dependent wife and children from being homeless if he cannot make bail and thus loses his job. Conversely, private counsel might argue that the fact that her client is a professional with a high-paying, respectable job gives the defendant an incentive to make his court appearances. Although it is inappropriate to reward or penalize a defendant based on his economic situation, a court may still take into consideration any fact that bears on the defendant's likelihood to make court appearances, including ties to the community, such as having a family or a job. It is unfair to reduce someone's bail solely because he has a prestigious career, such as that of a doctor, or even a judge. A defense attorney, however, could legitimately make the argument that her client would be unlikely to jeopardize his job, his financial well-being, and consequently his reputation, by fleeing the jurisdiction. Likewise, a defendant whose family relies on him to pay rent might be likely to encourage him to appear in court so as to ensure that he stays out of custody so he can support his family. Thus, the pivotal facts are not the defendant's financial status, but rather his incentive to make court appearances and obey the laws or to flee the jurisdiction.

From an ethical perspective, the bail system has also been the subject of much criticism. One major criticism is that the current system favors the wealthy and puts the poor and those without significant financial means at a disadvantage. Often with indigent defendants, the amount of bail that a judge sets is irrelevant as they typically cannot afford bail, regardless of the amount set by the court. Many have questioned why a rich defendant can go free while an indigent defendant must remain in custody awaiting trial for the same offense. This is a legitimate concern and one that all parties must consider when determining how to approach bail hearings.

Some defendants and cases present unusual circumstances, and the judge must take these into account during the bail determination proceedings. To ensure that the judge is properly informed, the defense attorney must notify the court of her client's needs and unique circumstances. For instance, a defendant might be old and feeble or might suffer from a serious medical condition that requires extensive medical treatment unavailable in a jail facility. Often defendants will require medication while in custody: for example, those who suffer from withdrawal of narcotics or from psychiatric illnesses are especially likely to require medical treatment. Furthermore, it is the responsibility of defense counsel to apprise the judge if the defendant needs a medical or psychological evaluation; the court has the authority to order medical, dental, and psychological evaluations and treatment for defendants in custody, even if they are in custody only for a short time. Courts must also consider possible risk to a defendant if he is introduced into the general jail population, whether because of the type of charges against him (e.g., sex offenses such as child molestation), or because of his sexual orientation, gang affiliation, or psychiatric issues, or because of his past or present cooperation as a police informant. If the defense attorney suspects that the defendant is at risk of being injured by the other inmates, it is her responsibility to request "keep away" status for her client. Typically defendants with such status wear jail uniforms of a particular color to identify them to prison authorities, and are separated from the general jail population.

B. STRATEGY

Judges are usually impressed when a defense attorney presents a packet containing favorable information about the defendant for the bail review hearing. This packet should include all positive aspects of the defendant's past, as well as any favorable efforts the defendant has made after arrest. For example, if the defendant has a clean record, this should be included in the bail review work-up packet. If the defendant has been gainfully employed, is in school, or has made significant community service contributions, an effective defense lawyer will bring these mitigating facts to the court's attention. Savvy defense counsel will, depending on the charges, have the client pay past-due child support, demonstrate an ability or willingness to make restitution, or attend Alcoholics Anonymous meetings, Narcotics Anonymous meetings, or counseling for anger management or other psychological issues. Importantly, such efforts are not an admission of guilt. Rather, they demonstrate that the defendant is taking the charges seriously and is willing to do what is necessary to gain a favorable bail resolution and case settlement. Indeed, in addition to the positive effects on bail determination, these efforts also go a long way to helping the defendant obtain a favorable case resolution. When a judge is presented at the arraignment and bail hearing with a packet showing that a defendant is making efforts to be sober and law-abiding, and if applicable, to reimburse a victim for any monetary loss, this shows respect for the judge and the criminal justice system. These case packets can also include character reference letters for the defendant. Judges grant significant consideration to statements that vouch for the defendant's good character and efforts to rehabilitate. Such letters are especially helpful if they come from respected members of the community, such as clergy, teachers, or employers. Attorneys who regularly present such packets to a judge tend to get more favorable bail determinations and case settlement resolutions. Coming to the arraignment and bail hearing with documents that help the client, or witnesses who will make statements on the client's behalf, furthers the defendant's case and reflects well on the advocate's sense of professionalism.

C. BE CREATIVE

Judges appreciate efforts by attorneys to clarify what the appropriate bail should be. Most judges strive to be judicious and fair when facing difficult decisions like bail determinations. The more prepared the lawyer and the more favorable the information presented to the court, the more likely the judge will rule in that lawyer's favor. For example, if a defense attorney brings to court a comprehensive packet about the defendant's background and efforts to be law-abiding and responsible, and also has a witness who will make a statement on the client's behalf, the judge is much more likely to reduce or modify bail. It is highly effective to have a drug rehabilitation counselor, clergy, employer, or family member make a statement on the defendant's behalf, especially if that person agrees to monitor the defendant or help make sure the defendant makes court appearances. Particularly in cases with youthful defendants, if a parent is in the courtroom and is willing to take responsibility for the defendant and to help ensure that the defendant makes court appearances and obeys all criminal laws, it is much more likely that a judge will allow that defendant a reduction in bail or O.R. release. Conversely, if a prosecutor has documentation that a defendant has a serious criminal record, has a history of failures to appear in court, is on probation or parole, or has violated a court order, the court is much more likely to remand the defendant into custody with higher bail. The prosecutor may also want to provide the court with a packet, such as the defendant's rap sheet, bills indicating restitution allegedly owed to a victim, hospital records showing a victim's injuries, or evidence of violation of a restraining order or other court order. If the prosecutor has filed a bail deviation request, he can also call witnesses, such as a police officer, to show that the defendant has improperly contacted or threatened the victim, or committed some other act that would warrant high bail.

Defense counsel should, if appropriate, present the court with alternatives to bail. For instance, the defense might suggest subjecting her client to house arrest or electronic monitoring. The defendant might not be allowed to leave his home, or might only be allowed to go to work and medical appointments, with the aid of an electronic device that would notify authorities if the defendant went outside a designated geographic area. Such devices are typically paid for by the defendant and therefore raise some concerns that defendants with financial means have an unfair advantage over those who are indigent. Retained counsel can also point out that the fact that her client hired an attorney is some evidence that the defendant intends to be responsible and make court appearances.

All of these considerations present challenges to a judge striving to determine what constitutes fair bail. Courts, moreover, are under increasing pressure to reduce the number of defendants in custody because of jail overcrowding. In cities where the jails are overcrowded, defendants assigned a low bail will often be released by the jail authorities, even without the posting of bail. All the same, a judge's determination may not take these factors into account. In other words, when there are no aggravating factors, courts cannot ethically increase bail above the guideline in the schedule just because it is likely that a defendant with a low bail will be released. Likewise, it is unethical for the prosecutor to request higher bail in an attempt to raise the chances that the defendant will remain in jail. Ultimately, courts should set bail based on the severity of the offense, as well as on an impartial evaluation of factors such as whether the defendant is likely to flee, whether the defendant has prior convictions or a history of failing to make court appearances, and whether the defendant poses a public safety risk. It is the court's duty to weigh the aggravating and mitigating circumstances of each case, in order to determine a fair amount for bail (if any is permitted at all). Similarly, it is the responsibility of both prosecution and defense counsel to present the relevant factors that will aid the court in making just such a fair and appropriate ruling.

SAMPLE MOTION

BENJAMIN RAFFITY
District Attorney, # 168346
MELISSA PRODER,
Deputy District Attorney, # 193278
3451 West Richmond Street
Maliwood, Oceana 90120
Telephone: (809) 392-2521

Attorneys for the Plaintiff

SUPERIOR COURT OF THE STATE OF OCEANA
FOR THE COUNTY OF MALIWOOD

PEOPLE OF THE STATE OF OCEANA,
 	
                                   Plaintiff,
 	
          v.
 	
JOHN STEVEN BRIGGS,
 	
                                   Defendant.
	CASE NO.: C223574
	
	PEOPLE'S REQUEST FOR BAIL DEVIATION; POINTS AND AUTHORITIES; DECLARATION THEREOF
	
	Date: August 15, C.Y.
	Time: 9:00 a.m.
	Dept: 33

TO THE HONORABLE JUDGE OF THE ABOVE ENTITLED COURT:

The People respectfully request the Court to set bail in the amount of one-million dollars ($1,000,000).

Dated: August 3, C.Y.

Respectfully Submitted,
BENJAMIN RAFFITY
DISTRICT ATTORNEY

By: *Melissa Proder*
        Melissa Proder
        Deputy District Attorney

BENJAMIN RAFFITY
District Attorney, # 168346
MELISSA PRODER,
Deputy District Attorney, # 193278
3451 West Richmond Street
Maliwood, Oceana 90120
Telephone: (809) 392-2521

Attorneys for the Plaintiff

SUPERIOR COURT OF THE STATE OF OCEANA
FOR THE COUNTY OF MALIWOOD

PEOPLE OF THE STATE OF OCEANA,
 	
       Plaintiff,
 	
  v.
 	
JOHN STEVEN BRIGGS,
      Defendant.
	CASE NO.: C223574
	
	PEOPLE'S REQUEST FOR BAIL DEVIATION; POINTS AND AUTHORITIES; DECLARATION THEREOF
	
	Date: August 15, C.Y.
	Time: 9:00 a.m.
	Dept: 33

I. **PENAL CODE SECTION 1275 DICTATES THAT THE PUBLIC SAFETY SHALL BE THE PRIMARY CONSIDERATION WHEN SETTING BAIL.**

Penal Code section 1275(a) in part states:

"In setting, reducing, or denying bail, the judge or magistrate shall take into consideration the protection of the public . . . ***The Public safety shall be the primary concern.***" (Emphasis added; *See In re Weiner* (1995) 32 Cal.App.4th 441; *In re Horiuchi* (1930) 105 Cal.App. 714.)

In the case at hand, Defendant is clearly a predator who took advantage of an eight year old boy. Defendant admitted to massaging the victim's groin area. Clearly, this predatory behavior is an extreme threat should Defendant get out of custody.

More importantly, Defendant is a flight risk. Defendant already has a ticket to El Salvador for this week, where he stated he has a son that he visits regularly. Furthermore, Defendant has been working for American Airlines for fourteen years and has access to the computer system and additional employees should he wish to purchase a ticket in a rush and leave the country.

Should the court not increase the bail schedule, the People respectfully request that the Court confiscate Defendant's passport prior to the allowance of posting bail and Defendant's release.

II.   CONCLUSION

Based on the foregoing, the People respectfully request the Court to set bail in the amount of one-million dollars ($1,000,000).

Dated: August 3, C.Y.

Respectfully Submitted,
BENJAMIN RAFFITY
DISTRICT ATTORNEY

By: *Melissa Proder*
        Melissa Proder
        Deputy District Attorney

SUMMARY

Every criminal defendant has the right to an arraignment, at which he is informed of the charges against him. Generally, the arraignment must occur within forty-eight hours after a complaint has been filed. At the arraignment, the accused is also advised of his constitutional rights: the right to a speedy trial, the right against self-incrimination, the right to confront and cross-examine witnesses, and where applicable, the rights to counsel and to a trial by jury. Indeed, the right to counsel attaches at the defendant's first appearance before a judicial officer after a formal charge is made. Adversarial proceedings, in other words, are generally initiated at the arraignment. For indigent defendants, this is usually when they first meet a public defender or decide to represent themselves. Other defendants may not yet have retained private counsel. Because the arraignment is often the first time an attorney appears before the court in a specific case, both attorneys will want to appear competent and professional, and the defense attorney will also want to make a positive impression on her client. Furthermore, any issues regarding defects in the complaint should, furthermore, be resolved at the arraignment.

Although defendants usually enter a not guilty plea at arraignments, it is common for arraignments to be postponed, and a "continuance" granted when the accused agrees to a time waiver. A continuance will also postpone when the accused will enter a plea. Minor cases may be settled at the arraignment; however, because of potential repercussions that could impact a client long after a case is settled, defense counsel should be sure, even if the charge is a misdemeanor, that she has explained the consequences of a plea to the defendant. For example, legal residents might find it difficult to become citizens if they plead guilty to felonies or certain misdemeanors, so they should be counseled accordingly. If the arraignment is postponed, it is possible that an offer will be made when the defendant returns to court to enter a plea, and the case may be settled with an early disposition. If a defendant charged with a felony does not accept a settlement offer, the case will likely proceed to a preliminary hearing (unless there has been a grand jury indictment). Again, defense counsel will need to advise the client throughout these early stages, and should try to procure favorable offers, while also preparing for a possible preliminary hearing and trial. Notably, both the prosecutor and the defense attorney should be working on their respective case theories as early as the arraignment stage.

While some defendants are in custody during the arraignment, others have posted bail or have been released on their own recognizance. The Eighth Amendment prohibits excessive bail, but bail itself is not guaranteed to every defendant. Bail is unavailable for some offenses, and for others, it is assigned according to a schedule. The amount of bail can increase depending on the seriousness of the offense. At arraignment, the magistrate will release the accused on his own recognizance (a promise to appear before the court at a future date), set an amount for bail, or in some cases (especially when capital offenses are charged), deny bail. The judicial officer will have to consider aggravating and mitigating circumstances as presented by counsel. Before releasing the accused on his own recognizance, the judicial officer will consider whether the defendant should be considered a flight risk or whether he presents a danger to the community. Even if release is granted, there may be conditions, such as surrendering a passport, which defense counsel must explain to the defendant. Release from custody aids the attorney-client relationship in several ways; above all, when the defendant is not in custody, an attorney can interview and communicate with her client more frequently, thoroughly, and intimately.

Counsel should use the arraignment and bail review to their advantage. At these earliest stages, it is crucial to make a good first impression and to set an appropriate tone for the case. If the defense attorney is diligent and well prepared at these early stages, both the court and the client will have more faith in her advocacy skills. Likewise, a professional, skilled prosecutor will be more impressive to any victims or witnesses who are present in the courtroom.

CHECKLIST

✓   When an attorney first appears in court, the impression she makes will have a lasting impact, not only on her client, but also on colleagues, adversaries, and the court.

✓   Remember that the arraignment and plea, as the first procedural step on the way to trial, can be just as important, if not more important, than the trial itself. Always use arraignment and bail proceedings to your advantage.

✓   Know the procedural timing for pretrial hearings. Be sure to consult relevant statutes for the particular jurisdiction and any appropriate local rules.

✓   Understand and protect the rights of the criminal defendant, including the right to the effective assistance of counsel, which it is the criminal defense attorney's duty to provide.

✓   Whether a criminal defendant is released on bail or on his own recognizance, he must fully understand the conditions of the release.

✓   Keep in mind protective orders and how they may impact a criminal defendant or victims.

✓   Remember the benefits of creativity when making bail motions, and consider the aggravating and mitigating circumstances that might affect these motions.

✓   Maintain familiarity with the bail schedule of your jurisdiction, ensuring that your requests to the court are realistic and do not threaten your credibility.

CHAPTER 5
INTERVIEWING AND COUNSELING WITNESSES

"There are always three sides to a story: your side, my side, and the right side."
–Ralph Kenyon

Witness preparation is not undertaken in a vacuum. By the time an attorney has completed his list of witnesses and has started scheduling meetings with them, he should have already completed the bulk of the background research for the case and begun to formulate a case theory. When preparing for the initial interview, a litigator should remember that witnesses may be entirely unfamiliar with the legal process, reluctant to testify, or simply uncomfortable with a stranger asking them questions about an alleged crime. Successful attorneys will therefore cultivate a comfortable environment for witnesses that will pave the way for a collaborative and trusting relationship. The more comfortable witnesses are with the attorney, the more likely it is that they will be forthcoming with information and generally helpful in providing crucial information when necessary. This openness will, in turn, translate into more credible and persuasive testimony. Witnesses, especially defendants and crime victims, may feel uneasy about discussing a criminal incident, particularly one that involved violence.

Just as crime victims and witnesses to violent crime are often shaken up by the experience of being interviewed and giving testimony when required, defendants are also often distraught over being arrested and facing criminal charges. Attorneys need to counsel both types of witnesses to help them get through what is surely one of the most difficult ordeals of their lives. This chapter explores the most effective methods of interviewing witnesses in general, while Chapter 6 will specifically focus on attorney-client interviews.

THE INTERVIEW

A. COLLECTING INFORMATION

A trial is analogous to a large puzzle. By the time witness interviews begin, the shape and form of the puzzle should have begun to emerge. The interview should aid the attorney in identifying the missing pieces of the puzzle, thereby providing a clearer picture of what happened. Since a witness interview serves, primarily, to obtain information, the bulk of the witness interview should focus on exploring the witness's recollection. Counsel should not rely on the police to have asked every relevant question or to have considered every motive or viewpoint. Further, an astute criminal defense attorney should realize that police have a law enforcement bias, which may have had an effect on the content of the witness's statement to the police. This pro-prosecution bias may also have affected the way in which the detectives have conducted their interrogations and written police and supplemental reports. For example, perhaps the police officer conducted the interview by using leading questions, or an eyewitness to a crime was given hints or might have been subtly coerced into identifying a suspect as the perpetrator of a crime. An attorney should ask questions that can reveal such circumstances. <u>Prior to the interview, the attorney should be intimately familiar with the police report and any prior statements the witness has given.</u> This background research is necessary for a productive and efficient interview process.

By the time an attorney meets with a witness, it is likely the witness will have already been asked many of the same questions about the case two or three times over. A witness may resent the amount of time the case takes up, and therefore be reluctant to help. Recognizing such concerns and working to overcome them, will facilitate a healthy relationship between an attorney and witness. Because the statements an attorney obtains from witnesses will be crucial to completing the puzzle, the preparation is worth the effort. Moreover, it is important to remember that collecting information is an ongoing process. Primarily, attorneys will gather most of the information about a case before trial, but fact gathering may well continue during trial and sometimes even afterwards. <u>Trial preparation is a fluid process that requires flexibility and a willingness to alter a case theory when the evidence warrants.</u> — *tell that to Judge Mason*

1. Preparing for the Interview

Expert lawyering requires meticulous preparation, and the best attorneys know their cases better than anyone else. It is imperative to review and outline the police report, any supplemental reports, and toxicological or other forensic reports, if available, before conducting witness interviews. Having an outline of the areas to explore can help facilitate a smooth interview. Before the interview begins, the attorney should be prepared to confirm the statements previously made by the witness and seek to clear up any inconsistencies at that time. Where there are gaps, she should be ready to explore, and hopefully clarify, what the witness remembers. This preparation will ensure that the witness's time is not wasted. Still, attorneys should anticipate resistance from some witnesses and make an effort not to alienate them.

HYPO: *Oceana v. Hardy*

Consider the following hypothetical scenario. You are the prosecutor in a case where the defendant, Jude Hardy has been charged with murder. Hardy is allegedly part of a gang, and if you can prove that he is a gang member, then his sentence upon conviction will be significantly lengthened. In order to prove that Hardy is a gang member, however, you may have to call another member of the same gang as a witness. Hardy's affiliate in the gang is currently serving time for an unrelated crime. For these reasons, it is likely that this witness will be reluctant to testify. How might you, as the prosecutor, obtain the cooperation of the witness and prepare to conduct a jailhouse interview? (Refer to "Section D: Dealing with Challenging Witnesses").

---

2. Diplomacy of the Interview

An attorney must possess a great many skills, and one skill that is often overlooked but can determine the course of a case is the ability to create productive relationships with witnesses. Being personable and conversing easily with others is one of the most useful attributes of a skilled trial attorney. In addition to being eloquent in front of a judge and jury, persuasive litigators have good "people skills" and can readily establish a positive rapport with witnesses.

As noted earlier, just as an effective attorney will work to make each client or victim feel comfortable and appreciated, the lawyer must do the same with each witness. This means being considerate of the witness's needs and understanding his concerns as he raises them. When scheduling an interview, the attorney might consider meeting at a time that does not require the witness to sit in rush-hour traffic or miss work. When a witness arrives at an attorney's office, the attorney should consider his comfort and, if at all possible, the witness should not be kept waiting. The attorney should also be mindful to offer the witness a comfortable chair and a glass of water or a cup of coffee.[1] Moreover, an attorney should make sure that her witness understands the interview process; at times, this might mean printing out a schedule outlining the format for the meeting so that the witness can understand the goals of the interview process.

As simple as all of these ideas may seem, together they demonstrate to the witness that he is valued, and this will more likely encourage his cooperation. Even the best witness can hurt a case if he dislikes an attorney. Ill will towards an attorney can cause a witness to be less than candid and may cause not just the attorney but also the jury to distrust his testimony.

B. CONDUCTING AN INTERVIEW

When a witness first arrives at an interview, an advocate should identify the goals of the interview and articulate her case strategy. It is common for a witness to be apprehensive about meeting with an attorney, especially in a criminal case. It is hoped that putting witnesses at ease will help alleviate their anxiety. The most effective demeanor for the attorney is to be confident without ever appearing arrogant. Exuding confidence is reassuring, while exhibiting arrogance is unappealing.

Be clear about what your plan is and what you want for the witness

The primary goal of the interview is to obtain relevant information by learning the witness's version of the events. Although the witness may already know the nature of the case, it is a good idea to remind him of the charges. Finally, the attorney must come away from the interview understanding how this witness's piece of the puzzle fits into the rest of the case. It is also advisable to record any witness interviews as this will have the dual effect of ensuring that nothing is missed, and will further help avoid future inconsistent statements. Recording an interview, however, can be unsettling for witnesses, so the attorney should be sure to explain the importance of recording the interview while remaining flexible. If a witness is uncomfortable with audio recording, then the attorney should simply take notes.

---

[1] The Model Rules of Professional Conduct prohibit attorneys from providing food or money to witnesses, although non-alcoholic beverages may be served within reason. Similarly, witnesses (with the exception of expert witnesses) cannot be paid for their time. Any appearance of impropriety can raise questions of undue influence and potential charges against an attorney. *See* MODEL RULES OF PROF'L CONDUCT R. 3.4(b) (2010); *see also* MODEL CODE OF PROF'L RESPONSIBILITY EC 7-28 (1983). Some limited witness expenses are paid by the government.

Since some witnesses, such as Jude Hardy, the reluctant gang member in *Oceana v. Hardy*, may not be forthcoming, there should be at least one other person present during any interview. For a prosecutor, this other person will often be the detective assigned to the case. For the defense, it could be an investigator, paralegal, or even a law clerk. In the event that the witness recants a statement or refuses to testify when called, the other person in the room can accurately testify to what the witness said earlier. The attorney does not want to be placed in a position of having to testify as to what a witness said, as this might put the attorney in the predicament of having to recuse himself.[2] This is particularly crucial in domestic violence cases and in gang cases, where it is common for witnesses to recant.

At other times, an attorney will have to arrange for a translator. Since legal matters can be complex and often involve an intricate understanding of language, it is critical to make sure that the attorney and witness understand each other. Many words and phrases have a completely different meaning to someone who speaks English as a second language or comes from a different culture. Witnesses accustomed to conversing in English on a daily basis might still decide, given the tense environment of a courtroom where precision of language is required and the terminology is oftentimes complex, that they would prefer to testify through an interpreter. If an attorney determines that the witness might be more comfortable using an interpreter, then the attorney should arrange for one to be provided. In criminal cases, the court provides interpreters (at the attorney's request) at no cost to the witness or lawyer.[3]

1. The Initial Interview

The most effective approach for the initial interview is to allow the witness to explain what he knows about the incident without interrupting him during this first recounting of the story. One of the best skills an attorney can develop is to be a good listener, as this helps develop trust between the attorney and the witness. After the witness explains the event, it is appropriate to reframe or confirm the information the witness has shared, and only then should the attorney ask questions, focusing on the points still in need of clarification. Most attorneys find it helpful to have the witness review prior statements (or, in the case of a police officer, have him look over his report), and explain any discrepancies or inconsistencies. In addition, inquiring into the witness's personal background and biases might explain why he remembers a particular event or perhaps why he is out to help or harm certain individuals. An attorney, furthermore, should obtain information that can be used in trial to personalize the witness in front of the jury.

During the interview, it is possible that the information received from a witness will only confirm what is already known. All the same, thorough preparation is necessary for an efficient interview to take place because a principal goal of a witness interview is to discover other witnesses or evidence that can corroborate another witness's version of events or undermine opposing counsel's case theory. For instance, the witness may be aware of another witness's reputation for

---

[2] *See* MODEL RULES OF PROF'L CONDUCT R. 3.7 (2010).

[3] *See* 28 U.S.C. § 1827(d) (2006); *see also* CAL. EVID. CODE § 752 (Deering 2012).

truth or his propensity for violence, or he may have knowledge of another witness's prior convictions or bad acts. The witness may provide information that sheds light on the motive or bias of another witness (perhaps the defendant, victim, or other percipient witnesses). For instance, a witness might inform the defense attorney that the complaining witness has a grudge against the defendant. Perhaps the witness is aware that the defendant cheated on his girlfriend, the alleged victim, and her motive is to retaliate. It is possible that the defendant was too embarrassed to reveal such personal information and withheld it from the attorney. Clearly, this type of information could be grounds for establishing bias and it would also provide the defense attorney with powerful ammunition when cross-examining the complaining witness. Further, this type of information can provide much needed leverage during case settlement negotiations. A more detailed discussion of case settlement is located in Chapter 12. Prosecutors and defense lawyers alike should always ask witnesses whether they know of any reason why other witnesses (particularly the complaining witness and the defendant) would fabricate a story or mislead investigators.

2. The Pretrial Interview

The pretrial interview should take place shortly before the trial date. The pretrial interview is not a rehashing of the initial interview. The initial interview is more about fact-finding and understanding the witness, while the pretrial interview is more about preparing for testimony. Because the attorney needs to prepare the witness for testifying in court, and sometimes she must calm down an anxious witness, the witness should be informed of the general areas that will be covered in direct examination. The attorney should explain to the witness the concept of "blocking," a method by which different aspects of the testimony are covered in separate parts of the direct examination. Blocking is a way to break the testimony down into sections that make sense to the witness, judge, and jury. Typically, the first block of the testimony will be the personalization of the witness, then the next block will be the setting of the event, then next will be the action section of the criminal event, and finally conclusions, such as the certainty of the identification of the defendant.[4] The attorney should remind the witness to tell the truth, not to guess at answers, and not to digress when testifying. At this interview, attorneys should familiarize witnesses with any trial exhibits they intend to use. Witnesses should also use this opportunity to practice explaining the events relevant to their case by using diagrams and other exhibits. Finally, the attorney should role-play the part of opposing counsel and thoroughly prepare the witness for the experience of cross-examination.

C. EVALUATING THE WITNESS

When evaluating the interview, a preliminary determination must be made as to the witness's competence. Before an attorney can call a witness, she must ensure that four criteria have

---

[4] *See, e.g.,* L. TIMOTHY PERRIN, H. MITCHELL CALDWELL & CAROL A. CHASE, THE ART & SCIENCE OF TRIAL ADVOCACY (2d ed. 2011) (providing an in-depth explanation on the concept of blocking).

been met: (1) the witness must be willing to swear under oath or affirm to tell the truth;[5] (2) the witness must have percipient knowledge of legally relevant information;[6] (3) the witness must be able to remember what was perceived as having taken place; and (4) the witness must be able to communicate this information in an articulate manner. If an attorney doubts a witness's ability to satisfy these requirements, she is ethically prohibited from calling that witness to testify.[7] Additionally, an attorney cannot call a witness to testify if she knows the witness intends to perjure himself.[8] A further discussion of this last point is located in Chapter 6.

All relevant information, not just helpful information, should be garnered from witnesses. Advocates should keep in mind, however, that relevant facts and concerns that hurt the case theory should not be ignored. They should be confronted and if at all possible, they should be resolved. When such damaging facts cannot be resolved, efforts must be made to mitigate the damage they may cause to the case. Since opposing counsel will be sure to focus on such weaknesses, it is, of course, best to be prepared and confront these types of potential concerns well in advance of trial. When evaluating a witness's testimony, it is important for the attorney to be aware that opposing counsel may call witnesses or produce evidence that contradicts the version of events her witness has provided. It is appropriate to test a witness's credibility based on the statements of opposing witnesses or other evidence, such as DNA, ballistics, or any other available forensic evidence that might be produced in court. It is certainly preferable to obtain information that threatens one's case during the interview process, rather than being blindsided in trial by evidence that undermines the attorney's case theory. Once the witness has divulged damaging information to the attorney, the attorney should evaluate the potential consequences of moving to exclude the damaging evidence by bringing a pretrial motion. As there is always the possibility that such a motion might fail, the attorney should have a strategy in mind by which to present such information to the jury in a light that is the least damaging to her case.

While remembering the importance of evaluating witness interviews, it is also critical to separate what the witness says from how he actually says it. One's impression of a statement might

---

[5] FED. R. EVID. 603; *see also* CAL. EVID. CODE § 710 (Deering 2012).

[6] FED. R. EVID. 602; *see also* CAL. EVID. CODE § 702 (Deering 2012).

[7] MODEL RULES OF PROF'L CONDUCT 3.4(b) (2010) ("A lawyer shall not falsify evidence, counsel or assist a witness to testify falsely . . . .").

[8] *Id.*

change depending upon whether one heard the statement spoken, or only regarded it in written form. For example, someone who has only read Martin Luther King, Jr.'s "I Have a Dream" speech, but has never heard the recording of Dr. King's actual delivery, will miss much of the significant emotional effect of his legendary words. Certainly, the text version of his words is powerful and moving, but the heart-felt conviction with which Dr. King delivered his speech contributed immensely to its now significant place in American oratory history. Because witness testimony is presented orally, the way in which the words of that testimony are delivered can significantly influence their effect upon the listener.[9] For this reason, attorneys must consider the subjective evaluation of jurors and how those evaluations will affect counsel's case theory. Litigators should tell witnesses that the jury could analyze the way they testify in terms of word choice, inflection, pace, tone, and body language and use that in assessing the witnesses' credibility and impact of their testimony. Although a myriad of factors should be considered when conducting a witness interview, primary among these are a witness's ability to recollect facts, the witness's ability to communicate his story of the manner in which the events unfolded, and, of course, his general demeanor.

For example, in the mid-1980s, allegations of sexual abuse were made against the directors of the Virginia McMartin Preschool in Manhattan Beach, California. Given the incendiary nature of the crimes alleged, the prosecutor's office began a lengthy investigation. The mother who initially made the allegations claimed that satanic rituals and sodomy had taken place at the preschool, and the investigation that followed included interviews of hundreds of preschool students. Based on the children's statements and some medical evidence, 321 counts were brought against the owners, directors, and teachers at the preschool. Ultimately, two defendants, facing a total of sixty-five charges, were brought to trial.[10]

Every child who indicated that they had been victimized had been counseled at the same child psychology center before making incriminating statements. This fact raised questions in the eyes of jurors. Additionally, the children were interviewed in a manner that was later determined to be leading and suggestive. Ultimately, the jury failed to convict either defendant of any charges. Juror comments indicated that the children's lack of credibility doomed the prosecution's case.[11] Consequently, after a thirty-month trial costing approximately $15 million, the case was lost because prosecutors failed to accurately evaluate the credibility of the witnesses essential to their case. The prosecution in *McMartin* should have considered the following components of

---

[9] While juries may have access to transcripts of witnesses' testimony after deliberations begin, the impression a witness makes when taking the stand can taint the objective presentation of the words in a transcript.

[10] Eventually, all charges were dropped and no convictions were obtained, however, for the sake of clarity, this case will be referred to as *McMartin* throughout the text.

[11] Robert Reinhold, *The Longest Trial—A Post-Mortem; Collapse of Child-Abuse Case: So Much Agony for So Little*, N.Y. TIMES (Jan. 24, 1990), http://www.nytimes.com/1990/01/24/us/longest-trial-post-mortem-collapse-child-abuse-case-so-much-agony-for-so-little.html?src=pm.

recollection, communication, demeanor, and how the jury might have perceived the child witnesses at trial.

1. Recollection

A witness's strength of recollection consists of his ability to recall the facts accurately. Consideration of a witness's ability to recollect information, however, requires more than just an evaluation of the facts presented by the witness. During the interview process, an attorney should evaluate how quickly a witness recalls the information in addition to assessing how confident he seems to be about the accuracy of his recollection.

To clarify, all of the children who testified in the *McMartin* trial discussed above had spoken with the same counselors at the counseling center. How might the influence of child psychologists eliciting responses from children affect a juror's evaluation of the children's veracity? Also important to consider is the fact that the children's testimony came years after the alleged crimes. In the mind of a juror, how likely is it that an eight or nine year old child will accurately recollect events that took place five years earlier? A prosecuting attorney who plans to put a child victim on the witness stand must first consider whether he believes the child, and then whether the child's testimony will be credible. If an objective attorney observes a child struggle to remember facts or give inconsistent statements, this should influence the decision as to whether or not the child should be called as a witness.

Another reality of witness testimony is that some people, despite their sincere belief in the truth of what they are saying, are simply not believable. This is especially important to consider when dealing with children: jurors might sympathize with young children, but they may not find them credible. Whether the witness is a child or adult, it may not matter if the witness is telling the truth if he does not come across as trustworthy; sometimes *how* the words are spoken can be more significant than the words themselves. A witness who cannot maintain eye contact with the lawyer or jurors, who shifts around uncomfortably and fidgets, or who gives evasive or inconsistent

answers, may simply appear unconvincing. Prosecutors must keep in mind that the standard of proof of beyond a reasonable doubt is a very high standard. If a case hinges on a witness who appears to be only somewhat convincing, this might be insufficient to eliminate a reasonable doubt that the witness is mistaken or lying. When making the evaluation of whether to call a particular witness, especially a child witness, an attorney must be as objective as possible and weigh the benefits of the testimony against the potential damage it might cause to his case.

Isn't it true you didn't see the robbery, am I wrong?

2. Communication

In addition to appearing trustworthy, it is imperative for a witness to communicate effectively. An attorney can ask questions and seek to clarify answers, but he cannot ultimately speak for the witness. Counsel must always feel confident that his witness can communicate ideas clearly on his own. During direct examination, the focus should be on the witness, and the testimony should be in the witness's own words. Although leading questions are proper on cross-examination, they are not permitted during direct examination.[12] Rather, attorneys should ask simple, clear questions in order to facilitate the process.

As demonstrated by the children who testified in *McMartin*, young children will not generally communicate as clearly as adults. Moreover, that case called for testimony on sexual topics, an area in which a child would not be expected to have much knowledge and even less comfort in discussing. A prosecutor must consider whether or not a child can communicate the facts clearly. What if the child cannot articulate what happened? Will the child's description of sexual acts be confusing? Will that hurt the witness's credibility? And again, how will a witness's difficulty communicating affect the case theory? What if no child can describe, with clarity, what happened? These types of considerations, and many others like them, must be carefully thought through by the attorney before calling a witness. If, for example, a witness requires a translator during trial, the attorney should consider how hearing witness testimony through a translator might impact the jury.

3. Demeanor

When evaluating a witness's demeanor, the attorney should also consider non-verbal communication. It is a reality (both in and out of the courtroom) that prejudice often guides an individual's perceptions. In truth, jurors may start to form opinions about the case as early as *voir dire*. Before a witness ever takes the stand, a jury will have already begun to formulate opinions about him. Jury opinions are influenced by the witness's body-language, the way he walks, dresses, sits in the chair, as well as the degree of respect he demonstrates for the attorneys, jury, and judge. Witnesses who look unkempt or who have offensive tattoos (such as Nazi or gang insignia) will alienate jurors. Attorneys must therefore instruct witnesses to dress and groom conservatively for court.

Often, the demeanor of a witness is also affected by his willingness to cooperate. If a gang member has been subpoenaed, he will likely resist testifying. This uncooperative attitude might be reflected in his tone or disrespect for the authority of the court. Part of effective trial preparation is to explain to jurors in *voir dire* and opening statements that criminal cases often necessitate calling witnesses whom the jurors may find unsavory. On the other hand, although a witness may remain completely composed during an interview, a harsh cross-examination may unsettle a once calm demeanor. When a witness's emotions take control, the jury's impression of the witness can be affected. This is especially true when a witness becomes combative with an attorney.

---

[12] *See, e.g.*, CAL. EVID. CODE § 767 (Deering 2012).

D. ORGANIZING TESTIMONY

When evaluating how each witness functions as a component within her case strategy, it is critical for the attorney to consider the way in which each witness's actual testimony will be presented. As discussed earlier, counsel must determine the role of each witness in supporting the case theory. The following concepts can aid an attorney in organizing and evaluating the testimony a witness might give and thus help guide its incorporation into the case theory.

1. Primacy and Immediacy

Jurors will best remember the first and last statements they have heard. This entails the importance not only of the opening statement and closing argument, but also the beginning and end of witness testimony.

2. Chronology

Sometimes a story is best told chronologically. An attorney should consider the evidence that each witness will provide and how the telling of that witness's story fits into the larger picture.

3. Overview Witness

Certain witnesses may be able to provide a comprehensive picture of the case. If they are credible, they can effectively lay out the presentation of a case. These witnesses might include the victim's close friend or the investigating officer on the case.

4. Adverse Witness

Some witness testimony will hurt an advocate's case theory. Confronting this testimony will demonstrate to the jury that the attorney has nothing to hide. At the same time, by burying harmful content in the middle of witness testimony, the attorney can reduce the damage of the testimony by limiting the extent to which jurors will focus upon it as a result of such strategic incorporation.

5. Lay and Expert Witnesses

Complicated cases often require expert testimony. An attorney should consider whether expert testimony would help the jury understand subsequent lay witness testimony, or whether it would be preferable for a lay witness to tell the story and then have an expert explain its significance.

6. Availability

Because not all witnesses can testify whenever required, limitations to witness schedules must frequently be accommodated. Part of trial preparation is planning the opening statement so that it tells a persuasive, logical story that alleviates any confusion should counsel need to call witnesses out of order.

7. Defendant

Generally, in criminal cases, the defendant, if he testifies, will do so last. This provides defense counsel the opportunity to evaluate the impact of each witness's testimony relative to the rest of the case and then modify trial strategy accordingly. While defendants have the right to speak on their own behalf, most attorneys will typically discourage their clients from taking the stand. When questioned by opposing counsel, mistakes, hesitation or incoherent statements in a defendant's testimony might raise a doubt in jurors' minds about the defendant's innocence. Additionally, defendants who choose to testify run the very real risk of having their credibility impeached with prior convictions, bad acts, or prior inconsistent statements.[13] Sometimes, this may simply be too high a risk for an attorney to take. Of course, advising defendants whether or not they should testify must be undertaken on a case-by-case basis and the ultimate decision always belongs to the defendant. This will be further explored in Chapter 6.

8. Witness Demeanor

However credible some witnesses appear during private conversation with the attorney, they may not be cut out for the stress of testifying during a criminal trial. An attorney must consider many things when deciding whether or not a witness is suited to providing trial testimony: can the witness stand up to rigorous cross-examination; will the jury sympathize with the witness; will the witness appear weak or untruthful; will the witness come across as biased or hostile. When confronted with any one of these concerns, an attorney must further consider how they might diminish the jury's ability to believe the witness's statements.

9. Credibility

As this chapter has emphasized, a witness's credibility is of paramount importance to a juror and hence should be of equally significant concern to the attorney asking him to testify. It is the attorney's responsibility to bring out credible testimony and to diffuse the potentially harmful effect of unfavorable information by strategically locating it midway through the witness testimony. Furthermore, an attorney must ready her witness to offer a reasonable explanation for any damaging testimony such as prior inconsistent statements or inaccurate prior statements that resulted from a shocking ordeal. Credibility is judged by the content of the testimony, the way the witness testifies, and whether or not any prior inconsistent statements, biases, motives, or prior convictions or bad acts might be exposed.

E. WORK PRODUCT DOCTRINE

Much of what an attorney discusses during a witness interview is discoverable, although work product is not.[14] For a successful interview process, the attorney must understand the distinction between what is discoverable and what is not. Conversations between an attorney and a witness may be discoverable, but an attorney's thoughts and ideas about the witness are not.[15] Keeping these two categories distinct and separate will make the attorney's job much easier. The following is an example of an attorney's interview sheet.

---

[13] FED. R. EVID. 609.

[14] See FED. R. CIV. P. 26(b)(3). See also FED. R. CRIM. P. 16(b)(2).

[15] FED. R. CIV. P. 26(b)(3)(B).

CHART 5.1
Witness Statements

Statement	Work Product
Here the attorney would record witness statements, which are discoverable generally.	Here the attorney writes thoughts and impressions of the witness's statements–these are protected work product.

The left side of the page includes facts and statements made by the witness. Generally speaking, this information is discoverable. The right-hand side of the page, on the other hand, has notes that are the attorney's thoughts and impressions of the witness. These ideas include the attorney's evaluation of the credibility of the witness as well as evidentiary concerns and ideas for establishing a persuasive case theory. All of the attorney's impressions that are listed on the right side of the sample work sheet are not discoverable, as they are protected by the work product doctrine.[16]

F. A NEW WITNESS

Sometimes, as previously mentioned, an attorney may have to interview a witness about whom she has little or no knowledge prior to the interview. This raises a new sort of challenge, and the following case hypothetical, *Oceana v. Burton*, puts it into perspective.

HYPO: *Oceana v. Burton*
For the last week and a half, a definitive issue in an on-going murder trial has been revealing the identity of the shooter. The prosecution has sought to use witnesses and circumstantial evidence to prove that the defendant, Jack Burton, is the same man who shot the victim, Sandy Talons, outside a grocery store. As the trial nears its conclusion, the prosecutor has now called a key witness, Sally Carter, who works the cash register inside the store.

Carter testified that she had "a decent look at the guy with the gun." Identifying Burton, she said, "He kind of looks like the guy. It was hard to see, though, because there was a customer walking out who passed between me and the shooter when he was kind of turned towards me."

Carter's statement on the stand marked the first time she ever identified this "customer," and security images did not capture the area where he was allegedly standing at the time of the shooting, so he has never been identified. Certainly, this mysterious "customer" might be a critical witness for both the prosecution and the defense.

Locating this person, however, will not be easy. At this critical phase of trial, a lengthy continuance is unlikely. Thus, each side faces two tasks: preparing to interview this person about whom they know little and locating the witness—already no small task.

Oceana v. Burton demonstrates, first, the need to be thorough; it should be clear by now that an attorney cannot merely rely upon police and investigators to collect all the information necessary

---

[16] FED. R. CIV. P. 26(b)(3).

for trial. Moreover, *Burton* illustrates the challenges that attorneys face when a new witness is discovered so late in the process. Interviews conducted under these circumstances must be much more exploratory than is typically the case and will require the attorney to take a more open approach. The majority of the work, however, will be in the evaluative stage.

After gathering the information from the new witness, the attorney may discover that the additional evidence introduces a host of legal issues. What if, for example, the new witness's statement—the unidentified customer—suggests that self-defense may have precipitated the defendant's actions? This will likely affect the case theory. Moreover, the new witness's testimony may, in turn, require interviewing yet further witnesses. What if the witness informs the attorney that there were at least two people in the getaway car? Up until this point, the evidence available indicated that Burton was alone in the car. The attorney must now try to find the second occupant of the getaway vehicle, in addition to re-evaluating the overall case theory. Like all other aspects of trial preparation, an attorney must be ready to account for anything that might affect the case strategy. An ability to address unfavorable rulings, adeptly handle evidentiary challenges, and integrate the appearance of new witnesses, will only benefit the overall case presentation. Although it is impossible to anticipate every conceivable obstacle that might arise, being prepared to take the unexpected in stride can result in a confident appearance in the courtroom. The following section discusses the ways in which to adapt case theory to witness interviews.

PREPARING WITNESSES FOR TRIAL

ETHICS

The *Model Rules of Professional Conduct* govern an attorney's actions and limit the extent to which an attorney may advise a witness prior to testimony. Model Rule 3.4(b) states that a lawyer "shall not counsel or assist a witness to testify falsely."[17] This black-letter rule must be clearly understood and followed.

A. COUNSELING WITHOUT COACHING

While a lawyer can and even should counsel a witness, it is unethical for a lawyer to "coach" a witness prior to testifying, or, in other words, tell the witness what to say. Despite the sometimes blurry boundaries between coaching and counseling, there are still some acts that are clearly permissible and others that clearly are not. An attorney cannot tell a witness what to say, but an attorney can preview the questions she intends to ask her witness and practice the testimony. The attorney can also advise the witness about what demeanor will come across as credible to a jury.

In preparation for trial, witnesses should be told to tell the truth, to avoid guessing at an answer or digressing from what is being asked, and to avoid giving lengthy answers or arguing with opposing counsel or the judge. Witnesses who give lengthy answers that go beyond the scope of the

---

[17] MODEL RULES OF PROF'L CONDUCT R. 3.4(b) (2010).

questions risk confusing the jury and are more likely to bring up damaging information that opposing counsel would not otherwise have been able to admit into evidence. For example, if a witness testifies to good character evidence, this then opens the door for opposing counsel to bring up bad character evidence. Attorneys should instruct witnesses to listen carefully to the questions and to give only answers that directly relate to the questions, whether under direct or cross-examination.

Counseling a witness can make the witness more comfortable about testifying; this calmness can lend credibility. Although a witness's hesitation before answering a question may not, in fact, indicate dishonesty, such a delay can still affect a juror's opinion of that witness's credibility. Practicing testimony can be extremely useful for familiarizing the witness with his answers and putting him at ease when he is called to testify. Discussing the content of the answers and working to frame them as favorably as possible will also maximize the positive effects of a witness's testimony. By the same token, the attorney should not practice direct examination with questions that are fully written out and she should not over-prepare the witness. Answers that sound scripted will not be believable and will also be boring. It is better to prepare witnesses for subject areas of direct and cross-examination, rather than expect them to recite answers memorized verbatim.

Counseling can also include familiarizing a witness with the procedure of testifying. While police officers and expert witnesses will probably be comfortable in the courtroom setting, most witnesses will not have testified before and may find the surroundings of a courtroom intimidating. Explaining to the witness when he will be called, the nature of the oath he will take, and the process of direct and cross-examination should help ease his anxiety.

Attorneys might also benefit from explaining to witnesses that they will be eliciting information in the direct examination that seems negative or counterintuitive. For example, if there are facts that will come out in the trial that will be harmful to an attorney's side (such as the fact that the witness is a gang member, or has prior felony convictions, or has had extra-marital affairs) and counsel believes that the opposing side will bring up these points in cross-examination, then it is imperative to preempt the cross-examination and bring these damaging aspects of the case out on direct examination to deflect the impact of the cross-examination. This strategy is referred to as "pricking the boil" or "taking the wind out of the opponent's sails."[18] If a litigator is certain that the prejudicial information will come out in the course of the trial, it is much better to bring it up in direct examination and acknowledge it. The advantages of this approach include having the opportunity to put a more positive spin on the information, burying it in the middle of direct examination, and looking more credible to the jury by demonstrating that the attorney is not trying to hide weaknesses in the case from jurors. If counsel does not discuss this strategy with her witness before putting him on the stand, the witness will not understand the process and might even feel betrayed by the lawyer's questions, which might be embarrassing to answer or might seem to hurt the case (such as questions about prior convictions).

---

[18] PERRIN, CALDWELL & CHASE, *supra* note 4, at 65, 110.

The following is an example of diffusing the impact of damaging evidence about the defendant by bringing it out on direct examination during the defense's case-in-chief.

Q: **Now that we know a little about you, I am going to ask you some questions about your past, so the jury can have a complete picture. Were you ever a member of a gang?**
A: Yes, Ma'am, when I was a teenager I ran with a gang called '77th Street.' I'm not proud of this, but I want to be straight with my testimony.
Q: **Do you have any gang affiliations now, sir?**
A: Absolutely not.
Q: **When did you quit the gang life?**
A: Eight years ago, when I was twenty-two.
Q: **Why did you join a gang?**
A: It's hard to explain if you didn't grow up on the streets. I had no dad, my mom worked as best as she could to pay the rent, so she wasn't around much, and the neighborhood was tough. It was either join the neighborhood kids or get beat up. I did it for protection.
Q: **What made you quit the gang life?**
A: My wife really guided me to seek a better way. Well, she was my girlfriend then, but now we're married. You know they say that behind every good man is a great woman. Becky is the best, and she showed me how to get my act together. She encouraged me to go to trade school and learn a skill where I could be a man and support a family.
Q: **And did you go to trade school?**
A: I sure did, and I learned to be a mechanic. I'm real proud of that, because it's such practical knowledge and now I've got a good job. Becky is proud of me and I feel like I have made something of myself.
Q: **Where do you work now?**
A: Coast Mechanics.
Q: **What is your job title?**
A: I'm the assistant manager.
Q: **So do you have employees that work under you?**
A: I sure do. I supervise five mechanics.
Q: **Do you enjoy your job as an assistant manager?**
A: I sure do, and the job is stable.
Q: **Are you ever tempted to go back to the gang life?**
A: Are you kidding? No way, absolutely not.
Q: **Would you do anything to jeopardize your job?**
A: No, ma'am. Absolutely not.
Q: **Would you do anything to jeopardize the family life you have built with your wife?**
A: No, ma'am. That's why these charges are false. There's no way I would steal anything from anyone. I have a good job and a stable home life. I've worked hard to create that. I put my rebellious teen years far behind me. I'm a man now and I have responsibilities that I take seriously.
Q: **The State has records showing that you were behind in your rent, Mr. Brown.**
A: Yes, that's true. Like lots of people struggling in this tough economy, Becky and I got behind with some bills.

But I was not tempted to steal.
Q: Did you have a plan in place to pay your back rent?
A: As a matter of fact, I did. I had worked out a payment plan with my landlord. We get along real good. He knows I'm a good guy.
Q: Did you make any arrangements at your job to increase your salary?
A: Yes I did. I arranged to work an extra shift twice a week. So I had no reason to steal, and even if I was broke, I would not steal. I've come too far to slip back into a criminal lifestyle.
Q: Did you take the watch that the State is accusing you of stealing?
A: No, ma'am, I did not.
Q: Did you take anything that did not belong to you?
A: Absolutely not. I'm a family man now, and I have a respectable job where people look up to me. I wouldn't do anything to mess that up.
Q: Thank you for being so candid with us, Mr. Brown. Now that we understand your job responsibilities, I am going to ask you some questions about the day you were arrested.

In the above example, the criminal defense attorney was able to put a positive spin on the damaging evidence that her client was a former member of a criminal gang. Of course, the appropriate way to handle this type of damaging background information is to bring a motion under the *Federal Rules of Evidence*, Section 403, that any probative value of this evidence is substantially outweighed by the undue prejudice.[19] If the attorney loses this motion, it is crucial to bring the damaging material up during her own direct examination so that she can introduce it in a way that substantially mitigates the damage.

Notably, the damaging evidence is also brought out in the middle of the direct examination where it will have the least impact. The attorney has the witness explain the behavior in a way that the jurors can understand and that can elicit their empathy for the defendant. By appearing forthcoming, the defendant shows that he is not hiding his unsavory past from the jury. The attorney also shows the jury that she is not being deceitful or keeping information from them. The witness's explanation for joining a gang when he was a teenager is believable and his denials of current criminal conduct sound credible. The witness appears mature and likeable, and has demonstrated that he has too much at stake to commit a theft.

Had the defense attorney not brought up the gang affiliation, the damage on cross-examination could have been devastating to her case. The prosecutor would have asked a question such as, "Isn't it a fact that you were affiliated with a violent criminal gang, the 77th Street Gang, from the age of fifteen to twenty two?" Any cross-examination in this area will be greatly diffused by the direct examination. The jury will likely be thinking, "Oh, we already heard about that. He

[19] *See also* CAL. EVID. CODE § 352 (Deering 2012) (court may exclude evidence if the probative value is substantially outweighed by undue prejudice or consumption of time); CAL. PENAL CODE § 1538.5 (Deering 2012) (motion to suppress evidence).

doesn't seem like someone who would jeopardize everything to steal a watch."

The criminal defense attorney in the above sample direct examination also deals with the motive of financial desperation and diffuses the impact of this damaging fact. When interviewing the witness, it is imperative to explain the concept of "pricking the boil" to the defendant so that he understands the attorney's line of questioning during trial and does not feel as though his answers will harm the case. By meticulously preparing for direct examination and employing the skills of counseling without coaching, lawyers can ethically present information in the light most favorable to their side.

In order to have the direct and cross-examination flow smoothly, it is crucial to use the device of "blocking." Blocking, as discussed previously, is the attorney's strategy of organizing the direct and cross-examination into sections. An advantage of this technique is that it signals to the

witness, judge, and jury when the attorney is moving from one subject area to another. The following is an example of blocking that a prosecutor may use on direct examination of a victim. The transitions between the blocks give a brief conclusion to the prior block and introduce the new block so that the judge and jury can easily follow along.

1. Scene Visualization

The attorney should start off by having the witness briefly describe himself in order to personalize him before the jury.

> "OK, Mr. Green. Now that we know a little about your background, let's turn to the night that you were robbed, February 3rd of last year. I am going to ask you some questions to set the scene . . ."

The attorney should then ask questions about the lighting and the witness's ability to see and hear the events. Questions such as whether the witness was wearing glasses or contacts, the distance, lighting, time of day, and his vantage point, should be posed. Setting the scene is crucial so that the narration of the action is not interrupted.

always establish

2. Action Sequence

> "Now that we know what the scene looked like, let's turn to what actually occurred the night of the robbery."

Then the witness answers questions about the robbery. The questions need to be short, making sure the focus is on the witness and allowing the drama to unfold.

> "Now that we know what happened to you when you were robbed, I want to ask you some questions about the identification you made to the police."

The attorney should then have the witness identify the defendant (by what the defendant is wearing in the courtroom and where he is currently seated). He should also have the witness explain why she is certain that the defendant is the person who robbed her and he should follow up with questions about the nature of the identification to give the jury a clear understanding of what the witness saw.

If an attorney goes over these blocks of testimony with a witness before trial, the testimony will be much clearer and better organized. The witness will also know what to expect without following a script. Although it is effective for counsel to outline the testimony in advance, it is unwise to write out the questions in full beforehand because the attorney will become too tied to the notes. Not only will the questions and answers sound stilted, but it will also be difficult to listen to the witness's answers and ask appropriate follow-up questions.

By going over these subject areas to block out the direct examination, both the attorney and witness will be well prepared for the courtroom. To prepare witnesses for the possibility that the attorney may use the "refreshing recollection" technique on direct examination, it might be wise to inform the witness during the interview that a question such as "Are you sure about that answer?" is designed to imply to the witness that he misstated testimony or forgot something. If the witness states that he is unsure of the answer, or does not remember, the attorney's follow-up question would be something like, "Would it help refresh your recollection if I showed you your preliminary hearing testimony?" The item used to refresh the witness's recollection might be a statement made to the police, or a photo, or any item that might jog the witness's memory.[20] Key words such as "would showing you [whatever the item is] help refresh your recollection" should signal to the witness that the witness misspoke. The witness should listen carefully and cooperate with the attorney as long as the testimony is truthful. Going over techniques, such as refreshing recollection before trial, will therefore help the witness to be well prepared for the courtroom.

Attorneys should counsel the witness to testify in a manner that is clear and simple without sounding condescending to the jury. Witnesses should be advised to wait until the attorney finishes asking a question before answering it. In addition, witnesses need to be counseled that if an objection is made, he must wait until *after* the court rules on the objection before answering. If the judge sustains the objection, then the witness should not answer the question. If evidence is

TAKE NOTE

excluded in a pretrial motion, the witness must be informed of this and cautioned not to bring up the excluded evidence. If a witness mentions evidence that was ruled inadmissible, such as the defendant's prior convictions, it could result in a mistrial even if the answer was not in response to a question and even if the attorney was not acting in bad faith.

Counsel should review the elements of the crime with the witness. Prosecutors should prepare a sheet with all of the elements of the crime, all allegations, and enhancements. This should also include proving the jurisdiction, which means demonstrating that the offense occurred in a particular county, borough, or parish. Likewise, the witness should be prepared to answer a question that proves jurisdiction. For instance, the prosecutor would typically ask, "Did the crime occur in the county of Los Angeles?" The attorney must also go over any relevant legal concepts with the witness, such as state of mind requirements. For example, a necessary element for proving rape is vaginal penetration; the prosecutor must go over this area of questioning with the victim

---

[20] *See* FED. R. EVID. 612. *See also* CAL. EVID. CODE § 771 (Deering 2012).

before the testimony, so that the witness understands why the attorney is asking such a personal, and perhaps embarrassing, question. Likewise, certain crimes might require a showing that the victim was in fear for her life. In such a case, it would be wise for the prosecutor to explain this to the witness before direct examination so that the witness does not deny being in fear out of a desire not to appear weak. This latter point is especially important with male witnesses who may worry about not appearing masculine enough if they admit to fear. The prosecutor, without coaching the witness as to what to say, should simply point out that he plans to ask whether the witness was in fear of the defendant because it is a necessary element of the crime in question that must be proved. This is also an area where legal research and thorough understanding of the elements of a crime can pay off; in many jurisdictions fear does not necessitate being afraid but only requires a reasonable belief that the other person can and will act–such explanation can help the witness understand the nature of the attorney's questions. Further, attorneys need to inform the witness about questions that might sound silly because the answer is needed to help prove an element, such as "Did you give the defendant permission to take your car?" when the witness knows full well that the defendant stole his car.

Effective attorneys will be thoroughly familiar with the police report and preliminary hearing transcript by the time of the trial; they also will have compiled a trial notebook, which can be used to retrieve an item such as a prior inconsistent statement for impeachment. This area will be covered in more detail in Chapter 13.

B. ANTICIPATING CROSS-EXAMINATION AND OTHER OBSTACLES

Cross-examination has been described as a crucible; certainly, it is a formidable test for a witness and can subject even the most composed and experienced witness to extreme pressure. Cross-examination has the potential to devastate a case, thus underscoring the importance of preparing a witness for cross-examination and identifying any obstacles that might arise at this juncture.

Opposing counsel will often take one of two general approaches to questioning a witness during cross-examination. If the attorney believes the witness can offer some testimony helpful to her case, she would be wise to first elicit that testimony. Alternatively, with an uncooperative witness, it is preferable to go on the offensive immediately. As to the first, why would an attorney call a witness for direct examination if his opponent will use that witness against him? The answers are varied. Some witnesses provide information that cuts both ways. Sometimes a prosecutor realizes that the defense will definitely call a witness, and the prosecutor determines that the most effective way to minimize the impact of the witness is to call him first.[21] Circumstances may arise when both sides will want to extract favorable testimony from the same witness. Anticipating this

---

[21] Remember that in criminal cases, the prosecution always presents its case first. For that reason, the option of calling witnesses during the case-in-chief prior to an opponent is only available to the prosecutor. Of course, the prosecutor can never call the defendant as a witness. *See* U.S. CONST. amend. X; Akhil Reed Amar & Renee B. Lettow, *Fifth Amendment First Principles: The Self-Incrimination Clause*, 93 MICH. L. REV. 857 (1995).

and preparing for the unexpected will help mitigate the damage that can occur during cross-examination. The general expectation of cross-examination is that the opponent's case will be attacked and the examiner's case bolstered. There will also be an attempt to destroy the witness's credibility. Thus, it is important for attorneys to conduct mock cross-examinations and to prepare witnesses for a grueling cross-examination. Witnesses should be counseled not to show anger or take the bait of the opposing attorney. Witnesses who remain composed when being attacked on cross-examination often score big points with jurors. It is also crucial to remind witnesses that they should seek clarification if they do not understand a question and never guess at an answer. It is important for an advocate to remind a witness before he takes the stand that if he does not know the answer, then he should respond by saying "I don't know." Witnesses who guess or feel the need to answer a question, even if they do not remember the answer, create potentially hazardous inconsistencies. For instance, it can destroy the prosecution's case if the opposing counsel asks whether the robber had a beard, and the witness who does not remember guesses and says "yes," and then it turns out that the defendant did not have a beard on the day of the robbery. Additionally, witnesses should be instructed not to answer a question until the question is finished, and the witness should likewise be counseled to listen carefully to the questions and not agree with the cross examiner's questions unless they are truly accurate. Whether considering a witness's demeanor or his ability to recollect or communicate clearly, opposing counsel will attack any perceived weaknesses. Thus, it is important to limit a witness's exposure to such tactics. Fortunately, through pretrial interviews, attorneys can work with witnesses to eliminate some of the characteristics or habits that might impede an otherwise successful examination.

Opposing counsel may also try to impeach a witness through the use of prior statements on cross-examination. To counsel her witness effectively, the preparing attorney must be thoroughly familiar with every witness statement that is potentially available to the other side. An attorney should clarify any inconsistent statements during the counseling process. Moreover, an effective attorney will tell her witness to expect that opposing counsel will attempt to impeach his testimony, and she should also rehearse this scenario with the witness so that he feels comfortable with his response. Of course, attorneys are forbidden from telling their witnesses to lie. Furthermore, as

discussed above, an attorney may not call a witness to the stand knowing that the witness intends to lie.[22] Attorneys must always be conscientious of the rules that govern ethical conduct and must take care to avoid any behavior that could compromise a case or their professional reputation. This will be further covered in Chapter 6.

---

[22] MODEL RULES OF PROF'L CONDUCT R. 3.4(b) (2010).

C. PRACTICAL CONSIDERATIONS

The setting of a courtroom can intimidate many witnesses and despite the proliferation of courtroom dramas suggesting the process to be straightforward, participating in a real trial can be complex and confusing. As discussed above, familiarizing a witness with the general procedural aspects of criminal trials can go a long way in providing comfort in an otherwise stressful setting. In particular, an attorney should review demonstrative evidence, such as diagrams and photos, with the witness before calling him to the stand. If an attorney plans to have a witness make a diagram or chart while testifying, it is crucial to have the witness practice drawing the exhibit before he actually takes the stand. Even if the witness is a law enforcement officer or expert witness who is used to testifying, the attorney should familiarize the witness with exhibits and go over the planned testimony before calling the witness. Otherwise, such a witness may use past experience to infer incorrectly what the attorney is trying to accomplish, and it can be exceedingly difficult for the attorney to correct or to explain what is needed from the witness while the witness is on the stand, especially on direct examination when leading questions are not allowed. The following pointers can prove valuable for a witness:

1. Logistical Information

An attorney should make sure the witness knows where the courthouse is, when to arrive, where the attorney or an associate will meet him, and what the witness should do after he is done testifying. A witness who has to leave work just to wait around the courthouse all day before being called to the stand may become a hostile witness. The logistics of objections should also be explained to the witness, as well as the judge's role and the fact that the witness must show respect towards the judge. If the witness ever responds to the judge, he should address the judge as "Your Honor." If the witness responds to opposing counsel, it might be helpful if he addresses the attorney as "sir" or "ma'am," at least at the beginning of cross-examination. As described earlier, this type of helpful information will reduce the witness's stress and will further cultivate a positive relationship between attorney and witness.

[handwritten margin note: — Don't be a schmuck,]

2. Appearance and Behavior

Witnesses should dress in accordance with the respect that a courtroom warrants. Expert witnesses should wear a suit. Lay witnesses need not be quite as formal, but slacks and a collared shirt are appropriate for a man; a conservative dress or slacks and a blouse are appropriate for a woman. If a witness wears a uniform to work, it is usually appropriate for him to wear the uniform to testify. Jurors can often relate to a hardworking blue-collar worker. Also, if a witness is not accustomed to ever wearing a suit, he may appear uncomfortable or phony wearing one to court. What is important is that the witness appears clean and neat and does not dress in a manner that is provocative or in any way disrespectful of the court. Witnesses, like attorneys, should not wear showy jewelry to court as this can alienate jurors.

[handwritten margin note: — Dress like you are being judged by a bunch of old prudes.]

Defense attorneys who completely transform their client's appearance for trial run the risk that the prosecutor will show the defendant's booking photo and argue that the defense is trying to mislead the jury. While proper grooming and attire and the covering up of offensive tattoos is a wise strategy, witnesses should not look as if they are trying to deceive the jury with their appearance. Of course, it is proper for defendants who are in custody to change out of jail jumpsuits and into appropriate courtroom attire for each day of the trial so that they do not look like a "criminal." Defendants have the right not to wear jail clothing in front of jurors, and, to the extent that they do not pose a security risk, judges will generally have handcuffs and shackles either removed for court, or at least not visible to jurors.

The dress and behavior of a witness may be specific to the case at hand. In a highly publicized 2011 trial, Casey Anthony was accused of murdering her young child to free herself from the responsibilities of motherhood.[23] The prosecution presented both testimony and photographs to portray the defendant as a wild party girl. Throughout the trial, the defendant wore her hair back in a simple manner, wore no makeup, dressed conservatively, covered up her tattoo, and maintained a serious demeanor. The presentation of the defendant at the counsel table (she did not testify) provided a stark contrast to the party girl depicted by the prosecution. A similar strategy was used in the high publicity case *People of California v. Menendez*,[24] in which brothers Eric and Lyle Menendez were accused of murdering their parents. Their attorneys dressed the defendants in pastel sweaters that made them look young and vulnerable, ostensibly to gain empathy with the jurors and support the defense theory of abused children and a claim of modified self-defense. In sum, there is no "one size fits all" attire for trial appearances; attorneys must assess what will be effective for each case.

Witnesses should also be counseled to be respectful of the judge and the jury and not to argue with opposing counsel. Of course, witnesses, like lawyers, should not have any contact with the jury outside of court proceedings. It is up to witnesses if they want to meet with opposing counsel to give a pretrial interview. Most attorneys will instruct a witness that this is the witness's decision, but they usually request the witness to notify them if they plan to speak to opposing counsel so that the attorney can either be present for the interview or send an investigator in his place. Prosecutors, of course, are not allowed to speak directly with criminal defendants.[25]

DEALING WITH CHALLENGING WITNESSES

Like fingerprints, witnesses have their own individual characteristics. Each witness is unique and must be handled accordingly. The idea that all witnesses are intelligent, dependable, and cooperative is,

---

[23] Florida v. Anthony, No. 48-2008-CF-13331-AO, 2011 WL 3531470 (Fla. Cir. Ct. Aug. 12, 2011) (Trial Order); Nancy Grace, *Casey Anthony Defense Fighting to Keep Photos Out (transcript)*, CNN TRANSCRIPTS (April 29, 2011), http://transcripts.cnn.com/TRANSCRIPTS/1104/29/ng.01.html.

[24] *See* Menendez v. Superior Court, 834 P.2d 786, 788 (Cal. 1992).

[25] MODEL RULES OF PROF'L CONDUCT R. 3.4(b) (2010).

of course, a fallacy. Dealing with difficult witnesses can pose a challenge for attorneys, but it is one that must be confronted. While all witnesses must be dealt with individually, attorneys can benefit by identifying general categories of witnesses and anticipating ways in which counsel can work to alleviate the difficulties that witnesses can sometimes pose.

A. THE RELUCTANT WITNESS

Many witnesses, for one reason or another, are reluctant to cooperate with the attorneys who have called them as witnesses. Some witnesses will refuse to testify against a criminal defendant because they fear retaliation. In gang trials, gang members who are called to testify will often conceal information out of allegiance to the "code of the streets." Other witnesses will resist simply because cooperation creates an inconvenience for them. Additionally, some witnesses are reluctant to testify or will testify falsely because they are covering for someone else.

Trial lawyers in encountering these challenges have options: they can involve the court and its powers to compel cooperation or they can work to persuade the witness to cooperate. This latter tactic may prove more difficult, but if applied effectively, it is much more likely to generate positive results.

HYPO: *Oceana v. Jerome*

A known gang member, Anthony Jerome, faces trial for the murder of a rival gang member, Riff Robbins. There are only two witnesses to the crime, but as trial approaches, neither has been cooperative. Both insist they did not see anything and could not clearly discern the identity of the shooter. A traffic camera, however, distinctly shows both witnesses with a clear line of sight to the shooter.

The first witness, a middle-aged woman named Anita, was carrying groceries across the street just as the shooter stepped out of his car to shoot at Robbins. While the shooter fired six rounds over a period of five seconds, Anita stood in the street less then fifteen feet away. Still, she insists she cannot give any description of the shooter.

The second witness, Maria, is a rival gang member who was not targeted by the shooter, but was standing ten feet from Robbins at the time the shooting took place. She took the victim to the hospital where she admitted seeing the shooter, but gave only a vague description to officers. In subsequent police interviews, however, she has refused to give any more information and has said only, "I can't be sure."

As the prosecutor in the case, you believe that both Anita and Maria can identify the defendant. Anita, you suspect, fears that the shooter's gang will take revenge on her if she testifies. Maria, meanwhile, will not help for two reasons: cooperating with law enforcement is taboo among gang members, and gangs tend to prefer to dole out their own street justice.

Trial is rapidly approaching. How would you try to convince Maria and Anita to testify?

In evaluating each witness, the prosecutor should consider the different approaches for urging each to cooperate. Following one approach, he may seek to persuade a witness through empathy and reasoning.[26] With this method, a good place to begin is explaining the legal process. Additionally, the prosecutor may seek to explain the nature of gang crime and activity in the area, showing the effects in terms of damage to the lives of innocent victims and also the damage to property. The attempt to appeal to the witness's compassion for others may help her identify with the victim. This approach might be used on Anita in *Oceana v. Jerome*, because she is more mature and probably cares for her community.

A second option is to offer the witness protection. This can come in the form of individual police officers stationed outside her home or some greater degree of witness protection, such as relocating the witness.[27] The reality, of course, is that prosecutorial and other law enforcement resources are not limitless. Moreover, while the public interest in protecting witnesses is significant, the degree to which the government will provide this protection often depends on the nature of the crime. It is also important to consider that the witness may have spent her entire life in the neighborhood and has no desire for protection. Citizens of neighborhoods where crime is rampant often fear the "justice" of the criminals patrolling the streets more than the threat of a prosecutor's office. Further, some people distrust law enforcement in general and will be deeply reluctant to cooperate with police or prosecutors in almost any circumstances.

An effective approach to convincing a reluctant witness to testify can be to explain to the witness that testifying will "empower" her. In other words, as long as a gang member or other criminal can brutalize people and then intimidate them not to testify, the victims are powerless. Once victims and other witnesses come forward and testify, it can give them some control over their future. They are sending the message that they will not be intimidated into silence. Such tactics can make neighborhoods much safer. Likewise, in domestic violence cases, when a woman is repeatedly battered and consistently refuses to testify against her abuser, she is allowing the abuse to continue. Only by being strong and cooperating with law enforcement can a victim of abuse aid the prosecution in putting a batterer in custody, thus allowing the victim to seek safety and leave the abusive relationship. Many victims also find that they gain emotional closure if they are able to testify against a violent criminal. The process of testifying can be cathartic and, especially in cases of sexual abuse, can allow a victim to move on with her life.

None of these tactics is failsafe; however, by incorporating the methods discussed earlier, by seeking to forge a healthy and trusting relationship with the witness, and by providing a comfortable atmosphere where the witness feels safe, the prosecutor may be able to cultivate the witness's willingness to cooperate. All the same, in some cases, no amount of gentle prodding can bring the witness to testify. It is important to keep in mind, too, that the stakes for the witness—perhaps she fears physical violence against herself or her family if she testifies—are often much higher and more tangible than for the prosecutor. Unfortunately, it is also a reality that financial hardships can play a part in a witness's reluctance to testify against an abuser who is supporting her and her children. If a woman believes that

---

[26] Recognize that while reluctant witnesses will plague both prosecutors and defense attorneys, a much larger number of witnesses will resist testifying on behalf of the prosecutor's office. Typically, the fear of retribution by the criminal is the prevailing factor.

[27] *See* 18 U.S.C. § 3521 (2006).

her husband will lose his job if he is placed in custody, this may deter her from testifying, even if she realizes that the defendant is a danger to her. In such cases, it is imperative for prosecutors to make the witness aware of victim advocates, victim restitution resources,[28] battered women's shelters, and other assistance that may be available to her.

When a witness cannot be convinced to cooperate, courts and attorneys can employ tools to compel testimony. For example, the gang member in *Oceana v. Jerome*, Maria will be a challenging witness to convince to testify. Understanding the dynamics of gangs is fundamental in working to persuade the gang member. Certainly, gang members have no love for law enforcement officers, including prosecutors. The act of helping a district attorney or detective with an investigation is likely forbidden, and the consequences for the gang member may be fatal. If a gang member willingly testifies, he will almost certainly become a target of the gang against which he testifies. Moreover, he may become a target within his own gang. Street gangs are predicated on the idea of respect, and any member who cooperates with the police or prosecution may be viewed as bringing disrespect on his own gang. Of course, the same rule holds true for more sophisticated members of organized crime and political corruption. Prosecutors who specialize in cases of corrupt police officers or politicians face unique challenges presented by the "code of silence" ~~believed~~ known to exist among law enforcement officers. In these types of cases of reluctant witnesses, a prosecutor will likely not be able to employ the methods that may work for the innocent bystander. Still, empathizing with the witness may at least encourage cooperation.

Similarly, the reality is that in many circumstances involving informants and other witnesses who may have criminal culpability, the prosecution will have to offer some type of immunity in order to persuade the witness to testify. Witnesses who testify for the prosecution under immunity grants must be counseled to admit to the jury that they are testifying truthfully in exchange for the promise that they will not face prosecution. Informant witnesses, sometimes referred to disparagingly as "snitch" witnesses, pose their own particular challenges since jurors are often understandably suspect of witnesses who testify in exchange for leniency. Jurors are especially distrustful of witnesses who admit to criminal wrongdoing and yet will get off scot-free by inculpating the defendant. The prosecutor needs to carefully prepare informant witnesses for scathing cross-examination. It is crucial that this type of witness remains composed and gives the jury the impression that, as the "small fish," he represents the lesser of two evils. In other words, the prosecutor must be able to convince the jury that it is appropriate that the informant witness escapes punishment (or receives a lighter sentence) in exchange for testifying truthfully against the criminal with the greater culpability. For example, while distasteful, it is logical and preferable that the get-away driver in an armed robbery is offered leniency if he agrees to testify truthfully against the armed robber, if such testimony is necessary to convict the robber.

When dealing with reluctant witnesses, it is imperative that attorneys try a variety of approaches

---

[28] *See* 18 U.S.C. §§ 3663, 3664 (2006) (explaining orders for restitution and procedures for issuance and enforcement). *See also* Violence Against Women Act of 1994 (VAWA), 42 U.S.C. §§ 13925–14045 (2006). *See, e.g.*, CAL. HEALTH & SAFETY CODE § 124250 (Deering 2012) (shelters for victims of domestic violence); CAL. PENAL CODE § 13823.15 (Deering 2012) (comprehensive statewide domestic violence program); CAL. WELF. & INST. CODE § 18294 (Deering 2012) ("[d]omestic violence shelter-based programs shall provide all of the following basic services to victims of domestic violence and their children").

until they find the one that convinces the witness to cooperate. Empathizing with the witness and offering practical solutions is the preferred approach to gaining the witness's trust. If, at last, the attorney exhausts his options and the reluctant witness still refuses to cooperate when he is on the witness stand, then there is little an attorney can do. A court can hold a witness in contempt (contempt charges attach legal consequences) if the judge has cause to believe the witness knows the answer to a question and refuses to testify.[29] A judge can incarcerate a witness who refuses to answer questions, but there is no weapon in a judge's arsenal that will allow her to force a witness to testify. While all witnesses will be subpoenaed, not all will respond. When the gang member or innocent bystander fails to appear, courts may issue a bench warrant.[30] The bench warrant means that the witness can be arrested for disobeying the subpoena. Unfortunately, many witnesses will accept the penalties associated with a bench warrant or contempt charges rather than testify. Further, a witness who is hauled into court pursuant to an arrest warrant will likely be an extremely hostile witness.

The challenges of dealing with reluctant witnesses can also affect defense attorneys. Sometimes the defense is faced with a witness who has exculpatory information that could help exonerate her client, but the witness refuses to cooperate. In these instances, the defense should adopt persuasive tactics similar to those suggested for the prosecution. Additionally, the defense attorney can try to shame the witness into how difficult it would be to live with the consequences of having an innocent person sent to prison because of the witness's unwillingness to testify to the truth. It is a difficult fact that not all witnesses are willing to cooperate; certainly it makes an attorney's job more challenging. Recognizing this obstacle and being prepared to deal with it, however, will allow an advocate to evaluate a case objectively and form a persuasive case theory.

B. CHILD WITNESSES

When children become participants in the legal system, they present a unique challenge to the interviewing attorney. It is essential to develop a rapport with child witnesses. Successful lawyers learn to adapt their vocabulary to meet the needs of their witnesses, and with children it is necessary to converse in a way that they can understand. Questions need to be especially clear and simple. If possible, the attorney should introduce the child witness to opposing counsel before direct examination, as this often results in a less combative cross-examination. When the adversary attorney has had a chance to meet the witness and sees that it is a vulnerable child, she would be wise not to be too rough on the witness for fear of alienating the jury. In fact, some attorneys, when they know the case will involve a child witness, will ask jurors during *voir dire* if they would be averse to an attorney who has to go through the exercise of cross examination with such a vulnerable figure.

With child witnesses it is crucial to take the time to get to know the witness before asking any questions about the case. Counsel should not make assumptions about maturity levels, as young people's maturity levels vary greatly. The attorney should tell the child something about her own hobbies and

---

[29] FED. R. CRIM. P. 17(g). *See also* FED. R. CIV. P. 45(e).

[30] *See* 18 U.S.C. § 401 (2006).

background to break the ice, so to speak, so that the child will feel more comfortable discussing serious matters like criminal activity and charges; however, attorneys need to be careful not to over-prepare witnesses, especially child witnesses, who may become overwhelmed and confused. Opposing counsel will also likely ask the child if he was prepped for trial and counseled on what to say. Thus, while it is effective to go over concepts, subject areas, and terminology, there should not be scripted questions and answers.

It is also often helpful, when dealing with child witnesses, to allow them to have a trusted person in the courtroom with them for moral support when they testify.[31] Another idea is to let the child bring a comforting stuffed animal, blanket, or a toy up to the witness stand to hold during testimony. When children are asked to describe matters of a sexual nature, it is helpful to provide them with anatomically correct dolls to make it easier for the child to explain what happened. Attorneys should be familiar with victim advocates, children's advocates, and other resources and agencies, such as Child Protective Services, whose function it is to aid child victims.

In the *McMartin* case discussed earlier, the jurors struggled with the credibility of the children who testified. Establishing credibility is just one of the issues that attorneys face when dealing with child witnesses. Perhaps the primary concern is creating a comfortable environment for the child. Children are even less likely than adults to be familiar with the criminal justice system. Moreover, the likelihood that a child is intimidated by her surroundings is a necessary consideration; young people will have likely spent little to no time in an office setting where the interview can take place. Almost certainly they will have never been in a courtroom. How can an attorney mitigate the intimidating world of an office? Perhaps, it is best to conduct the interview somewhere other than at an office, for finding a setting that may be more familiar to a child can help put a child at ease. A defense attorney or prosecutor may even have a room specifically for interviewing children.

When dealing with child witnesses, even more than when dealing with adults, it is crucial to develop trust. While the idea of confidentiality may be difficult for a young person to understand, explaining in simple terms that an attorney is bound by certain rules may create a heightened sense of trust and comfort. In some instances, it may be appropriate to have the child's parent present during the interview and throughout other phases of the process.[32] Of course, the nature of the case will dictate the appropriateness of the parent's presence. For instance, if a parent or the parent's significant other is suspected of abuse, it would be unwise to have that parent present during the interview.

Cases in which a child will be a witness against a parent present their own issues. Consulting a child psychologist and having the psychologist present during the interview process may facilitate a productive interview during which the child feels comfortable and willing to divulge sensitive material. An attorney will have to prepare the child if she will have to testify against a parent while that parent is present. This can be a particularly difficult situation for a child to deal with. To overcome this potential difficulty and to underscore the importance of testimony, an attorney must explain the importance of

---

[31] 18 U.S.C. § 3509(i) (2006) (stating that a child testifying has the right to an adult attendant for emotional support).
[32] *Id.*

truth. As part of this explanation, an attorney should detail the nature of the oath the child will have to take before testimony begins. Because telling the truth is a notion that children understand, the oath can serve as an additional tool to ensure that the witness tells the truth. Experts in the field of interviewing abused children in preparation for testimony recognize that open-ended, non-judgmental questions are more likely to generate detailed, accurate accounts from child witnesses. University of Southern California law professor and psychologist Thomas Lynn explains, "Anyone who works with abused kids knows the kids are afraid and threatened and reluctant and ashamed."[33] Lyons, an expert in interviewing abused children, emphasizes that it is essential to establish rapport with the child witness, ask open-ended questions, and ask the child to promise to tell the truth.[34]

Throughout the process of creating a level of comfort for the child witness, an attorney must always consider the veracity of the child's statements during an interview and during future testimony. In the *McMartin* case, suspicion arose that the children had been fed answers through suggestive questioning and via a letter sent to the parents alleging misconduct. The concern was that parents had planted seeds of the claimed misconduct in the minds of children, and those seeds germinated as a result of the interviews with child psychologists. This type of influence must always be considered and weighed against the statements that come from child witnesses. Particularly with children who can be influenced by parents or people in positions of authority, an attorney has a duty to ensure that any prosecution is based only upon credible testimony. A crucial lesson for attorneys and psychologists that came out of the *McMartin* case is that witnesses, especially children, are easily coached; they need to be asked questions separately from other witnesses and in a non-leading fashion. Phrasing questions in such a manner as "Johnny said that the teacher touched his private parts; did the teacher touch your private parts, too?" are unduly suggestive and likely to solicit unreliable answers.

More than just ensuring the truth of the statements, something that is essential with all witnesses, the attorney must objectively evaluate how the child witness will appear to the jury. Children, particularly those who are victims, are sympathetic witnesses; however, knowing that a juror will sympathize with a child should not entice an attorney into calling a child who is an otherwise unreliable witness. In *McMartin*, although many children testified and described the sexual acts committed against them, the jury still found the testimony unbelievable and acquitted the defendants. As with all witnesses, child witnesses must be adequately prepared and counseled during trial preparation. They must be readied for cross-examination, and this must be accomplished without coaching. A child's ability to recollect, communicate, and remain composed will affect the child's credibility and can thereby ultimately affect, if not determine, case theory.

C. THE WITNESS WITH SUBSTANCE ABUSE ISSUES

Many defendants who come through criminal courts face drug charges. Some of these defendants will be addicts, and their associates—often other addicts—will be critical witnesses to a case. This raises

---

[33] Larry Gordon, *Coaxing children to talk—about crime*, L.A. TIMES (Mar. 19, 2012), at A1.
[34] *Id.*

the very real possibility that witnesses will be under the influence of drugs during both the interview process and at trial. Another realistic possibility is that the defendant or witness will be suffering from withdrawal or perhaps brain impairment resulting from long-term substance abuse. Drug abuse or alcoholism, for example, can affect a witness's ability to perceive or recollect events. Such impairment can also affect the ability of a defendant or other witness to relate information clearly and accurately. Some addicts have extreme difficulty articulating their thoughts and many even struggle to put together coherent sentences. Clearly, witnesses with substance abuse issues present particular challenges.

These problems are not unique to drug cases, but may arise in all types of criminal cases. Any witness, whether the charge is drug-related or not, may potentially have substance abuse issues. Unfortunately, attorneys cannot wait for the witness to complete rehabilitation or stand by hoping that another witness comes along so that they might proceed with their case. When an attorney encounters any witness who is under the influence of drugs or alcohol, or if the witness is otherwise chemically dependent, she will be faced with the task of guiding that person through the witnessing process. Attorneys need to have a referral list of psychologists, addiction counselors, and substance abuse experts available in order to help witnesses with issues find the help they need. Attorneys should also be prepared to refer witnesses to Alcoholics Anonymous or Narcotics Anonymous meetings, or other resources for drug or alcohol rehabilitation. These issues often arise when the witness with the substance abuse issue is the defendant. This situation will be fully explored in Chapter 6.

It may be necessary to emphasize the importance of telling the truth all the more with a client who has a less than exemplary background. It is likely that opposing counsel will know about the witness's history of substance abuse, and it will almost certainly be revealed in cross-examination. A prudent attorney will thus encourage the witness to be truthful about this fact when questioned. An attorney will be the first to question her client, and the first to present the delicate issue of her client's substance abuse to the jury in a sympathetic manner; this will take the sting out of a potentially harmful piece of information that opposing counsel could have planned to use against the witness. In some cases, a motion *in limine* can be filed to exclude a client's or other witness's prior bad acts from the trial.[35] This will most likely not be helpful in a case relating to a defendant's substance abuse problem, because opposing counsel will argue that the addiction affects the defendant's credibility, memory, and state of mind. While addiction itself is probably not relevant, anything that affects the witness's ability to perceive or recollect the incident in question is fair game for cross-examination.

HYPO: *Oceana v. Cruz*

Mirtha Cruz has a history of cocaine use and is on the stand to testify that she witnessed a store robbery. Defense counsel, Johnny Jung, does not mention the drug use so as not to prejudice the jury against Cruz. Opposing counsel starts his cross-examination. He immediately asks Cruz about her history with cocaine abuse. Even if Jung objects, the prosecution will argue that it is possible that she was under the influence at the time of the robbery and that her recollection may therefore be in doubt. The prosecution

---

[35] *See* FED. R. EVID. 403. Courts have their own rules for filing motions *in limine*.

then has the opportunity to delve into Cruz's history of drug abuse. He will discredit her as much as possible. It will be difficult for Jung to rehabilitate Cruz as a witness after the cross-examination.

If, however, Jung had instead agreed with Cruz to reveal the abuse to the jury on her own terms, then the situation could have turned out much differently. By "pricking the boil," or taking the wind out of the opponent's sails, the jury may also begin to see Cruz's drug problems as harmless.

A jury would not think that an attorney would intentionally discredit her own witness, so the information about the drug abuse might not come to be viewed as being of particular importance. The defense attorney can have the witness explain that she was not using drugs on the day that she witnessed the robbery if that was the case. She can also testify to any sobriety efforts. If it is left for the prosecutor to interpret and present the witness's history, then the information could potentially be much more destructive.

With regards to the rest of the witness-attorney relationship, an attorney should treat a witness with a history of substance abuse in much the same manner as any other witness. An advocate will strive to develop a relationship with the witness that will encourage the witness to relate his story to the attorney in full. With an addict, it is imperative to find out every detail, as the opposition will be sure to use the addiction against the witness on the stand. An addict is more vulnerable to his past history than other witnesses because his past is seen as disreputable and untrustworthy to begin with.

Another challenge that criminal defense attorneys face, especially with clients who are chemically dependent, is that the client might not have a solid grasp of reality. Some clients are falsely convinced that the case against them is weak. As a result, attorneys in these circumstances have an uphill battle trying to convince some clients to accept a plea agreement or to stay off the witness stand altogether. In contrast, some clients have the inability to face facts or to evaluate the evidence against them in a realistic fashion. It is important to note that this deficiency can be caused by a variety of issues, but regardless of the cause, a defendant who is unable or unwilling to assess incriminating evidence presents a particular challenge to a defense attorney. Especially when dealing with youthful defendants or those with notable impairments, it can be useful to have a family member, such as a parent or spouse, help the attorney to persuade the client to be reasonable. Of course, the attorney needs to have the client's permission before having another person present during attorney-client discussions. Attorney-client issues will be more fully explored in Chapter 6.

D. ELDERLY WITNESSES

Witnesses who are elderly, or who suffer from memory issues, may be reluctant to testify or they might find themselves bewildered by the criminal proceedings. They may be particularly emotional or uncomfortable with the courtroom proceedings or with discussing personal issues, especially if the testimony involves a violent crime. As with child witnesses, it is essential to establish a rapport with elderly witnesses and to put them at ease from the outset. Attorneys need to reassure elderly witnesses that their role is only to tell the truth, and that it is okay if they do not remember certain details. The rules of the courtroom should be explained. The attorney should let the witness know that he needs to explain what happened or what he saw or heard, even if it involves graphic language that makes the witness uncomfortable. It is common for elderly people to have hearing issues, so it is the lawyer's job to make

↳ sisly? These people fought in korea and made "The Exorcist"

sure that she speaks loudly enough for the witness to hear her and also that the witness project his voice enough for the jurors to hear him. It is important for attorneys to be respectful of elderly witnesses and to use language that the witness can understand without coming across as condescending. While a frail witness might be intimidated about testifying, he will likely evoke the jurors' sympathy, as long as he appears to be truthful.

E. INFORMANT WITNESSES

Attorneys need to use extreme caution when putting informant witnesses on the stand. These witnesses are often very unappealing and unsympathetic to jurors. It is inadvisable to use accomplice witnesses, for that matter, unless it is absolutely necessary. Prosecutors sometimes need to call to the stand a co-conspirator to a crime or another type of partner in crime and offer that person immunity in order to convict the more culpable criminal; however, jurors tend not to trust such witnesses. Moreover, the accomplice witnesses sometimes purposefully sabotage the prosecutor's case. Immunity deals should

 always be predicated on the witness's promise to testify truthfully, with the understanding that if the witness does not keep up his end of the bargain, the deal is off. The immunity deal must be in writing and must be made clear to the jury and judge. Ethics are extremely important when dealing with accomplice witnesses; it is crucial to be entirely forthcoming with opposing counsel, the judge, and the jury when a witness is offered immunity. It is imperative that a prosecutor's interview with an accomplice witness be carried out with an investigator or another prosecutor present. Additionally, it is almost always essential to tape the interview because the accomplice might make false claims about what was promised to him or might later deny the statements that he made during the interview. The witness should be informed that during direct examination, the attorney will bring out any of the witness's relevant criminal convictions in order to diffuse the impact of such convictions and make the cross-examination less damaging. This is also an opportunity for the lawyer to show the jury that he has integrity by acknowledging facts that are harmful to his case and by not hiding any evidence from them. This is true for all witnesses with criminal backgrounds. Prosecutors should not ingratiate themselves with accomplice witnesses; the prosecutor needs to clearly explain any deal that is offered and make it abundantly clear that the only thing the prosecutor is bargaining for is truthful testimony.

F. SEXUAL ASSAULT VICTIMS

Prosecutors need to be especially sensitive to the needs of victims of sexual assault. Large prosecution offices typically have special units where the prosecutors are trained to handle these types of cases. It is particularly important to gain the trust of the witness who is a sex crime victim. Further, since these types of offenses are particularly dependent on the victim's credibility, the prosecutor must scrutinize the believability of the alleged victim. The prosecutor needs to try to get to know the victim so that he can explain the victim's actions if that seems necessary. For instance, if the victim suffered from rape trauma syndrome and was frozen out of fright so that she did not try to get away from her attacker when given the opportunity, then this is something that must be fully examined in the interview so that it can be explained to the jury. Testifying is also especially traumatic for victims of sexual assault. The prosecutor needs to be sensitive about how difficult it will be for the witness to discuss the crime and how traumatic it will be to testify in front of the defendant and a group of total strangers. The prosecutor should explain to such victims that testifying and putting the perpetrator behind bars would empower them while protecting others from being victimized. The prosecutor can explain that many victims find the process of testifying to be cathartic and a milestone towards closure.

Most jurisdictions provide victim advocates and allow the victim to have a support person in the courtroom during testimony.[36] The prosecutor should counsel the victim to dress conservatively when she comes to court. The victim should be cautioned about her behavior in front of the jurors, including how she might appear when she is in the court hallway or parking lot. The prosecutor must prepare the victim for the fact that the crime will have to be addressed in detail both during the interviews and at trial. Of course, it will be uncomfortable to testify about a sexual attack, but the prosecutor needs to make it clear that the details are necessary in order to prove all the elements of the case. For example, the crime of rape requires proof of penetration, and the victim will need to testify, for example, that the defendant's penis penetrated her vagina in order for the element of rape to be proven. Most courts will allow leading questions due to the sensitive nature of this testimony, but it is crucial that the victim understand what the elements of the offense are and why the prosecutor needs to ask questions that the victim will naturally find embarrassing and uncomfortable.[37] Preparing the victim to remain calm and focused on cross-examination is particularly important in cases involving sexual assault.

G. WITNESSES WHO NEED INTERPRETERS

It is the attorney's responsibility to make sure that the witness understands the court proceedings, and that the jury can understand the witness. Even if the witness is reluctant to use an interpreter despite English being the witness's second language, the attorney should insist on one if he thinks it will be helpful to the case. Some non-native English speakers with a fairly good grasp of the English language are still not comfortable testifying in English. The attorney should explain to the witness that he will not be viewed in a negative light if he chooses to testify through an interpreter. Litigators should keep in mind that under some circumstances, prior inconsistent statements or omissions can be explained away due to a language barrier. The attorney must always be certain to clarify with the witness and the interpreter if a word might have a different meaning in the witness's native language versus when it is translated into English for the jury. Furthermore, it should be kept in mind that many languages have different dialects, so the attorney must make sure that the interpreter understands the witness's particular dialect so that he does not overlook nuances of language that might be present. At the same time, the

---

[36] *See* 18 U.S.C. § 3509(i) (2006). *See, e.g.*, CAL. PENAL CODE § 868.5 (Deering 2012); People v. Adams, 23 Cal. Rptr. 2d 512, 525–31 (Cal. Ct. App. 1993).

[37] FED. R. EVID. 611(c) (noting that leading questions are allowed on direct examination in order to develop the witness's testimony). *See also* United States v. Grassrope, 342 F.3d 866, 869 (8th Cir. 2003) (holding that the district court did not abuse its discretion by allowing the government's use of leading questions in examination of the victim). Various state statutes also list this rule regarding leading questions. *See* CAL. EVID. CODE § 767 (Deering 2012); TEX. R. EVID. 611; ARIZ. R. EVID. 611; MICH. R. EVID. 611; ILL. R. EVID. 611.

attorney's questions should be directed to the witness, not the interpreter. Likewise, the witness should answer the attorney directly. It is particularly important when using an interpreter to keep the questions short, clear, and simple so that there is a reduced risk of lost meaning or misinterpretation during the process of translation.

H. EXPERT WITNESSES

It is imperative that experts testify in clear and simple language free from technical jargon that a jury can readily understand. The key to effective expert testimony is for an expert to appear knowledgeable, without being arrogant. Expert witnesses who come across as condescending can alienate jurors to the point that the jurors vote for the opposing side due to such unfavorable testimony. It is also crucial that experts do not appear to be "hired guns." Because experts are paid for their time preparing for a case and also for the time spent testifying, it is always a good idea for an attorney to ask all experts whether they are being paid. This type of challenge question gives the expert witness the opportunity to demonstrate that he has nothing to hide and that he is not being paid to come up with a conclusion for the side that engaged him. All professionals are paid for their services and the fact of compensation should be brought up in direct examination in a matter-of-fact way. Ignoring the issue of compensation on direct examination provides opposing counsel with powerful ammunition on cross-examination.

It is crucial during an interview to prepare the expert to testify that her compensation is also not affected by the outcome of the case. Attorneys must do their homework and try to discover whether an expert always testifies exclusively for one side or another, as this suggests a bias. It constitutes powerful ammunition for cross-examination, moreover, if counsel can obtain a transcript of court testimony from a previous trial in which the expert witness arrived at a conclusion different from that in the current case in spite of similar evidence. This situation can occur, for example, when a forensic expert who has worked for the State then retires and makes herself available as a witness for the defense, as in the following hypothetical scenario.

 ### HYPO: *Oceana v. Currey*

Assume a chemist expert, Mary Currey had a history of testifying that all persons are under the influence of alcohol for purposes of driving a motor vehicle at a blood alcohol level of 0.08%. Currey also testified for years as a crime lab law enforcement scientist that the gas chromatograph used to measure blood alcohol levels is a reliable instrument. After retiring from the sheriff's crime lab, Currey hires herself out as a defense expert for $800 per hour and completely reverses her conclusions. She now testifies regularly at trial that because of individual differences such as tolerance levels, people may or may not be impaired for purposes of driving a motor vehicle at 0.08% blood alcohol content and that the boundary for being under the influence is actually 0.10%. Further, she now states that the gas chromatograph is unreliable and fraught with problems. A prepared prosecutor will obtain transcripts of Currey's previous testimony and use it to impeach her on cross-examination.

Blocking, as described above, is particularly important with expert witness testimony because this testimony can be complicated and filled with technical terminology. Generally, the witness should testify about his background and qualifications first and then explain the procedure or data by which he arrived at his opinion. He should then render his opinion, providing reasons for his conclusions. Each of these areas should be a separate subject "block." Attorneys should go over any hypothetical questions with the expert before putting him on the stand. If an attorney anticipates that the adversary will also call an expert, it would be helpful to ask the expert how he would counter the opposing side's expert's conclusions and/or qualifications.

 It is generally unwise to accept an opponent's offer to stipulate to an expert's qualifications. Attorneys are not required to accept stipulations proposed by opposing counsel. Since it is the jury's role to assess the credibility of witnesses and the weight to be attached to each witness's testimony, it would be helpful for the jury to hear the specific qualifications of the expert, such as education, training, experience, publications, honors, and how many times the expert has previously qualified to testify as an expert witness.

Trial attorneys need to gain familiarity in the subject area that the expert will testify about as well. They should be familiar with any report an expert has used in order to arrive at his conclusion. An attorney should remember that leading questions can be used when conducting direct examination of an expert witness.[38] The expert also needs to explain to the attorney any tests that he performed. It is generally considered impressive to have the expert use visual aids when testifying; however, the attorney should go over any exhibits with the witness before he testifies. One way to gain insight into an expert's area in preparation for trial is to ask the expert to recommend publications on the subject in question. Additionally, the expert should help prepare the attorney to cross-examine the opposing side's expert.

Police officer experts present their own set of issues. Make sure that police officers do not testify in police jargon. Instead of stating, "I activated my overhead lights and, pulled over the subject, then exited the patrol vehicle," the officer should state, "I turned on my lights, pulled the suspect over, and got out of my car." The witness should refer to time as "a.m." and "p.m." instead of military time. Attorneys need to go over the police report with the witness before he testifies and make sure that he is familiar with all of its content. The officer should not be permitted to read from the police report on the witness stand. All witnesses are expected to testify from their recollection. Make sure the officer is familiar with the elements that need to be proved. Patrol officers should generally wear their uniforms to court, while it is appropriate for detectives to wear a suit, or in the case of a female detective, a conservative dress or pant-suit is acceptable.

---

[38] FED. R. EVID. 611(c).

SUMMARY

Witness testimony is perhaps the greatest variable in criminal trial work. When a litigator receives an unwelcome surprise in court, it is typically due to unexpected and damaging witness testimony. The best way to guard against evidence that is damaging to the case is to be thoroughly prepared and to carefully interview witnesses. This chapter has detailed the ways in which to advise witnesses, to prepare them for testimony, and to mitigate the potential for harm on the witness stand. Ultimately, however, an attorney cannot control what a witness might say when called to the stand. The best tool to combat the "danger of the unknown," is preparation and counseling of the witness. It is proper and advisable to role-play with witnesses in order to prepare them for trial. Counsel should go over areas of testimony on direct examination, as well as playing the role of opposing counsel and asking simulated questions in order to prepare the witness for cross-examination. It is permissible to give the witnesses advice regarding how to dress for court and how to conduct themselves appropriately during trial. It is unethical, however, to coach a witness in terms of *what* to testify. A witness should be told to tell the truth, not to guess at an answer, and never to digress or discuss irrelevant matters. Witnesses should answer in a clear, concise, and truthful manner and should ask for clarification if they do not understand a question. Witnesses should not argue with attorneys or with the judge and should remain composed throughout their testimony. Challenging witnesses require special preparation. By applying the methods described, an attorney gives herself the best chance to advance her case theory and earn a favorable verdict.

CHECKLIST

✓ Prior to a witness interview, an attorney should familiarize herself with any police reports (including toxicology and forensic data), background research or prior statements the witness has provided. The interview should allow for the opportunity to confirm the statements previously made by the witness, in addition to clarifying any inconsistencies that the attorney has identified in these statements.

✓ At the initial interview, the witness should be asked to provide his complete recollection of the incident without interruption. Good listening skills on the part of the attorney are essential to a successful information-gathering process.

✓ After obtaining the witness's account, the attorney can reframe or confirm anything that seems in need of clarification. She may also inquire as to whether or not additional potential witnesses might exist.

✓ Witnesses, particularly crime victims, are oftentimes uncomfortable when it comes to discussing a criminal incident, especially if it involved violence. As a result, attorneys should always attempt to foster a comfortable and safe environment when interviewing victims of crime.

✓ Witnesses need to be thoroughly prepared for testifying in court. The attorney should go over the areas that will be covered in direct examination, explain the concept of "blocking," remind the witness to tell the truth and never guess at answers, and that he should avoid digressing when testifying. Further, the attorney should familiarize the witness with any trial exhibits they intend to use.

✓ Critical to the preparatory process is thoroughly preparing the witness for the experience of cross-examination. The attorney should role-play opposing counsel in order give the witness a sense of the potential rigors of this aspect of trial procedure.

✓ The attorney must determine a witness's competence to appear and testify at trial. Such competence can be determined by the witness's willingness to swear an oath to tell the truth, his possessing percipient knowledge of legally relevant information, his ability to recollect the events of the incident, and his ability at all times to clearly communicate any information.

✓ Much of what an attorney discusses during a witness interview is discoverable, although attorney work product is not.

✓ From the first moment jurors see or hear a witness, they will have begun to formulate an opinion about him; the attorney must therefore remain aware of the witness's body-language, manner of dress, posture, and the degree of respect he demonstrates for the attorneys, judge, and jury, advising him accordingly.

✓ Counsel should always review the elements of the crime with the witness in advance.

✓ When dealing with reluctant witnesses, it is imperative that attorneys try a variety of approaches until they find the one that convinces the witness to cooperate. Empathizing with the witness, offering protection, or counseling the witness that testifying can be an empowering process might work to gain the witness's trust.

✓ Children represent a unique challenge to the interviewing attorney, and it is essential to develop a rapport with child witnesses well in advance of trial, always speaking to them in a manner they can easily understand.

✓ When the defendant or witness suffers from substance abuse, withdrawal or brain impairment might be a very real concern. The attorney must keep in mind that such problems might affect the witness's ability to perceive or recollect events clearly.

✓ Elderly clients also pose concerns relating to their ability to testify reliably and effectively. Memory issues or a reluctance to testify for any number of reasons makes it necessary for the attorney to establish a rapport with elderly witnesses and put them at ease from the outset. The rules of the courtroom should be explained well in advance of trial.

✓ Informant witnesses are of particular concern, as they tend to come across as unappealing and unsympathetic to jurors. It is advisable to use accomplice witnesses only when absolutely necessary, and immunity deals should always be predicated on the witness's promise to testify truthfully.

✓ If an interpreter is deemed necessary for the delivery of witness testimony, the attorney must ensure that she is made aware of any differences in the translation of the witness's native language into English in order to safeguard against misrepresenting or misstating any testimony to the jury.

✓ When it comes to expert witnesses, they must be advised to testify using straightforward language that is free from technical jargon. The expert will ideally appear knowledgeable and never arrogant. The attorney should not avoid confirming her expert witness's fee schedule for the jury, as such an approach deflates any opportunity for opposing counsel to suggest the expert is nothing more than "a hired gun."

✓ A police officer witness must also be counseled to avoid testifying in police jargon, and he should be further prepared for trial by being familiarized with all of the elements of the crime requiring proof.

CHAPTER 6
CLIENT INTERVIEWS

"Preparation is the be-all of good trial work. Everything else—felicity of expression, improvisational brilliance—is a satellite around the sun. Thorough preparation is that sun."
                                                                    –Louis Nizer

Success as a trial lawyer often rests on the preparation that takes place outside the courtroom, in some cases long before trial ever begins. For a criminal defense attorney, a significant portion of that preparation is directly linked to the relationship she has with her clients. Gaining a client's trust, learning a client's story, and adopting an approach that works effectively with each client are all critical steps that lay the foundation for thorough trial preparation. Beginning with the first client meeting and up until a case settlement or a trial verdict, the advocate's ability to initiate and maintain clear lines of communication with her client is essential, since an effective attorney-client relationship may go a long way towards achieving a favorable case outcome.

As noted in Chapter 2, developing a case theory that will guide an advocate's focus throughout the case is of utmost importance. For a defense attorney to formulate a case theory, knowing the client's story is essential, and although many factors may help the attorney understand his story, the most direct route is through client interviews. This chapter explores the many dimensions of the interviewing process, from professional obligations to strategies for overcoming the challenges that arise while cultivating this important relationship between attorney and client.

PROFESSIONAL OBLIGATIONS

Perhaps the best way an attorney can begin to build trust is by providing the client with an explanation of an attorney's professional obligations as early on as possible. These obligations are detailed in the *Model Rules of Professional Conduct* and the *Federal Rules of Evidence*, as well as state and local statutes. Many of these ethical principles are designed to protect the client and some apply specifically to client interactions.

A. THE ATTORNEY-CLIENT RELATIONSHIP

The first and most significant principle of the attorney-client relationship is the attorney-client privilege. Tracing its origins back to common law, it is the oldest and most protected of testimonial privileges. The United States Supreme Court has said the privilege serves to encourage "full and frank" disclosure between clients and their attorneys.[1] The relationship of trust made possible by confidential communications is necessary to enable lawyers to defend their clients zealously. Since understanding how and when the privilege is formed is critical to both attorney and client, the relationship should be defined when representation begins. Explaining the nature of this relationship early in the counseling process helps a client understand the attorney's professional obligations to him, and, not least of all, it

---

[1] Upjohn Co. v. United States, 449 U.S. 383, 389 (1981).

allows the attorney to sow seeds of trust with the client.[2]

B. FORMATION OF THE ATTORNEY-CLIENT RELATIONSHIP AND PRIVILEGE

The attorney-client relationship is formed when a client first meets with a defense attorney. From the moment a prospective client walks into the attorney's office to seek legal advice, a formal relationship is created and the attorney has a fiduciary responsibility to that individual.[3] Even if further counseling is not sought, the initial consultation—provided that it is for the purpose of seeking legal services—initiates the attorney-client relationship, and the communications that take place between the attorney and client are privileged. It is important that the client understand the meaning of the privilege, as it can provide the foundation for candid conversations. Often, this explanation is best provided to the client in writing at the initial formation of the attorney-client relationship.

The attorney-client privilege, as a basic principle of legal representation, is often misunderstood. The privilege belongs to the client, and it is for the client to exercise it.[4] Thus, a client has a privilege to refuse to disclose confidential communications he has made with his attorney. Perhaps more significantly, the client can prevent others—specifically, his attorney and his attorney's representatives— from disclosing any of the client's confidential communications during the course of representation. The privilege, which can take many forms, presents layered complexities. For example, when the client is a corporation, corporate officials' or employees' statements may be protected if the statements were authorized or directed by the corporation. This means that a corporation can assert its privilege over statements made by individuals.

Additionally, the privilege may apply to more people than just the attorney retained by the client. An attorney's representative—anyone employed by the attorney to assist in rendering professional services—is also subject to the privilege. Thus, a paralegal who sits through meetings with a criminal defendant, but is not a member of the bar, can be precluded from testifying about confidential communications made by the defendant. In order to ensure respect for the rules governing an attorney's behavior, it is essential to understand the privilege's intricacies and the ways in which it impacts a defense attorney's representation of a criminal defendant. This aspect of the attorney-client privilege places a burden on attorneys to educate all of their employees about the characteristics of the privilege and the professional requirements to which they are held.

The privilege also survives the end of representation, and can even extend beyond death.[5] Consider the story of Alton Logan, an Illinois man convicted of murder in 1983. Shortly after Logan's conviction, two attorneys representing

REAL CASE

---

[2] In addition to verbally explaining the nature of the privilege to the client, it is often effective to provide the client with a written explanation.

[3] Generally speaking, this fiduciary responsibility requires attorneys to place the interests of the client first, insofar as there may be conflicting interests regarding representation.

[4] The privilege is one of common law, but some jurisdictions have codified it by statute. *See, e.g.,* N.J. STAT. ANN. § 2A:84A-20 (West 2012); OHIO REV. CODE ANN. § 2317.02 (LexisNexis 2012).

[5] Swidler & Berlin v. United States, 524 U.S. 399, 410 (1998).

another man accused of killing two police officers were told by their client that he committed the murder for which Logan was convicted. For twenty-six years, the attorneys kept secret the information their client, Andrew Wilson, disclosed in confidence. Because Wilson exercised the attorney-client privilege to prevent his attorneys from disclosing the confidential communication, Logan remained in prison until Wilson's death. Only because Wilson's attorneys persuaded him to let them reveal after his death that he was the real killer, the attorneys were finally able to come forward with statements exonerating Logan. This extreme example underscores the importance of the privilege and illustrates the strict confidentiality that the attorney owes her client.

All the same, the privilege does not apply in some instances. For instance, if the client seeks legal advice to facilitate future criminal conduct, there is no privilege. If, furthermore, a dispute arises between the client and his attorney related to malpractice, or a client's failure to pay attorney fees, the privilege may not apply.

C. CONFIDENTIALITY

The Logan example stresses the point that confidential communications may not be disclosed to third parties except those who have a role in providing legal services. When Wilson confessed to his attorneys, he did so in confidence, realizing they could not reveal the statement. Moreover, the statement does not fall within the exception regarding criminal conduct because the communication dealt with *past* acts and did not seek assistance with a future crime; however, had Wilson's communication been made knowingly in the presence of a stranger—a cellmate or even a family member—Wilson could not later assert the privilege and protect the communication because it would not meet the requirements of confidentiality.[6]

The *ABA Model Rules of Professional Conduct* (Model Rules) expand on the requirements involving confidential communications. Model Rule 1.6(a) states: "A lawyer shall not reveal information relating to the representation of a client unless the client gives *informed consent*, [or] the disclosure is *impliedly authorized* in order to carry out the representation . . . ."[7] Explaining this rule and the obligations it places upon an attorney can help a client understand that he can trust his attorney because only the client can waive the privilege.

D. COMPARING THE ATTORNEY-CLIENT PRIVILEGE AND CONFIDENTIALITY

It should be noted that a difference exists between the attorney-client privilege and confidential communications. The Model Rules regarding confidentiality are different from those concerning the attorney-client privilege. Attorneys cannot disclose confidential communications to anyone at any time without the client's consent. The client, meanwhile, can only assert the privilege during a judicial proceeding. It is the attorney's duty to guard her client's right to have privileged communications. If an attorney thinks a defendant desires confidential communications to be shared with anyone else, the

---

[6] *See* MODEL RULES OF PROF'L CONDUCT R. 1.6(b)(2) (2006).

[7] MODEL RULES OF PROF'L CONDUCT R. 1.6(a) (2006) (emphasis added).

attorney must obtain an explicit waiver from the defendant and should never assume that a waiver is implied.

Figure 6.1 illustrates that the duty of confidentiality affects attorneys more broadly than the attorney-client privilege. The duty of confidentiality covers any facts learned about the client, whether directly or indirectly, during the course of representation. The attorney-client privilege extends only to actual communications between the attorney and client in the pursuit of legal advice. Although an exception may arise for the attorney-client privilege, a duty of confidentiality may still remain.

CHART 6.1
Duty of Confidentiality and the Attorney-Client Privilege

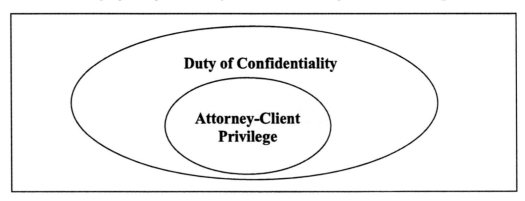

HYPO: *Oceana v. Quijana*

Your client, Alonso Quijana, wants to meet with you at his favorite restaurant, The Windmill, to discuss his upcoming trial. When you and your paralegal arrive, he has already chosen a table in the middle of the restaurant—surrounded by crowded tables and booths. As Quijana begins discussing the events of the day of the crime, he describes his participation in the crime and lists specific details about the events of the robbery. A couple at the table next to you seems to be listening to your conversation with Quijana, but you are not certain they can hear what he is saying.

While considering this hypothetical situation, practice keeping in mind not only the provisions of the *Federal Rules of Evidence* and Model Rules, but also strategies for influencing the situation to best suit Quijana's needs. For the purposes of this hypothetical example, assume that Quijana has already been informed of the attorney-client privilege and the attorney's duties concerning confidential communications.

Given these circumstances, how should you approach the situation? What, if anything, should you say to Quijana regarding his disclosures? Would it be appropriate to interrupt him? If so, at what point? Consider the following additional facts: after meeting with Quijana for some time, the restaurant begins to empty. You, your paralegal, and Quijana become the only remaining customers. As your conversation continues, however, Quijana's close friend, Dulce, arrives and joins the table. How does Dulce's presence change the nature of the communications between counsel and client? How does it change how the attorney-client privilege should be applied? Are statements made by Dulce considered confidential? Are those statements protected by the attorney-client privilege?

It should be apparent that the communications in *Oceana v. Quijana* might not be "confidential," because the information the client provided could have been readily obtained by a third party not affiliated with the client's legal representation. Thus, if the couple at the next table heard Quijana confess that he participated in the robbery, the communication is not considered "confidential" and will not be protected by the attorney-client privilege. As zealous advocates required to provide effective assistance of counsel, it is incumbent upon attorneys to consider the impact of communications like the one in *Oceana v. Quijana* and to manage communications with clients in a way that serves their best interests while always preserving trust.

If the attorney feels a need to discuss the client's case with another party (perhaps a therapist, a drug counselor, an investigator, etc.), then these communications are normally considered confidential because the attorney is consulting with these people as part of her representation of the client. In these types of situations, however, it is safer for the lawyer to obtain a written waiver of confidentiality from the client. At the outset, the client may want the lawyer to discuss his case with outside consultants, but after he sees a written report from one of those individuals he might not be happy and could accuse the attorney of breaching confidentiality.

E. FEE ARRANGEMENTS

Attorneys are sometimes characterized as greedy liars who will do anything for a buck. While the vast majority of attorneys do not fit this stereotype, there are specific rules in place to deter behavior associated with this misconception. These rules, with both professional and practical justifications, guide attorneys' actions when charging fees.

Model Rule 1.5(b) states: "The scope of the representation and the basis or rate of the fee and expenses for which the client will be responsible shall be communicated to the client, preferably in writing, *before or within a reasonable time after commencing the representation . . . .*"[8] This rule stipulates a requirement that attorneys should bear in mind when conducting all initial client interviews. In addition to meeting the ethical demands of legal representation, this disclosure can also bring practical benefits. Ultimately, most criminal defendants are concerned with two issues: avoiding a conviction or minimizing their sentences and how much the legal representation will cost. Although all clients want effective representation to avoid conviction—or at least receive a reduced sentence—not all clients can afford it. Clarifying a fee arrangement, often in writing, eliminates the possibility of misunderstanding and generates trust at the outset of the relationship. It can also reduce the chances of misunderstandings, which can lead to a bad attorney-client relationship and waste time and effort.

The Model Rules also prohibit attorneys from charging an "unreasonable" fee, though such a term is subjective.[9] For example, $400 an hour may be the typical rate a seasoned criminal defense attorney charges in a large metropolitan city, but it may not be a reasonable fee for an inexperienced attorney in a small town. An attorney should consider several factors when setting fees: level of

---

[8] MODEL RULES OF PROF'L CONDUCT R. 1.5(b) (2006) (emphasis added).

[9] *See* MODEL RULES OF PROF'L CONDUCT R. 1.5(a) (2006).

expertise, practice area, relative market value, the seriousness or complexity of the case, and the financial situation of the client.

Although attorneys are required to discuss fees at the beginning of client representation, they may set fees in several ways. An attorney can charge an hourly rate, set a single fee for each portion of the case, or set a single fee that covers the entire case. For example, some lawyers charge a flat fee if a case is settled before the preliminary hearing, another flat fee if it there is a preliminary hearing, an additional fee if the case settles before trial, and then either a flat fee or hourly rate if the client requests a trial. Further, attorneys can take a case *pro bono*—without charging a fee—or develop a payment plan for a client who has limited financial means. Despite the different options available, the Model Rules make it clear that a criminal defense attorney cannot "enter into an arrangement for, charge, or collect . . . a contingent fee for representing a defendant in a criminal case."[10] Since, unlike civil cases, criminal cases are not outcome-determinative, an attorney cannot charge more for obtaining a favorable result, whether that result is a negotiated plea or an acquittal. Likewise, a criminal defense attorney cannot accept a bonus from the client for the work performed. It is presumed that the attorney will do her best regardless of the fee charged, so it would be improper for the attorney to ask for or accept additional fees for an exceptional result. Ultimately, criminal cases revolve around seeking justice and this concept would be undermined if fees were determined by the outcome of the case.

Attorneys who bill on an hourly basis must accurately and specifically document how time is spent.[11] A client bill must clearly account for every moment with sufficient detail about the work conducted on the client's behalf, whether by counsel or associated persons. These details serve several important purposes: they give the client an accurate bill explaining the costs associated with his legal representation; they safeguard counsel if a fee dispute arises; and they help counsel to maintain an organized record of all work, thereby encouraging efficiency in the office. Often, fees that an attorney collects are placed in what is called a client trust. The purpose of such a trust is to avoid unethical commingling of money paid by a client with an attorney's private funds.[12] An attorney's failure to comply with Model Rule 1.5 or any other Model Rule can result in sanctions or disbarment. One effective way to avoid the risk of non-compliance with Rule 1.5 is to hand out a fee schedule or an explanation of standard fees. Providing a fee schedule to a client in writing allows him to review the fee information and make an informed choice about whether or not to further pursue the representation. This helps to ensure that a client receives accurate information and helps thwart potential disputes that may arise later.[13] Since this discussion of fees is not exhaustive, it is important for attorneys to familiarize themselves with the Model Rules and the relevant statutes specific to the jurisdiction in which they

[10] MODEL RULES OF PROF'L CONDUCT R. 1.5(d) (2006).

[11] Attorneys that bill hourly often do so incrementally. For example, an attorney may bill by the half-hour or quarter-hour. Some attorneys might even bill by the tenth of an hour—that is, in six-minute increments.

[12] *See, e.g.*, MODEL RULES OF PROF'L CONDUCT R. 1.15(d) (2006).

[13] ROBERT F. COCHRAN, JR. ET AL., THE COUNSELOR-AT-LAW: A COLLABORATIVE APPROACH TO CLIENT INTERVIEWING AND COUNSELING 70 (2d ed. 2006).

practice. Learning local rules helps attorneys understand their obligations and enhances advocates' ability to represent their clients. Attorneys should also check with their State Bar for guidance on setting fees; some states, for instance, provide sample fee forms.[14]

The remainder of this chapter discusses goals of the interviewing process, techniques employed to achieve these goals, professional and ethical dilemmas that might arise, and methods for dealing with those dilemmas effectively. Attorneys should be familiar with the requirements imposed by the Model Rules and always remain mindful of how these requirements can strengthen relationships with clients.

F. DUTIES TO INFORM AND ADVISE

Attorneys are required to inform and advise clients about the distribution of decision-making powers. Model Rule 1.2(a) defines the allocation of authority between the client and the lawyer. Rule 1.2 gives attorneys the power to make strategic decisions, while recognizing that clients retain specific constitutionally protected rights.[15] The client must be informed of these rights, which include the sole authority to decide the following: whether to accept a plea deal; whether to demand a jury trial; whether to testify; whether to waive the right to a speedy arraignment, preliminary hearing, or trial; and, if convicted, whether to appeal. An attorney's violation of the client's right to make any of these decisions can lead to sanctions and may result in a mistrial or plea withdrawal.

Just because the Constitution preserves these rights for defendants does not mean that attorneys may not influence clients' decisions. Because of their experience and expertise, attorneys should use their skills to persuade clients to make decisions that, in the attorneys' best judgment, will be most advantageous to their clients. Persuasive tactics can be aggressive as long as the attorney acknowledges and respects the client's right to make the specified decisions himself.

Consider the hypothetical situation below. Keep in mind that while outcome-determinative decisions are ultimately left to the criminal defendant, it is the defense attorney's responsibility to advise the client to the best of her ability. Clients count on attorneys for expertise and counseling—the reason, of course, why attorneys are called "counselors at law."

HYPO: *Oceana v. Varo*

Frida Varo is accused of murdering her ex-husband, Diego. As you prepare to present your defense, she asks you whether it would help her case if she testified. Given the following circumstances, consider whether you would encourage your client to take the witness stand.

Frida has a prior felony conviction and the judge ruled in a pretrial motion that the prosecution can introduce the conviction for impeachment purposes if she testifies. She has also expressed concern that jurors might have a difficult time acquitting her if she does not look them in the eye and deny that she killed her ex-husband. You have told her the jury will be instructed not to draw

---

[14] For example, the forms for attorneys practicing in California can be found at http://www.calbar.ca.gov/Portals/0/documents/mfa/Sample-Fee-Agreement_%20r.pdf. A sample fee form is included at the end of this chapter.

[15] MODEL RULES OF PROF'L CONDUCT R. 1.2 (2006).

conclusions if she chooses not to testify, but she fears (and rightly so) that the jurors may not heed this admonition. In light of these facts, how would you advise your client? If the prosecution's evidence is weak, how might this affect your advice?

THE INITIAL MEETING

An attorney's professional obligations and responsibilities play an integral part in the actual mechanics of effective representation, beginning with the initial client interview. The first meeting that takes place between a criminal defendant and his attorney significantly affects the development of their relationship. Often, the first encounter occurs during the initial interview, and it will provide a foundation—good or bad—for the attorney-client relationship. While the attorney-client relationship is one built on trust that evolves over time, the initial meeting is a crucial component of building a positive working relationship. Thus, before an attorney ever meets with a client, she must identify the goals of the initial meeting and what she hopes to accomplish at this critical stage. This helps to ensure that the meeting will be as effective and efficient as possible. Although some of these goals may seem fairly obvious, they are nevertheless integral to successful representation; articulating and achieving a set of precise goals will help cultivate a fruitful attorney-client relationship.

A. PLANNING THE INTERVIEW

Everything a criminal defense attorney does should have a clearly defined purpose. Many inexperienced attorneys tend to focus on *voir dire*, evidentiary issues, or what questions to ask a witness on cross-examination, but do not devise a plan for the initial client consultation. This initial meeting, however, deserves just as much attention as the more exciting aspects of trial preparation. As an attorney prepares to meet with a client or prospective client for the first time, she must consider the primary goals of the meeting. Some of the goals, such as establishing a good rapport with the client, are universal and apply to all attorney-client interviews. There are many ways to approach the client interview and diverse clients can present unique challenges. Recognizing one's own style and considering general strategies will help meet these goals, but these steps alone are not enough. No less valuable is an advocate's ability to adapt her style to the individual client.

The following discussion clarifies some common goals that are applicable to all attorney-client interviews, identifies methods to achieve these goals while maximizing efficiency, and explores a variety of issues an attorney may confront during these meetings.

B. INITIAL CONTACT

Whenever possible, a defense attorney should speak with the potential client before the initial office meeting. Even a brief phone conversation can achieve several goals, both legal and practical. Contacting a client by phone, e-mail, or text message prior to an interview can allow an attorney to inform the client of his legal rights and potentially preserve them. An attorney, for instance, can advise a client to refuse to speak with law enforcement without her present. Since refusing to give a statement to the police may be the wisest decision that a defendant makes, this crucial piece of advice should be the first thing an attorney tells a potential client. Anything the defendant says to law enforcement may be used against him either to make the prosecution's case stronger or for impeachment at trial. There might also be legal deadlines that the lawyer and client might want to discuss before the first office meeting. In a case of driving under the influence (DUI), for example, failure to request a hearing with the Department of Motor Vehicles, or other licensing authority, within a certain number of days of the arrest may result in a suspension of the defendant's driver's license. These legal advisements can drastically affect a client's well-being and can foster confidence in the attorney's representation.

An initial conversation might also preserve evidence or facilitate the discovery of evidence. In a case in which drug charges or driving under the influence may be filed, a prompt blood test from a reputable hospital could be greatly beneficial to the client's case. If an attorney is retained promptly, it might allow her to send an investigator to the scene of the arrest and/or crime and interview witnesses. Acting quickly might make the difference between finding a key witness and having no defense. Additionally, the defense may find it advantageous to take photographs of a location as soon as possible after the alleged crime in order to accurately record any pertinent details. Indeed, there are myriad reasons why a defense attorney might take actions to aid the potential client even before the first in-person interview takes place.

By speaking with the client, an attorney can also learn significant facts about him. Is the client fearful or confident, knowledgeable or entirely unfamiliar with the criminal justice process? Will the client come to the interview alone or will he be with someone else? If the client is a minor, his parents might accompany him, or if he is married, his spouse might attend the interview. These facts are critical because they allow the attorney to plan accordingly for the initial consultation. When a person besides the client meets with an attorney, there are several factors to consider. When the client is a minor, securing a retainer and discussing fees will likely require the presence of a parent or guardian. If the client's spouse will attend the meeting, an attorney might seek to meet individually with the client before meeting with the spouse as well. Meeting privately with the client might help to build rapport, and might cause the client to be more honest and open than he would be if a family member were present during a meeting. The presence of individuals besides the client during meetings will also affect issues of confidentiality. Even if the client is a minor, once the attorney is retained, she will want to have a private meeting with the defendant, and then, with the defendant's permission, conduct a meeting with a parent, either with or without the defendant present.

A conversation prior to the interview can also help an attorney determine what type of case her client faces. A preview of the facts of the case prior to meeting will allow the attorney to determine if she is the right person for the job. The charges against a potential client might be unfamiliar to the lawyer or the case might present unusual circumstances. Perhaps the case involves a juvenile client, for example, or a type of charge, such as child molestation, that the attorney does not handle. Or perhaps the case is a complicated charge such as tax evasion, which requires an attorney who is an expert in tax law. If so, discovering this over the phone saves the defendant and the attorney from wasting valuable time.

C. COURT-APPOINTED COUNSEL VS. PRIVATE COUNSEL

The nature of the attorney-client relationship depends on whether the attorney is court-appointed or privately retained. If the court-appointed counsel is a public defender, she will likely already have a police report and may have received a discovery packet from the prosecutor's office.[16] The initial meeting with a court-appointed attorney is typically much quicker than it might be with a private attorney, and it may take place with the client in custody. A private attorney is more likely to initiate conduct by phone, e-mail, or text message, as discussed above. Still, it is important for private counsel to gather as much information as practical and secure the discovery packet as soon as possible.

Since a court-appointed attorney is paid by the government, there is no need to discuss fees with the client; however, it is still imperative to instill confidence in the client and to forge a positive attorney-client relationship. Court-appointed attorneys are generally passionate about criminal defense and are highly-trained, experienced lawyers. Because court-appointed defense attorneys work daily with prosecutors and judges in a particular courthouse, these defense attorneys have likely built relationships that are helpful for settling and trying cases. All the same, a court-appointed attorney should still make clear to her client that she cares about the case and will advocate for him, even though such lawyers typically have very high caseloads.

D. BACKGROUND RESEARCH

Failure to prepare adequately for a client interview can cost an attorney future business and harm her reputation. Adequate preparation includes conducting appropriate research into the charge against a client, familiarizing oneself with the pertinent laws, anticipating questions, and generally demonstrating competence in representation. Because this meeting will provide the client with a first impression, it is vital that the attorney instill in the client confidence that she is the right person for the job.

---

[16] A discovery packet should provide all information the prosecutor has at his disposal that demonstrated probable cause for the charges to be filed. This will likely include a police report, witness statements, and if applicable, a chemist's report.

CONDUCTING THE INTERVIEW

The execution of the interview must build upon the preparations the attorney has already made for the initial interview. Since criminal defense attorneys often have limited opportunities to meet with clients, the first interview is a critical moment, as it will set the tone for future interviews and, indeed, the entire course of representation. If the defendant is incarcerated at the time of the meeting, the interview will most likely take place in the jail interview room, where attorneys are nonetheless afforded privacy during client interviews, which must still remain confidential.

A. CLARIFY PROFESSIONAL OBLIGATIONS

At the outset of any initial consultation or meeting, attorneys must articulate the nature of the attorney-client relationship and explain the fee arrangement to their clients. Even though this explanation should not take more than a few minutes, it is nevertheless essential to explain these professional obligations in order to build a trusting relationship. In addition to the obligation to explain attorney-client privilege, confidentiality, and applicable attorney fees, an attorney also has the duty to inform and advise clients as required by Model Rule 1.2. Explaining the character of this relationship should strengthen trust between the attorney and client—a critical goal of the initial interview.

B. BUILD THE CLIENT'S TRUST

The initial attorney-client meeting might influence how the relationship will unfold during the remaining period of legal representation. While trust can be lost at any critical juncture, it is crucial to demonstrate to the client at this initial meeting that the lawyer can be trusted. Just as building the relationship between client and attorney is a fundamental element of preparation for trial, as well as settlement negotiations, the advocate must actively maintain the relationship over the course of representation in order to retain and further deepen the client's trust.

Dealing with a client is much like dealing with people in ordinary, day-to-day life. Each client has a unique temperament and set of expectations. Except, in the case of court-appointed representation, the client is *paying the lawyer* to understand his personality and meet his expectations. Also, the client is most likely going through one of the most traumatic episodes of his life: being charged with a crime and facing potential incarceration is an emotional ordeal for all but the most jaded defendants. Building a client's trust will require adapting to that specific client since if, at any point from the initial meeting onwards, an attorney cannot gain and keep her client's trust, she may soon lose that client. Although this discussion of building trust is geared towards attorneys in private practice, it is equally essential for public defenders to gain the trust of the indigent clients that they represent. Even though defendants do not have the right to choose between court-appointed lawyers, it is still crucial to develop a cooperative relationship between the defendant and the court-appointed attorney.

Whether acting as court-appointed or private counsel, the attorney must exude confidence without offering false hope. The attorney needs to convey to her client that she has confidence both in her own abilities and in her case theory, while respecting the fine line between being confident and overselling one's abilities. Attorneys need to adopt the style that works for them. When the famous winery owner Robert Mondavi was seeking a lawyer to represent him in a complex litigation, he asked John Martel (the lawyer whom he eventually decided to hire) why he should pick him. Martel purportedly responded, "Because I don't lose cases and I don't intend to start with yours."[17] While the reality is that almost all lawyers lose cases sometimes, and it can backfire to come across as overly confident, exuding confidence in one's abilities can reassure an anxious client.

One way for an attorney to gain a client's trust is to show the client that she genuinely cares about him as a person and that she is committed to obtaining a favorable outcome for him. Although it is generally not advisable to become friends with one's client, the attorney may still respect the boundaries of a professional relationship while demonstrating her compassion for the criminal defendant as he contends with the predicament of facing charges. As acclaimed criminal defense attorney Leslie Abramson has remarked:

> I don't try to hide the affection I feel for my clients from the jury, either. I want them to understand that my advocacy isn't an act or a pose. They should know that I'm not faking this; this is not just a job. I really, really believe this guy and you should too.[18]

C. LEARN THE CLIENT'S STORY

When a person is charged with a crime, the prosecutor has determined that enough evidence exists to prove that a crime was committed and that the named defendant is the individual who committed it. That is the prosecutor's story. When a prospective client walks into a defense attorney's office for an initial meeting, he too will have a story. Learning this story is a fundamental goal of the first meeting.

In order to gather as much information as possible about the client and his version of the facts, the defense lawyer should examine the charges filed against the defendant and the events surrounding the charges. It is also important for the lawyer to carefully study all of the elements that the prosecutor must prove for each alleged crime. Often, the facts and the law point to a defendant, but there might be a missing element of the crime that the prosecutor will have difficulty proving. Since the prosecution must prove each element beyond a reasonable doubt in order to obtain a conviction, it is imperative to go over details with the client while trying to locate holes in the prosecution's case. Getting a sense of the events that occurred—at least as far as the defendant knows them or is willing to divulge—is only the beginning, however. It would be naïve to believe that the story a criminal defendant tells his attorney will always be a complete and fully accurate description of what happened. Sometimes a client may not remember things clearly, sometimes he may insist that the police or prosecutor's depiction of events distorts the truth, and sometimes the defendant will fabricate part or all of his story. Learning the client's version of what happened requires more than just inquiring about his accounting of the facts.

As the saying goes, there are two sides to every story. The reality, however, is typically much more complicated. In the context of a criminal trial, while there may be two sides to the story, there may also be several versions of the "truth." A thorough client interview can help clarify the actual events.

---

[17] JULIA FLYNN SILER, THE HOUSE OF MONDAVI: THE RISE AND FALL OF AN AMERICAN WINE DYNASTY 103 (2007).

[18] LESLIE ABRAMSON, THE DEFENSE IS READY: LIFE IN THE TRENCHES OF CRIMINAL LAW 12 (1997).

Few cases are black and white, and even if the defendant admits responsibility and wants to plead guilty, there are gradations of culpability. The attorney must seek out any facts that may mitigate the client's guilt in order to facilitate a beneficial case settlement.

Hand-in-hand with learning the story is the need to ascertain what it is that the client hopes to achieve from counsel's representation. Often, a criminal defendant is most interested in receiving a favorable settlement offer from the prosecution. Sometimes a client's biggest concern is the collateral consequences of a conviction, such as losing a professional or driver's license, being deported, or suffering damage to his reputation. A thorough discussion of case settlement and collateral consequences is located in Chapter 12.

For example, Juan Catalan was charged with murder in early 2004. After a witness identified him out of a photo lineup, Los Angeles detectives were convinced, despite Catalan's protests, that he had murdered a sixteen-year-old girl. Catalan's criminal defense attorney, Todd Melnik, however, worked diligently to confirm an alibi—Catalan insisted he was at a baseball game when the murder was committed. After poring over television footage of the Dodgers game Catalan said he attended, his attorney learned that the HBO show *Curb Your Enthusiasm* was filming at the stadium the same day. Ultimately, Melnik was able to find footage from HBO's cameras that exonerated his client.[19]

Catalan's story illustrates the importance of taking time to learn a client's version of events. If the client insists he has an alibi, the attorney should seek out other people or evidence that can corroborate it. A criminal defense attorney should consider the following questions: Does the client have any prior charges or convictions? Is he on parole or probation? Are there witnesses who can corroborate an alibi or cast further light on the events surrounding the crime? Are there individuals who can provide character references for the defendant? What is the accuser's reputation in the community? Is there any reason why the accuser or other witnesses might be biased against the client? Does the client have anything against the accuser? Are there mitigating circumstances that might reduce the charge or provide grounds to have it dismissed entirely? A checklist or questionnaire can provide a framework for effectively learning a client's story, and can also ensure that nothing is overlooked at this critical preliminary stage.

D. MAKING THE MOST OF THE INTERVIEW

At the beginning of the interview, there are other basic steps an attorney can take to promote a productive and efficient meeting. Offering a client a cup of coffee or a glass of water, although seemingly insignificant, can go a long way towards demonstrating the attorney's concern and interest in her client. Providing the client with a printed agenda for the meeting can also get things off to a good start. As simple as it may seem, a sheet of paper that details what the attorney hopes to accomplish during the meeting can help ease the client's mind and keep his thoughts focused. Providing the client with a pen and paper can also be helpful, so that he may record his thoughts or questions.

Another important consideration should be scheduling a follow-up meeting. Setting a time to

---

[19] David Rosenzweig, *Man with TV Show Alibi Sues LAPD*, L.A. TIMES (Aug. 5, 2004), http://articles.latimes.com/2004/aug/05/local/me-alibi5.

meet again accomplishes several goals. First of all, it demonstrates to the client that the lawyer is focused on the client's case, since a further meeting can build upon the initial interview and allow for follow-up on any questions that arise. When scheduling this second meeting, it may be helpful to provide a list of outstanding items not yet discussed at the first meeting. Not least of all, for clients in custody, there can also be a psychological benefit to planning an upcoming meeting, since the defendant can be confident of further contact with his attorney and avoid feeling abandoned during his ordeal.

E. OBTAIN BACKGROUND INFORMATION

In addition to learning the client's version of events, the astute defense attorney also needs to obtain background information about her client that will aid in the client's defense, as well as in any settlement negotiations. The client's history, for example, may contain mitigating factors, such as mental health issues, or hardships, that might elicit sympathy from the prosecutor, jury, or judge. In some cases, the client can refer the attorney to other individuals who have information that would either exonerate him or at least reduce his culpability. The attorney should, furthermore, try to discover the biases of prosecution and defense witnesses, including any reasons why someone might have a grudge against the client or might fabricate a story about him. Lastly, the attorney should make an effort to find out whether her client knows facts about any witnesses that could affect their credibility, including criminal history or substance abuse issues.

EVALUATING THE INTERVIEW

During the client interview, the primary goal is to collect as much information as possible; immediately after the interview, the main goal is to objectively evaluate that information. This requires assessing the credibility of the client and the substance of the information obtained. A defense attorney must also identify areas where further investigation is needed, including any possible legal issues that would require additional research.

A. CREDIBILITY

Evaluating a client's credibility is a critical step, given that the truthfulness of a client's story can significantly affect the case theory and bear on the attorney's decision whether to advise her client to testify. A miscalculation here could cost the client his case and could have damaging professional ramifications for the attorney, if she puts the client on the stand knowing that the client is likely to commit perjury. The client's credibility, moreover, is a key factor the attorney should consider when advising the client whether to accept a settlement offer.

When an attorney meets with her client, she should consider how a jury will interpret the client's demeanor. Even when evidence supports a client's story and counsel believes in the client's sincerity, a jury might not find the defendant credible. The jurors' distrust could result from bias on their part against criminal defendants, a client's physical appearance, or even the client's manner of speaking. While the oft-quoted aphorism, "Justice is blind," suggests a rigorously impartial system, jurors can, unfortunately, bring imperfections and prejudices into their deliberations. An attorney should recognize how the client will likely be viewed and prepare accordingly. As discussed earlier, the Model Rules allow the client to make the ultimate decision about whether to testify or accept a plea agreement, but the Rules also require effective assistance of counsel. Since advising the client in this regard can be critical, an attorney should consider her honest assessment of a client's demeanor. If the client's credibility is a concern, a skilled lawyer will find alternative ways to present the evidence. Creative litigators will formulate a persuasive case theory through the presentation of other witnesses (including experts), conflicts in the statements of the state's witnesses, physical evidence, and demonstratives.

HYPO: *Oceana v. Whitman*

Richard Whitman is charged with robbery, and while the evidence favors him, during the initial interview he is evasive in answering questions. Furthermore, he has a slight stutter that can give the impression he is not being entirely forthright. The client is also entirely unfamiliar with the criminal justice process, as he is a first-generation American whose English is intelligible but not fluent. He expresses his desire to testify and tell his side of the story, even if it means testifying through an interpreter. You believe he is sincere and that his testimony would be truthful and could exonerate him. You do not believe, however, that he will be a credible witness in his own defense. How would you advise Whitman?

B. FOLLOWING UP

After the initial interview, the defense attorney must determine how she will proceed in order to represent her client successfully. This critical period marks the beginning of trial preparation. After speaking with the client and evaluating the information garnered during and after the interview, counsel should begin developing a case theory. As the attorney is developing her theory, she should work to fill in any gaps left over after the initial interview. This will involve pursuing leads generated during the initial interview, including interviewing other witnesses and collecting additional information. The attorney must continue exploring the case and the ways in which she can advocate on her client's behalf. This can be accomplished through discovery, continued interviews with the client, or further investigation.

The journey towards trial requires the attorney to constantly nurture the relationship with her client. Ongoing communication with the client is fundamental, and scheduling future interviews allows an attorney to monitor and strengthen the case. Returning a client's phone calls, e-mails, or texts can go a long way in demonstrating dedication to the client. Defense attorneys can demonstrate to the client that they are actively working on the case by sending a copy of a motion that was prepared on the client's behalf. Subsequent client interviews will update the client on the progress of his case and will provide an opportunity to answer questions that may arise either for client or counsel. These interviews will strengthen the trust that is developed during the initial consultation.

ALTERNATIVE APPROACHES TO THE INTERVIEW

The harsh reality that the client will not always be entirely truthful might complicate an attorney's duty to provide effective assistance of counsel while abiding by both the client's wishes and her own ethical obligations. For example, a client might admit to committing a crime but insist on going to trial and testifying falsely. The defendant alone can decide whether or not to testify, however, the attorney may not call a witness whose testimony she believes would constitute perjury. In situations that present such ethical complications, a defense attorney may vary her approach to the client interview. It is important for attorneys to keep in mind that there are degrees of culpability. For instance, a client who is charged with aggravated battery may have been engaged in a fight, but he may not have been the aggressor, or he may have made efforts to retreat and the "victim" may have used unreasonable threats or force on the defendant. Or, a defendant charged with murder may have killed the victim, but he may have been acting in self-defense, or in the heat of passion. Or, a client who sold drugs to an undercover police officer may have the defense of entrapment. Thus, even a client who assumes he is "guilty" may not actually be guilty of a crime in the eyes of the law, or he may be guilty of a lesser crime than the one charged against him. It is the attorney's job to ferret out facts from the interview, pursue further investigation, determine how the facts fit with the law, and formulate a case theory that affords the client the strongest, most credible defense, or the most advantageous settlement strategy.

HYPO: *Oceana v. Curtain*

Don Curtain has been charged with murdering his wife, Betsy. He insists that he found her body in the kitchen after coming home from work. She had bled to death by the time he found her with a gun lying next to her on the floor. His prints are found on the gun, which he admits to owning. There are no signs of breaking and entering, but the safe in which the gun was stored is open, and Don insists that jewelry is missing. The jewelry is insured. Don and Betsy recently purchased a life insurance policy and he is due to collect $1 million unless he is found guilty of murder. You have reviewed the prosecutor's discovery packet. At the beginning of the initial interview, Don insists on proceeding to trial. How should you advise Don?

Most criminal cases—more than 95% in most jurisdictions—will eventually settle. But in those instances in which clients insist on going to trial, several potential ethical issues may arise. During the initial client interview, attorneys might address the possibility of trial in one of two ways: either an "open-ended" or a "closed" approach.

A. OPEN-ENDED INTERVIEW

During an open-ended interview, the attorney will ask questions that permit the client to tell his story without limiting the nature of the response. Generally, the format of the client interview outlined in this chapter is consistent with the open-ended approach. Consider the following hypothetical scenario:

With a murder charge, as in *Oceana v. Curtain*, the client will almost certainly be in custody and the attorney will likely have access to the prosecution's discovery packet before meeting with the client.

Using that discovery as a foundation for the interview, the attorney can seek to develop her understanding of the charges by posing open-ended questions:

1. Open-Ended Questions

- What happened the night your wife was murdered?
- Can anyone verify your story?
- What happened when you entered your home?
- Is there any reason someone might want to kill your wife? Please explain.
- Can you explain why your prints were on your gun? Do you ever target shoot or take the gun out of the safe? Can you elaborate?
- Did anyone know about your home safe? Who might have known?
- Do you think people were aware that Betsy had valuable jewelry at home? Did she wear her jewelry in public or at parties? Why might someone have targeted Betsy?
- Do you think your home was a target for burglary? Why? Can you explain how someone might have gotten in your home without leaving signs of breaking and entering? Can you explain your practice regarding securing your home? What was Betsy's routine regarding leaving doors unlocked or locked when she was home?
- Tell me about the insurance. Tell me about your financial situation.

The potential responses the client might give to these questions are numerous. Counsel will have already explained attorney confidentiality to the client, so some questions might elicit unexpected answers. What if the client admits he committed the murder but he insists on going to trial? What if the client wants to testify that he is innocent? How will that affect representation?

B. CLOSED INTERVIEW

The closed interview, on the other hand, is structured to limit the nature of a client's responses. Rather than asking open-ended questions, a closed interview might focus on the evidence the prosecution has offered and potential defenses that might be successful given the evidence against the client.

1. Closed-Ended Questions

- Are you aware that your blood alcohol level tested at 0.09% at the police station?
- Do you know that the legal blood alcohol limit for driving in Oceana is 0.08%? Do you understand that it is not illegal to drive with a blood alcohol level less than 0.08% as long as you were not impaired?
- The police report states that the test took place about thirty minutes after you were pulled over, does that sound right to you?
- Do you understand that to be guilty of the charge, the prosecutor needs to prove that your blood alcohol level was above the legal limit at the time of driving? If it was below the legal limit at the time of driving, you are not guilty of a crime, even if the level was above the limit at the time of the test. Does this make sense to you?
- Do you realize that it takes time for alcohol to absorb into the blood system? Experts conclude that it takes at least thirty minutes after drinking alcohol before the alcohol reaches a peak blood alcohol level. Are you aware of this? Did you tell the police when you started drinking? Did you tell the police when you stopped drinking? Did

you tell the police what you drank? Did you tell the police how many drinks you had? Were you nervous or scared when you spoke to the arresting officer?

- Please read over the police report including the breath test results. Please tell me when you had your first and last drink in relation to when you drove. How many drinks did you have that night? How many minutes went by after your last drink and when you drove? How long did you drive before you were pulled over? How much time passed between when you were pulled over and when you were given the alcohol test at the police station? Did you feel intoxicated when you were driving?

HYPO: *Oceana v. Cost*

Lane Cost was arrested for suspicion of driving under the influence of alcohol. In the State of Oceana, the legal limit is 0.08%. Cost's blood alcohol level registered 0.09% when he was tested at the police station. The test at the police station occurred approximately thirty minutes after he was pulled over. The arresting officers administered field sobriety tests, the results of which were inconclusive. You have reviewed the prosecutor's discovery packet. At the onset of your initial interview, Cost insists on pushing the case to trial. How should you advise the client? Consider how this case would be handled using a closed interview style.

Consider the following additional facts and apply the closed interview approach: Assume scientific data shows that it takes thirty to forty-five minutes for a person to reach his peak blood alcohol level from the time of the last drink. Cost has two drinks in the half hour prior to driving, finishing the last drink within ten minutes of the stop. Thus, his blood alcohol level will be rising from the period of time between the stop and the breath test. What questions might you ask?

The closed interview approach is much less common than the open-ended interview. One very real concern with the closed interview approach is that counsel, ignorant of specifics, might compromise her ethical obligations by supplying the defendant with possible defenses for him to adopt. While attorneys are permitted to guide a client regarding demeanor and the nature of the testimony, an attorney cannot instruct her client to perjure himself, nor can an attorney knowingly call any witness that intends to commit perjury. For instance, in the hypo *Oceana v. Cost*, counsel cannot suggest that the client posit a delayed rising blood alcohol defense, since it is improper to coach a witness—including the defendant—by suggesting a defense. One ethical way to conduct the closed interview, however, is to show the defendant the police report, medical test results, or any other evidentiary documents collected against him, then ask the defendant to explain the evidence and tell his side of the story. It is also ethical to comment on the defendant's version of what happened, including informing the client that his story is not credible in light of the incriminating evidence. In no event, however, is it permissible to suggest to the client what his testimony should be.

ETHICS

Both the open-ended and closed approaches raise potential ethical issues. What if the defendant discloses criminal conduct? What if he insists on testifying? The Model Rules require an attorney to urge her client to be truthful or otherwise the attorney should recuse herself. If an attorney cannot withdraw, she can disclose confidential communications to rectify the issue. For example, in the investigation of President Clinton in the Monica Lewinsky matter, President Clinton's attorney sought to use Lewinsky's signed affidavit to show that the two did not have sexual relations. Upon learning that Lewinsky perjured herself, the attorney disclosed the necessary information to the presiding judge.

It is unethical for an attorney to put the defendant on the stand knowing he is going to lie. The attorney should try to convince the defendant not to testify if she believes the client intends to perjure himself. Of course, it is also possible that a client's initial admission of guilt to his defense attorney was fabricated. Sometimes people falsely admit complicity, either to try to gain notoriety or to take the rap for someone else. It is also important to note, as previously explained that there are gradations of guilt; the client may have some complicity yet not be legally guilty of the crime with which he is actually charged. It is likely that the client does not even realize what legal elements must be proven by the prosecution before he can be convicted. Certainly, he may be unaware that under the law he has a partial or complete defense to the charges. Given a scenario in which a client fully admits to his lawyer that he is "guilty as charged," and in which the evidence against the defendant is compelling, the attorney should encourage the client to agree to settle the case. If the client in this scenario insists on going to trial, the attorney should make every effort to persuade him not to testify and she should advise the client that he cannot testify because that would be committing perjury. If the client insists on trial, and demands to testify even though he admits he will testify falsely, the lawyer must still represent the client to the best of her abilities, but she cannot call the client as a witness, because that would be suborning perjury. If the client still insists on testifying, the lawyer can sit quietly and not participate in the false testimony (not ask questions that would call for a lie and not offer the false testimony as part of her case in closing argument) or alternatively, counsel can request the judge to remove her from the case. It is imperative for defense attorneys to keep in mind that, regardless of whether the client admits the truth of the charges, he has the right to the zealous representation of counsel, and he can hold the prosecution to the burden of proving every element of every charge beyond a reasonable doubt.

C. DEALING WITH DIFFICULT CLIENTS

In some cases, interacting with clients can be a difficult task. The pressures of an impending trial can create a stressful environment for clients and can lead to difficult client demands and strained communications. Additionally, especially in the case of court-appointed defense attorneys, advocates may not be able to pick and choose among clients. For example, clients can bring with them a host of concerns that may impact their interaction with their attorney, such as drug addiction, psychiatric issues, racist tendencies, anti-social behavior, or linguistic or cultural barriers. Detailed suggestions for interacting effectively with difficult clients and witnesses can be found in Chapter 5.

A common challenge when representing defendants in criminal cases is that they often have substance abuse issues, which can diminish the client's good judgment or clarity of thought. Since substance abuse can damage the client's ability to perceive and recollect events, his version of events may be mistaken or skewed. If the client's account of what happened is not credible, the attorney must inform him, just as she must when the best option is to settle the case. Because people with addictions often have difficulty facing reality, the attorney may have an uphill battle convincing the client that jurors may not believe his story or that it will be wise to accept the prosecutor's plea deal.

SAMPLE RETAINER AGREEMENT

THIS ATTORNEY-CLIENT FEE CONTRACT ("Contract") is entered into by and between
_____ and Lauren A. Hailey ("attorney").

1.   CONDITIONS

This Contract will not take effect, and Attorney will have no obligation to provide legal services until Client returns a signed copy of this Contract and pays the fixed fee and or deposit called for under paragraph 3.

2.   SCOPE AND DUTIES

Client hires Attorney and any associates that Attorney should designate to provide legal services in connection with the following (brief description of alleged offense):

_____

_____

_____

INITIAL APPROPRIATE BOX. ANY BOX NOT INITIALED DOES NOT APPLY

[ ]   Misdemeanor Pre-Trial

Attorney shall represent Client at the arraignment, file and argue pretrial motions, if necessary, conduct pretrial investigation, conduct plea negotiations and attempt to settle the matter during the pre-trial period. Attorney is not retained for any post-conviction court appearances (fine payments, progress reports, extensions of probation obligations, probation violation hearings). Attorney is not retained for court or jury trial. If such appearances (post conviction, court or jury trial) are required an additional fee will be required.

[ ]   Felony (Preliminary Hearing)

Attorney shall represent Client at the arraignment, file and argue motions prior to preliminary hearing, if necessary, conduct pre-preliminary hearing investigation, conduct plea negotiations, attempt to settle matter before the preliminary hearing and conduct the preliminary hearing itself. Attorney will not represent the Client beyond the preliminary hearing unless subsequent fee arrangements are made.

[ ]   Misdemeanor or Felony Trial

Attorney shall make all appearances for jury or court trial proceedings including jury selection, opening statements, prosecution case, defense case, closing statements, verdict and if necessary, probation and sentencing hearing. If a mistrial occurs attorney is not responsible for a retrial unless an additional fee is paid. Attorney is not retained for appellate or write services.

[ ]   Pre-Filing Investigation

Client hires attorney to consult with Client, his family members and relevant persons, to counsel Client regarding his or her legal rights and remedies and generally to provide legal advice and guidance. In the case of a criminal matter where criminal charges may or may not be brought by the prosecuting agency (District Attorney, City Attorney, City Prosecutor) attorney is retained to consult with Client, family members of Client and relevant parties through the pre-filing period, to contact the appropriate law enforcement agency and the appropriate prosecuting agency and to attempt, if possible, to negotiate or otherwise obtain a non-filing or rejection of criminal charges by the appropriate law enforcement prosecuting agency. In this regard, if criminal charges are not filed by the law enforcement or prosecuting agency, attorney will be deemed to have provided the necessary and required legal service contracted for herein. Client will be entitled to no refund of the attorney fee should criminal charges be not filed by the appropriate law enforcement agency or rejected for filing by the appropriate prosecuting agency.

[ ]   Other
        Attorney shall provide the following services (describe):

_____

_____

_____

3.   FEE ARRANGEMENTS
        (For services described in section 2 of this agreement)

        INITIAL APPROPRIATE BOX. ANY BOX NOT INITIALED DOES NOT APPLY.

[ ]   Fixed Fee
        Client agrees to pay a fixed fee of $_____ for Attorney's services under this Contract.
Attorney shall have no obligation to provide services to Client until the required deposit is paid. No
portion of the fee will be refunded once this retainer agreement is signed. Attorney hereby acknowledges
receipt of $_____. Client hereby agrees to pay the remaining balance of the fixed fee as
specified below under "Payment Arrangements" on page 3. Should any payment be 30 days delinquent
the entire amount of all outstanding fees shall become due and payable immediately.

[ ]   Trial Fee (Optional)
        As indicated herein Attorney has not been retained at this time to represent Client for jury or
court trial proceedings. If such services (jury or court trial as described on page 2 of this retainer
agreement) are required Client agrees to pay an additional fixed fee of $_____.

[ ]   Hourly Fee with Non-Refundable Retainer
        Client agrees to pay attorney a total non-refundable retainer of $_____. Attorney
acknowledges receipt of $_____. This minimum retainer is non-refundable and will be
Attorney's minimum fee but hourly charges of $350 per hour will be credited against it. When this
amount becomes exhausted based on the hourly charges, Attorney reserves the right to demand further
fees.

[ ]   Payment Arrangements

_____

_____

_____

_____

4.   EXCLUDED SERVICES
        Attorney is not retained to conduct administrative hearings, (except DMV Admin Per Se
hearings), appear before government agencies or represent the client regarding possible civil claims,
lawsuits either on behalf of or against the Client. Attorney is not retained for any post-conviction services
including fine payments, progress reports, extensions of probation obligations, probation violation
hearings, Penal Code section 1203.4 expungement or Penal Code section 851.8 factual innocence
proceedings. Post Conviction Appearances payable at $_____ per appearance.

5.   COSTS AND EXPENSES

In addition to the fixed fee, Client shall reimburse Attorney for all out of pocket costs and expenses incurred by Attorney. Costs include, but are not limited to, investigation costs, expert fees and expenses, laboratory costs, messenger service fees, process server fees, messenger service fees and photocopying expenses.

6.   DISCLAIMER

The Client agrees that Attorney cannot promise or guarantee and does not promise or guarantee any specific result, judgment, verdict sentence or compromise of any kind or nature and that no such representation has been made by Attorney.

7.   DISCHARGE AND WITHDRAWAL

Attorney may withdraw with Client's consent or for good cause. Good cause includes Client's breach of this Contract, Client's refusal to cooperate with Attorney or to follow Attorney's advice on a material matter or any other fact or circumstance that would render Attorney's continuing representation unlawful or unethical.

8.   IMMIGRATION

Attorney advises Clients that they do not practice immigration law. Further, Attorney advises any Client who is not a citizen to contact an Immigration lawyer immediately.

Date: _____

Client: _____

Date: _____

Client Guarantor: _____

Date: _____

Lauren A. Hailey, Attorney: _____

SUMMARY

An attorney's success depends largely on the preparation that takes place outside of the courtroom, and, for the defense, a significant part of that preparation includes interviews with the client. Just as positive first impressions before a jury play a vital role in successful litigation, forming a trusting attorney-client relationship right from the outset of representation is likewise essential for obtaining a satisfactory outcome. The defense attorney must work to gain her client's trust, effectively communicate with him, and ascertain his needs and goals. Meanwhile, she must also uphold standards of professional and ethical conduct. She must bear in mind—and explain to her client—the attorney-client privilege, the character of confidential communications, and relevant fees, all the while informing and advising the client in a competent and professional manner.

Defense counsel should never underestimate the importance of her initial meeting with a client, for this first interview sets the tone of the remainder of the representation. She should plan, come prepared, and be willing to listen to her client. Above all, she needs to build trust with her client, with whom interaction may be difficult, seeing that he is likely facing one of the most upsetting and confusing predicaments of his life. Although he is very likely feeling anxious and helpless, defense counsel can, at the very least, provide some reassuring support. Counsel needs to exude confidence and professionalism, without appearing arrogant or giving the client false hope.

Client interviews can pose a myriad of difficulties. The defense attorney needs to learn the client's story, even when that task proves challenging. The client may be reluctant to communicate candidly, he may be afraid or embarrassed, or he may not remember details. The attorney's patience and tact can be particularly valuable qualities in such situations. In addition, humor or anecdotes, when appropriate, may help diffuse tension.

After the interview, the information acquired should be used to build a defense, or prepare for case settlement and sentencing. Elements for the case theory should already begin to materialize, and directions for further investigation should start becoming evident. While gathering facts from the client, counsel should also be evaluating his credibility and how the client will come across to the judge and jury. Will a jury sympathize with him? If the client testifies, will a judge or jury believe what he says? Is the client a likeable person? Counsel will need to consider these factors when planning case strategy.

After the initial interview, trial preparation gets fully underway. The defense attorney should remain in contact with her client as her case theory develops and moves forward. If the initial interview was particularly challenging, counsel should consider alternative approaches when following up with subsequent interviews. In most cases, she should ask open-ended questions, although, if a more directed approach seems more effective in certain situations, she may ask closed ended questions. Most importantly, she must proceed ethically. It is defense counsel's obligation to represent her client zealously, while remaining within the bounds of ethics and the law. Since over 95% of criminal cases settle, counsel should keep case settlement in mind, from the initial interview to the conclusion of the case.

CHECKLIST

✓ Counsel must be familiar with the *Model Rules of Professional Conduct*, the relevant evidentiary rules, applicable local rules, and the different ways in which they affect interaction with clients.

✓ Counsel must detail for the client her obligation to inform, and advise of the allocation of authority that exists between that attorney and client.

✓ Prior to the initial interview, counsel should prepare by making initial contact with the client, securing discovery documents, and researching the relevant legal issues.

✓ Counsel should maximize the opportunity at the initial meeting to develop rapport and demonstrate competence, being sure to communicate with the client the nature of the professional obligations and the ways in which they influence the attorney-client relationship—including confidentiality, the attorney-client privilege, and fee arrangements.

✓ Counsel should learn the client's story during the interview. Ultimately, this, along with the research completed and the evidence gathered, will help form the case theory.

✓ Counsel must remember that the first interview provides the foundation for future interviews and directs the course of trial preparation. During the first interview, strive to establish a safe and welcoming environment, asking open-ended questions whenever possible.

✓ Counsel should clearly present the goals and structure of all interview sessions.

✓ Counsel must keep in mind a client's credibility when evaluating the case and developing the case theory. Remember, too, that the case theory can change throughout preparation for trial and even during trial.

✓ Counsel must be aware of the different approaches to conducting a client interview and be mindful of how ethical obligations can be put to the test by clients who admit guilt.

CHAPTER 7
DISCOVERY

"Discovery consists of seeing what everybody has seen and thinking what nobody else has thought."
–Albert Szent-Gyorgyi

The overriding purpose of discovery is simply to gather information. As a legal term of art, discovery is the process during which opposing counsel exchange information. Discovery enables advocates to gather material that is used to formulate case theories and bui ld cases. The knowledge gained from the discovery process often leads to uncovering information which may, in turn, lead to the revelation of additional evidence, witnesses, or further "ammunition" for trial, such as identifying prior convictions and statements that can be used to impeach or corroborate witnesses.

Don't hide the ball with discovery!

Discovery can take many forms such as written, recorded, or even an electronic format. The actual discovery process can potentially span from the time of arrest until trial. In a criminal trial, however, discovery will generally be much more limited than in a civil trial, for several reasons. First, the Federal Rules of Criminal Procedure place limits on the discovery available to both defendants and the prosecution. For example, depositions are very rarely, if ever, used when it comes to criminal discovery. There may also be limitations placed upon discovery by state law or local rules. Also, because the Seventh Amendment and the Due Process Clause of the Fourteenth Amendment guarantee the criminal defendant a speedy trial, there may be discovery limitations simply as a result of time limits. Other reasons discovery in the criminal case might be limited include concern for the protection of victims, witnesses, informants, and the public. Of course, the Fifth Amendment provides the defendant facing criminal charges with the right to remain silent, thus the prosecution has no right to question the defendant or even obtain a statement from him. Finally, criminal discovery is distinctly more informal than its civil counterpart, where voluminous paperwork, such as written motions to compel, interrogatories and depositions, might be requested. As this chapter discusses, criminal discovery is often an informal process whereby an attorney often times can simply make an oral request to opposing counsel to provide the information required.

Besides being a significant step in trial preparation, discovery is the area of litigation in which attorneys, especially prosecutors, are most likely to be sanctioned. This is unsurprising. Although an area ripe with strategic possibilities, discovery is also an aspect of pretrial preparation in which the rules are sometimes manipulated with the purpose of trying to gain the upper hand (such as when an attorney attempts to classify evidence as immaterial in order for it to remain undiscoverable). If a statute requires

that an attorney turn over recorded interviews with witnesses, unethical attorneys may choose not to record them at all in order to keep information secret. It is imperative to understand that it is always unethical to hide information that should be disclosed to opposing counsel. Moreover, it is critical that material be turned over in a timely fashion. Playing "hide the ball," by unfairly delaying discovery, is one of the most common ways for attorneys to infuriate a judge. Indeed, the potential loss or remedy available to opposing counsel for violations of the rules of discovery can far outweigh any short-lived advantage gained by deceiving one's opponent. What remedies are available for such violations? If the violation occurs post-trial, then a conviction could be overturned and a new trial ordered. If the trial has not concluded, then a mistrial, sanctions for the attorney being found in contempt, or even the complete exclusion of particular evidence could be ordered. Discovery violations are the most common form of prosecutorial misconduct and are one of the leading causes for the reversal of verdicts.

CONSTITUTIONAL DISCOVERY: *BRADY* AND ITS PROGENY

A. *BRADY* DISCLOSURE

In the landmark case, *Brady v. Maryland*, the Supreme Court held that the Due Process Clause of the Fourteenth Amendment required the prosecution to disclose to defendants all favorable evidence that is materially relevant to guilt or punishment.[1] It is irrelevant whether or not the prosecution suppressed the favorable evidence in bad faith,[2] and the prosecution's duty to disclose arises even in the absence of the defendant's specific request.[3] Ultimately, a conviction may be reversed if the prosecutor fails to provide *Brady* materials.[4]

What is favorable evidence? *Brady* determined that exculpatory evidence is favorable, and in *Giglio v. United States*, the Supreme Court held that impeachable evidence was favorable as well.[5] An example of favorable impeachment evidence is when prosecutors make agreements with witnesses. Plea agreements with government witnesses must be disclosed, even if the prosecutor of the current trial was not informed about them.[6] Because juries might discredit informant testimony given in exchange for immunity or a lighter sentence, such deals constitute evidence that would be considered exculpatory to the defense under *Brady*.

While the prosecution is responsible for turning over *Brady* material, the prosecutorial team also includes other government agencies. The prosecution has an affirmative duty "to learn of any favorable

---

[1] Brady v. Maryland, 373 U.S. 83, 87 (1963).

[2] *Id.*

[3] United States v. Agurs, 427 U.S. 97, 107 (1976).

[4] Kyles v. Whitley, 514 U.S. 419, 421–22 (1995).

[5] Giglio v. United States, 405 U.S. 150 (1972).

[6] *Id.* at 150–51.

evidence known to the others acting on the government's behalf in the case."[7] This means that the prosecution has a duty to learn of any materially exculpatory evidence from other assisting and investigating agencies (such as the police), and turn it over to the defense.

HYPO: *Oceana v. Bird*

A renowned sculpture by an artist named Jon Moon was stolen from the Oceana County Museum of Art. An art enthusiast named Tanya went to the police and implicated the famous artist Joel Bird as the thief. Bird was arrested at the airport on his way to Paris.

As the prosecutor, you were gathering evidence for the government's case against Bird. You interviewed Tanya. When you asked Tanya what information she had, she said: "Well I was surprised to see Mr. Bird at the OCMA. You see, I'm a big fan of his work. Anyway, we were both looking at Moon's sculpture when Bird looked at me and said, 'That sculpture is such a piece of junk that . . .'"

At this point, you asked Tanya to pause since you noticed the interview was not being recorded. You turned the recorder on and signaled for her to proceed. Tanya then said, ". . . so, then while staring at the sculpture, Mr. Bird said, 'I'm sure if it suddenly disappeared no one would notice.'"

Although you and Tanya both casually critiqued the stolen statue, that was the extent of the interview regarding Bird's statements. Is the recorded statement exculpatory or impeachment evidence? How about the unrecorded statement? As the prosecutor, are you required to disclose favorable evidence that is unrecorded?

In 2007, the above hypothetical case was partly answered by the Second Circuit case *United States v. Rodriguez*.[8] In *Rodriguez*, the Second Circuit held that the government's obligations under *Brady* do not require the government to record witness statements; however, the prosecution is required to disclose *Brady* material for the purpose of seeking fairness and truth.[9] Thus, the *Brady* obligation to provide favorable evidence, even if unrecorded, arises because it would be unfair to the defendant for the trial to be conducted without informing the defendant of such information, and not producing such evidence might cast doubt on the reliability of the verdict.[10]

While the *Brady* rule mandates specific prosecutorial disclosure, it is not a "blank check" with which the defendant can make unreasonable demands. Prosecutorial non-disclosure does not violate due process when the undisclosed information is already either in the possession of the defendant or when the defendant, using reasonable diligence, has access to the information through other channels.[11] The defense does not have a constitutional right to search through the prosecution's entire case file.[12]

---

[7] *Kyles*, 514 U.S. at 437.

[8] United States v. Rodriguez, 496 F.3d 221 (2d Cir. 2007).

[9] *Id.* at 225.

[10] *Id.* at 226.

[11] United States v. Whitehead, 176 F.3d 1030, 1036 (8th Cir. 1999). *See also* United States v. Ladoucer, 573 F.3d 628 (8th Cir. 2009).

[12] Giglio v. United States, 405 U.S. 150 (1972).

Moreover, legal privileges, such as doctor-patient privileges, are still maintained. Finally, the prosecution's trial strategy and work-product (material prepared for trial by the attorney and those working directly under the attorney's direction) are also not discoverable. Work product includes the attorney's thoughts about a case, development of a case theory, evaluation of the credibility of witnesses, evaluation of the strength of the case, position on case settlement, or jury selection strategy. Neither side is entitled to discover work-product at any time.

B. MATERIALITY AND AGGREGATION

The Supreme Court has required *Brady* disclosure to involve only evidence that is material.[13] When determining materiality, appellate courts analyze how the undisclosed evidence would have affected a verdict of guilt or the form or degree of punishment. In *United States v. Bagley*, the Court held that "evidence is material only if there is a reasonable probability that, had the evidence been disclosed to the defense, the result of the proceeding would have been different."[14] Reasonable probability is not as low a standard as the preponderance of the evidence standard, but, instead, is "a probability sufficient to undermine confidence in the outcome."[15] Another way to look at reasonable probability is whether the absence of the undisclosed *Brady* material resulted in an unfair trial, such that the underlying verdict is not "worthy of confidence."[16]

What if the prosecution fails to disclose *Brady* or *Giglio* material? The Court held in *Bagley* that when courts decide what evidence must be disclosed, they must consider the cumulative impact of all undisclosed favorable evidence and how it relates to other evidence presented in trial.[17] Even if the evidence individually fails to meet the "reasonable probability" test, *Brady* will still be violated if the aggregate impact of *all* the undisclosed favorable evidence undermines confidence in the outcome of the trial.[18] If, however, the evidence against the defendant is overwhelming, then the materiality of the undisclosed favorable evidence will be less significant as it is less likely to undermine confidence in the outcome. It should be noted that this standard of appellate review should not interfere with the prosecution's ethical duty to disclose all potentially favorable evidence in a timely manner. The practical aspect of whether a conviction is likely to get reversed is a separate concern from the ethical duty binding counsel to comply with discovery rules.

When determining materiality, courts not only look at factual matters, but to rules and statutes as well. For example, in *Wood v. Bartholomew*, the prosecutorial team did not disclose a polygraph test of

---

[13] Brady v. Maryland, 373 U.S. 83, 87 (1963).

[14] United States v. Bagley, 473 U.S. 667, 682 (1985).

[15] *Id.*

[16] Kyles v. Whitley, 514 U.S. 419, 434 (1995).

[17] *Bagley*, 473 U.S. at 700.

[18] *Id.* at 682–83.

one of the witnesses that showed he might have given deceptive answers.[19] The Court held, however, that it did not rise to the level of "reasonable probability" to be deemed material because polygraph tests were not permitted under state law for substantive or impeachment purposes.[20] Thus, the Court found that there was no *Brady* violation since the result of the trial would probably not have been different had the prosecution disclosed the polygraph test. This is known as the "harmless error standard." Be that as it may, the Second Circuit in *United States v. Gil* held that favorable evidence required to be disclosed need not be admissible in court if it could still be used for impeachment purposes or reasonably lead to admissible evidence.[21] When in doubt as to whether information is material, prosecutors should err on the side of disclosure.

CHART 7.1
Forms of **Brady** *Suppression*

Evidence Suppressed in *Brady* Context	
Prosecution	Prosecution fails to provide material favorable evidence
Government Agencies	Prosecution fails to learn of material favorable evidence from other government agencies or fails to provide such evidence to defendant
Time	Prosecution fails to disclose material favorable evidence at a time defense "can not effectively use at trial"

C. TIMING OF DISCOVERY

Brady and subsequent cases have not provided specific timing guidelines regarding disclosure. The general standard is that the disclosure must be made in time for the defense to efficiently use it at trial, or it will be deemed prejudicial to the defendant and will result in a *Brady* violation. The courts, both state and federal, have varied their approach to the question of timing. Some courts have chosen not to impose any specific time restrictions for disclosure, and these courts will usually permit *Brady* disclosures late in the process unless prejudice is shown.[22] In contrast, other courts have stringent requirements pertaining to timing requirements for the production of discovery. Here are some examples of these requirements as they pertain to certain states and districts:

---

[19] Wood v. Bartholomew, 516 U.S. 1, 4 (1995).

[20] *Id.* at 5.

[21] United States v. Gil, 297 F.3d 93, 104 (2d Cir. 2002).

[22] *See Gil*, 297 F.3d at 95–108 (finding that prosecution turning over exculpatory evidence two business days before trial ineffective and would be treated as suppressed evidence).

CHART 7.2
Sample Jurisdictional Disclosure Time Requirements

State	Disclosure Period
Massachusetts	At or prior to the pretrial conference[23]
New York	Within 15 days after service of discovery request[24]
California	No later than 30 days prior to the trial[25]

Finally, the *Brady* duty is a continuing one. If, during the trial, the prosecution team learns of any exculpatory evidence or impeachable evidence favorable to the defendant, then the prosecution has the duty to disclose this evidence to the defendant.[26] The law, however, is unsettled with regard to post-conviction evidence that comes to light. If the prosecutor becomes aware of exculpatory evidence post-conviction, it is unclear if he must notify the defendant with regard to such material.[27] On the other hand, the prosecution has an ethical duty that obligates him to seek justice, and thus disclosure of any such exculpatory materials should be made.[28]

D. DEFENDANT GUILTY PLEAS

Brady disclosure is required to ensure a fair trial, but is disclosure required during plea agreements for the defendant? In *United States v. Ruiz*, the Supreme Court held that the Due Process Clause does not require the government to disclose impeachment evidence (evidence that can be used to challenge the credibility of a witness) at the time of a defendant's guilty plea.[29] Although providing impeachment material is necessary for a fair trial, guilty pleas can, nonetheless, be considered voluntary without it.[30]

In *Ruiz*, it was held that a plea agreement offered in exchange for the defendant waiving impeachment evidence was also not a violation of the Constitution. It is possible for the prosecution to ask, as part of a plea agreement, certain waivers of defendants' rights. The Court held that in respect to a defendant's awareness of relevant circumstances, the Constitution does not require complete knowledge of such facts, but permits a court to accept a guilty plea with its accompanying waiver of various constitutional rights.[31]

---

[23] MASS. R. CRIM. P. 14(1)(A).

[24] N.Y. CRIM. PROC. LAW § 240.80(3) (Consol. 2010).

[25] CAL. PENAL CODE § 1054.7 (Deering 2012).

[26] FED. R. CRIM. P 16(c).

[27] For further discussion regarding the post conviction duties, see Fred C. Zacharias, *The Role of Prosecutors in Serving Justice After Convictions*, 58 VAND. L. REV. 171 (2005).

[28] MODEL RULES OF PROF'L CONDUCT R. 3.8(d).

[29] United States v. Ruiz, 536 U.S. 622 (2002).

[30] *Id.* at 623.

[31] *Id.* at 630.

HYPO: *Exploring Guilty Plea Disclosure*

Thomas, a gifted musician, was accused of stealing five instruments from a local shop. After stealing the instruments, he went home and slept. His roommate, Colin came home and saw the instruments scattered in their living room. Assuming the instruments were stolen, Colin moved out, called the police, and never spoke to Thomas again.

During a preliminary meeting, the prosecution offered Thomas a deal in exchange for a guilty plea. The prosecution, in turn, was willing to recommend that the court reduce his sentence. Although Thomas was hesitant at first, the prosecution informed him that their key witness was Colin. Somewhat paranoid, Thomas was immediately more willing to accept the offer and agreed to plead guilty.

The prosecution did not tell Thomas that one week after moving out, Colin himself was arrested for felony drug possession and the prosecutor offered him a reduction to a misdemeanor in exchange for his testimony against Thomas. Were Thomas's constitutional rights violated?

Although not required to disclose impeachment evidence during plea negotiations, the courts may analyze non-disclosure as a factor to be considered when determining whether or not the defendant "knowingly and voluntarily" pled guilty. Indeed, the defendant may possibly have a *stronger* claim that he did not enter a valid guilty plea if the prosecution did not disclose the favorable evidence to the defendant. Nevertheless, many scholars and attorneys are disturbed by the fact that plea bargaining is such an extensive part of the adversarial system, yet the prosecution is held to reduced discovery requirements when settling cases than the standards by which it would be held to at trial.[32] Certainly, such criticism is not unwarranted.

E. PRESERVATION OF EVIDENCE: GOOD FAITH AND BAD FAITH

The Supreme Court distinguishes the duty to disclose favorable evidence that is material, from the duty to preserve evidence that is of an unknown nature under the Due Process Clause, and based upon the holding in *California v. Trombetta*.[33] In *Trombetta*, the Court carefully addressed the issues regarding unpreserved evidence when the nature of such evidence is unknown. Since the Court is hesitant to make constitutional rules based on evidence when the contents are unknown and possibly disputed,[34] the holding in *Trombetta* limited preservation requirements to those that are expected to play a role in the suspect's defense.[35] The evidence must have an exculpatory value that was apparent *before* it was

---

[32] For a general discussion critiquing criminal discovery and impeachment evidence during plea negotiations, see R. Michael Cassidy, *Plea Bargaining, Discovery, and the Intractable Problem of Impeachment Disclosures*, 64 VAND. L. REV. 1429 (2011).

[33] 467 U.S. 479 (1984).

[34] *Id.* at 488–89.

[35] *Id.* at 488.

destroyed, and it must also be of a type that would prevent the defendant from obtaining comparable evidence by other reasonably available means.[36]

In *Arizona v. Youngblood*, the Court elaborated on *Trombetta* and held that a defendant must show bad faith on the part of the government for the defendant's due process rights to have been violated.[37] Negligence on the part of the state is insufficient.[38] If the defendant claims a *Trombetta-Youngblood* violation, courts will look at the police preservation practices, actual procedures that minimize the likelihood that evidence was exculpatory, as well as seeing if there are alternative means by which the defendant might demonstrate his innocence.[39]

HYPO: *Oceana v. Rickshaw*

Police arrested Adam Rickshaw for drug possession while patrolling the neighborhood of West Oceana. Undercover Agent Carlisle noticed Rickshaw on a street corner talking to three people individually and passing them each white baggies as they, in turn, handed over cash. Agent Carlisle approached Rickshaw and arrested him. When frisked, Agent Carlisle noticed four baggies in his right pocket containing crack cocaine. After Agent Carlisle called for backup, he kept the baggies on the front passenger seat of his car and put Rickshaw in the back.

When backup arrived, they took Rickshaw from Agent Carlisle's car to their own and went back to the police department. While Agent Carlisle was talking to witnesses, it turned out that the police car windows were open. When he came back, Agent Carlisle noticed that the baggies of drugs were no longer on the front passenger seat but had been stolen.

As the defense attorney for Rickshaw, is it likely that the destruction of the bags of evidence would be ruled to be a violation of Rickshaw's due process rights? What would you argue if you were the prosecutor?

CHART 7.3
Constitutional Discovery

Cases	Rule
Brady-Giglio	Prosecution must disclose exculpatory and impeachment evidence of accused that is material to either guilt or punishment
Agurs	Prosecution's duty to disclose exists even if defendant does not request favorable evidence.
Kyles	Prosecution has affirmative duty to learn of favorable evidence from other government agencies.
Bagley	Evidence is material only if there is a reasonable probability that, had the evidence been disclosed to the defense, the result of the proceeding would have been different.
Kyles	Undisclosed suppressed evidence can be analyzed cumulatively to see whether, if disclosed, the result of the proceeding would have been different.

---

[36] *Id.* at 479–480.

[37] Arizona v. Youngblood, 488 U.S. 51 (1988).

[38] *Id.* at 58.

[39] *Id.* at 56.

Giglio	In the *Brady* context, there is no distinction between impeachment and exculpatory evidence.
Ruiz	Prior to a plea bargain agreement, prosecution need not disclose impeachment evidence.
Trombetta-Youngblood	With regards to preservation of evidence, defense must show bad faith on the part of the government for the destruction of evidence to be a due process violation.

STATUTORILY MANDATED DISCOVERY RULES

A. JURISDICTIONAL RULES: LIMITED JURISDICTIONS AND OPEN-FILE STATES

The Supreme Court, through *Brady* and its progeny, has established mandatory disclosure rules for criminal discovery; however, every jurisdiction has statutes and rules that further govern discovery. In fact, states often allow for broader discovery than the minimum mandated in *Brady*. It follows, then, that the prudent lawyer should always take the time to fully familiarize himself with the discovery rules of his particular jurisdiction.

Some state courts and the federal courts provide limited discovery beyond *Brady*. Some examples of materials discoverable aside from *Brady* material in these "limited" discovery jurisdictions include disclosure of a defendant's statements and criminal record, witness statements, and expert reports.[40] On the other end of discovery rules, the "open-file" states provide very broad discovery. In Florida, for example, if the defense files a notice of discovery, then the defendant must be provided with any and all information regarding witnesses, even if some of the witnesses will not be called to testify at trial.[41] The Florida rules also enable the court to prohibit the state from introducing into evidence any of the material not disclosed but required by the statute.[42] Most of the states have discovery rules that rest somewhere between "limited" and "open-file" jurisdictions.

B. DEFENSE DISCLOSURE

1. Defense Notices and Reciprocal Agreements

Many statutes and rules require defendants to provide disclosure as well. Notices involving alibis, insanity pleas, or the presentation of special evidence, are examples of disclosures that most states and the Federal Rules require. Indeed, over the past thirty years, reciprocal disclosure agreements have emerged in the majority of courts. "Notice-of-alibi" statutes, for example, require the defense to give notice to the government when they intend to provide an alibi.[43] Moreover, in *Williams v. Florida*, the Supreme Court held that notice-of-alibi statutes do not violate the Fifth Amendment because the prosecution may request a continuance to seek rebuttal evidence should an alibi be provided at trial.[44]

---

[40] FED. R. CRIM. P. 16(a), 26.2.

[41] FLA. R. CRIM. P. 3.220.

[42] FLA. R. CRIM. P. 3.220(b)(3).

[43] *See* FED. R. CRIM. P. 12.1.

[44] Williams v. Florida, 399 U.S. 78, 85 (1970).

Insanity and alibi plea notices remain a valid disclosure requirement; however, two years after *Williams* was decided, the Supreme Court conditioned these notices upon reciprocity of disclosures. In *Wardius v. Oregon*, for example, the Supreme Court held that defendants must have equal discovery opportunities before the prosecution can obtain discovery material from them.[45] Distinguishing Oregon's "one-way-street" discovery rules from Florida's discovery statute, the Court found that Florida's notice-of-alibi, validated in *Williams*, is carefully "hedged with reciprocal duties requiring state disclosure to the defendant."[46] Thus, in pursuit of truth and fairness in the criminal trial, if the defense is required to disclose material, then the prosecution must be required to disclose material as well.

Reciprocal disclosure requirements are statutes that allow the prosecution to request certain types of disclosure from the defendant, and are often triggered when the defendant requests material from the prosecution. How effective are such rules? If the defendant fails to disclose materials under reciprocal disclosure agreements, then the courts may preclude the defense from using such evidence in court. In *Taylor v. Illinois*, for example, the Court found that preclusion of evidence based on a discovery statute violation was not a violation of the Compulsory Process Clause of the Sixth Amendment.[47] The Compulsory Process Clause is not automatic and must be affirmatively employed by the defendant.[48] The Sixth Amendment also does not give defense counsel the right to present testimony free from the legitimate demands of the adversarial system. For example, the defendant cannot testify without being subjected to cross-examination.[49] The adversarial system cannot function properly without adherence to procedural rules, including those pertaining to discovery.[50] The Court concluded that if a party willfully fails to comply with discovery rules and is motivated by a desire to hamper opposing counsel's cross-examination tools and rebuttal evidence, then it would be consistent with the purpose of the Compulsory Process Clause to simply exclude the witness's testimony.[51] It should also be noted, however, that reciprocity rules do not apply to situations involving non-testimonial evidence. This means that the prosecution and law enforcement can request blood samples, handwriting samples, fingerprints and the like from the accused, without violating reciprocity rules.[52]

2. Notice of Offering and Specific Evidence

There are also particular rules that govern notice and hearings when certain types of evidence are to be presented. The Supreme Court held in *Michigan v. Lucas* that there is no per se violation of the defendant's Sixth Amendment rights when evidence is precluded as a sanction for violating special

---

[45] Wardius v. Oregon, 412 U.S. 470 (1973).

[46] *Id.* at 474.

[47] Taylor v. Illinois, 484 U.S. 400 (1988).

[48] *Id.* at 410.

[49] *Id.* at 411–12.

[50] *Id.* at 411.

[51] *Id.* at 415.

[52] Schmerber v. California, 384 U.S. 757 (1966).

evidence notice and hearing requirements.[53] As part of their rape shield statute, for example, Michigan required the defense to file a written motion and offer of proof within ten days after arraignment, if the defense intended to present evidence at trial that the alleged rape victim had previously engaged in sexual conduct with the defendant.[54] At no time did the defendant, Lucas, who allegedly raped his former girlfriend, provide a written notice or offer of proof.[55] The Michigan Court of Appeals held that the trial court violated the Sixth Amendment by precluding the evidence.[56] The Supreme Court, however, disagreed and held that although the statute implicates the Sixth Amendment, (since it prevents the defendant from presenting probative evidence) legitimate interests in criminal trials may preclude such evidence from being presented without necessarily violating the Sixth Amendment.[57] The case was remanded to the Michigan courts to determine the validity of the preclusion and whether or not the specific preclusion in *Lucas* violated the Sixth Amendment.

In much the same way that *Brady* and its progeny redefined the disclosure duties of the prosecution, the Supreme Court has provided the contours of modern criminal defense discovery and disclosure through *Williams*, *Wardius*, *Taylor*, and *Lucas*. In *Williams*, the Supreme Court held that pretrial procedures and deadlines are nothing new for counsel, and that the prudent defendant should be mindful of pretrial notice requirements. In *Wardius*, fairness in pretrial discovery requires statutes to include reciprocity of disclosure if the defendant is to disclose evidence to the prosecution. In *Taylor*, counsel are instructed that willful violation of discovery requirements and ambushing opposing parties through surprise witnesses are no longer a valid tactic without the threat of preclusion of testimony. Finally, *Lucas* establishes that even specific evidence to be presented may require notice and approval by the court prior to being admitted in trial. Thus. the criminal trial is no longer a covert "poker game in which players enjoy an absolute right" to conceal their cards until played,[58] but has been redefined to consider such legitimate and critical interests of the adversarial system as fairness and truth.

C. PROSECUTION DISCLOSURE

Under the Federal Rules of Criminal Procedure, the defendant can make a request to the government for discovery, at which point the prosecution is required to turn over any statements made by the defendant that are relevant; these include statements that are written, recorded, or made by the defendant during an interrogation or given to an individual that the defendant knew was a government agent.[59] On its face, this might seem generous; however, in reality, it is restrictive. A statement that is unrecorded or made to an undercover agent remains undiscoverable under such a rule. Most states,

---

[53] Michigan v. Lucas, 500 U.S. 145 (1991).

[54] *Id.* at 146–47.

[55] *Id.* at 146.

[56] *Id.* at 151.

[57] *Id.*

[58] *Id.* at 150.

[59] FED. R. CRIM. P. 16(a)(1).

however, allow for enhanced discovery with regards to defendant statements. In California, all non-privileged defendant statements are discoverable.[60] In contrast, in *Booker v. State*, the Court of Appeals of Indiana held that a defendant's oral statement given to a police officer did not have to be disclosed.[61] In sum, the rules vary widely among the states and attorneys should adjust their strategies accordingly.

1. Witness Statements

As mentioned above, sometimes there exist reciprocal disclosure requirements and if this is the case, then at the time the defense or prosecution request materials for discovery, the other side will have to reciprocate. For example, in many jurisdictions where the defense is required to turn over their witness statements, the prosecution must do the same. In fact, most state courts require that the defense disclose their witness lists and their corresponding recorded statements. Some states, Oklahoma for example, even require a summary of an oral statement.[62] In California, by contrast, the prosecution must disclose witnesses they intend to call at trial.[63] Further, California requires that both the prosecution and defense must, within reason, also disclose the whereabouts of witnesses.[64] If, however, a specific factual showing can be made demonstrating that disclosing witnesses' whereabouts will place them in danger, then their location need not be revealed.[65] And again, in those jurisdictions in which the defense is required to turn over their witness lists, the prosecution will likely be required to do the same.[66]

2. Reports and Statements

Some states also allow the defense access to all police reports related to the case,[67] while other states only allow for partial discovery of such reports. Either way, even in jurisdictions in which the defense is able to inspect a police report, this does not mean that the police will have written down or included all the materially exculpatory evidence they became aware of at the scene of the crime in their report. For example, in one case, a woman in Oregon was charged with driving under the influence of intoxicants. Two officers arrived at the scene, one wrote the report, and another interviewed a witness but did not write down the witness's statement in the report. That witness was later called to testify at trial, the woman was convicted, and her attorney objected by arguing that there was a discovery violation. The district attorney had notified defense counsel regarding the witness as soon as she became aware of his existence, but this was the night before the trial. The Supreme Court of Oregon found no violation, reasoning that while the statute imposes obligations on the prosecution, it does not impose an obligation

---

[60] CAL. PENAL CODE § 1054.1(b) (Deering 2012).

[61] Booker v. State, 903 N.E.2d 502, 505 (Ind. Ct. App. 2009).

[62] OKLA. STAT. ANN. tit. 22, § 2002 (B)(1)(a) (West 2012).

[63] Izazaga v. Superior Court, 815 P.2d 304 (Cal. 1991).

[64] *In re* Littlefied, 851 P.2d 42 (Cal. 1995).

[65] Reid v. Superior Court, 64 Cal. Rptr. 2d 714 (Cal. Ct. App. 1997).

[66] Nor does this requirement violate any Fifth Amendment right against self-incrimination. United States v. Nobles, 422 U.S. 225 (1975).

[67] *E.g.*, ARIZ. R. CRIM. P. 15.1(b)

on the police.[68] Lastly, some states do not allow the discovery of police reports by classifying them, in whole or in part, as work-product.[69]

In contrast, expert reports are usually open for discovery by both the prosecution and the defense. This means that both sides will often have to notify each other of the names of their experts and their reports; however, this does not necessarily mean that if an expert's testimony goes beyond the report, that there will be a violation. For example, in Kentucky, an expert for the defense submitted his report regarding the analysis of DNA, but did not state in that report that he would be criticizing the methodology of the prosecution's DNA expert. The Supreme Court of Kentucky held that the defense expert was not confined to the four corners of his report.[70]

Of course, as discussed in Chapter 1, prosecutors and defense attorneys are officers of the court and have a duty to conduct themselves at all times with integrity. Lawyers should not be devious nor should they ever "sandbag" opposing counsel by disclosing evidence for the first time once the trial is underway and it is too late to investigate the information. Instead, prosecutors should strive to seek justice and not to obtain convictions at any cost. A crucial aspect of ensuring that the defendant receives a fair trial is for the prosecutor to timely disclose exculpatory evidence and other material evidence to the defense. Prosecutors who do not comply with discovery rules are inviting the wrath of the judge.

GENERAL STRATEGY

A. INFORMAL DISCOVERY MEETINGS

Criminal discovery is governed by extensive constitutional and jurisdictional rules. While it is imperative to be aware of the applicable discovery rules, the most effective approach to criminal discovery is typically for defense counsel and the prosecution to confer informally. Not only are informal meetings permitted by the courts, they are encouraged as they clear court time and allow the courts to focus on specific discovery disputes.[71] During the informal meetings, opposing counsel should discuss the discovery material to be disclosed. The prosecution should provide available *Brady* and *Giglio* material. The defense may also want to provide notices of certain defenses or presentation at this time. Depending on the jurisdiction, defense counsel may want to request that more discovery material be made available to them. If such material is requested, there may be reciprocal discovery agreements, and the prosecution may then also ask for certain discovery material.

Once the meeting has occurred, a discovery hearing date should be set. Both parties should inform the court if there are any discovery disputes. In this way, counsel can show what disclosure the applicable statutes and constitutional laws allow or require, and the court can make its rulings accordingly. It also provides an opportunity for the disputes to be on the record, in case subsequent

---

[68] State v. Divito, 5 P.3d 1103, 1107 (Or. 2000).

[69] *See, e.g.*, State v. Coe, 684 P.2d 668 (Wash. 1984).

[70] Jones v. Commonwealth, 237 S.W.3d 153 (Ky. 2007).

[71] *See* CAL. PENAL CODE § 1054 (Deering 2012).

appeals are filed. The court should also be informed of the materials already provided and agreed upon for future disclosure. In this way, if there are any subsequent disputes, the agreed upon disclosures are on the record. It is typically much more advantageous for both sides to conduct discovery informally. The court will appreciate that the attorneys are not wasting valuable court time, and this will keep costs, appearances, and paperwork to a minimum. Further, judges appreciate when lawyers can resolve issues such as discovery without being acrimonious. Of course, while the trial itself often resembles a battle, it benefits both sides if the pretrial conferences, including discovery meetings, are calm and fruitful. Advocates should keep in mind that the ultimate goal is to seek justice. Being forthright with discovery and not playing games or skirting the rules is not only ethical, but it is also a more practical avenue by which to get to the truth and obtain a fair result for both sides.

B. WORK PRODUCT SEPARATION

When interviewing potential witnesses, the prosecution, defense counsel, and those working immediately under them should be mindful of how they memorialize witness interviews. In *Hickman v. Taylor*, the Supreme Court held that work product is generally exempt from discovery in civil litigation.[72] In *United States v. Nobles*, that exemption was also held to apply in criminal cases.[73] There, the Court explained that "[a]lthough the work-product doctrine most frequently is asserted as a bar to discovery in civil litigation, its role in assuring the proper functioning of the criminal justice system is even more vital. There is an interest that both society and the accused obtain a fair and accurate resolution of the question of guilt or innocence, and this demands that adequate safeguards assure the thorough preparation and presentation of both sides of the case."[74] It should be noted, however, that the doctrine is not absolute and can be waived.[75] Since work product is generally privileged, such materials should be separated from the actual witness statement. In this way, the opinions, strategies, and tactics of the prosecution or defense will be protected and not disclosed along with the statement of the witness. One way to do this is to take notes that split the work product and the witness statement. Another way would be to split the files or notes into "work product" and "statement" files.

CHART 7.6
Work Product Statement Split

Work Product	Statement
The attorney's impression of the witness' statement and demeanor.	The actual witness' statements.

---

[72] Hickman v. Taylor, 329 U.S. 495 (1947).

[73] United States v. Nobles, 422 U.S. 225 (1975).

[74] *Id.* at 238.

[75] *Id.* at 239.

PROSECUTORIAL STRATEGY AND ETHICS

Prosecutorial ethics is at the core of discovery. Proper discovery, for the most part, relies on the judgment of the prosecutor. While *Brady* clearly established that the prosecution must disclose favorable evidence that is materially relevant to guilt or punishment, it is the prosecution who must determine before trial what evidence may or may not be *Brady* material. This duty has led many to criticize the rules that govern criminal discovery. Many feel that it is an area in which the prosecution bends the rules and strategizes in order to classify evidence as non-*Brady*, and thereby keep it out of the hands of the defense.[76] Prosecutors should, however, "seek justice rather than victory."[77] Because "*Brady* depends upon the integrity, good faith, and professionalism of the prosecutor for its effectiveness," ethical concerns are paramount in this area of litigation.[78]

There are other practical reasons why prosecutors should not play games and should, instead, disclose required materials in a timely manner. Failure to disclose could result in a new trial, and delayed disclosure could result in the evidence being excluded or the trial being delayed. Since it is sometimes difficult to predict the materiality of a certain piece of evidence from the outset of trial, the Supreme Court has indicated that "the prudent prosecutor will resolve doubtful questions in favor of disclosure."[79] While disclosing such evidence may seem unfavorable to the prosecutor's case, it is critical to remember the role of a prosecutor. A prosecutor's job is not to try to obtain a guilty verdict for every possible defendant who is charged with a crime. There are many falsely accused defendants, and disclosing exculpatory evidence justifies the trust placed in prosecutors as officers of the court seeking justice.[80] As the Supreme Court in *Banks v. Dretke* stated, there is a "special role played by the American prosecutor in the search for truth in criminal trials."[81]

Even though trials are sometimes referred to as "battles," it is critical to remember that trials are not games. The outcomes of criminal trials affect individuals' lives in myriad and significant ways. Prosecutors have an ethical duty to be forthcoming with discovery and should consistently remember that fairness and seeking justice mandates that all potentially exculpatory material and all information that requires disclosure be made available to the defense as soon as possible.

In 2006, three members of the men's lacrosse team at Duke University were falsely accused of rape. The Durham County District Attorney, Mike Nifong, drew attention for his overly zealous prosecution of the case and failure to disclose

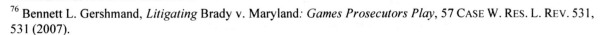

---

[76] Bennett L. Gershmand, *Litigating* Brady v. Maryland: *Games Prosecutors Play*, 57 CASE W. RES. L. REV. 531, 531 (2007).

[77] *Id.*

[78] *Id.* at 533.

[79] United States v. Agurs, 427 U.S. 97, 108 (1976).

[80] Kyles v. Whitley, 514 U.S. 419, 439 (1995).

[81] Banks v. Dretke, 540 U.S. 668, 696 (2004) (citation omitted).

exculpatory evidence in a timely manner, including inconsistencies in the accuser's testimony, solid alibis, and DNA evidence vindicating the players.

In 2007, Prosecutor Nifong was found guilty of fraud, dishonesty, deceit, and misrepresentation by the State Bar of North Carolina's disciplinary panel, and was subsequently disbarred. In 2007, he was also found guilty of criminal contempt for making false statements during criminal proceedings. The players later sued him, and he has since filed for bankruptcy.

DEFENSE STRATEGY AND ETHICS

Discovery presents a different set of obstacles for defense counsel. Whereas the prosecution must decide what should be disclosed, the defense has to be proactive. They must, without knowing exactly what investigation is taking place, anticipate the investigation and the possible materials being uncovered. Unlike the prosecution, which has more access to discovery tools such as grand jury subpoenas, forensics, and detectives, the defense generally relies on the prosecutor to turn over discovery that is favorable and material. The fact is that there will be times when one's opponent may not be ethical, so the defense must not simply sit back and wait for discovery materials to be disclosed. Instead, they can apply for protective orders (to prevent destruction or loss of evidence), hire private investigators, in addition to filing motions requesting disclosure to supplement that which they have received.

Because the defense has no general right to discovery, defense counsel should constantly consider whether or not sufficient investigation has taken place.[82] Even in "open-file" policy jurisdictions there is no guarantee that all the necessary investigation has been completed. The defense should, if they can afford to, conduct independent investigations and push the prosecution to fill in any gaps that might exist. It should be noted that if defense counsel makes a showing to the court that an investigator is needed, it is likely that the court will order the appointment of a defense investigator at no cost to the defendant. The defense should not rest easy even when they believe that they have been given ample discovery. If evidence is discovered after trial, the court must then ask if the defense should have known about it or should have, with reasonable diligence, found it themselves.[83] Accordingly, the prosecution is not responsible for such materials.

Although the defense should advocate zealously, in cases in which the allegations are highly sensitive they should be careful not to generate an adverse reaction by their efforts. For example, in the Jerry Sandusky case, the defense was criticized for their discovery tactics. Sandusky, a former assistant football coach, was arrested, charged, and convicted of the sexual abuse of young boys. It was reported

---

[82] Pennsylvania v. Ritchie, 480 U.S. 39 (1987).

[83] *Agurs*, 427 U.S. 97.

that Sandusky's attorney requested information related to the victims' pasts.[84] Some of the materials requested included school transcripts, cellphone records, Facebook account information, employment documents, medical records, Twitter records, etc. Lawyers for Sandusky's victims were quoted as saying that the requests were "an act of cowardice."[85] Some felt that the defense was attacking the victims, and because the alleged acts were the sexual abuse of children, that the defense needed to balance advocacy with ethics and tact. While the defense was likely trying to discredit the victims and suggest that the accusations were false, they should have been careful to avoid being viewed as needlessly insensitive. On the other hand, the defense is obligated to advocate on behalf of their client, and zealousness on behalf of their client must be their primary priority.

The defense has several strategic issues it must sort out with regard to discovery. First, as discussed throughout this chapter, some discovery material is required to be turned over by the prosecution. In addition to *Brady* material, the defense may have to notify the prosecution if they are mounting an affirmative defense, pleading insanity, or providing an alibi. Lastly, in some cases, and depending on the jurisdiction, the defense may be subject to reciprocity. In other words, if they request materials of the prosecution, they may have to reciprocate by turning over the same or similar materials to their opponents. The consequences of revealing discovery materials to the prosecution will have to be carefully weighed by defense counsel. They must balance the consequences of the revelation with their compliance with discovery requests, only then determining which course of action is in the best interest of their client. Of course, attorney-client confidential communications and privileged conversations are not discoverable.

In sum, in addition to the legal and ethical obligations of providing required discovery, counsel for the prosecution and defense would be wise to be mindful of protecting their reputations as reputable lawyers. Consistently providing full and timely discovery is one of the critical ways that litigators can establish a reputation among judges and the bar for being respectable trial attorneys.

COMPLIANCE FAILURE: REMEDIES AND SANCTIONS

Federal Rule of Criminal Procedure 16(d)(2) governs the actions to be taken after a discovery violation is committed: "If a party fails to comply with this rule, the court may: (A) order that party to permit the discovery or inspection; specify its time, place, and manner; and prescribe other just terms and conditions; (B) grant a continuance; (C) prohibit that party from introducing the undisclosed evidence; or (D) enter any other order that is just under the circumstances."[86] The court is given broad discretion on deciding how to remedy a violation and whether or not a sanction would be the appropriate step to take. If a discovery violation is made very early on in the pretrial stage, then a motion to compel disclosure is

---

[84] *Sandusky's Attorney Digging into Accusers' Pasts*, SI.COM (May 8, 2012, 5:23 PM), http://sportsillustrated.cnn.com/2012/football/ncaa/05/08/penn-state-abuse.ap/index.html.

[85] *Id.*

[86] FED. R. CRIM. P. 16(d)(2)

often the appropriate remedy. Discovery violations, however, can become increasingly more complicated if it is revealed just before trial or during trial that a party has failed to comply with the discovery request.

The court should not impose a sanction that is harsher than necessary to accomplish the goals of FRCP 16.[87] There are a number of factors to be considered in determining what sanction to impose for a discovery violation. Such factors are (1) reasons for a failure or delay and whether this was in bad faith, (2) prejudice to the opposing party,[88] and (3) feasibility of continuance. The defendant's remedy for the prosecution's discovery violation may hinge upon the stage of the proceedings when the violation is discovered. If a *Brady* violation is revealed following the completion of the preliminary examination, the court may choose to dismiss the charge or allegation to which the exculpatory evidence relates.[89] If the defendant has already entered a guilty plea due to his reliance on the absence of discovery material, then the defendant can withdraw his guilty plea.[90] If the *Brady* violation is discovered following the defendant's conviction, the appropriate remedy may be to set aside the conviction and order a new trial.[91] Therefore, the issue turns from one of remediation, to the consideration of whether or not the discovery violation prevented the defendant from receiving a fair trial.[92]

If the defense is the party that has incurred the discovery violation, the defense cannot argue that the Sixth Amendment creates an absolute bar to the preclusion of surprise testimony.[93] "The Sixth Amendment does not confer the right to present testimony free from the legitimate demands of the adversarial system; one cannot invoke the Sixth Amendment as a justification for presenting what might have been a half-truth."[94] Defense evidence may be excluded by the court if the court finds that the exclusion is necessary to maintain the integrity of the adversary process, uphold the interest in the fair and efficient administration of justice, or prevent the potential prejudice to the truth-determining function of the trial process.[95] Judicial opinions and statutory provisions, however, also recognize several other sanctions or remedies, including (1) a charge directing the jury to assume certain facts that might have been established through the non-disclosed material, (2) granting a mistrial, (3) holding in contempt the party responsible for the nondisclosure, and (4) dismissal of the prosecution.[96]

---

[87] United States v. Gee, 695 F.2d 1165, 1169 (9th Cir. 1983).

[88] While prejudice might be a factor, it is not a requirement when a party has made a willful violation of a discovery order. *See* United States v. Talbot, 51 F.3d 183, 187–88 (9th Cir. 1995); United States v. Garcia, 730 F. Supp. 2d 1159, 1167 (C.D. Cal. 2010).

[89] Stanton v. Superior Court, 239 Cal. Rptr. 328 (Cal. Ct. App. 1987); People v. MacKey, 221 Cal. Rptr. 405 (Cal. Ct. App. 1985).

[90] Sanchez v. United States, 50 F.3d 1448, 1453 (9th Cir. 1995).

[91] *See* People v. Robinson, 37 Cal. Rptr. 2d 183 (Cal. Ct. App. 1995).

[92] People v. Bowles, 129 Cal. Rptr. 3d 290 (Cal. Ct. App. 2011).

[93] Taylor v. Illinois, 484 U.S. 400, 410 (1988).

[94] *Id.* at 412–13.

[95] *Id.* at 414–15.

[96] *See, e.g.*, United States v. Carrigan, 804 F.2d 599, 603 (10th Cir. 1986) (discussing the trial court's ability to implement sanctions when certain discovery requirements are not met).

SUMMARY

Discovery, or the means by which attorneys gather information in order to mount their cases, comes in many forms and is governed by constitutional and state law. Discovery in criminal trials is much less formal and more limited than in civil cases, and while the prosecution is required to turn over evidence that is potentially materially exculpatory, nothing more is generally required of them. Most states, however, have additional rules that implicate both the prosecution and the defense. For example, some states require reciprocal discovery and because the rules are less developed for criminal discovery than other areas of the law, this is an area suited to many strategic possibilities. On the other hand, it is also an area in which ethics are extremely important, as this area of pretrial advocacy is easily subjected to sanctions. Moreover, the court has broad discretion in terms of how to remedy a failure to comply with a discovery order, and in some cases, a *Brady* violation can cause a conviction to be overturned.

CHECKLIST

✓ Discovery enables advocates to gather material that is used to formulate and then build case theories.

✓ The information acquired during the discovery process often uncovers information that may reveal important additional evidence, or even previously unknown witnesses.

✓ Discovery can take the form of written, recorded, or even electronically stored information.

✓ The discovery process can potentially span from the time of arrest until the commencement of trial.

✓ In a criminal case, discovery will typically be of a much more limited nature than what is found in civil cases. Criminal discovery is also often a much more informal process than its civil counterpart, and may take place as the result of nothing more than an oral request for information from either party.

✓ Discovery is an area of litigation in which attorneys, especially prosecutors, can find themselves subject to sanctions if they do not err on the side of disclosure.

✓ It is of great importance to remember that it is *always* considered unethical to hide information that should be disclosed to opposing counsel, and it is equally critical to remember that materials must be turned over in a timely fashion.

✓ The prosecution is required to disclose *Brady* material for the purpose of seeking fairness and truth in the adversarial process, and in order to insure that the defendant's trial be conducted with *all* favorable evidence having been disclosed to the defendant's counsel.

✓ During discovery, legal privileges are still maintained and the prosecution's trial strategy and work product are always *non*-discoverable.

✓ Every jurisdiction has statutes and rules that govern discovery and attorneys should always take the time to familiarize themselves with the discovery rules governing their particular jurisdiction.

✓ For defense counsel, discovery presents particular considerations as counsel must, without knowing exactly what investigation is taking place, anticipate the outcome of such an investigation and the possible materials being uncovered by their opponents.

✓ Defense counsel may be obligated to notify the prosecution if they are mounting an affirmative defense, pleading insanity, or providing an alibi and, depending upon the jurisdiction, might be subject to reciprocity in terms of any discovery disclosures.

CHAPTER 8
PRELIMINARY HEARINGS

"Let us watch well our beginnings and results will manage themselves."
–Alexander Clark

The preliminary hearing, also known as the preliminary examination, is a critical stage of the criminal justice process and is likely to be the first adversarial proceeding of the case. After the preliminary hearing, if the presiding judge decides that there is probable cause to support the charges, then the defendant is "bound over," or held to answer. A second arraignment then occurs, at which point, the original complaint is superseded by a document referred to as the "information," or by an indictment in the case of a grand jury proceeding. Even though the hearing is truly "preliminary," in the sense of laying the necessary groundwork for trial, it nevertheless represents a pivotal opportunity for both the prosecutor and defense attorney to learn more about their case.

A preliminary hearing serves primarily as a screening device, whereby the prosecution must show probable cause to bind the case over, and before the defendant is subjected to the pressures associated with a criminal prosecution. Another benefit is that taxpayers are spared the expense of frivolous or malicious criminal trials. Preliminary hearings, moreover, provide a preview of the case, which is instrumental in developing a case strategy as well as in formulating realistic case settlement goals.

The preliminary hearing should not be confused with the probable cause hearing, also known as a *Gerstein* hearing, at which incarcerated defendants are entitled to a probable cause determination by a judicial officer within forty-eight hours of a warrantless arrest.[1] Further discussion of the *Gerstein* probable cause hearing appears in Chapter 1.

WHAT IS A PRELIMINARY HEARING?

A preliminary hearing is a condensed version of a trial with a few notable differences. In fact, while a preliminary hearing is also an adversarial hearing conducted in court, it is more limited than a trial. First, the prosecution has a lower burden of proof than at trial. During a criminal trial, the prosecution has the burden of proving guilt "beyond a reasonable doubt." At a preliminary hearing, on the other hand, the prosecution need only show a "strong suspicion" that the alleged criminal activity has occurred and that the defendant is responsible for it. A "strong suspicion" standard is equivalent to the "probable cause" standard.

Second, the trier of fact is a judge because there is no right to a jury at the preliminary hearing stage. Third, the proceedings are not as extensive as would be expected at trial. Typically, there are no opening statements, only limited closing arguments, and both parties will usually not present all witnesses and evidence. Some testimony, such as the conclusion of a chemist, is often merely stipulated, rather than

---

[1] Gerstein v. Pugh, 420 U.S. 103, 122 (1975); County of Riverside v. McLaughlin, 500 U.S. 44, 56 (1991) (establishing that a forty-eight-hour period complies with the promptness standard of *Gerstein*).

proven by presenting witness testimony. It is not unusual for the defense to present no witnesses or affirmative defenses. As a result, a preliminary hearing is much shorter than a trial.

DEFENDANT'S RIGHT TO A PRELIMINARY HEARING

In *Hurtado*, the Supreme Court held that the Fifth Amendment right to a grand jury indictment did not apply to the states.[2] As previously discussed, the Court in *Gerstein* held that a non-adversarial *ex parte* procedure is a sufficient vehicle to make a probable cause determination to keep a defendant incarcerated following a warrantless arrest. Once a state chooses to provide preliminary hearings, however, then certain constitutional protections, such as the right to counsel, are triggered.[3]

In federal court, the Fifth Amendment requires screening by a grand jury in felony cases. Federal Rule of Criminal Procedure 5.1(a) states that the requirement of preliminary hearings in felony cases is rendered moot when there is already a grand jury indictment. Therefore, United States Attorneys almost always opt for the procedure of a hearing before a grand jury instead of a preliminary hearing. A comprehensive discussion of grand jury proceedings appears in Chapter 9. State jurisdictions vary considerably regarding whether they proceed by preliminary hearing or indictment.[4] The majority of states that provide the defendant with the right to a preliminary hearing specify that this right can only be lost by an express waiver. Whenever the defense attempts to waive the preliminary hearing in felony cases in these jurisdictions, prosecutors should ensure that the defendant receives an explanation of his right to a hearing and that both the defendant and his counsel make a clear and express waiver on the record. Some jurisdictions allow the prosecution to insist on a preliminary hearing, even if the defense waives this right. The most common reason for the prosecutor to demand a preliminary hearing would be to perpetuate testimony in order to preserve it as an exception to the hearsay rule if a witness becomes unavailable.[5]

The proceedings of a preliminary hearing are similar to that of a trial. The prosecuting authority, having the burden of proof, will start by eliciting relevant testimony from a series of witnesses. For each direct examination conducted by the prosecutor, the defense attorney will have an opportunity to cross-examine. Although the defendant's lawyer may mount a defense, this is not required. Once the defense has rested, both parties are given an opportunity to argue whether there is probable cause for each element of the charged offense(s). The judge will then decide whether probable cause exists for each charged crime. If so, then the judge will hold the defendant to answer to the charges, and the defendant will be bound over for trial. If not, the judge will dismiss the charges; if no charges remain, the judge will discharge the defendant. Since the constitutional prohibition against double jeopardy does not apply at

---

[2] Hurtado v. California, 110 U.S. 516, 534–35 (1884).

[3] Coleman v. Alabama, 399 U.S. 1, 9–10 (1970).

[4] United States v. Coley, 441 F.2d 1299, 1301 (5th Cir. 1971) ("Failure to hold a preliminary hearing, without more, does not amount to a violation of constitutional rights . . . .").

[5] Crawford v. Washington, 541 U.S. 36, 68 (2004); California v. Green, 399 U.S. 149, 165–66 (1970).

this stage of the case, the prosecutor may re-file charges if he did not receive the desired outcome at the preliminary hearing.

Probable cause, for the purposes of a preliminary hearing, means that reasonable grounds for believing the defendant's guilt exist. The Supreme Court has explained that probable cause is the equivalent of trustworthy information that would lead a reasonable person to believe that an offense has been committed, and that the defendant is the person responsible.[6] When determining whether there is a strong suspicion that the defendant committed the crime in question, the magistrate should view the evidence in the light most favorable to the prosecution.[7] Probable cause is the same standard of proof to which a grand jury is held when bringing an indictment and constitutes a far lower standard of proof than the reasonable doubt standard required for conviction at trial.

CHART 8.1
Criminal Standards of Proof

Reasonable Suspicion	• Amounts to specific and articulable facts, not a mere guess, hunch, or gut instinct • Necessary for a "*Terry* frisk"[8]
Probable Cause	• Higher standard than reasonable suspicion • Standard required for an officer to make an arrest or obtain search warrant • Equivalent to a "strong suspicion" standard for preliminary hearings • Refers to a state of facts that would lead a person of ordinary caution and prudence to believe and conscientiously entertain an honest and strong suspicion that the person arrested is guilty of the crime charged
Beyond a Reasonable Doubt	• No other logical explanation can be derived from the facts except that the defendant committed the crime; such is the only reasonable conclusion • Commonly referred to as an "abiding conviction"

In federal courts, defendants charged with felonies are entitled to either a grand jury hearing or preliminary hearing, usually at the prosecutor's discretion.[9] In some instances, defendants charged with non-petty misdemeanors may also be entitled to a grand jury hearing or a preliminary hearing.[10] In contrast, defendants charged with misdemeanor crimes are not normally entitled to a preliminary hearing in state courts. Attorneys should research the rules in their jurisdiction to learn which misdemeanor crimes, if any, entitle the defendant to a preliminary hearing.

---

[6] Brinegar v. United States, 338 U.S. 160, 175–76 (1949).

[7] Williams v. Kobel, 789 F.2d 463, 468–69 (7th Cir. 1986). *See also* People v. Holder, 658 P.2d 870, 871–72 (Colo. 1983).

[8] Terry v. Ohio, 392 U.S. 1, 27 (1968).

[9] United States v. Coley, 441 F.2d 1299, 1301 (5th Cir. 1971) ("submission of an accused's case directly to a grand jury, even absent a preliminary examination, is not constitutionally impermissible").

[10] FED. R. CRIM. P. 5.1.

A. TIMING REQUIREMENTS

The Sixth Amendment of the United States Constitution guarantees criminal defendants the right to a speedy trial. The purpose of the preliminary hearing and its timing requirement is to prevent unreasonably long periods of incarceration for criminal defendants prior to trial. Additionally, because of the stigma associated with felony charges, it would be unfair to force defendants to face these charges without demonstrating some merit to the allegations. An in-custody criminal defendant, therefore, has a right to a preliminary hearing within a reasonable time, not to exceed fourteen days after his initial appearance in court.[11] Out-of-custody defendants can also request a preliminary hearing, which must be held within twenty-one court days from the first court appearance. As with any court-timing requirement, defendants are permitted to waive this constraint and have their preliminary hearings outside the allotted timeframe if they choose. Waiving time for the preliminary hearing does not obligate defendants to waive their right to a speedy trial. By the same token, however, the prosecution is also entitled to have a case proceed to trial in a timely manner. Thus, even if the defense waives time for a preliminary hearing, it is impermissible for the defense to delay the case so long that it jeopardizes the prosecution's ability to meet its burden of proof. For instance, if the State's most important witness is elderly, ill, or fearful of testifying, then undue delays might prevent the prosecution from proceeding because of consequent witness unavailability.

B. JURISDICTION AND IDENTITY OF DEFENDANT

Besides presenting sufficient evidence for every element of each charged offense, the prosecuting authority must demonstrate that the jurisdiction requirement is met. In the federal criminal system, proper jurisdiction needs to be established in one of two ways. First, the alleged criminal activity can be a federal crime, such as tax evasion or bank robbery. Second, if not a federal crime, the alleged offense must take place on federal property, such as a post office or national park. In order to prove the requisite jurisdiction during a preliminary hearing, the prosecuting agency will typically lay the jurisdictional foundation through a law enforcement official or other qualified witnesses. For states, jurisdiction is established by identifying the relevant county in which the alleged crime has been committed. During the preliminary hearing, the prosecutor will usually ask a simple question such as, "Did this attack occur in the county of [X]?"

The prosecutor must also prove the identity of the defendant, specifically, that the defendant, present in the courtroom, is in fact the one responsible for the alleged crime. This is usually accomplished by asking a testifying witness who knows the suspect's identity and has seen him before whether the individual being prosecuted is in the courtroom. A prosecutor will also commonly ask the witness to point out the suspect in the courtroom and to describe briefly the clothing that the suspect is wearing at the time of the proceeding. Once a witness has identified the defendant, a prosecutor should ask the presiding judge to have the record reflect that the testifying witness has identified the defendant.

---

[11] FED R. CRIM. P. 5.1(c).

Since the stenographer's transcript serves as the official record of the preliminary proceedings, it is crucial to properly preserve this record in anticipation of trial, and a copy of the transcript will be made available to both parties. Any time a witness performs a material and relevant non-verbal act, such as identifying the defendant, or estimating dimensions or distances by physical demonstration, the attorney should attempt to express this non-verbal act in words in order to memorialize it. Doing so serves two significant purposes at the trial stage. First, should a case be appealed, the appeals court will have access only to the court reporter's records, which will then provide the sole account upon which the later court will base its judgment. Unless it is verbalized as part of the record, the physical demonstration, for all intents and purposes, never occurred. Second, at the initiative of the jury, a court reporter may read back testimony during deliberations. Because physical demonstrations may be no less relevant than actual testimony, it is important for both parties to make sure the record can serve as a complete and accurate basis for the jury's verdict.

1. Sample Court Identification of Defendant

Attorney: Mrs. Carter, is the man who attacked you on September 7th here in the courtroom today?

Witness: Yes, sir.

Attorney: Ma'am, can you please point to where he is sitting and tell us what he is wearing today?

Witness: Yes, he is sitting over there at counsel table wearing a blue jumpsuit.

Attorney: Thank you, ma'am. Your Honor, may the record reflect that the witness has pointed out the defendant, Joe Bradley, as the man who attacked her on September 7th.

Judge: The record will so reflect.

Attorney: Thank you, Your Honor. Mrs. Carter, after the defendant attacked you, what was going on in your mind?

C. SUBPOENA

A preliminary hearing subpoena operates similarly to a trial subpoena or grand jury subpoena. The subpoena, a written court order compelling either production of evidence or testimony from a specific individual, will specify the time, date, and location for the named individual to make a mandatory court appearance. For preliminary hearings, attorneys from both sides will want to serve each testifying witness with a subpoena and ensure that each subpoena is duly received.

PREPARATION FOR THE PRELIMINARY HEARING

Although a preliminary hearing is, in many ways, a condensed version of a trial, the standard of proof is lower, the testifying witnesses are fewer, and the time in court is considerably less. Even if not identical, some of a prosecutor's preparation for a preliminary hearing is also similar to that for a trial. The prosecutor must still subpoena the relevant witnesses, produce and elicit evidence, and make appropriate objections and arguments. Nevertheless, unique strategic considerations, different from those at trial, also arise for prosecutors and defense attorneys at the preliminary hearing. The following sections focus on strategic considerations to bear in mind during the preparation and performance of a preliminary hearing.

A. EVALUATING EVIDENCE AND WITNESSES

At this stage in the criminal justice process, the assigned prosecutor should have a case file containing all relevant documents needed for prosecution. For instance, in a felony vehicular manslaughter case in which the driver was impaired by alcohol, the prosecutor should have the toxicology reports, police narratives, results of the field sobriety test exercises, and any statements made by the defendant. In such a case, the likely witnesses to be subpoenaed for the trial are the arresting officers, criminal analyst, coroner, and any civilian witnesses. At the preliminary hearing, however, a prosecutor is unlikely to call all relevant witnesses for a number of reasons. First, since the objectives and burden of proof at a preliminary hearing are less demanding than at trial, all that the prosecutor must demonstrate to the presiding judge is that there exists probable cause to believe that the defendant has committed the charged offense. Second, because the preliminary hearing is not an end in itself, but rather a step towards trial or settlement, preparation and presentation of evidence are condensed. Lastly, prosecutors make a beneficial strategic decision to shield their witnesses from cross-examination.

From the opposing perspective, the defense attorney must also evaluate her own witnesses and evidence. All jurisdictions allow the defense to call witnesses at a preliminary hearing, although this right is rarely exercised. At this stage in the criminal justice process, the defense may not yet know what the most effective defense will be. Even if, in fact, defense counsel already does know, it is typically not advantageous to use the preliminary hearing to test out the presentation of witness testimony before the trial. Attempting to defeat charges at the preliminary hearing is normally not worth the risk of subjecting defense witnesses to cross-examination and giving the prosecutor an early opportunity to learn more about the defense's side of the case. Additionally, testimony offered at the preliminary hearing can be used to impeach witnesses at trial.[12] Not least of all, since the preliminary hearing serves as a screening device to show probable cause, it is highly likely that the judge will decide that, when witnesses' statements appear inconsistent with other evidence, their credibility should be determined by the fact finder at trial. Thus, as a general rule, the defense attorney should not call any witnesses to testify at the preliminary hearing. The exception to this rule is when the state's case is so weak that it will unlikely meet the low burden of probable cause; the defense attorney may then choose to present a defense in hopes of having the case dismissed. It should also be noted that, while defendants are allowed to present evidence that disproves an element of any charge, state jurisdictions differ as to whether defendants are

---

[12] Coleman v. Alabama, 399 U.S. 1, 9 (1970).

precluded at the preliminary hearing stage from producing an affirmative defense such as insanity or entrapment.[13]

B. EVALUATING THE OPPONENT'S STRENGTHS

In addition to evaluating the strength of their own evidence and witnesses at the preliminary hearing, both parties will gain a critical perspective on their case when they place themselves in their opponent's shoes. As discussed in Chapter 2, an effective case theory will target the shortcomings of the opponent's case. Thus, the preliminary hearing is an ideal opportunity to test out and revise case theories.

As a defense attorney, one will want to evaluate the strength of the prosecution's case. Are any elements of the offense in question? Are all the testifying witnesses credible? Is there an affirmative defense, such as self-defense, available? Is there a mistake of identity? Even if none of these options is available, defense attorneys can still attack allegations concerning the opportunity, intent, and especially motive of their client. At the trial stage, reasonable doubt can arise from a failure of the prosecution to prove a certain element. Reasonable doubt can also arise when jurors are unable to understand how the defendant sitting in front of them could have committed the alleged crimes. Similarly, judges at preliminary hearings might be influenced by the appearance and manner of the defendant in court.

TAKE NOTE

The defendant's physical appearance is an important matter, which defense attorneys often discuss with their clients. Defense attorneys will generally advise their clients to come to court dressed in their "Sunday best," or groomed in a way that makes them appear more innocent. There is reason to believe that the emphasis placed on appearance has been taken to new heights recently. The recent "nerd defense" phenomenon illustrates how extraneous and irrelevant factors can sometimes influence perceptions.[14] A 2008 study, conducted by the *American Journal of Forensic Psychology*, found that acquittals are made at a more frequent rate for defendants who wear glasses at their trial than for those who do not. The tactic, which usually occurs during violent cases, seeks to soften the image of the defendant and perplex jurors who are confronted with a "nerdy" defendant and heinous crimes. If attempts, such as having the defendant wear glasses, or cover up gang tattoos, are made to help a defendant appear less threatening, prosecutors should introduce photos (such as booking photos) to show the defendant's appearance on the day of the crime.

C. PREPARING FOR DIRECT EXAMINATION

At the preliminary hearing, the prosecutor will present evidence in the form of testimony given by a series of witnesses. During this direct examination, a prosecutor needs to establish three key elements:

---

[13] Jennings v. Superior Court, 428 P.2d 304, 306 (Cal. 1967) (allowing affirmative defense at preliminary hearing); State v. Altman, 482 P.2d 460 (Ariz. 1971) (determining that affirmative defense is not allowed at the preliminary hearing and should be resolved at trial).

[14] Michael J. Brown et al., *The Effects of Eyeglasses and Race on Juror Decisions Involving a Violent Crime*, 26 AM. J. FORENSIC PSYCHOL. 25 (2008).

jurisdiction, identity of the defendant, and the elements of the offenses charged.[15] To do so, a prosecutor will frame his questions in a way that directs witnesses to provide the necessary evidence. The following tips in this chapter provide a basic idea of how to create questions for direct examination at a preliminary hearing.

The chart below details a sample charged offense and the accompanying elements that must be proved. A common method prosecutors use to determine each element of the offense is to review the jury instructions for each charged offense. In crafting questions, the prosecutor should be able to pinpoint the specific facts that each witness will provide to satisfy each element of the offense. Consider the example below in which the alleged crime is grand theft.

CHART 8.2

Factors to Prove	Sources of Proof	Facts	Evidentiary Issues
Element #1: **Taking of Property**	Security Tapes, Eye-Witness Customer	As tapes and witness reveal, suspect took several pieces of jewelry and placed into handbag	Admissibility of tapes?
Element #2: **With Intent To Permanently Deprive Owner of Property**	Security Tapes, Store Owner, Eye-Witness Customer, Arresting Officer	Suspect left the store with store merchandise	N/A
Element #3: **Value is Worth > $950.00**	Store Owner	Price of the jewelry	N/A
Jurisdiction	Arresting Officer, Store Owner	Identifying that the store lies in the county of Oceana	N/A
Identification	Store Owner	Identified defendant as suspect	Could only identify suspect after watching the security tapes

The prosecutor should determine the witness testimony that can best establish the requisite jurisdiction for the court and the identification of the defendant. It is important to remember the audience at a preliminary hearing, where the presentation of evidence is directed towards a presiding magistrate or judge, and not towards a jury. Consequently, attorneys should avoid questions intended to tell a story or build emotion but should instead focus their questions solely on the facts. Accordingly, questions should

---

[15] Depending on the respective state rules, a prosecutor might also need to establish probable cause for any prior convictions, enhancements, and special circumstance allegations.

be concise, open-ended, and allow the witness to tell the story. As a common saying goes, when it comes to direct examination during preliminary hearings, "get in and get out." When in doubt as to what the next question should be, the attorney should simply ask: "What happened next?"

It takes time and experience for a prosecutor to develop his skills in choosing which witnesses to call and which evidence to present during a preliminary hearing. As previously discussed, a prosecutor will not want to call every witness and will aim to present just enough evidence to demonstrate to the court the requisite jurisdiction, identification of suspect, and each element of the offense(s) charged. The meeting of these requirements should guide the selection of witnesses and evidence to present at the hearing.

HYPO: *Oceana v. Shades*

Johnny Shades is charged with armed bank robbery. Assume that armed bank robbery elements are as follows:

1. Shades took money that was in the care, custody or possession of Ocean Bank from Ocean Bank employees while person(s) were present;
2. Shades used force and violence or intimidation;
3. Shades intentionally assaulted or put the life of a person in jeopardy by the use of a dangerous weapon or device while taking the money; and
4. The deposits of Ocean Bank were insured by the Federal Deposit Insurance Corporation. (FDIC).

The following is a list of potential witnesses who can be called at the preliminary hearing.

A. William Whitworth: Ocean Bank manager who was on duty the day of the robbery. Mr. Whitworth was in his office throughout the entire ordeal, and later reviewed the security tapes. The tapes reveal a man who appears to be in his thirties wearing a black hat, black sunglasses, blue jeans, and a grey sweatshirt. Mr. Whitworth is leaving on a vacation to Hawaii the following week.

B. Officer Roger McKenzie: Assigned police officer patrolling the City Courtyard; Ocean Bank is one of the several businesses located there. Officer McKenzie was the first officer to arrive on the scene and the only individual to witness the bank robber get into a silver Toyota Camry, license plate starting with #4AB, and drive off in great haste. He obtained witness statements from Ms. Evans, Mr. Cruz, Mr. Whitworth, and Mr. Sweeney.

C. Officer Renée Parker: 911 dispatcher who radioed to local police officers immediately following the bank robbery.

D. Officer Eric Mayberry: Arresting officer, Officer Mayberry, pulled over Shades, who was driving a silver Toyota Camry, license plate number 4ABX3010. Officer Mayberry found an unloaded, registered nine-millimeter pistol along with $2,400 in miscellaneous bills. Shades, 43, was wearing blue jeans, black sunglasses, and a grey sweatshirt. No other clothes were found in the vehicle.

E. Marie Evans: Bank teller who was approached by the bank robber. The bank robber passed Marie a note demanding all the money in her drawer or else. Marie handed the man $4300 in various bill amounts. Marie noticed a bulge in the front pouch of the bank robber's sweatshirt.

F. John Sweeney: One of two customers in the bank at the time of the robbery. He had a clear view of the bank robber from the time he entered the bank until he fled. He was reluctant to give any information to the police. Mr. Sweeney is genuinely nervous about the idea of testifying in court.

G. José Cruz: Ocean Bank customer who overheard demands made by the bank robber to Marie Evans. Mr. Cruz told the police that he believed his life was in danger. A native Spanish speaker, Mr. Cruz understands English very well but has trouble speaking the language. Mr. Cruz was once convicted of counterfeiting money.

Assume that you are the attorney on this case and consider the following questions you will need to answer prior to the start of the preliminary hearing:

- What is the standard of proof? Is it necessary or advisable to call more than one witness to prove an element of the offense?
- What is the risk to the prosecution of calling more than one witness to prove a particular element of the charged offense?
- What must the prosecutor prove in order to have the defendant held to answer for trial? Which witness or witnesses can prove the necessary elements of bank robbery?
- Is there any advantage to calling more witnesses than are necessary to demonstrate probable cause that the defendant committed the bank robbery?
- Which witnesses would you call for the preliminary hearing?

D. DIRECT EXAMINATION SAMPLE

Below is the transcript of a direct examination of an arresting officer at a preliminary hearing. It is brief but still accomplishes the three primary objectives of direct examination; it establishes the elements of the offense, the jurisdiction, and the defendant's identity.

Proceedings OFFICER PETER NASH The Witness, called for Direct Examination by the Prosecution, having declared and affirmed under the penalties of perjury to tell the truth, was examined and testified as follows: DIRECT EXAMINATION BY MR. MILLER	←Along with perjury, witnesses also face impeachment at trial.
Q: Good afternoon, Officer. Could you please state your name, spelling the last for the record. A: Peter Nash, N-A-S-H.	
Q: Mr. Nash, are you currently employed? A: Yes, I am a patrol officer for the County of Maliwood. **Q: How long have you been an officer there?** A: For the past 5 years. **Q: Were you on duty February 10th at 9:54 pm?** A: Yes, I was in my patrol car on Ocean Breeze Parkway at Sun Gas Station.	←See section on "Hearsay." In some jurisdictions, to use the hearsay exception, the officer must have 5 years of experience as a law enforcement official or have taken a requisite training course.
Q: At that time, what, if anything, did you observe? A: I noticed a Caucasian male, medium build, in a black sweatshirt and blue jeans tagging a wall at the gas station.	←Helps lay the necessary foundation for the identification of the suspect that will come later in the direct examination.
Q: Is that gas station located in Maliwood County? A: It is.	←Establishes the requisite jurisdiction. One question, one answer.
Q: What, if anything, did you do in response to observing this? A: I turned on my overhead siren and positioned my	←As pointed out earlier, "What happened next?" can be a useful question during direct examination.

patrol unit right behind this individual. I then exited my patrol car.

Q: **What happened next?**

A: As I approached him, he dropped a can of spray paint he had been using and told me he was just messing around.

Q: **What did you do?**

A: I informed him that tagging is a crime and that I needed to see some identification.

Q: **What happened next?**

A: As he went to pull out his wallet, a baggie containing a white substance fell to the ground.

Q: **As police officer, do you have training or experience with the recognition of controlled substances?**

A: Yes, I do. At the police academy, we had a forty-hour course focusing on the recognition of controlled substances. We learned what they look like, smell like, the physical effects that can have on people, instruments that are used to smoke them, and so forth.

← Here, the officer avoids a lack of foundation objection by not identifying the substance as a drug.
← The prosecutor is establishing the necessary foundation for the officer to claim that the substance he observed is contraband (i.e., drugs).

Q: **As a police officer, do you have any experience with the recognition of a particular controlled substance, cocaine?**

A: Yes, I have made over a dozen investigations leading to arrest with individuals caught with possession of cocaine.

← After laying foundation for the officer's recognition of controlled substance in general, the prosecutor wants to elicit foundational testimony for his recognition of a particular controlled substance (i.e., cocaine).

Q: **Did you form an opinion as to the contents of the baggie that dropped from the individual's sweatshirt?**

A: Yes, based off the white color and powdery texture, I believed the substance to be cocaine. I then arrested the individual for possession of cocaine.

Q: **Do you recognize this individual in court today?**

A: Yes.

Q: **Could you please point him out by providing to the court his location in the courtroom and articles of clothing he is wearing?**

A: He's seated at the defense counsel table wearing a white shirt with a blue tie.

Judge Thomas: The record reflects that the witness has identified the defendant.

← Build up question for the actual identification of the suspect. Demonstrating to the court that the witness is capable of making an identification.

← Identification has been properly established.

Knowing exactly how you want each witness to testify in order to satisfy the element requirements is one thing, whereas eliciting that information is another task entirely. Testifying witnesses may be unresponsive, inconsistent, forgetful, or just nervous about being involved in a legal proceeding.

It is the attorney's duty to tailor his questions and conduct to meet the needs of the witnesses. The following witness breakdown sets forth three types of witnesses that prosecutors and defense attorneys are likely to encounter at the preliminary hearing:

1. Civilian

A civilian witness may be the person least familiar with courtroom proceedings. Prosecutors can therefore anticipate that nerves will play a role in a civilian's testimony. He may stumble over his words, modify previous statements, or fail to understand questions. Attorneys should be sensitive to the witness's nervousness and do their best to make him or her feel comfortable. Attorneys should, without providing grounds for objections, guide these witnesses more, by asking follow-up questions for clarification or rephrasing a question when necessary. Lastly, civilian witnesses may also be prone to answer questions with non-verbal communication. To preserve such an answer in the record, an attorney should follow up to elicit a verbal response.

2. Expert

An expert witness is compensated for his time in court. The attorney conducting the direct examination should elicit testimony with regards to an expert's compensation. It is important to make it clear that the fee is not contingent upon a particular case outcome; experts are frequently paid hourly for their time, regardless of the results, and providing testimony in criminal cases is one of their duties. Attorneys can expect these types of witnesses to be far more comfortable in a courtroom setting than a civilian witness. The task for the attorneys will be to clarify the expert's answers and make sure that the expert explains terms of art in a manner that the judge will understand. The challenge with an expert witness is to ensure that the witness comes across as competent without being arrogant. Of course, expert witnesses present unique challenges when the case proceeds to the trial stage. Moreover, expert witnesses who are condescending and egotistical alienate the trier of fact. Oftentimes, a crucial question in a case, such as whether a killing was in self-defense, may turn into a battle of the experts.

3. Law Enforcement

A law enforcement officer is the type of witness who will most often testify in a criminal case. Like expert witnesses, law enforcement officers tend to be more seasoned in the courtroom. Because officers frequently make arrests, their testimony is often based almost entirely on their arrest or police report. As a result, such testimony comes across in a matter-of-fact fashion. Having an officer appear confident and credible is fundamental to the success of any prosecution's case. Typically, that ideal level of objectivity is achieved when an officer does not embellish or provide recently discovered insight when testifying at the preliminary hearing or trial. While it is true that the police report is only a summary of the events and the officer may testify to additional minor points, the substance of the officer's testimony should also be in the report, especially when the officer knows the prosecution is relying upon the officer's report. Otherwise, the defense attorney can and should question the officer as to the omission in the report. As long as the officer provides an honest account of the events, sticking primarily to the basic facts of the arrest report may be a prosecutor's and the witness's best course of action.

E. CROSS-EXAMINATION

Since the defense rarely presents evidence at the preliminary hearing, defense counsel typically focuses instead on cross-examining prosecution witnesses.[16] To begin with, attorneys need to be wary of pre-conceptions regarding cross-examination, since television shows and movies often inaccurately portray courtroom proceedings. Depictions of witnesses who, after being backed into a corner on cross-examination, break down and reveal case-resolving testimony are fictionalized dramatizations and rarely, if ever, occur during an actual courtroom proceeding. Because achieving this type of breakthrough is not a realistic objective, prosecutors and defense attorneys do not need to go for the "home run" during cross-examination. An effective cross-examination at trial will raise doubts in the minds of the jurors that will be magnified during closing arguments. An effective cross-examination at the preliminary hearing will "lock in" testimony for trial as well as point out discrepancies and omissions in the witness's testimony. Demonstrating that a witness's testimony is inconsistent, either with other witness testimony or even with his own prior statements, can be devastating to the opponent's case. Getting a witness to make contradictory statements or to admit to fabrications or mistakes can be pivotal to case settlement or to preserving testimony that can be used to impeach the witness at trial. Another effective tool of cross-examination is to point out that the witness's version of events simply does not make sense. Carefully worded questions and adopting an incredulous tone of voice can be helpful tools for impeaching a witness. It is important to remember that well-crafted, controlled questions can persuade the trier of fact, regardless of whether the witness agrees with the attorney's insinuations. Thus, sometimes questions on cross-examination simply serve to convey the attorney's case theory to the judge or jury. For the sake of clarity, it is advisable to limit cross-examination questions to one point per question.

1. "Locking In" Witness Testimony

At a preliminary hearing, the aim of defense attorneys will be to prepare for trial or gain leverage to negotiate a favorable case settlement. While the Supreme Court has ruled that defendants are not entitled under the Sixth Amendment to cross-examine witnesses at the preliminary hearing, all jurisdictions allow at least some cross-examination of any witnesses called by the State.[17] Typically, state courts do not allow cross-examination questions specifically directed towards gaining discovery. It is unlikely at this stage that cross-examination will be sufficient to defeat the charges and dismiss the case. Thus, defense attorneys primarily set out two objectives when conducting cross-examination at the preliminary hearing. First, determine the scope of the prosecution's evidence, and second, "lock in" witness testimony for later impeachment.

For the first objective, even though discovery should give the defense access to all pertinent documents relating to the case, defense attorneys will want to acquire an all-encompassing view of the prosecution's evidence, including evaluating the credibility and recollection ability of witnesses called at

---

[16] For a more in-depth coverage of cross-examination in a trial advocacy setting, see L. TIMOTHY PERRIN, H. MITCHELL CALDWELL & CAROL CHASE, THE ART & SCIENCE OF TRIAL ADVOCACY (2d ed. 2011).

[17] *See, e.g.*, Commonwealth *ex rel.* Buchanan v. Verbonitz, 581 A.2d 172, 174 (Pa. 1990); People v. Horton, 358 N.E.2d 1121, 1123 (Ill. 1976).

the preliminary hearing. In order to present the best defense possible, defense attorneys will need to understand fully the case against their client. The preliminary hearing provides such an opportunity.

In regards to the second objective, ignorance is not bliss when it comes to conducting criminal trials. Not knowing what witnesses will testify about, or whether their testimony will suddenly change at trial, presents a significant issue for both sides. Thus, defense attorneys will "lock in" prosecution witness testimony for trial. Any witness who testifies at the preliminary hearing may be impeached by their testimony at trial. Effective defense attorneys will extensively question witnesses about any material aspect of the case at the preliminary hearing.

A common example of "locking in" witness testimony occurs during the cross-examination of law enforcement officials at the preliminary hearing. Since law enforcement officials generally base their testimony upon an arrest or police report, defense attorneys seek to confine such testimony to their report in preparation for trial. The following is a series of questions one may expect from a defense attorney's cross-examination of a police officer at a preliminary hearing.

> **Defense Attorney: Officer, did you ever memorialize the events in question?**
> Officer: Yes, I wrote and filed a police report.
> **Defense Attorney: Isn't it true that you've been trained to write these reports?**
> Officer: Yes.
> **Defense Attorney: In fact, part of your training is to include all pertinent information relating to a case?**
> Officer: That is correct.
> **Defense Attorney: You've had an opportunity to review this report prior to testifying today, correct?**
> Officer: Yes.
> **Defense Attorney: Is there anything in the report that you would like to change at this time?**
> Officer: No.

Cross-examination is just as much about technique as it is content. In crafting their questions and conducting cross-examination, prosecutors and defense attorneys should follow the seven "truths of cross" as described below.

CHART 8.2
Seven Truths of Cross

1. Use close ended, leading questions. The "question" should be a statement in question form.

> Good Example: Isn't it true that you never actually saw a gun?
> Bad Example: Did you ever see a gun?

2. One point per question. Keep the questions concise and simple. This allows the questioner to control the examination and avoids confusion and ambiguity.

> Good Example: You were not wearing your prescription glasses, correct?
> Bad Example: You were not wearing your prescription glasses and you were a long distance away from the intruder, correct?

3. Stay calm and in control. The appearance of confidence is more important than confidence itself.

4. Do not damage your case on cross-examination. Avoid asking a question to which you do not know the answer, or the "*one question too many*." Save the point for closing argument.

> Attorney: Doctor, I noticed while looking at your résumé that you took a considerable time off after completing your residency, correct?
>
> Doctor: Yes.
>
> Attorney: Wouldn't you agree with me that to practice medicine competently, one needs to remain up-to-date with the changes in the medical field and protocol?
>
> Doctor: Yes, definitely.
>
> Attorney: And wouldn't you also agree with me that someone who begins practicing after completing their residency would be more up-to-date with medical protocol than someone who took several years off between the residency and working as a practicing physician?
>
> Doctor: Yes.
>
> *Attorney: So this considerable time off has affected your ability to competently practice medicine?*
> **[One Question Too Many]**
>
> Doctor: On the contrary, the period of time you designated as "time off," I volunteered my time to serve our nation as a medic in Iraq. By saving a number of lives in the battlefield, I learned far more than I would have in any medical office.

5. Control the witness. Insist that the witness answer your question.

> Attorney: Isn't it true that you never actually performed a complete investigation in this matter?
>
> Witness: We had all the information we needed.
>
> Attorney: Thank you for your response, but directing you back towards my question: You never actually performed a complete investigation in this matter?
>
> Witness: No, I did not.

6. Avoid quibbling over minor details. Pick your battles wisely.

> Attorney: After the party, you went straight home, correct?
>
> Witness: Yes, we arrived at 11:45 p.m.
>
> Attorney: You told the police that you arrived home at 11:43 p.m. Are you now changing your story?
>
> Witness: Well, I guess it depends what I meant by arrived. Did I mean pull into our parking spot? Did I mean entering the apartment door?
>
> Attorney: Are you telling me that you did not tell the police you arrived home at 11:43 p.m.?

7. Go out with a bang. Save the last question or series of questions that are most damaging to your opponent's case until the end.

F. CROSS-EXAMINATION SAMPLE

Below is a sample cross-examination of the arresting officer who testified in the above direct examination for the prosecution. The questions conform to the "Seven Truths of Cross."

CROSS-EXAMINATION	
BY MR. JACKSON	
Q: Officer Nash, isn't it true that you did not see my client actually tag the wall?	←The question is leading and close ended.
A: Well no, it was an inference given the fact he had a spray paint can and there was graffiti on the wall.	←Here, the officer adds more than he's asked. Instead of objecting or asking the question again, the defense attorney proceeds with a series of questions that investigate how reasonable this "inference" actually was.
Q: Officer, have you see this wall before?	
A: Yes, I regularly patrol this area.	
Q: So then could you tell me what graffiti, if any, was present the day before this incident?	
A: Well, I mean I've seen the wall regularly but can't remember all the details.	←The officer is once again unresponsive to counsel's question. The defense attorney in not concerned with the officer's excuses and reiterates the question again to get the facts straight.
Q: Is that a no, Officer, that you cannot recall if graffiti was present the day before this incident occurred?	
A: No, I can't recall.	
Q: You didn't examine the wall after arresting my client, did you?	
A: I photographed the wall.	
Q: But you didn't physically touch the wall did you?	
A: No.	
Q: And you didn't smell the wall?	
A: No.	
Q: So isn't it possible then that the graffiti that you photographed was old graffiti done by someone other than my client?	←Even though the defense attorney does not get a statement from the officer that could exonerate his client on a charge, he nevertheless effectively attacks the officer's credibility and elicits "newfound" evidence.
A: I do not believe so. The defendant's spray paint can was not new. It appeared to have been used. There was also a slight hint of corresponding black spray paint on the tips of the defendant's fingers.	←Even though the new evidence is unfavorable to his client's case, the defense attorney now has immense firepower at trial should the officer once again provide evidence outside his arrest report.
Q: Did you include in your arrest report that the defendant had black spray paint on the tips of his fingers?	
A: No.	
Q: And you are trained to include all potentially relevant information in these reports?	
A: Yes.	
Q: And you do remember that you had the opportunity to review and update where necessary?	←As noted before in this chapter, this is a common series of questions and technique used by defense attorneys to
A: Yes.	

Q: **Officer, is there anything else you'd like to add to your report at this time?** A: No, I believe that was the only relevant fact left out of the report. Q: **You mentioned on direct that the baggie fell out of the defendant's sweatshirt pocket, correct?** A: Yes. Q: **Did you ever ask the defendant whether or not that sweatshirt belonged to him?** A: No. Q: **No further questions, Your Honor.**	"lock in" officers to the facts provided in their arrest reports. ←The final two questions are purposefully asked for trial. It's not likely that the defense attorney is defeating this drug charge at the preliminary hearing because of a failure of the officer to ask questions about possession. This may, however, be the preparation for exploring a possible case theory at trial. It is also helpful for case settlement.

G. FISHING EXPEDITION

In addition to using cross-examination to "lock in" witness testimony for trial, defense attorneys often use this opportunity to go on a "fishing expedition." Defense attorneys will ask questions, entirely unaware of their answers, in an attempt to uncover evidence that may support a motion to suppress evidence or bolster a potential defense at trial. Since the criminal justice process is an adversarial system, it is up to the attorneys, not the judge, to limit evidence to what is admissible according to the rules of evidence. Thus, prosecutors will want to guard vigilantly against such "fishing expeditions." Since the preliminary hearing serves to

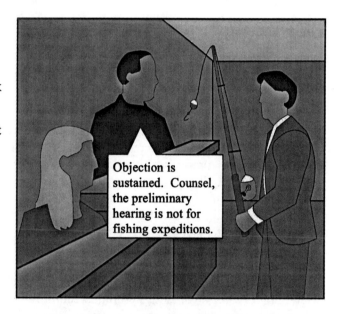

Objection is sustained. Counsel, the preliminary hearing is not for fishing expeditions.

determine the sufficiency of the evidence against the defendant, counsel's questions that go beyond that purpose can and should be objected to as irrelevant. Even though both the defense and prosecution gain insight into the case from the preliminary hearing, the proceeding is not intended to be a vehicle for discovery. Jurisdictions vary, however, on the amount of discovery that is permissible at a preliminary hearing. Skilled defense attorneys will treat the preliminary hearing as an opportunity to conduct extensive cross-examination of prosecution witnesses to lock in their testimony. Since criminal cases, unlike civil cases, do not have depositions, preliminary hearing testimony (through transcripts) provides a fertile source of grounds for impeachment at the trial stage, whether by prior inconsistent statement or by omission at trial.

CONDUCTING THE PRELIMINARY HEARING

A. DEFENSE STRATEGY

Defense strategy at a preliminary hearing goes far beyond conducting an effective cross-examination. The defense attorney, at this stage, should keep the prosecutor in check and ensure that each element of the offense, jurisdiction, and identification has been demonstrated. As mentioned above, it is unlikely that a defense attorney will succeed in getting a case dismissed at the preliminary hearing stage. Getting a charge dropped or reduced, however, is a realistic objective for defense attorneys. For example, in some jurisdictions, state legislatures have designated certain crimes as "wobblers," which are crimes that could be charged as either misdemeanors or felonies. A misdemeanor is a crime for which the maximum possible sentence is a year or less at a local jail, while a felony entails a potential sentence of more than a year in state or federal prison.[18] At the preliminary hearing, once the prosecution has laid out the evidence against the defendant, a defense attorney may be able to ask the judge, where appropriate, to reduce a charged felony to a misdemeanor.

HYPO: *Oceana v. Stone*

Troy Stone has been charged with possession of cocaine. In the state of Oceana, the crime is considered a "wobbler." The drugs were found during a routine traffic stop. Even though Stone, known as "Tough Troy," has a criminal nickname, he has had a clean record since acquiring the nickname in an assault fifteen years ago. The prosecutor files the crime as a felony. At the preliminary hearing, the prosecutor establishes the requisite jurisdiction, identification, and elements of the offense. The defense attorney requests the presiding judge to reduce the crime to a misdemeanor. What kinds of arguments should the defense attorney seek to make?

The first matter that a defense attorney should consider is the alleged crime itself. What are the details surrounding the crime? In this case, how much cocaine was found? Were there children or other passengers in the car? Are there any mitigating factors of the crime that could push the judge to reduce the charged "wobbler" to a misdemeanor? Second, does your client have a criminal record? Here, Stone, while possessing a criminal record, has been "crime-free" for a significant number of years. Moreover, there are no drug-related charges on his record. By convincing the judge that the alleged drug possession is an aberration, rather than part of a pattern of criminal behavior, the judge will be more inclined to reduce a felony to a misdemeanor.

A defense attorney, regardless of skill and expertise, is not likely to defeat charges at this stage in the criminal justice process. By setting realistic objectives and avoiding the "home run" mentality, the defense attorney can better position her client for case settlement and/or trial, as well as garner a reputation for professionalism and honesty from her client, the prosecutor, and the court.

---

[18] Jurisdictions vary in the way offenders are incarcerated. For example, California felonies underwent a significant change in October 2011, through the California Legislative initiative known as realignment. The change was introduced to address the issue of overcrowding in state prisons. Now in California, usually only sentences for violent felonies are served in state prison, whereas sentences for most non-violent felonies are served in local, or county, jails.

Another goal during a preliminary hearing is to carefully analyze all the elements for each charge to see whether they have each been proven or whether a lesser but related charge may be more appropriate. For example, in the case of a "strong-arm" robbery prosecution, defense counsel may argue that her client should be held to answer only on a charge of grand theft. In such situations, the judge should be asked to weigh the evidence to determine which charge most closely describes the defendant's behavior. Sometimes the main goal of the defense is to have the charge reduced from a felony to a misdemeanor.[19]

Additionally, the preliminary hearing judge has the discretion to drop enhancements or allegations charged against the defendant. These enhancements and allegations can include: special circumstances added to a murder charge, use of a firearm, intent to commit great bodily injury, prior convictions, excessively high blood alcohol level when driving, allegations relating to the age of the victim, sex offense allegations, and myriad other allegations that can significantly increase the sentence if the defendant is convicted. Sometimes the major goal of the defense at the preliminary hearing is to have allegations or enhancements dismissed.

B. LEGAL REPUTATION AND TAKING CUES FROM THE JUDGE

Even in large cities like Los Angeles or New York, the legal community is relatively small, even more so in the field of criminal law. As either a prosecutor or defense attorney, one will frequently interact with the same judges and attorneys on a regular basis. Consequently, reputations are made and become well-known quickly. It is important for inexperienced attorneys to keep this in mind as they begin practicing criminal law. Starting at the preliminary hearing, likely the first adversarial proceeding of a case, relationships are formed between each attorney and the presiding judge. How attorneys choose to conduct themselves at the preliminary hearing can set the tone for the current case, as well as for future cases. Successful attorneys realize that it is not advantageous to bring frivolous objections. Similarly, taking an unreasonable stance with settlement negotiations will alienate the court. Developing a professional reputation takes time and experience, but starting with the preliminary hearing and tailoring the case to cues from the judge can be a good start.

The presiding judge at the preliminary hearing is there to weigh the evidence against the defendant. In fulfilling their roles, however, judges are not mere passive observers. Rather, judges, through body language and tone, drop significant hints that attorneys would be wise to follow. For example, less is sometimes more. Nervous, inexperienced attorneys are sometimes tempted to present too much evidence or to call too many witnesses during a preliminary hearing—strategically unwise steps, as explained above. All the same, even when novice prosecutors effectively limit the number of witnesses, they still tend to draw out lengthy and unnecessary direct examinations. Alertly following cues from the presiding judge will allow a prosecutor to conduct a preliminary hearing successfully. If a judge states, "I assume the People are not going to call any more witnesses," the prosecutor should take the cue that the judge has heard enough evidence to make a ruling. One caveat to bear in mind, however, even after the

---

[19] FED. R. CRIM. P. 5.1. *See also* CAL. PENAL CODE §17(b)(5) (Deering 2012).

defendant has been held to answer, the defense may still make a motion to a different judge to dismiss the case on the basis of insufficient evidence. Thus, although it is wise to take cues from the judge, if a prosecutor believes that more evidence should be presented in order to prove each element (even with the lower standard of probable cause), he should not be bullied into presenting a weak case.

C. RULES OF EVIDENCE AND OBJECTIONS

State jurisdictions vary widely as to the extent that the rules of evidence apply during preliminary hearings. Only a small minority of states limit the rules of evidence to the rules applicable at trials. Be that as it may, the term "preliminary" should not lull attorneys into a false sense of security when it comes to making objections. In fact, attorneys often feel more inclined to make objections since, in contrast to a trial setting, there is no risk of alienating the jury. Further, it is the attorney's duty to protect her witnesses. Testimony that is given at the preliminary hearing can and will be used for impeachment purposes at trial. Attorneys on both sides will want to protect their witnesses from future impeachment by limiting testimony to what is admissible according to the local rules of evidence.

Whether at trial or during a preliminary hearing, attorneys issuing objections should rise before addressing the court. Unless an attorney is familiar with a more informal practice in a particular courtroom, it is wise to employ a more formal approach to court proceedings.

1. Objections

Typically, objections are made to challenge either the form of the attorney's question or the response given by the witness. Listed below are common objections attorneys might need to make at a preliminary hearing.

CHART 8.4

Hearsay	Hearsay is an out-of-court statement offered for the truth of the matter asserted. Look for tipping words such as "he said" or "he told me." However, there are a number of hearsay exceptions.
Speculation	Does the question or response engage the witness in reasoning not founded on adequate knowledge or experience? If not, a speculation objection may be proper.
Relevance	Only relevant evidence is admissible. Relevant evidence goes to prove or disprove a fact of material significance in the case.
Beyond Scope of Direct	Is opposing counsel's question related to the issues mentioned during direct examination? If not, such an objection may be proper.
Leading	Typically, leading questions are not allowed on direct examination. A leading question is one that suggests the answer.
Lack of Foundation	Before testimony or documents may be admitted as evidence, there must be a sufficient preliminary demonstration of their authenticity and relevance. This is often a consideration with expert witnesses, but is certainly not limited to them.

Privilege	The rules of evidence have labeled certain communications as confidential. For example, the "attorney-client privilege" protects communications made between an attorney and her client.
Best Evidence Rule	Generally speaking, secondary evidence, such as a copy, might not be admitted into evidence if the original exists and is available.
Vague	To guard against courtroom confusion, attorneys may object to a vague or ambiguous question.
Cumulative	To guard against inefficient use of the court's time, attorneys may object when the examiner is rehashing evidence that has already been established.
Argumentative	When a question provides no additional relevant evidence and is brought to incite an argument with the witness, that question is argumentative.
Narrative	Direct examination follows a question and answer format. Attorneys can object when witnesses launch into prolonged responses.
Character Evidence	Generally, evidence tending to try to prove that a person has a particular character based on past actions is inadmissible. Evidence as to a person's credibility, though, is always admissible.
Compound Question	When a question touches upon more than one issue, it is objectionable as a compound question.

2. Applying Objections

In jurisdictions where rules of evidence are strictly enforced, both attorneys will want to issue appropriate objections in order to limit evidence to what is admissible. The above objection chart will be helpful when determining if the following questions are proper.

1. **Attorney:** After the incident, you told Officer Gregory that the defendant brandished a gun, right? **(On direct examination of the victim).**

2. **Attorney:** Do you often feel the inclination to lie in such circumstances? **(On cross-examination of the complaining witness.)**

3. **Witness:** John had mentioned to me in passing that he had a grudge against Bob and would do something about it soon.

4. **Witness:** If I had to guess, I would say he was standing about thirty feet from me.

5. **Attorney:** You didn't see him do anything to her, did you?

D. HEARSAY

Depending on the jurisdiction, hearsay may operate differently at a preliminary hearing than at trial. To review, hearsay is an out-of-court statement offered to prove the truth of the matter asserted. For example, a testifying witness may be offering inadmissible hearsay when he says, "Gene told me that he had no money on him prior to being robbed." If this statement is offered as evidence to prove that Gene, in fact, had no money on his person, then it is hearsay. Unless an applicable exception exists, such testimony will not be admitted as evidence.

Some states, such as California, have passed legislation to allow qualified law enforcement officials to testify to one level of hearsay at the preliminary hearing.[20] California Proposition 115, referred to as the Crime Victims' Justice Reform Act, modified preliminary hearings to make them more expedient, less expensive, and more convenient for witnesses.[21] This was primarily achieved by allowing single-level hearsay by a police officer, as long as minimal requirements are met.[22]

It is certainly less burdensome for witnesses not to have to testify at a preliminary hearing, especially when their testimony is about an issue that is not in dispute. For example, in a stolen car case, the Crime Victims' Reform Act alleviates a witness from having to take time off work and go to court just to testify that the witness did not give the defendant permission to take the witness's car. If the witness directly told this to the police officer, then the officer can relate it as single layer hearsay. Officer "A" would not be allowed, however, to testify as to what the witness told Officer "B." It is important for prosecutors to recognize that there are circumstances where it is preferable to call a victim or other significant witness instead of having this evidence related by a police officer. This is often the case in serious offenses, such as sex assault cases, where the victim's credibility is crucial. In such circumstances, it is usually advantageous to see how the witness holds up during cross-examination.

Proposition 115 also gives prosecutors the choice of proceeding by grand jury indictment or preliminary hearing, limits the hearing to a probable cause screening, and prohibits using it as a vehicle for discovery. This saves the court's time and resources as it allows the prosecutor to call fewer witnesses to meet his burden. Using hearsay at the preliminary hearing also allows prosecutors to "shield" their witnesses so that they cannot be cross-examined by defense lawyers. Prosecutors should check with their respective jurisdiction regarding hearsay and the rules of evidence at the preliminary hearing stage. Even though many jurisdictions permit hearsay at preliminary hearings, there is still some protection of the integrity of the evidence, as the person (usually the police officer) who is testifying to the hearsay information is subject to cross-examination. Since the preliminary hearing, unlike a *Gerstein ex parte* hearing, is an adversarial proceeding, the defense attorney has a chance to show that there is not sufficient probable cause to hold the defendant to answer for the offenses.

The majority of jurisdictions do not apply the exclusionary rules to suppress physical evidence or confessions obtained in violation of the Fourth or Fifth Amendments at the preliminary hearing stage.[23] All jurisdictions, however, apply the rules of testimonial privileges, such as attorney-client, or doctor-patient privileges. Most jurisdictions follow 1101(d) of the *Federal Rules of Evidence*, which states that,

---

[20] Such a hearsay exception does not violate the Confrontation Clause since the purpose of the preliminary hearing is not to decide guilt.

[21] *See* CAL. CONST. art 1, § 30(b); Crime Victims' Justice Reform Act, Initiative Measure Proposition 115 (approved June 5, 1990).

[22] CAL. PENAL CODE § 872(b) (Deering 2012) ("Any law enforcement officer or honorably retired law enforcement officer testifying as to hearsay statements shall either have five years of law enforcement experience or have completed a training course certified by the Commission on Peace Officer Standards and Training that includes training in the investigation and reporting of cases and testifying at preliminary hearings.")

[23] FED. R. CRIM. P. 5.1(e).

other than protected privileges, evidentiary rules do not apply to preliminary hearings. [24] It is left to the magistrate's discretion at the preliminary hearing to determine whether the proffered evidence is reliable. Thus, hearsay evidence is allowed at preliminary hearings in federal court. [25] Although the majority of states prohibit challenges to evidence on the grounds that it was unlawfully obtained, some jurisdictions, such as California, give the defense the option to bring a motion to suppress evidence at either the preliminary hearing stage or after the defendant is bound over but before trial. [26] In jurisdictions that allow a motion to suppress evidence to be brought in conjunction with the preliminary hearing, the prosecutor will need to prove the reasonableness of a search or seizure as part of the proof at the preliminary hearing. Since there is a wide discrepancy in the ways in which different state jurisdictions apply the rules of evidence at the preliminary hearing stage, it is crucial for attorneys to research the relevant statutes and court rules in the jurisdiction in which they will practice.

POST-PRELIMINARY HEARING

After hearing the evidence presented, the presiding judge will determine whether sufficient evidence exists to hold the defendant to answer for the charges. The judge may decide to hold the defendant to answer for all charges, some charges, or no charges. It is also well within the discretion of the presiding judge even to add charges to conform to the proof. The judge may also choose to add or to dismiss enhancements or allegations. For example, if the victim testifies at the preliminary hearing that the defendant, who was charged with grand theft, actually pointed a gun at her and took property from her person, then the judge would likely add a charge of robbery and the enhancement of personal use of a firearm. Witnesses are unpredictable, thus judges have the discretion to add, reduce, or dismiss charges after hearing the evidence and arguments at the preliminary hearing stage. Post-preliminary hearing charges cannot be added that do not conform to proof at the preliminary hearing, which is why it is imperative for the prosecution to develop charges before and during the preliminary hearing. [27] In any event, the decision by the judge is not final, as it may be challenged.

In federal court and most state courts, both parties are entitled to challenge the decisions made by the presiding magistrate at the preliminary hearing. [28] The process is initiated when the challenging party files the respective written motion. As indicated earlier, a court reporter will transcribe the proceedings at the preliminary hearing, and a copy of the transcript is made available to each party. When a challenge to the judge's findings at the preliminary hearing has been filed, the transcript is provided to a fresh pair of

---

[24] FED. R. EVID. 1101(d)(3) (stating that the rules of evidence, other than privilege, do not apply to miscellaneous proceedings like a preliminary examination in a criminal case).

[25] FED. R. CRIM. P. 5.1(a).

[26] People v. Lazlo, 206 Cal. App. 4th 1063 (Cal. Ct. App. 2012).

[27] See CAL. PENAL CODE § 1009 (Deering 2012); People v. Peyton, 176 Cal. App. 4th 642 (Cal. Ct. App. 2009).

[28] The prosecution is also entitled to the "two bites at the apple" rule. If faced with an unfavorable decision at the preliminary hearing, the prosecution can simply dismiss the case and re-file, however, this can only be done once during the whole history of a case. See FED. R. CRIM. P. 5.1(f).

eyes: a new magistrate. This magistrate will review the transcript along with the filed written motion and response and will conduct a hearing. Like the preliminary hearing magistrate, she will look at the elements of the offense, identification, requisite jurisdiction, and any allegations or enhancements that needed to be proven at the preliminary hearing. For the most part, the reviewing magistrate is concerned with issues of law and not issues of fact. In other words, whether or not a testifying witness is credible is generally within the discretion of the preliminary hearing judge. Successful motions will generally be based on issues of law, as a reviewing magistrate is likely to give deference to factual findings of the preliminary hearing judge.

If the magistrate has violated the defendant's rights at the preliminary hearing, the standard of review is typically a harmless error standard. Sometimes even a clear violation, such as when a magistrate does not allow cross-examination, can result in a wrong without a remedy. For instance, if a grand jury indicts the defendant after the preliminary hearing, then any error at that hearing will likely be moot. Similarly, if the defendant has been convicted after a trial, then even an egregious error at the preliminary hearing will unlikely result in a dismissal because the standard of proof is much higher at the trial. A possible exception to this rule would be when the preliminary hearing judge's error affects the defendant's opportunity to later have a fair trial. For instance, if the defense was not allowed to call a crucial witness and the witness died before the trial, this could present a reason to reverse a conviction. The Supreme Court in *Coleman v. Alabama* held that the harmless error standard should be applied if a defendant was denied his Sixth Amendment right to counsel at a preliminary hearing, subsequently indicted by a grand jury, and then convicted at trial while represented by counsel. The *Coleman* Court remanded the case to the lower court to determine whether the defendant actually suffered prejudice at the preliminary hearing.[29] State courts vary as to remedies when a defendant's rights have been violated at the preliminary hearing level.

Many states allow a prosecutor to appeal a magistrate's decision not to bind a defendant over. A trial court magistrate will hear the prosecution appeal and determine whether the preliminary hearing judge abused her discretion when she dismissed the case.[30] Generally, the magistrate who rules on the appeal will grant it only if there was an error of law, since the reviewing judge did not have the chance to assess the credibility of the witnesses at the preliminary hearing. Some states do not allow this appeal, but they sometimes allow an extraordinary writ. Furthermore, since jeopardy has not attached, the prosecutor may have the option of bringing the case to a grand jury to obtain an indictment, even though a judge has dismissed the case after a preliminary hearing. The vast majority of jurisdictions allow the prosecution to re-file the charges and seek another preliminary hearing (sometimes before a different magistrate) as long as the defense does not prove that the charges are frivolous and intended to harass the defendant. It is beneficial for prosecutors to re-file charges in instances where the charges are solid but there was a problem of proof at the first preliminary hearing, such as witness unavailability. In some circumstances, after re-filing charges, the prosecution will obtain additional evidence that strengthens its

---

[29] Coleman v. Alabama, 399 U.S. 1 (1970).

[30] *See, e.g.*, CAL. PENAL CODE § 995a(b)(1) (Deering 2012).

case. Prosecutors, however, would be wise not to re-file charges in a weak case. If the victim, or other crucial witness was found not to be credible after the preliminary hearing, or there were other major problems of proof, then it does not behoove the prosecution to re-file charges.

Similarly, the defense may bring a motion to appeal the decision to bind the defendant over.[31] Again, the standard for the reviewing magistrate is whether the magistrate who heard the preliminary hearing abused her discretion. An example of when the defense might prevail on this motion would be a jurisdictional error, such as a lack of proof that the crime occurred in the court's jurisdiction. Another example would be when a necessary element of the offense is missing. For instance, in California, Penal Code section 487 requires that, to constitute grand theft, the stolen property must have a value of at least $950. If there is no testimony to support this element of the offense, then that charge should be dismissed, or reduced to Penal Code section 484, misdemeanor petty theft.

SUMMARY

Though not an end in itself, the preliminary hearing is a critical juncture in the pretrial advocacy of both the prosecutor and the defense attorney. The prosecutor has an opportunity to observe and evaluate the strength of both his case and the witnesses' credibility. Should the prosecution succeed in proving strong suspicion at the hearing, the credibility of the prosecutor's case will gain him greater leverage in future plea negotiations. Even if the evidence against her client is sound, the defense attorney still has a significant opportunity on cross-examination to "lock in" witness testimony in anticipation of trial and to highlight problems with the prosecution's case. By also getting a preview of the case against her client, the defense attorney can better prepare an effective defense at trial.

---

[31] *See, e.g.*, CAL. PENAL CODE § 995 (Deering 2012).

CHECKLIST

✓ A preliminary hearing is like a condensed trial in which the prosecution's burden of proof is "strong suspicion."

✓ The prosecutor must demonstrate jurisdiction, each element of the offense(s), and identification of the suspect, but generally should not present every witness or piece of evidence.

✓ The prosecutor ought to tailor his direct-examination style to suit each type of witness: civilian witness, expert witness, or law enforcement official.

✓ The defense attorney should "lock in" witness testimony on cross-examination.

✓ Statements made at the preliminary hearing may later be used to impeach witnesses at trial for inconsistency.

✓ Follow the "Seven Truths of Cross-Examination" when crafting questions.

✓ Certain rules of evidence apply during the preliminary hearing, though these rules are generally less stringent than those at trial.

✓ Watch for cues from the judge as to when sufficient evidence has been presented.

✓ Make appropriate objections, beware of "fishing expeditions," and make sure the court record is complete, including indications of witnesses' non-verbal communication.

✓ Both parties may appeal the findings of the preliminary hearing judge in most jurisdictions.

CHAPTER 9
GRAND JURY

"A good prosecutor can get a grand jury to indict a ham sandwich."
–Criminal law cliché

Preliminary hearings, as discussed in Chapter 8, have a particular role in the criminal justice system. Subsequent to the filing of any charges and arraignment, the prosecuting authority will proceed with a preliminary hearing, at which a magistrate is required to decide whether there is probable cause that the accused has committed the charged crime. If there is sufficient evidence, then the defendant is held to answer and a date is set for trial. If not, charges cannot proceed and the case ends unless the prosecutor re-files and succeeds at the second preliminary hearing. A preliminary hearing, however, is not the only way to bind an accused over for a trial.[1] In some cases, a grand jury proceeding is more desirable or even necessary.

A grand jury, like the magistrate in a preliminary hearing, can be summoned to evaluate evidence presented by the prosecuting authority in order to determine whether there is probable cause that the accused committed a crime. The grand jury is primarily an instrument of the federal court system, and is empanelled only in the case of felony charges. Since the grand jury clause of the Fifth Amendment of the U.S. Constitution has not been incorporated,[2] it is not mandatory for the states and only about one-third of the states rely on the grand jury to issue indictments for either felonies or capital cases.[3] In many state courts, prosecutors have the discretion to proceed by way of a preliminary hearing or a grand jury hearing. Meanwhile, in the federal court system, a grand jury hearing is the most common mechanism for meeting the probable cause requirement and is, in fact, required when the charge is for an "infamous crime."[4] In this way, grand juries, like preliminary hearings, serve a filtering, or screening, role.

---

[1] In most instances, the prosecuting attorney has the authority to re-file charges once more and begin the process anew, when, for example, new evidence has strengthened a previously weak case.

[2] Hurtado v. California, 110 U.S. 516, 538 (1884).

[3] The states requiring a grand jury when initiating serious criminal charges are: Alabama, Alaska, Delaware, Georgia, Kentucky, Maine, Massachusetts, Mississippi, New Hampshire, New Jersey, New York, North Carolina, Ohio, South Carolina, Tennessee, Texas, Virginia, and West Virginia. For capital cases, Florida, Louisiana, Minnesota, and Rhode Island require the use of a grand jury.

[4] Infamous crimes are felonies. Campbell v. Louisiana, 523 U.S. 392, 397 (1998).

In addition to its screening function of determining whether indictments should be issued, the grand jury also acts as an investigative body. Indeed, in some cases, the prosecuting authority may believe that a crime has occurred, but will require further investigation by a grand jury in order to determine precisely what took place and whether the accused is the culpable party. For instance, in cases of fraud or misappropriation of public funds, the details of the crime are obscure by their very nature. The grand jury can be summoned to investigate such activities in order to determine what, if any, charges can and should be brought by the prosecuting authority and against whom.

During the grand jury proceedings, the prosecutor's role is similar to his role in a preliminary hearing or trial: to hold the defendant to answer. In order to do so, he must present sufficient evidence, mostly consisting of testimony from subpoenaed witnesses, but sometimes including physical evidence. The actual proceedings, however, are more informal than those of a preliminary hearing or trial. There is no presiding judge to rule on objections and matters of law, just as there is no defense attorney to initiate objections or conduct cross-examination. Witnesses are allowed to give accounts and tell their stories without being limited to merely answering a prosecutor's questions. Moreover, the grand jury panel, unlike a petit jury, is an active participant in the proceedings.

In this chapter, the processes and procedures of grand jury hearings are examined, paying particular attention to the various issues that prosecuting authorities face when deciding whether to proceed with a grand jury hearing, rather than a preliminary hearing.

A. HISTORY OF THE CRIMINAL GRAND JURY

The origins of the criminal grand jury can be traced back to King John's signing of the Magna Carta in 1215. This key document in the history of common law provided a check on the King of England's power, particularly in regards to criminal prosecution. Specifically, Clause 38 of the charter held that "no bailiff for the future shall, upon his unsupported complaint, put anyone to his 'law,' without credible witnesses brought for this purpose."[5] This provision paved the way for citizens of the community to screen cases of those individuals accused of criminal conduct. As this practice came to be viewed as an effective measure, the group of citizens later became officially known as the "grand jury." What was originally intended as a device by which nobles could prevent the king from arbitrarily exercising his prosecutorial power, ultimately turned out to be an effective limiting mechanism that was integrated into the American legal system.

---

[5] MAGNA CARTA ch. 38, *reprinted and translated in* WILLIAM SHARP MCKECHNIE, MAGNA CARTA: A COMMENTARY ON THE GREAT CHARTER OF KING JOHN 370 (2d ed. 1914).

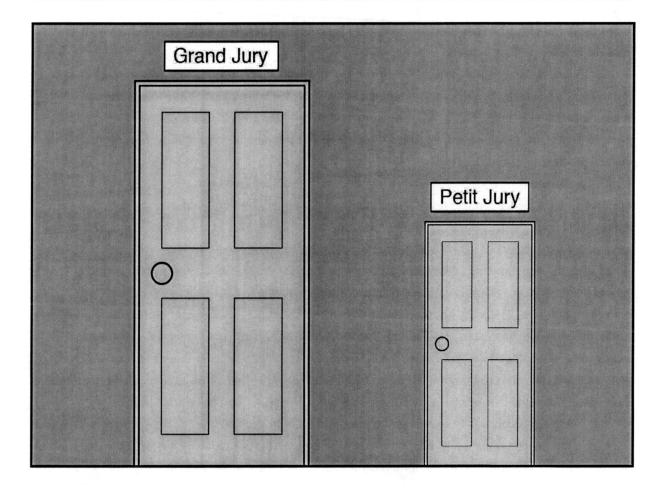

1. The American Grand Jury

The Fifth Amendment of the United States Constitution stipulates, "No person shall be held to answer for a capital, or otherwise infamous crime, unless on a presentment or indictment of a Grand Jury."[6] While the legal origination of grand juries lies in the Constitution, the rules by which they function are set out in the *Federal Rules of Criminal Procedure.* Under the federal rules, a grand jury panel can range from sixteen to twenty-three jurors. Sixteen jurors constitute a quorum, with twelve of the sixteen required to return an indictment. Potential grand jurors are selected at random in order to ensure that the pool is drawn from a fair cross-section of the community in which the federal grand jury sits. Generally, prospective jurors are selected from a list of registered voters. It is imperative that this process provide equal opportunity for all members of the community to serve, since the principal requirement of grand jury selection forbids discrimination against protected groups.[7] In fact, a defendant or attorney for the government may challenge the composition of a grand jury on these grounds.[8] After selection, each member of the jury is sworn in, and the court selects a foreperson and deputy foreperson.

---

[6] U.S. CONST. amend. V.

[7] FED. R. CRIM. P. 6(a)(2).

[8] FED. R. CRIM. P. 6(b)(1).

A federal grand jury panel sits until discharged by the court—generally for eighteen months, with a possible extension of six months.[9]

Whereas the selection process for a petit jury provides safeguards against juror bias, and actual pre-existing knowledge by the jurors about the facts of the case, no analogous restrictions apply to the selection of grand jurors. This is likely because the threshold for probable cause is low, and should a case proceed to trial, the evidence will be tested under the usual and more stringent burdens of proof demanded at the trial stage.

Surprisingly, one rare exception to the lax requirements of grand jury selection occurred in what media commentators have called the most publicized criminal trial in American history, the O.J. Simpson murder trial. In June of 1994, O.J. Simpson was arrested for the murders of his ex-wife Nicole Brown Simpson and Ronald Goldman. A day after the arraignment, a grand jury was convened to decide whether Simpson should be indicted and charged with two counts of murder. Just two days after the grand jury was convened, Simpson, guided by his attorneys, filed a motion seeking the dismissal of the sitting grand jury on the grounds of media exposure, claiming that the jurors' ability to remain impartial had been jeopardized. The judge ruled in favor of the defense and discharged the grand jury. Instead of calling another grand jury, the prosecution proceeded by a preliminary hearing, allowing the defense to build its case starting with the cross-examination of prosecution witnesses at the preliminary hearing.

The judge's decision to discharge the grand jury was an unusual one. Although outside influence during trial or deliberations is a significant concern for courts, it is not typically a major concern in grand jury proceedings because they do not ultimately decide the fate of anyone's liberty.

B. TIMING OF THE GRAND JURY

While preliminary hearings follow arraignment, grand jury hearings may actually initiate the criminal justice process. If a grand jury's investigation leads to an indictment, then an arrest and arraignment will follow. Thus, when the prosecutor proceeds with a grand jury, the person suspected of a crime may not even know that he is a suspect until he becomes aware that he has been indicted.

C. SECRECY OF THE PROCEEDINGS

The activities of the grand jury are conducted in secrecy. Unlike preliminary hearings, which are open to the public, grand jury procedure limits who may attend and what information from its proceedings, if any, may be disclosed. The rationale for keeping these matters private is rooted in the grand jury's history; as the United States Supreme Court has held, "the proper functioning of our grand jury system depends upon [it]."[10] A public grand jury hearing would undermine the goal of the proceeding to discover the facts. For example, if a material witness to an alleged federal crime knows

[9] Special grand juries also sit for eighteen months, but in some cases they may be extended an additional thirty-six months.

[10] Douglas Oil Co. v. Petrol Stops Nw., 441 U.S. 211, 218 (1979).

that the prosecution plans to use his testimony to pinpoint a suspected local gang leader, the witness might be unlikely to cooperate without the anonymity and secrecy afforded grand jury proceedings.

Other important considerations justify keeping grand jury proceedings secret. First, the secrecy of the inquiry prevents the potential defendant from being alerted to the investigation and reduces the likelihood that he will flee. Second, since the grand jury may eventually find no sufficient grounds to indict the suspect, the secrecy of the proceedings will help protect his reputation from undue suspicion. In the case of high profile individuals, being accused of a crime can be nearly as stigmatizing as being convicted of one. As a result, it is common practice for prosecuting agencies suspecting public figures, celebrities, politicians, or police officers, of criminal activity to pursue prosecution by means of a grand jury indictment. A recent example of this occurred in the Michael Jackson trial.

In 2004, a Santa Barbara grand jury indicted the singer on four counts of molesting a minor, four counts of intoxicating a minor, one count of abduction, and one count of conspiring to hold the boy and his family captive. Although Jackson was ultimately found not guilty and cleared of all charges, the prosecutor had sought a grand jury proceeding, rather than a preliminary hearing. Indeed, the media attention surrounding Jackson's subsequent criminal trial was enormous. The use of the grand jury curtailed media involvement, despite public demand for details of the investigation.

In accordance with federal rules and most state rules, the privacy of grand jury proceedings entails that only the following parties may be present: the grand jury members, interpreters (when needed), relevant witnesses (when being questioned), an attorney for the government, and a court reporter or operator of a recording device.[11] There is no judge, no defendant, and no defense counsel. In addition, all parties that may be present during the proceedings are held to a strict obligation of secrecy and must not disclose any matter occurring before the grand jury. Violations of this order can result in sanctions or charges of criminal contempt, although grand jury witnesses are excluded from such an obligation and are free to disclose their testimony to anyone if they so choose. Prosecutorial agencies are held to such a high standard of secrecy that they are expected to create a firewall wherein grand jury testimony is not disclosed to anyone outside of the prosecutor's office. The Court rigidly enforces this secrecy requirement.[12]

D. THE GRAND JURY'S DUTY: SCREENING FUNCTION

The screening function of a grand jury is much like the function of preliminary hearings, namely, to determine whether there is sufficient evidence to charge the accused with a crime. When the grand jury's function is to screen, they will consider the evidence put forth, and determine whether probable cause exists for which a defendant can be charged.[13] In so doing, it can either examine the evidence presented and issue an indictment, or it can perform its own investigation (discussed below) into the

---

[11] FED. R. CRIM. P. 6(d).

[12] United States v. Sells Eng'g Inc., 463 U.S. 418 (1983).

[13] Texas v. Brown, 460 U.S. 730, 742 (1983).

alleged criminal activity and issue a presentment. A grand jury indictment, which has the same effect as a judge's probable cause finding during a preliminary hearing, acts as a magisterial body's stamp of approval, which allows the case to move towards the trial stage.

The prosecutor in deciding whether to proceed with a grand jury or preliminary hearing is faced with a tactical decision. At a preliminary hearing, the defendant and counsel are present and are entitled to cross-examine prosecution witnesses, call their own witnesses, and present affirmative defenses. Whereas a grand jury proceeding cuts the defense out of the picture entirely, thus eliminating the defense attorney's ability to undermine the prosecution's case. Furthermore, evidence will be presented without a defense attorney objecting to evidence or a magistrate ruling to limit evidence.

Nevertheless, there are some advantages to proceeding with a preliminary hearing. By calling essential prosecution witnesses and having them subjected to cross-examination, the prosecutor can better assess the strength of his witnesses and the cogency of his case as he decides whether to take the case to trial. It does not behoove a prosecutor to barely squeak by with the probable cause standard, and then proceed to a trial in which he cannot prove the defendant's guilt beyond a reasonable doubt. Further, assessing the witnesses' credibility and the strength of the case by way of a preliminary hearing is helpful for case settlement. This is particularly true in cases such as domestic violence and sexual assaults, wherein the case hinges almost entirely on the victim's credibility.

HYPO: *Oceana v. Brody*

Sergeant Brody, a police officer, responded to a call in the West Adams district of South Los Angeles in which a man was reportedly holding up a popular restaurant. The suspect reportedly shot at and killed several customers. After arriving at the scene when the suspect was no longer armed, it is alleged that Officer Brody shot and killed the suspect. The case has generated a high degree of media attention and many commentators have suggested that police brutality was an issue. The only survivor who had a clear view of both the suspect and Officer Brody is an eight-year-old girl named Carrie. The prosecuting authority in this case, the district attorney, is considering bringing criminal charges against Officer Brody. If the district attorney opts to file charges against Officer Brody should he proceed via preliminary hearing, or grand jury?

What are the pros and cons of each alternative? For example, the prosecutor may want to avoid subjecting young Carrie to defense counsel's questions. The prosecutor may also be worried that Carrie's age and the graphic nature of the scene might cause her to give inconsistent answers, thereby creating impeachable testimony for use at trial. Conversely, testing Carrie at a preliminary hearing will give the prosecutor a better gauge on whether Dorian will hold up as a credible witness at trial.

E. THE GRAND JURY'S DUTY: INVESTIGATIVE FUNCTION

As already set forth, grand juries are also investigative bodies with the authority to make recommendations to the respective prosecuting authority. Such recommendations are called presentments or reports. In July 2010, for example, a scandal in Southern California involving municipal corruption was investigated by a grand jury.

The *Los Angeles Times* reported that City of Bell officials were also under investigation for drawing exorbitant salaries and various additional financial benefits. Indeed, the extent of the criminal activity was unclear. Once the scandal had broken, additional allegations regarding voter fraud surfaced.[14] In order to probe the issues, a grand jury was summoned as the most effective way to investigate the matter, particularly because of its broad subpoena power.[15] Grand juries are often most useful in cases in which the true extent of criminal activity is unknown, and such was the case when the City of Bell scandal was first exposed. In that case, charges for misappropriation of public funds were eventually brought against several city officials.[16]

The grand jury's broad subpoena power is the primary reason for its effectiveness as an investigative body. "A grand jury has broad investigative powers to determine whether a crime has been committed and who has committed it."[17] In instances when the grand jury conducts its own investigations, the subpoena acts as a powerful magnifying glass, potentially revealing the valuable and intimate details related to the alleged criminal activity in question.

In contrast with the procedure in many other types of investigations, a grand jury subpoena is issued by the court.[18] If the grand jury wants to question someone or retrieve a document, it can issue a subpoena. Where other requests for information might meet resistance, the subpoena power requires an answer. For the most part, the only way to avoid providing an answer is to plead a particular privilege. The Supreme Court has said that "it is clearly recognized that the giving of testimony and the attendance upon court or grand jury in order to testify are public duties which every person within the jurisdiction of the Government is bound to perform upon being properly summoned . . . ."[19] All the same, according to a later Court decision, "the power to compel testimony is not absolute."[20] The Fifth Amendment privilege against self-incrimination is available during such testimony, but the prosecutor is not required to inform anyone that they have the right to refuse to answer the grand jury's questions.[21] Absent a specific

---

[14] Jeff Gottlieb et al., *L.A. County Grand Jury Serves Subpoenas Seeking Thousands of Documents from Bell*, L.A. TIMES (Aug. 9, 2010, 6:42 PM), http://www.latimes.com/news/local/la-me-08-09-bell-investigation-20100810,0,2914607.story.

[15] *Id.*

[16] *Bell City Officials Plead Not Guilty in Salary Scandal*, CBS L.A. (Mar. 18, 2011, 11:11 AM), http://losangeles.cbslocal.com/2011/03/18/bell-city-officials-plead-not-guilty-in-salary-scandal/.

[17] United States v. Dionisio, 410 U.S. 1, 15 (1973).

[18] A subpoena is a court order forcing individuals to appear at a specific court proceeding to provide relevant evidence before the court. There are two types of subpoenas. First, a *subpoena ad testificandum* orders an individual to testify in court. A *subpoena duces tecum* requires an individual to appear before the court with specific physical evidence. For example, this latter type of subpoena could be served on a cell phone provider who is required to produce phone call records to the court.

[19] Blair v. United States, 250 U.S. 273, 281 (1919).

[20] Kastigar v. United States, 406 U.S. 441, 444 (1972).

[21] United States v. Mandujano, 425 U.S. 564, 580–81 (1976).

privilege, however, failure to appear will constitute contempt of court.[22] Thus, the grand jury can command what other investigative routes may not.

In many instances, grand juries are convened solely to take on this more active role in the criminal justice system and to perform a detective-like role. Arguably, the investigative grand jury assumes more unregulated power than any other government law enforcement agency. When the grand jury investigates, compliance is mandatory. Investigating grand juries are unrestrained "by questions of propriety or forecasts of the probable result of the investigation, or by doubts whether any particular individual will be found properly subject to an accusation." [23] Moreover, its "investigation 'is not fully carried out until every available clue has been run down and all witnesses examined in every proper way to find if a crime has been committed.'"[24]

The grand jury's subpoena power is extremely wide-ranging, as the Supreme Court has held: "The function of the grand jury is to inquire into all information that might possibly bear on its investigation until it has identified an offense or has satisfied itself that none has occurred. As a necessary consequence of its investigatory function, the grand jury paints with a broad brush."[25] Nevertheless, the subpoena power is not completely unrestricted: "Grand juries are not licensed to engage in arbitrary fishing expeditions, nor may they select targets of investigation out of malice or an intent to harass."[26]

F. RULES OF EVIDENCE DURING GRAND JURY PROCEEDINGS

One reason that this broad subpoena power is effective is that the *Federal Rules of Evidence*, absent privileges and the exclusionary rule, do not apply during grand jury proceedings. Even evidence obtained in violation of a defendant's Fourth, Fifth, or Sixth Amendment rights can be offered by the prosecutor and used by the grand jury as a basis for indictment.[27] In general, rules of evidence that apply to trials do not apply to grand jury proceedings; thus, improperly seized evidence is admissible at the grand jury stage.[28] Although this may at first seem unfair, in actuality, the grand jury only determines whether a crime has occurred and whether there is probable cause to issue an indictment. The grand jury does not, in other words, determine guilt. By the same token, prosecutors should be wary if evidence presented to the grand jury rests on evidence that would be inadmissible at trial. Since inadmissible evidence will be precluded at trial, prosecutors should not base their cases on questionably admissible

ETHICS

---

[22] Failure to follow subpoenas, absent good cause, may result in criminal contempt charges. Likewise, lying to a grand jury may result in perjury or false declarations before grand jury charges.

[23] *Blair*, 250 U.S. at 282.

[24] Branzburg v. Hayes, 408 U.S. 665, 701 (1972) (quoting United States v. Stone, 249 F.2d 138, 140 (2d Cir. 1970)).

[25] United States v. R. Enterprises, Inc., 498 U.S. 292, 297 (1991).

[26] *Id.* at 299.

[27] United States v. Calandra, 414 U.S. 338 (1974).

[28] Costello v. United States, 350 U.S. 359 (1956).

evidence for both ethical and practical reasons. From an ethical standpoint, it is unfair for a defendant to be indicted solely on the basis of evidence that would not be admissible in trial. Not only is it upsetting for a person to find out that he has been indicted, but also an indicted individual will likely incur legal expenses in anticipation of trial. Additionally, there is a stigma to an indictment, and it can damage an individual's reputation, especially that of a public figure.

G. DOES THE DEFENDANT HAVE THE RIGHT TO TESTIFY?

Both the prosecutor and the defense attorney should be well-acquainted with the rules of court in their jurisdictions because exceptions to the general rules governing grand jury proceedings might significantly impact the defendant's rights. While defendants are not typically present during grand jury proceedings, and in fact, may not even be aware of the proceeding, this is not always the case. Depending on one's respective jurisdiction, the defendant may have a right to testify during a criminal grand jury proceeding. For instance, in New York, a defendant who files appropriate written notice may exercise his right to testify at the grand jury hearing.[29] Indeed, a denial of this right can be grounds for dismissing a grand jury indictment.[30] Under federal jurisdictions, however, there is no such right because the Sixth Amendment applies only to "criminal proceedings," and not to the activities of a grand jury.[31] For example, a federal prosecutor is not even required to inform a witness that he is the target of the grand jury's investigation and that he may be indicted.[32] Even so, in jurisdictions that allow the defendant to testify, most defense attorneys will advise a client against doing so, reasoning that it would not be in the client's best interest to commit to testimony that could later impeach him at trial.

H. DUTY TO PRESENT EXCULPATORY EVIDENCE

On the other hand, because the targeted individual, in most jurisdictions, does not know that he is being investigated, it is incumbent upon the prosecutor to bring exculpatory evidence to the grand jury's attention.[33] It is worth remembering that the prosecutor's overarching duty is to seek justice, not merely to obtain a conviction under any circumstances. Failure to bring forth such exculpatory evidence, in jurisdictions that require it, could result in the dismissal of an indictment.[34] Moreover, once a defendant is indicted, all exculpatory evidence must be presented to the defense per *Brady v. Maryland*.[35] An extensive discussion on the discovery requirements of disclosing information to opposing counsel is located in Chapter 7.

---

[29] N.Y. CRIM. PROC. LAW § 190.50(5)(b) (Consol. 2012).

[30] *Id.* § 190.50(5)(c).

[31] United States v. Mandujano, 425 U.S. 564, 581 (1976).

[32] United States v. Washington, 431 U.S. 181, 189 (1977).

[33] Federal jurisdictions, however, are split on whether there is a duty to provide such evidence.

[34] Though actual prejudice must be demonstrated, the withholding of information vital to the grand jury's ability to make an informed and independent determination may lead to a dismissal of an indictment or, should a conviction result, a reversal of the conviction.

[35] 373 U.S. 83 (1963).

I. WHY UTILIZE THE GRAND JURY TO INVESTIGATE?

HYPO: *Oceana v. Cartel*

Imagine being an attorney at the Department of Justice. You have just received new information regarding a sting operation undertaken by the Federal Bureau of Investigation. What had been previously thought to be a small but high-profile drug bust has turned into a wide-scale operation with up to fifty potential defendants involved. The extremely complex web of criminal activity and widespread conspiracy will require the testimony of dozens of witnesses and months of preparation. Is swift justice available in such a scenario? How would you proceed? Would you impanel a grand jury or proceed with preliminary hearings?

Should the prosecutor not impanel a grand jury, then after the arrests are made, each of the fifty defendants in the hypothetical above would be constitutionally required to make an initial appearance in court before a magistrate. During the appearance, the judge would inform each defendant of the charges, set bail, and if counsel has not been retained, appoint counsel. Then, a preliminary hearing would be scheduled for each of the fifty defendants. Although it may be possible to consolidate all the defendants' cases into a single preliminary hearing, there is no guarantee of such consolidation. At the preliminary hearing or hearings, a magistrate would need to return a finding of "strong suspicion" for each defendant.[36] Regardless of how many hearings take place, the sheer number of defendants and the amount of evidence linking each defendant would present a logistical problem that may well result in the undue consumption of court time and resources. A grand jury indictment can effectively avoid these inefficiencies in such a scenario. This is one sound reason why grand juries are used in the United States, on both federal and state levels, as an alternative to the preliminary hearing when moving matters to trial.

J. PROSECUTION STRATEGY

In the event that a criminal grand jury is convened, a prosecutor must contemplate strategic considerations. First, whom should the prosecutor subpoena to testify? It is common practice, during both preliminary hearings and grand jury proceedings, for a prosecutor to provide only minimal, yet sufficient, evidence to satisfy the charges. In this way, a prosecutor limits the defense attorney's ability to gain a clear picture of the prosecution's evidence, strategy, and witnesses. Moreover, the decision not to call witnesses shields those witnesses from being impeached at trial by inconsistent testimony at the preliminary hearing or grand jury stage. Similarly, a prosecutor may use the grand jury hearings as a way to evaluate potential witnesses for use at trial. No prosecutor wants a material witness who will appear untrustworthy to a jury. Should a prosecutor have multiple witnesses who can provide substantially similar testimony, a prosecutor can effectively shape and strengthen his case by choosing the best

---

[36] A strong suspicion standard is commonly interchanged with probable cause. "Probable cause is shown if a man of ordinary caution or prudence would be led to believe and conscientiously entertain a strong suspicion of the guilt of the accused." Bompensiero v. Superior Court, 281 P.2d 250, 254 (Cal. 1955).

witnesses to testify at trial. Since the hearings are conducted in secrecy, a prosecutor may also use grand jury hearings to protect young or vulnerable witnesses.

A prosecutor should also research the elements for each specific charge sought and confirm that the witnesses subpoenaed will present sufficient evidence for each element, while at the same time establishing jurisdiction and accurate identification of the defendant.

As indicated above, grand juries have the power to conduct their own investigations and issue subpoenas. This is an important feature of the grand jury process not only for the panel but, more importantly, also for the prosecutor, since he can treat the grand jury as a sounding board. As such, he can gain invaluable insight in preparation for trial. It is crucial for a prosecutor to be able to pinpoint in advance the weaknesses and strengths of his case, not only from his and the defense's standpoints, but also from the perspective of a jury member. Receiving direct feedback from members of the grand jury will enable the prosecutor to prepare better for later prosecution at trial.

Should no indictment be returned, a prosecutor should re-evaluate the merits of his case. So long as the prosecutor reasonably believes in its merit, he can present the case again to another grand jury or proceed with a preliminary hearing. Of course, it is imperative that prosecutors do not abuse their discretion by proceeding with a case that is too weak to prove, even if the prosecutor is personally convinced of the suspect's culpability. In this circumstance, the prosecutor should direct the investigating officer to conduct further investigation to see if he might strengthen the case. An extensive discussion of the factors that affect the prosecutor's charging decision is located in Chapter 3.

K. DEFENSE STRATEGY

For a defense attorney whose client is facing a grand jury indictment or investigation, no action may be required. Because of the secrecy of grand jury proceedings, it is highly likely that neither the client or defense counsel, should he already have one, will be aware of the proceedings. Even if the defense attorney and client are aware of the grand jury's investigation, they cannot attend the proceedings or participate in them, with limited exceptions, such as in New York courts. Rather, the primary duties and responsibilities of a defense attorney will arise after the grand jury has returned an indictment.

Since the defense attorney is entitled to receive a transcript of the proceedings, she should review it in order to verify the validity of the indictment. If the indictment is invalid, defense counsel should bring a motion to dismiss it. Circumstances that might lead to such a motion include failure to meet one or more criteria for the crime or crimes charged, bias and prejudice of the grand jury, prejudicial publicity, false testimony, or failure to bring exculpatory evidence. The burden the defense faces, however, is high. According to the Supreme Court, dismissal of an indictment "is appropriate only 'if it is established that the violation substantially influenced the grand jury's decision to indict,' or there is 'grave doubt' that the decision to indict was free from the substantial influence of such violations."[37]

After an indictment has been returned, the defense attorney, in addition to following the other pretrial steps suggested throughout this book, should open negotiations with the respective prosecutor.

[37] Bank of Nova Scotia v. United States, 487 U.S. 250, 256 (1988) (quoting United States v. Mechanik, 476 U.S. 66, 78 (1986) (O'Connor, J., concurring)).

As will be detailed in Chapter 12, much of an attorney's pretrial work will be completed with settlement in mind.

L. GRAND JURY RESOLUTION

After reviewing the evidence and deliberating, the grand jury will resolve its proceedings in one of four ways: indictment, no bill, report, or discharge. First, the grand jury may, by a vote of at least twelve members, return an indictment. Jurisdictions vary regarding the number of grand jurors and quorum indictment requirements, usually depending on the population of the jurisdiction. An indictment will act as the certification that probable cause exists that a crime has occurred and the defendant is the one responsible. Second, if the grand jury is not convinced to a probable cause standard or chooses not to indict after its investigation, the panel will issue a "no bill." A "no bill" finding indicates that there is not sufficient evidence to support a given charge against the defendant. The prosecutor, who is not bound by the decision, may still choose to resubmit the case to the same grand jury panel or to a future one; a subsequent hearing permits the grand jury to examine the case once again, notwithstanding the issuance of the previous "no bill." Third, the grand jury, under certain circumstances, may issue what is called a "report." A "report," which is most commonly compiled and issued alongside a grand jury investigation, will disclose whatever has been uncovered. The prosecuting agency then may seek to file formal charges. And finally, should the court with ultimate jurisdiction over the grand jury find cause, it may discharge the grand jury panel.

M. THE USE OF GRAND JURY TESTIMONY AT TRIAL

The secrecy of the proceedings prior to trial does not necessarily mean that the resulting evidence will be excluded at trial. Should the witness's testimony at trial conflict with prior testimony before the grand jury, the opposing party may, in accordance with Federal Rule of Evidence 613(a), attack the witness's credibility by pointing out the inconsistency with his prior statement to the grand jury.

To return to our earlier hypothetical scenario involving a high-profile FBI drug bust, assume that an eyewitness states during the trial of one of the indicted drug dealers that he no longer remembers what happened. The prosecutor senses that the defendant has very likely intimidated the witness. The

prosecutor should then approach the bench and inform the judge of his intention to introduce the prior testimony of this witness from his grand jury testimony. The defense attorney would likely object, arguing that the witness's grand jury testimony cannot be admitted. How should the judge rule? Is the witness's prior testimony admissible?

CHART 9.1
Internal and External Inconsistencies

Internal Inconsistency: An individual's current testimony is in direct conflict with his prior statements.

Example: Simon, an eyewitness to a bank robbery, tells the police officer that the robber had black hair. At trial, however, Simon is convinced that the robber's hair was blond. Simon's testimony at trial represents an "internal inconsistency."

External Inconsistency: An individual's current testimony is in direct conflict with other evidence, testimonial or physical.

Example: Simon, an eyewitness to a bank robbery, tells the police officer and testifies at trial that the robber had no facial hair. April, a bank teller and eyewitness, told the police the robber had a beard. Simon's statement to the police is "externally inconsistent" with April's account.

N. POLITICAL RAMIFICATIONS

As discussed throughout this chapter, there are a number of reasons why the prosecutor will seek a grand jury indictment in place of a preliminary hearing, such as cases with multiple defendants, complex evidence, or high-profile individuals. Public sentiment can also prove a factor in the decision. For instance, in controversial, sensitive, or difficult cases, it may be expedient for the prosecuting agency to involve the relevant community. As much as possible, a prosecutor will look to put justice into the hands of the affected community and let the people decide through their representatives on the grand jury. This can indirectly build a bond of trust between the citizens and the given prosecuting agency. By handing over the keys of justice to the community, the prosecuting agency has effectively shielded itself from criticism associated with high-profile cases, should a criminal grand jury return lesser charges than expected or no charges at all.

In cases involving politicians or law enforcement suspects, the secrecy provisions of a grand jury hearing make it less likely that the suspect will be alerted to the pending charges. This is particularly important in cases of political corruption and conspiracy. It would be nearly impossible to convict politicians or police officers of corruption charges, if they were made aware of pending investigations and had ample time to destroy evidence or flee. Conversely, if after a grand jury proceeding, it is determined that there does not exist probable cause to believe that the suspect committed a crime, his reputation will not be tarnished by a public accusation. It is especially important to bear this concern in mind when the suspect is a public figure or a member of law enforcement, so as not to unduly undermine the public's confidence in our elected officials and in those sworn to protect us. In a free society, it is crucial that public officials are not relieved of their duties or carted off to jail on the basis of allegations that cannot pass the scrutiny of a probable cause standard.

SUMMARY

        The grand jury is a useful instrument enabling prosecutors to bring an accused to stand trial without the scrutiny of the public, the accused, or his attorney. In federal court, grand juries are always used instead of preliminary hearings in felony cases. In states that permit them, grand juries are common in cases in which the targeted individual is a public figure, an affiliate of organized crime, or a celebrity. If the evidence is complex and potential defendants numerous, a grand jury indictment can be a more efficient route to trial than the preliminary hearing. A grand jury hearing can, moreover, yield invaluable insight into potential pitfalls and strengths for the prosecutor in preparation for trial, when the burden of proof is higher and the consequences are more significant. As either a prosecutor or a defense attorney, it is critical to understand the structure of the grand jury. By recognizing how the grand jury works, an attorney should be able to adjust her approach to a case and tailor a corresponding strategy that maximizes the benefits and accounts for the disadvantages.

CHECKLIST

✓ An indictment, issued by a grand jury, has the same effect as a probable cause finding at a preliminary hearing; a grand jury hearing thereby serves a screening function similar to that of a preliminary hearing.

✓ Provided that a quorum of sixteen jurors is met, twelve federal jurors are required to return an indictment. Besides an indictment, three other outcomes of a grand jury hearing are possible: no bill, report, or discharge.

✓ Grand jury proceedings are conducted in secrecy. There is no right for targeted individuals or their attorneys to be present.

✓ A grand jury, unlike a petit jury, can serve an investigative function and play an active role during proceedings, for instance, by issuing subpoenas and directly posing questions to witnesses and prosecuting attorneys.

✓ For the most part, the rules of evidence do not apply during grand jury proceedings.

✓ Grand jury testimony can be used for impeachment purposes at trial.

✓ During a grand jury hearing, the prosecutor may have a duty to present any exculpatory evidence, although he is not required to bring forth all relevant evidence.

✓ The defense attorney should review the validity of the grand jury indictment.

CHAPTER 10
DRAFTING AND ARGUING MOTIONS

"The object of oratory alone is not truth, but persuasion."
–Thomas Babington Macaulay

Pretrial criminal motions come in many forms and perform a variety of functions, which can range from an oral motion for a translator to a written motion to suppress evidence. Regardless of the type of motion, they are all subject to the same important truth: pretrial motions are pivotal in shaping the trial strategy and case theory. At the same time, they also play an integral role in influencing settlement negotiations. Therefore, even before a criminal litigator steps into the courtroom, she must be able to draft and argue motions effectively as well as be able to think on her feet.[1] This necessarily includes anticipating procedural and evidentiary issues that might arise during trial.

This chapter focuses specifically on pretrial motions.[2] In addition to providing a basic overview of motions, this chapter will also discuss methods to research, write, and argue such motions effectively and persuasively. Interspersed throughout the chapter are key strategies for prosecutors and defense attorneys.

THE BASICS

A motion is simply a request to the court for a ruling on some matter. Both the prosecution and defense can make motions; and generally motions are made either to "get evidence in" or "keep evidence out."[3] The party making the motion is called the "moving party," and the non-moving side is the "responding party." Any motion made before trial is called a "motion *in limine*."[4] Motions *in limine* are key tools for admitting or suppressing evidence; however, motions may be made to resolve all types of legal issues.

Motions may be prepared in written form or made orally depending on the court's rules.[5] For instance, in some jurisdictions, courts will permit motions to be made off-the-cuff during a preliminary hearing. In many state courts defense attorneys will typically make an oral motion to dismiss charges for

---

[1] The gift of wit and the talent of communication are necessary for all criminal litigators. Oral powers of persuasion are a combination of natural talent and practice. For essential trial advocacy advice, see generally L. TIMOTHY PERRIN, H. MITCHELL CALDWELL & CAROL A. CHASE, THE ART & SCIENCE OF TRIAL ADVOCACY (2d ed. 2011).

[2] *See* FED. R. CRIM. P. 12 (discussing criminal pretrial motions). *See also* FED. R. CRIM. P. 47.

[3] "The court may exclude relevant evidence if its probative value is substantially outweighed by a danger of one or more of the following: unfair prejudice, confusing the issues, misleading the jury, undue delay, wasting time, or needlessly presenting cumulative evidence." FED. R. EVID. 403.

[4] "'*In limine*' has been defined as '[on] or at the threshold; at the very beginning; preliminary.'" Luce v. United States, 469 U.S. 38, 40 n.2 (1984) (quoting BLACK'S LAW DICTIONARY 708 (5th ed. 1979)). However, this court also interprets the term broadly to refer to any motion made before, or even during trial, to exclude evidence before the evidence is actually offered. *Id.*

[5] FED. R. CRIM. P. 47(b) (stating that the court may permit a motion to be made "by other means").

insufficiency of evidence. These motions are standard: a public defender or defense attorney should be prepared to make this motion and argue it at the conclusion of a preliminary hearing. Similarly, a prosecutor should anticipate this motion and be prepared to argue on behalf of the People. Often these motions are cursory and do not merit consideration. Indeed, it is not unusual after a preliminary hearing for a defense attorney to state, "motion to dismiss for insufficiency of the evidence," and for the prosecution to respond, "submit it." Sometimes, however, there is a genuine issue, and both sides will vigorously argue the motion to dismiss. A judge may even request case law to support an argument, and an attorney's ability to anticipate a motion can prove critical to the court's ruling. If necessary, an attorney can ask the judge if each side may have time to conduct further research.

Attorneys should always have a copy of the local rules to calendar timing deadlines for specific motions in state court; if in federal court, one can refer to *the Federal Rules of Criminal Procedure* for procedural rules and requirements. Court rules regarding the making and bringing of motions can vary dramatically from jurisdiction to jurisdiction; therefore, referencing the local rules of court is an essential element in bringing and responding to motions. It is also wise to bring to court a book containing the *Federal Rules of Evidence*, or a book delineating the state rules when in state court. The making of *any* motion, however, requires consideration of its purpose and effect.

CHART 10.1
Common Criminal Pretrial Motions

Dismissal

- Double Jeopardy
- Lack of Evidence
- Speedy Trial Violation

Suppression

- Of Statements Made By Defendant
- Of Statements Made By Witnesses
- Of Evidence
- Of Identification
- Motion To Exclude Under *Crawford*[6]

Other

- Prior Convictions
- Uncharged Acts
- Continuance
- Bail
- Diversion
- Change of Venue
- Fitness Hearing
- Competency Hearing
- 402—Witness Relevance
- Appointment of Support Person For Witness
- Appointment of Interpreter
- Conflict of Attorney Waiver
- *Marsden*: Change of Public Defender
- Severance of Counts
- Severance of Defendants
- Appointment of Expert
- Discovery Violation
- Prosecutorial Misconduct
- Identity of Informant
- Live Line Up
- *Romero*: Strike A Strike
- Find Prior Invalid
- Reduce Felony to Misdemeanor
- Medical Examination
- Keep Away Order
- Psychiatric Evaluation
- Challenge the Judge
- Reverse Preliminary Hearing Ruling

---

[6] Crawford v. Washington, 541 U.S. 36 (2004).

A. THE MOTION AND ITS RELATIONSHIP TO THE CASE THEORY

Motions are a vessel through which a litigator influences the court; therefore, they must appeal to both reason and emotion. In order to do that, the moving party must consider its procedural and substantive goals when bringing the motion. Identifying these two aspects is crucial to drafting and arguing a motion effectively and, if done with precision, should also reflect and substantiate the moving party's case theory.

As discussed in Chapter 2, a case theory is an underlying legal and factual theme—a compelling story—that supports an advocate's case. Once developed, it is communicated to the trier of fact in anecdotes proffered by both the witnesses and the attorneys. When developing a case theory, many litigators find it useful to create their case theory with the end result in mind. Working backwards in this way, litigators will first determine what motions are required and then draft them in order to achieve that goal. Such a comprehensive strategy will ensure that no needless, redundant, or ill-advised motions will be made. For example, if a defense attorney realizes that her client's confession is devastating to the defense's case, she should try to find an evidentiary basis to exclude the confession. Perhaps the defendant's statement was coerced, in violation of his *Miranda* rights,[7] or is fruit of the poisonous tree resulting from an illegal arrest.[8] The attorney should research the case law and apply it to the facts of the case to determine whether there is any credible argument that the confession should be suppressed. The same logic of selecting damaging aspects of the case and working backwards to see if there is a legal reason to exclude the evidence applies to physical evidence. Both the defense and prosecution should engage in this type of ends-means analysis. Knowing how to develop a case theory is significant because this same strategy can and should be applied to the creation of a motion. A motion theory is substantially similar to a case theory in that it is created with an end result in mind and often reflects elements of the case theory itself.

B. DECIDING WHAT MOTIONS TO BRING: IT'S ALL ABOUT STRATEGY

The term "*in limine*" does not refer to the content of the motion but rather to the motion's timing. Any motion made before the start of trial is considered *in limine*. Rulings on motions *in limine* can influence the strategy employed by an attorney during the trial or even dictate the trial's outcome. Nevertheless, this does not mean that any motion that could conceivably be made before trial should be.

As a basic rule, any evidence that is susceptible to a pretrial motion to exclude will still be vulnerable to exclusion if there is a timely objection at trial. Thus, the decision not to raise an evidentiary matter before trial will not be a litigator's last bite at the apple. Allowing a matter to be handled at trial often has its advantages. Indeed, standing up to say "objection" is certainly easier than drafting, filing, and arguing a motion *in limine*, and it can result in the same outcome. Additionally, an advocate may wish to avoid bringing unnecessary attention to a piece of evidence by filing a written motion. Although a party is generally not entitled to hide information from a party opponent, a litigator can avoid

---

[7] Miranda v. Arizona, 384 U.S. 436 (1966).

[8] Brown v. Illinois, 422 U.S. 590, 591–92 (1975).

illuminating certain facts if she senses that opposing counsel does not realize its potential evidentiary weight. Raising a motion *in limine* may result in bringing some "hidden gem" to light and giving opposing counsel ample opportunity to rebut the motion. Certain issues, however, such as whether there was probable cause to arrest the defendant or whether a search and seizure violated the Fourth Amendment, must be brought as a pretrial motion or the issue is forfeited.[9] If the defense attempts to bring these arguments up at the trial stage, then the prosecution should object on the grounds of relevance.

To begin with, the timing and intricacy of the argument should be considered when deciding to file a motion *in limine* as compared to an objection. If a legal issue is complex or relies on an obscure set of legal intricacies, it may be prudent to flush out the details in a written motion. This will also provide the court an opportunity to properly evaluate the merits of the argument. Objections in trial are often limited to a few sentences from each party and are kept brief for the benefit of the jury and the flow of the trial. Motions *in limine*, on the other hand, allow for the moving party to fully express the grounds for the motion and to discuss in detail the logic and reasoning behind it. Additionally, they occur outside the presence of the jury, and an unfavorable ruling will not reflect poorly on an advocate or diminish her efficacy in the eyes of the jury.

The reasons to move to introduce or to exclude evidence before trial are typically far stronger than those for waiting until trial. The risk of opposing counsel or a witness mentioning the evidence in question is usually too great of a gamble for a litigator—as the adage goes, a jury cannot "un-hear" something; and, likewise, an advocate cannot "un-ring a bell." By winning a motion *in limine* to suppress evidence, a litigator guarantees that the evidence will not be admitted during the trial. Moreover, in the event a pretrial motion fails, an attorney will then have an opportunity to create a strategy that limits the harm that was caused by either her inability to introduce or to suppress a piece of evidence. In contrast, an unsuccessful ruling during trial will leave the attorney with no alternative.

Another significant strategic advantage to bringing a pretrial motion is obtaining a ruling as to whether certain evidence can be discussed in opening statements. The admission or exclusion of prior convictions might influence an opening statement. For instance, will a prosecutor be able to use crime scene photos in an opening statement? Without obtaining a ruling in advance, the flow and persuasiveness of the opening statement could be diminished. It is imperative to remember that motions *in limine* can be just as effective for getting evidence in as for keeping evidence out. For example, it is almost always wise to obtain a ruling in advance if an attorney is attempting to bring a witness's prior conviction or prior bad act before the jury, as it is often effective for a prosecutor to refer to a defendant's prior convictions in opening statement. If a prosecutor refers to a conviction or prior bad act that the judge ruled should not have been mentioned in the presence of the jury, then he might be sanctioned or cause a mistrial.[10]

---

[9] *See* FED. R. CRIM. P. 12(b)(3) (listing motions that must be made before trial).

[10] For instance, "where . . . the improper evidence was calculated to make such an impression on the jury that no direction from the court, however strong, can eliminate the prejudice thereby created, the trial court must declare a mistrial." Helton v. United States, 221 F.2d 338, 341 (5th Cir. 1955).

A motion *in limine* will also give the litigator a distinct preview of how the judge may rule on certain issues, and this insight can be advantageous when arguing future motions or making basic objections. The ability to mold a legal argument to fit the judge's outlook is invaluable and could pay dividends later in the trial. As it stands, a judge has several options when it comes to ruling on motions: she can make a ruling, defer a ruling, or make a ruling subject to limitations. The judge may choose either to admit or to exclude the evidence after hearing both sides' arguments on a motion. Alternatively, the judge may take the matter under submission to rule at a later time depending on how the case progresses, or until the judge has a chance to further research the law. For example, the judge might state, "Counsel, I am going to wait until I hear from the ballistics expert to determine if I am going to allow you to bring up a theory about a hair trigger, so I am not going to allow this to be mentioned in opening statements." Or the judge might state, "People, the defendant's prior conviction for petty theft will only become relevant to impeach his credibility if he chooses to testify. If he testifies, I will allow you to bring it up on cross-examination and to refer to it for credibility purposes in closing argument; however, you may not refer to it in opening statement." The third option the judge might take is to grant a motion to exclude certain evidence unless opposing counsel or the opposing side's witness "opens the door."

Opening the door means referring to an issue and, as a result, allowing opposing counsel to introduce evidence that would otherwise be ruled inadmissible. Thus, if a judge rules that the defendant's prior conviction for drug possession is inadmissible because it is not a moral turpitude offense, meaning that it does not go to credibility, and the defendant then testifies that he has never been convicted of a crime, this would open the door for the prosecutor to bring up the prior conviction. Likewise, if fingerprint evidence was suppressed because of a search and seizure violation, and the defense counsel argues to the jury that there is no fingerprint evidence in the case, then the judge may allow the prosecutor to present the fingerprint evidence. Opening the door can occur from the opposing side's attorney or witnesses, but a party who wants evidence to be admitted may not bring up an issue in an attempt to open his own door. It is important to instruct witnesses not to refer to evidence that has been excluded. This is especially true with prosecution witnesses. If, for example, a detective refers to a confession that has been ruled inadmissible, this would likely result in a mistrial, even if the prosecutor did not ask a question about the confession.

It serves to note that some courts, particularly in misdemeanor cases, will refuse to rule on a pretrial motion before trial. The idea behind this judicial strategy is to save time. The practice is known as "carrying the motion with the trial" and usually involves a motion to suppress evidence. In these infrequent instances where a judge has refrained from ruling during pretrial hearings, she will allow the evidence to be introduced at trial, and then determine whether to suppress the evidence or not. As a general rule, a decision to suppress the evidence may well result in an immediate dismissal, while a decision to allow the evidence will mean the trial will continue.

C. BOILERPLATE VS. CASE-SPECIFIC MOTIONS

"Boilerplate" motions are fill-in-the-blank, pre-drafted motions that are not case specific. Such boilerplate motions are less likely to be taken seriously by the court.

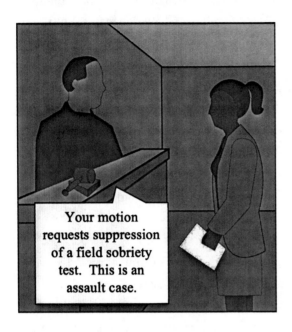 

Bench officers do not take flippant motions seriously, and an attorney's reputation for wasting the court's time can often follow her for the rest of her career. This not only affects the attorney, but also her client and her future clients. The following variation of a well-known children's short story demonstrates the danger in filing frivolous motions.

HYPO: *Frivolous Motions*

Imagine a defense attorney who spends her time entertaining herself by repeatedly filing needless motions. The motions are grandiose in their claims, alleging police misconduct or constitutional violations at a minimum and have no basis in fact. The motions are generic in nature and are nearly identical to each other, with the exception of items such as names, dates, and locations. Time after time, the court receives, reads, and hears testimony and oral arguments. Each time, the judge dismisses these claims as an irrelevant waste of time and judicial resources. Eventually, the defense attorney takes on a client who does indeed have a legitimate claim for the suppression of evidence gathered against him. Dutifully the attorney files the appropriate motion—the same motions she had filed needlessly many times before—only to have the judge summarily dismiss it based on the belief that this motion was as much a waste of the court's time as the others. The attorney has lost credibility with the judge. When an evidentiary issue is a close call, a judge will often rule in favor of the attorney who has built credibility.

Filing a motion spuriously, for no other reason than to bill a client for the time spent drafting and arguing the motion, is of course, unethical.[11] Attorneys are forbidden from passing on irrelevant costs to clients. It is also unethical to use boilerplate motions to mislead a client into thinking that an immense amount of time, effort, or expertise was employed for his specific case.

CHART 10.2
Common Boilerplate Motions **In Limine**

- Motion to exclude the personal beliefs of counsel about the justice of her client's case or the credibility of witnesses
- Motion to exclude representations about testimony which counsel does not have a good faith belief will be offered during the trial
- Motion to exclude expert testimony

Regardless of the type of motion an attorney drafts, all motions must have a clear purpose, be persuasively argued, and advance the case theory. It is also necessary to begin and end all motions with a clear request and to interweave case law and evidentiary rules with the specific facts of the case.

WRITING THE MOTION

It is one thing to determine which motion to bring, but it is quite another to actually draft it. Writing a motion can seem like a daunting task, particularly for a novice attorney, but writing it should be quite manageable if the attorney compartmentalizes the motion into its individual parts.

Each jurisdiction will have specific requirements detailing the components of a motion, although most are structured similarly. Still, it is sound practice to be familiar with the local jurisdiction's rules regulating the content and structure of motions. In fact, the rules of court can change from courthouse to courthouse. It should be noted that federal courts are much stricter than state courts in their motion requirements. Nevertheless, the basic elements of a motion typically remain unchanged from one jurisdiction to the next. The following discussion will present the most significant of those elements.

---

[11] MODEL RULES OF PROF'L CONDUCT R. 1.5 (2010) (discussing reasonable attorney's fees). Moreover, any counsel or attorney who "files a motion solely for the purpose of delay which he knows is totally frivolous and without merit" may be punished by the court. 18 U.S.C. 3162(b) (2006). Also, remember that it is the ethical duty for the lawyer to provide "competent representation to the client" requiring the "legal knowledge, skill, thoroughness and preparation reasonably necessary for the representation." MODEL RULES OF PROF'L CONDUCT R. 1.1 (2010). *See also* MODEL RULES OF PROF'L CONDUCT R. 1.3 (2010) (regarding lawyer diligence and promptness).

A. CAPTION

The first page of every motion begins with a caption; it is perhaps one of the most instantly recognizable aspects of a motion. The caption will include the case number, the title of the motion, the names of the parties, and the names of the attorneys or law firm. Generally, a caption will look something like this:

ALISTAIR FRANKLIN
District Attorney of County of Maliwood
Michelle Thompson, SBN: 654321
Deputy District Attorney
Maliwood Branch Office
200 W. Mali Blvd.
Maliwood, Oceana 90120
Telephone: (555) 555-1234

SUPERIOR COURT OF THE STATE OF OCEANA
FOR THE COUNTY OF MALIWOOD

PEOPLE OF THE STATE OF OCEANA,	Case No. 12345
Plaintiff,	
	PEOPLE'S OPPOSITION TO DEFENSE'S MOTION TO SUPPRESS EVIDENCE OF DRUG PARAPHANEILA; POINTS AND AUTHORITIES
v.	
IAN MCGREEVEY,	
	DATE: February 1st, C.Y.
Defendant.	**TIME:** 8:30 a.m.
	COURT: Department 1

B. NOTICE

Following the caption, most jurisdictions will use the remainder of the first page to introduce the motion and provide a brief statement of notice. It is important to note a distinction here between this form of notice and the notice required in civil actions. In a civil case, a separate statement of notice must be drafted and delivered to opposing counsel and requires compliance with a stringent set of guidelines. Motions made in criminal courts are made more informally and, in the course of a trial, are often made orally with opposing counsel waiving notice entirely. When written, this section of the motion may look something like this:

TO THE HONORABLE CHERYL PRESSLY, JUDGE OF THE ABOVE-ENTITLED COURT; STEWART DAY, COUNSEL FOR DEFENDANT; AND DEFENDANT:

PLEASE TAKE NOTICE THAT ON FEBRUARY 1, C.Y., or as soon thereafter as this matter can be heard, in Department 1 of the above-entitled court, the People will move to admit evidence of seized drug paraphernalia.

This motion is based on all pleadings, papers, transcripts and records in this action, the attached memorandum of points and authorities and any evidence received at the hearing.

DATED: January 21, C.Y.

Respectfully submitted,

Alistair Franklin

DISTRICT ATTORNEY

BY

Michelle Thompson

Michelle Thompson

DEPUTY DISTRICT ATTORNEY

The set up may appear peculiar, for under the phrase "Respectfully submitted," it states that the District Attorney submits the motion but then a deputy district attorney signs it. This is more of a symbolic step than a literal one. The suggestion is, of course, that the District Attorney himself is filing this motion on behalf of the people—but in reality it is wholly impractical to expect the District Attorney to file every single motion in every single case in his district. As a result, deputy district attorneys perform the task on behalf of the District Attorney.

C. STATEMENT OF FACTS

The statement of facts is, of course, a critical part of the motion. Although a motion's success largely depends on how well an advocate articulates the legal precedent and applies it to the current case, the manner in which the facts are presented can shape the entire argument. With that said, the factual presentation must be accurate. Misrepresentations should, and will, incur the wrath of the court and could prove to be far worse than any official sanctions. That does not mean, however, that a verbatim rendition of the facts from the police report is required. Instead, a good lawyer will present the facts in the light most favorable to her client without omitting information or misrepresenting facts. Superfluous wording or hyperbole should be avoided in favor of a clear and concise rendition of the relevant facts. Presenting the statement of facts can be a bit like walking a tightrope. On the one hand, it should not demonstrate bias and it should avoid issuing conclusions. On the other, it should be persuasive.

Consider what the fact pattern is in the controlling case you intend to cite as support for your motion. If the fact pattern in that case mirrors the facts found in your case, then it might benefit you to write your statement of facts to line up as precisely as possible with that case so that when it comes time to argue, the comparisons are already drawn. Conversely, if you know the fact pattern for the case that you hope to distinguish from your own, formulate your statement of facts in a way inapposite to the facts in that case. Remember, you don't want to misrepresent the facts, but you should state them in the light most favorable to your position.

D. ARGUMENT

This section, as its name indicates, allows an attorney to advance an argument for why her motion should be granted. The most important aspect to remember in preparing written arguments is to be concise, clear, and persuasive while avoiding hyperbole or misleading statements. Lengthy diatribes about nebulous issues risk annoying the court and impeding the argument. Instead, this section should be separated into logically organized parts. An attorney should not attempt to state her entire legal argument in one large paragraph. She should break up the elements of the argument into different, clearly defined sections. For example, in a jurisdiction that allows evidence of prior domestic violence perpetrated by the defendant, perhaps the first section of the argument will demonstrate that past acts are relevant to the case at bar with the second section arguing that they are admissible. Drafting a motion in this fashion will afford greater clarity to the judge, who is ultimately the motion's audience.

The importance of intertwining the facts with the law, however, cannot be overstated. An attorney should apply the facts to the law, citing cases that support her proposition. Attorneys should not ignore cases or statutes that contradict the primary points of their argument, as it is not only unethical but also foolish to "hide the ball." An attempt to get the judge to overlook certain relevant law can result in sanctions and hurt one's reputation. No judge wants to be overturned on appeal, so most will do their own research prior to ruling on a motion *in limine*, or the judge may already know the law from previous rulings. Additionally, opposing counsel may find the case that an attorney avoided. The revelation can be an embarrassing moment for the attorney who ignored or failed to find relevant case law. Instead, a persuasive lawyer will distinguish a negative case from the case at bar by bringing up the opposing case and convincing the judge that it is inapplicable. Interweaving the facts of her case and distinguishing the case's fact pattern from that of the negative case is the most effective way to deal with a case that appears to favor opposing counsel.

As this strategic approach illustrates, it is crucial to anticipate what opposing counsel will argue. Again, this can be achieved by raising opposing counsel's claims first and then dismissing them either by denying their legitimacy outright or by distinguishing them. Such a preemptive attack can provide an edge to both oral and written arguments. Generally, it is wise for an attorney to begin and end the argument section with her strongest points and put the preemptive argument in the middle. It is important to remember the rule of primacy and recency: a litigator's audience is most likely to remember the first and last things it is told.

In addition to case law and statutory law, it is often effective to include a public policy argument. For instance, in a case involving alleged police brutality, the defense can point out that if the police are overly aggressive, this can lead citizens to fear law enforcement to an extent that they cease to cooperate with the police. Conversely, the prosecutor can argue that an officer's safety is paramount and if society expects police officers to wait until they are shot at before they use force in self-defense, then no one will be willing to work in law enforcement. Public policy arguments are typically more effective when articulated orally; however, if public policy arguments are succinct, they can also help persuade a judge when they are included in the argument section of a written motion. Public policy arguments are most effective when attorneys do not resort to hyperbole and remember to make the argument proportional to the specific facts of the case.

E. CONCLUSION

The final section of a motion is the conclusion. While brief, the conclusion contains a few specific elements. The conclusion should contain a summary of the argument and specifically request a favorable ruling.

CONCLUSION

For the aforementioned reasons, this motion should be granted, *in toto*, and evidence of alleged drug paraphernalia should be deemed admissible pursuant to Oceana Evidence Code Section 352 because any prejudicial effect is not substantially outweighed by the probative value.

ORAL ARGUMENT

From the outset, it is important for attorneys to distinguish the differences between their audiences. During the pretrial phase of litigation and when arguing a motion *in limine*, an attorney will present her argument to a judge, not a jury. What will persuade a jury may not be convincing to a judge, and, accordingly, there are a few key factors to remember.[12]

A judge will most likely already possess at least a cursory understanding of the legal principles surrounding the motion at issue. It is, therefore, appropriate to spend far less time explaining what the governing legal principles are than one would when arguing in front of a jury. As such, it makes strategic sense to spend more of the argument explaining how these legal principles apply to the facts of the case. It is also important not to simply repeat the motion, as the judge should have already read it. Instead, the attorney should be prepared to answer the judge's challenges and be ready to expand on the argument if necessary.

---

[12] *See* PERRIN, CALDWELL & CHASE, *supra* note 1.

A. REMEMBERING YOUR AUDIENCE

When arguing in front of a judge, an advocate must realize she is speaking to someone who possesses a much deeper understanding of the law than the average juror. The following is an example of direct evidence versus circumstantial evidence as drawn from a commonly used jury instruction:

CHART 10.3

ATTORNEY TO JUDGE:	ATTORNEY TO JURY:
"As Your Honor is well aware, circumstantial evidence is to be given the same amount of weight as direct evidence."	"Circumstantial evidence is to be given the same amount of weight as direct evidence. An example of circumstantial evidence might be looking at a man who just walked into a room with no windows. He is wearing a raincoat that is dripping water, carrying an umbrella that is soaked, and wearing rain boots which are traipsing water onto the floor. From this, although you cannot see outside, you can infer that it is raining. That is circumstantial evidence. Direct evidence would be if you personally saw it raining. The circumstantial evidence where you inferred it is raining should be given the same amount of weight as direct evidence."

An attorney needs to be more concerned with maintaining the jury's attention than she would be with the judge. There is no doubt that it is difficult for a juror to sit through days of testimony, only to listen to both attorneys make their closing arguments. For that reason, it may benefit an attorney to use attention-grabbing language and visual aids. Conversely, a judge will be intent on hearing both the prosecution and defense arguments so that she can make an informed decision in order to ensure that justice is served and to lessen the likelihood of reversal. This means that a judge will be far less welcoming of hyperbole than a juror, and she may also wish to see the advocate be as concise and accurate as possible so as to not take up more time than is necessary.

There are a few basic rules that every attorney needs to remember. She should not refer to the judge as "judge"—this is too informal for the proceedings. "Judge" may be appropriate while passing each other in the courtroom cafeteria but certainly not for a hearing. Instead, the appropriate way to address the judge is "Your Honor."

It is always best to stand while addressing the judge. In state criminal courts, which are much more informal than federal courts, some attorneys do not always stand when addressing the court. Failure to do so is not necessarily improper, but it is best to show deference and respect to the court. Observing formal behavior is the ideal way to achieve this goal.

Further, the attorney should never speak directly to opposing counsel during legal proceedings. While it may be difficult to avoid engaging opposing counsel, it is inappropriate and can potentially hurt an attorney's credibility in the eyes of the judge and jury. If opposing counsel argue with each other or interrupt each other, it will likely anger the judge. Rather, an attorney should state, "Your Honor, perhaps

opposing counsel can explain why it was not coercive for the police to question my client for five hours?"
Or counsel might state, "Your Honor, would you please direct counsel not to interrupt my argument?"

Oral advocacy can become heated, especially in serious cases when a client's life may literally be
on the line; however, it is critical to remain respectful to opposing counsel, the judge, and the court staff.
Attorneys need to be mindful of the court reporter and, therefore, not speak too rapidly. Personal attacks
are inappropriate, unless opposing counsel has exhibited blatant unethical conduct. Overly aggressive
conduct is unprofessional and disrespectful to the court. Attorneys also need to retain a calm demeanor
even in the face of adversary rulings. While it is acceptable to ask a judge to clarify a ruling, or to request
the judge to reconsider a ruling, attorneys who overreact to unfavorable rulings by rolling their eyes or
criticizing the judge are inviting the judge's wrath. As always, litigators need to remember that they
should never jeopardize future cases by their choices made in the current case, and they should avoid
alienating the judge. Judges are not infallible, but counsel would be wise to be respectful when
questioning a judge's ruling. Most judges are receptive to an attorney's request to supplement a motion
with further written points and authorities and to take a matter under submission until each side has had
an opportunity to provide additional case law or statutory authority.

There are also ancillary matters that both defense attorneys and prosecutors must keep in mind.
A skilled defense attorney must be aware of her client's actions during the course of the trial. Any
outbursts, talking, or inappropriate facial expressions may reflect poorly upon the defendant and is usually
regarded as unacceptable by the court. Moreover, as the investigating officer on the case will often sit
next to the prosecutor through the course of the pretrial motions and the trial, the prosecutor must be
mindful of the officer's actions. Managing the investigator's demeanor and ensuring that he projects a
calm command of the case is critical for a prosecutor. It is advisable for the attorneys to communicate
with the client or investigating officer only by writing notes and not communicating orally during court
proceedings. Oral communication is not only disruptive, but also distracting to the attorneys.

For both the defense attorney and prosecutor, it is important to always take into consideration the
perceptions of other people in the courtroom, particularly the jurors. Any interaction with a client,
investigator, or another attorney should not diminish an attorney's authority. If communication is
necessary, it should be made in the form of a written note or a whisper. The practical consequence of any
distraction, of course, is that it may detract from an attorney's focus on the legal proceedings and can
compromise his ability as an effective advocate.

CHART 10.4
Oral Argument Principles

1. Be clear and concise	5. Maintain a professional demeanor
2. Structure arguments persuasively	6. Interweave facts with the law
3. Preemptively rebut your opponent's arguments	7. Distinguish opposing case law
4. Be prepared to answer the judge's questions	

The reasoning behind being clear and concise is not surprising. A court's docket is usually full, and trials often will not start until the late morning after other business is dispensed. Moreover, motions *in limine* are sometimes argued as the jury is waiting outside of the courtroom, so there is an added pressure on the judge to have the jurors brought in and seated as quickly as possible. Because of this, an attorney who can efficiently describe the evidence and the thrust of her argument at the outset will score major points with the judge and increase her chances of winning the motion.

In order to effectuate an efficient argument, the structure of the advocate's presentation is critical. It is the quality of an argument that will determine its success, so conflicting and weak arguments should be avoided. In addition to opting for only the strongest points, counsel should avoid a "shotgun" approach of multiple theories. It is wiser to pick the optimal theory and stay the course. Providing context is also an important element of a persuasive argument, as the facts of the case do not exist in a vacuum but are a part of a larger picture. Consequently, it makes sense to interweave the points of law and fact and bring them both back to the central issue of the case. This means that it may be advisable to broach opposing counsel's arguments before they can present them on their own terms. As discussed earlier, it is absolutely vital from an ethical and strategic standpoint that an advocate discloses, in good faith, the relevant law. In doing so, an effective lawyer has several methods by which she can disclose this information. She can distinguish the opposing authority from the current case; she can explain why the cited authority does not apply to the case at hand; or she can explain why the cited authority applies, but that it needs to be overturned in favor of a new rule. If this third approach is adopted, a public policy argument will probably be the most persuasive. Further, she should position the negative case law or authority between two good arguments supporting her proposition in order to lessen its impact.

Public policy arguments are tricky in that they may not be the most effective arguments to make. As any lawyer knows, the American legal system relies on precedent in order to maintain consistency. Making a public policy argument sometimes requires suggesting that the current status of the law is not appropriate and, as a result, should be changed. Judges are hesitant, more often than not, to enter the role of legislator or to buck precedent. As a result, public policy arguments may be more suited to the appellate courts. Public policy arguments, however, can sometimes be persuasive, especially when they refer to officer or public safety. In a case that is a close call, a judge may be inclined to err on the side of officer safety. For instance, a prosecutor may be able to convince a judge that it is reasonable for an officer to search a detained suspect for weapons without requiring the officer to wait until the suspect makes a move that could endanger the officer's or some third person's life.

CHART 10.5
Oral Argument Road Map

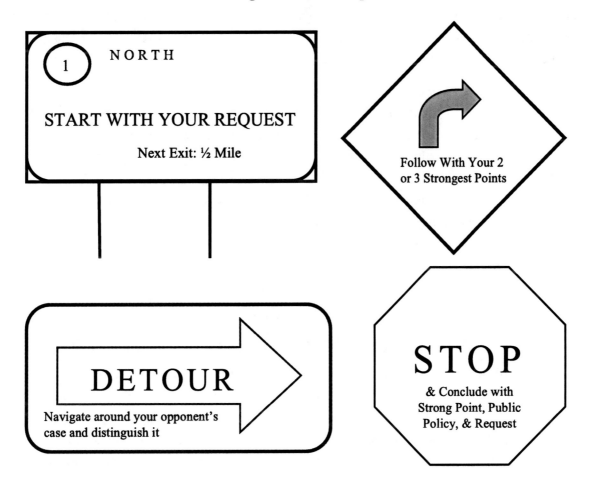

Finally, an attorney should be aware of the judge. She should not only consider the questions that the judge is asking, but also examine the non-verbal signs the judge may be providing. Many inexperienced attorneys fall into the trap of focusing exclusively on their own argument, ignoring the argument of opposing counsel or the non-verbal cues of the judge. Listening and reacting is a critical skill that all advocates must cultivate. An attorney should also be mindful of the fact that presenting the entirety of a prepared argument is not always essential to winning a motion, and a judge's reactions will often express that. If a judge asks a question, effective advocacy dictates that the question will be answered directly prior to moving forward with the argument. The remaining argument should be tailored to address the judge's concerns.

1. Role of an Advocate

Remember, it is the role of an advocate to educate and to persuade. A criminal defense attorney is charged with zealously representing her clients. A prosecutor's duty is to pursue justice on behalf of society, and he should not ignore his ethical duties in an effort to secure a conviction. If a prosecutor believes a defendant did not commit a crime or there is no reasonable probability of proving a case beyond a reasonable doubt, he should urge his superior to drop the charges.

The importance for an attorney of knowing her audience cannot be stressed enough. Judges have particular tendencies and researching a judge to gain insights into which arguments were effective with her in the past can provide an edge over an opponent. Private defense attorneys who are unfamiliar with a particular judge are wise to consult with a public defender that works within the court to gain insight into a particular judge's rulings on similar motions.

2. Argument Tips

In terms of public policy arguments, it may behoove the prosecution to suggest that the officer's actions in obtaining the evidence were reasonable given the need for officer safety. There is always strong public policy support for ensuring the safety of the officer.

For both prosecutors and defense attorneys, an effective catch-all phrase when attempting to introduce evidence at trial is, "This evidence goes to the weight, and not the admissibility." This phrase emphasizes that it is up to the jury to determine how strong the evidence is given a mistake in procedure.

THE AFTERMATH:
WHEN A MOTION IS GRANTED OR DENIED

It is, of course, problematic when an advocate—whether as a proponent or an opponent—suffers an adverse ruling. In such an event, effective advocates attempt to keep the issue open for future reconsideration. Judges will often either implicitly or explicitly allow for further argument of the issue at a later date. In the event of an adverse ruling, an attorney must make sure an objection is stated on the record in order to preserve the right to appeal.[13] Lastly, the advocate should be sure to seek clarification of any ambiguous ruling.

Adverse rulings require advocates to make tough choices, the most important of which is how to move forward strategically. If, for example, a motion to suppress evidence has been denied, the proponent of such a motion will likely have to decide how to temper the impact of the evidence. This strategy can usually be accomplished through one of two ways: either the attorney can raise the evidence through testimony first, in order to soften its impact, or she can attempt to avoid the evidence at all costs and renew the objection when opposing counsel introduces it. Either way, this decision will have to be weighed against any desire to appeal the ruling.

---

[13] FED. R. EVID. 103.

HYPO: *Oceana v. Watson*

The body of Laura Stewart was found in her home where she had been shot to death. Jared Watson, who was dating Laura prior to the incident, is suspected of committing the murder. Jared's fingerprints were found in Laura's home; however, this is not independently incriminating given the fact that the two were dating. More importantly, however, is the fact that Jared's fingerprints were found on the window of Laura's home, which is the suspected point of entry to the home, as the doors to the home were locked at the time of the murder in addition to the window being found open during the investigation. While there is no conclusive DNA evidence, there is fiber evidence that was found on Laura's body, which is consistent with the clothes that Jared was wearing the night of the murder. Jared also has scratch marks on his arms consistent with defensive wounds. The prosecutor has found a witness who will testify that Laura was going to break off her relationship with Jared. The prosecutor has also found another witness, Laura's neighbor, who will testify that she heard a man shouting at Laura the night she was killed, and the witness recognized the voice as belonging to Jared. The ballistics came back on the bullets found in Laura's body, which happen to be a positive match for the 38-caliber gun that was found in Jared's home. Defense counsel brought a motion to suppress the evidence of the gun based on a warrantless search of Jared's home. Unfortunately for the prosecution, this motion to suppress was granted.

- What options does the prosecutor have when the motion to suppress is granted? Can the prosecution possibly proceed without the gun evidence?

- What if after the prosecutor proceeds to trial, defense counsel "opens the door" to the gun evidence, such as by arguing that the prosecution's failure to produce a gun and tie it to Jared creates a reasonable doubt as to him being the one who committed the murder?

- Does the granting of the motion to suppress evidence of the gun create a strategic opportunity for the prosecution and defense counsel to discuss case settlement? If you were the prosecutor in this case, what would your settlement strategy be? What if you were defense counsel?

Rules dictating what can be appealed vary from jurisdiction to jurisdiction, but generally a party is not entitled to complain about evidence that they admitted. In practice, this means that attempting to mitigate the damage of certain testimony by introducing it first during direct examination may also destroy any chance of appealing the decision on the motion. Furthermore, parties are usually required to renew their objection at the time the evidence in question is introduced. A pretrial ruling on evidence alone will not preserve the error for appeal. Thus an advocate must decide between preserving the issue for appeal or mitigating the damage. Choosing the former means allowing opposing counsel to introduce the evidence and then objecting to its admission on the same grounds as argued in the motion *in limine*. That objection will almost certainly be overruled, and the evidence will be admitted. This will preserve the issue on appeal, but the jury will hear the harmful evidence.

1. Dispositive Motions

A dispositive motion is one that results in the resolution of the case. If a judge asks the lawyers, "is this motion going to be dispositive?" this is meant to inquire about whether the defendant will plead guilty if he loses the motion or if the prosecutor will dismiss the charges should the State lose the motion. For instance, in a possession of narcotics case, if the defense brings a motion to suppress the evidence of the drugs based on an illegal search, and the motion is granted, then the State will be unable to proceed. In this example, if the defense attorney tells the judge before the hearing that the motion is dispositive, this means that her client will plead guilty if she loses the motion. If the defense attorney does not know if the motion is dispositive, that is fine too. Another example of a dispositive motion is a challenge to the charge itself. For instance, if the defense can show in a hearing that the filing of charges is discriminating against a class of people, then the case would be dismissed if the motion were granted.[14] An example of a motion that would not be dispositive would be a motion to suppress a confession, wherein the state has enough evidence to convict the defendant without using his incriminating statement. If the prosecution did not have sufficient independent evidence to convict absent the confession, then this motion would be dispositive. The following is an example of a motion to suppress evidence.

---

[14] Murgia v. Mun. Court, 540 P.2d 44, 46 (Cal. 1975).

SAMPLE MOTION

LAW OFFICES OF THE PUBLIC DEFENDER
By: Cecily G. Bracknell, Deputy Public Defender
Bar No. 101654
Address: 711 Dublin Street, Second Floor
Rockport, Oceana 90122
Telephone: (555) 222-7759
Attorney for Defendant

IN THE SUPERIOR COURT OF THE STATE OF OCEANA
FOR THE COUNTY OF ROCKPORT

THE PEOPLE OF THE STATE OF OCEANA,	Case No.: RP101711
Plaintiff,	NOTICE OF MOTION TO SUPPRESS EVIDENCE (PENAL CODE 1538.5)
v.	
ERIK CLARK,	Date: March 12, CY
	Time: 8:30 AM
	Court: Department A
Defendant.	

TO OLIVER Y. FELIX, DISTRICT ATTORNEY FOR ROCKPORT COUNTY, AND/OR HIS REPRESENTATIVE:

PLEASE TAKE NOTICE that on March 12, CY-1, at 8:30 a.m., or as soon thereafter as the matter may be heard, in Department A of the above entitled court, the defendant Erik Clark will move under Penal Code § 1538.5 to suppress all evidence resulting from his arrest on February 21, CY-1, specifically but not limited to:

1. One black Yamaha motorcycle, license plate # 55VVS51.

2. One black motorcycle helmet.

3. Cigarette butts seized from Clark's apartment.

4. Photographs of Clark's apartment and its contents.

5. The analysis and results of any laboratory tests related to the above items, including but not limited to those performed by the Rockport County Sheriff's Department Officials at the location of the arrest, at the station, and/or any subsequent tests performed by the Rockport County Sheriff's crime lab.

6. Any and all statements made by Clark and his roommate River Coleridge during his detention, arrest, transport to the Rockport County station, and his subsequent booking.

7. Any observations made by officers before and subsequent to the search of Clark's

vehicle, Clark's apartment, and its contents.

The motion will be based on the attached memorandum of points and authorities, contents of the court file, and all the evidence and other matters to be presented at the hearing.

Cecily G. Bracknell _____
Cecily G. Bracknell
Deputy Public Defender

STATEMENT OF FACTS

On February 21, CY-1, police went to the home of Erik Clark, without a search warrant and entered his apartment. The police allege that they acted with the consent of Clark's roommate, River Coleridge. The police told Coleridge that they did not need a warrant to search the premises. Based on that information, only then did Coleridge allow the police to enter.

MEMORANDUM OF POINTS AND AUTHORITIES

I. THE SEARCH WAS CONDUCTED WITHOUT A WARRANT

A search without a warrant is presumptively illegal, and the prosecution bears the burden of establishing the legality of a warrantless search. (*See, e.g., People v. Osband* (1996) 13 Cal. 4th 622, 673; *People v. James* (1977) 19 Cal. 3d 99, 106). The police did not have a warrant to search Clark's apartment; and therefore, the search was illegal.

II. FRUIT OF THE POISONOUS TREE

Evidence that flows from an illegal search or seizure is tainted by the illegality and must be suppressed. "Such evidence includes not only what was seized in the course of the unlawful conduct itself—the 'primary' evidence as well as what was subsequently obtained through the information gained—the so-called 'derivative' or 'secondary' evidence. Therefore, the 'fruit of the poisonous tree,' as well as the tree itself, must be excluded." (*People v. Mayfield* (1997) 14 Cal. 4th 668, 760). The search of Clark's apartment and seizure of its contents was illegal; and therefore, any evidence recovered was illegally obtained and must be suppressed.

III. CONSENT WAS INVOLUNTARY AND THEREFORE INVALID

Where the police have not obtained a search warrant, or lack probable cause, they may conduct a search where they obtain valid consent. (*Schneckloth v. Bustamonte* (1973) 412 U.S. 218). In order to have a valid consent search, the police must obtain consent from someone with actual or apparent authority, and it must be voluntary. (*Illinois v. Rodriguez* (1990) 497 U.S. 177). It cannot be obtained as a result of coercion, duress, or fraud. Here, the police defrauded Coleridge by stating that a warrant was not required.

I declare under penalty of perjury that the foregoing is true and correct.
Executed at Rockport, Oceana.

By *Cecily G. Bracknell*
Cecily G. Bracknell
Deputy Public Defender

SUMMARY

Drafting and arguing pretrial criminal motions is a critically important skill because of its ability to affect all aspects of a case, whether on the side of the prosecutor or defense counsel. A number of factors must be considered in deciding whether a pretrial motion, otherwise referred to as a motion *in limine*, should be presented in written form or argued orally. Whether the motion is to exclude or admit evidence, one must consider all the potential advantages and disadvantages that could result to one's overall case theory, trial strategy, and credibility with the judge. An attorney should be wary of boilerplate motions and should never argue frivolous motions. Bringing a meritless motion is not only unethical, but also unwise because it harms the attorney's reputation. Attorneys who have earned a reputation for being forthright are more likely to win motions that legally could go either way.

All motions must be clear, persuasive, and advance the proponent's case theory. It is exceptionally important to anticipate what opposing counsel will argue so that these arguments can be made preemptively in the pretrial motion. When writing or orally arguing a motion, attorneys must always remember to interweave the facts with the pertinent and important case law and not ignore cases or statutory law that might contradict the primary points of their case. In drafting a motion, the most basic elements include the caption, notice, statement of facts, argument, and conclusion. It is important, however, always to refer to the rules of the local jurisdiction in order to determine how the motion should be drafted.

In presenting an oral argument, one of the most important aspects for an attorney to keep in mind is the audience being addressed. Motions are argued to bench officers, not to juries. It is proper to provide lengthier, attention-grabbing statements to the jury; however, an attorney must remember that judges are far more learned and are more concerned with obtaining answers to their questions. The attorney should also always be respectful of the judge and refer to her as "Your Honor."

Attorneys, likewise, should be well-prepared for the courtroom, thoroughly familiar with their case, and believe in their case theory. Confidence in one's case, and in one's own advocacy skills, goes a long way towards making an attorney a persuasive litigator. Because motions in criminal cases, unlike civil cases, can sometimes be brought with no notice, attorneys must be sure to be familiar with the statutory laws and local court rules of their jurisdiction. Attorneys should be prepared to "think on their feet" and respond to such spontaneous motions. Often, common sense arguments are the most persuasive to the judge.

Finally, if a motion is granted, this may significantly strengthen the proponent's case. On the other hand, if a motion is denied, the moving attorney must consider preserving the issue for appeal or mitigating the resulting damage to the case. Attorneys should be sure to clarify ambiguous rulings. Ultimately, pretrial motions play a pivotal part in any criminal case. When the ruling on a pretrial motion has a large impact on the case or is dispositive, this may present an ideal opportunity for settlement negotiation.

CHECKLIST

✓ When drafting a motion, attorneys should consider the interplay between the motion and their case theory. The motion should be drafted with the case theory in mind, so as to further it.

✓ In deciding what motion to bring, an attorney should consider all of the advantages and disadvantages of waiting to bring the motion before or during trial.

✓ Attorneys should be mindful when submitting any boilerplate motions. All motions should serve a purpose and not be frivolous, or an attorney may be subject to discipline for ethical violations.

✓ A motion should be written to contain all of its necessary sections. The motion should always contain a caption, notice, statement of facts, argument, and conclusion.

✓ The oral argument of a motion should be approached strategically, as the audience will be a judge and not a jury. The oral argument should be clear and concise, with the attorney maintaining a professional demeanor. Structurally, oral argument should begin with the request, followed by two or three of the argument's strongest points avoiding the "shotgun" approach. The argument should then navigate through the opponent's arguments and then follow with a conclusion.

✓ In the event of an adverse ruling where the motion is denied, an attorney should seek clarification of any ambiguous rulings. Moreover, an attorney should make sure that an objection is stated on the record to preserve the right to appeal. Finally, an attorney should carefully think through all of the remaining options.

CHAPTER 11
SPECIFIC MOTIONS AND EXAMPLES

"Lawyers with a weakness for seeing the merits of the other side end up being employed by neither."
–Richard J. Barnet

In preparation for trial, each side should seek to take advantage of its strengths, exploit its opponent's weaknesses, and control the nature of the confrontation. Perhaps the most effective way to do this is through the use of pretrial motions.[1] In general, such motions are made after the preliminary hearing but before the case goes to trial, and they can be brought by either side.[2] Either side may bring a motion for a variety of reasons, but each will impact the moving party's trial strategy because motions deal with provocative and contentious trial issues that can determine the outcome of a case. Such motions can determine what physical evidence may be introduced, what statements or confessions can be admitted, what testimony may be allowed, and what legal arguments may or may not be made. A pretrial motion might even be brought to contest the legitimacy of having the defendant stand trial at all. As such, pretrial motions are important tools and play a pivotal role of helping both the prosecutor and defense counsel define the scope of their respective cases and may also help them assess the relative strengths and weaknesses of a case.

Developing an intimate familiarity with the form and function of different motions can help an attorney to present a persuasive case theory that may ultimately lead to victory in the courtroom. Since a critical element of devising a persuasive case theory involves anticipating an opponent's actions, the manner in which attorneys anticipate and respond to opposing counsel's motions can critically impact their case. Moreover, success with pretrial motions puts a litigator in the most advantageous position to achieve a positive case settlement. While Chapter 10 explored pretrial motions in general, this chapter explains specific types of pretrial motions, such as: motions to suppress or include physical evidence, confessions, or statements; motions to dismiss; motions for severance and joinder; criminal demurrers; motions for writs of *habeas corpus*; bail motions; and motions to view privileged documents. In order to provide a context for this discussion of specific types of motions, this chapter will feature various hypothetical examples, case law, strategy, ethics, and a variety of sample motions. This discussion is meant to provide a sample of common motions and is by no means an exhaustive exploration of motions.

A. MOTIONS TO SUPPRESS OR INCLUDE

When an advocate brings a motion to suppress, she is asking the court to exclude, at trial, any evidence that was illegally or unconstitutionally obtained. Additionally, evidence can be excluded if its

---

[1] *See* FED. R. CRIM. P. 47(a) (According to the Federal Rules of Criminal Procedure, any application to the court for an order must be by motion.).

[2] *See* FED. R. CRIM. P. 12(b)(2) (Any defense, objection, or request, which is capable of determination without a trial of the general issue, may be raised before trial by motion.).

probative value is substantially outweighed by its prejudice, if it will unduly consume court time, or if it will mislead jurors.[3] Defense counsel will often bring motions to suppress evidence obtained from illegal searches and seizures, to bar the use of illegal identifications of the defendant, and to suppress a confession or statement obtained in violation of the accused's constitutional rights. Generally, when the defense brings a motion to suppress evidence based on a violation of the Fourth Amendment, the attorneys will stipulate that there was no search warrant, and then the burden will shift to the prosecution to prove the legality of the search. The exclusionary rule provides that if evidence was seized without a search warrant, the State must prove by a preponderance of evidence that the defendant's constitutional rights were not violated.[4] Thus, even though the defense brought the motion, the prosecution will call witnesses to meet its burden. It is standard practice to show that the police officer had probable cause to search or to arrest in order for the prosecution to meet its initial burden. On the other hand, if there was a search warrant, then the burden is on the defense to prove by a preponderance of the evidence that the search was illegal.[5]

HYPO: *Oceana v. Matthews*

David and Mary Matthews had a five-year, tumultuous marriage. Neighbors often called to report the sounds of fighting coming from their house. The Oceana police made several visits to the home but never arrested anyone. One night a woman who identified herself as Mary called 911.

The caller managed to say, "He's going to kill me!" and "He's coming at me with our gun!" before the call abruptly ended. When officers arrived at the address provided in the 911 call, they saw David Matthews standing in the driveway wearing bloody clothing. Without reading him his *Miranda* rights, Oceana police questioned David and took him into custody. The police entered the house and found a gun on the kitchen table.

At the Oceana police station, David told the police that he had nothing to do with Mary's death. Finally, after four hours of questioning, David confessed to murdering Mary with the gun found in the house.

Identify the potential evidentiary issues that might arise from this set of facts.

TAKE NOTE

Prosecutors should keep in mind that when an evidentiary ruling is a close call, it is often effective to argue that a minor violation by the police "goes to the weight and not the admissibility" of the evidence. This type of argument can be persuasive to judges who, in a close case, will typically rule to allow the finder of fact (the jury, unless it is a court trial) to hear the evidence and decide how much credibility to give the witness. This type of argument is effective for technical violations, such as not administering a blood alcohol breath test according to all the specifics of a checklist. This argument, however, would be ineffective where there is a violation of the defendant's constitutional rights. Other effective prosecution

---

[3] FED. R. EVID. 403.

[4] United States v. Scheffer, 463 F.2d 567, 574 (1972).

[5] Franks v. Delaware, 438 U.S. 154, 155 (1978).

arguments include: that the police were permitted to conduct a search because of officer safety concerns or other exigent circumstances; that officers were acting in good faith;[6] and lastly, prosecutors often make a "catch-all" argument that there would have been "inevitable discovery."[7] Astute defense attorneys, however, should point out that such "catch-all" arguments, especially inevitable discovery, can completely undermine the exclusionary rule. After all, the Fourth Amendment right of protection against unreasonable searches and seizures would be superfluous if the claim of inevitable discovery always prevailed.

Counsel, however, must be cognizant of timing when bringing motions to suppress. Rule 12(b) of the Federal Rules of Criminal Procedure states that the motion to suppress evidence must be raised prior to trial.[8] This is an important consideration for a defense attorney as under Rule 12(e), which states that if the motion is not made before trial and counsel cannot give an adequate reason why she did not seek pretrial relief, the defendant is considered to have waived his search and seizure objections.[9] The prosecutor should object as untimely to a defense motion to suppress that is made during trial. It should also be noted that if a defense attorney fails to bring a motion, the issue is waived for purposes of appeal. Many states also have a similar timing requirement. The motion to suppress is thus a powerful tool that can, if successful, exclude evidence vital to the prosecution's case. Of course, prosecutors also bring motions to suppress any prior convictions of their witnesses or defense evidence (through testimony or physical evidence) that they believe is unreliable or irrelevant.

In contrast to motions to suppress, counsel can also bring motions to include. Such motions are requests to the court to *include* evidence. If an attorney wishes to broach something controversial in the opening statement, such as prior convictions, prior uncharged bad acts, or graphic crime scene photographs, then they should obtain a pretrial ruling from the court to ensure that the contested evidence will be admitted. If the attorney mentions this evidence or shows bloody crime scene photographs during the opening statement without first getting permission, he not only risks having an objection sustained during the opening statement, but the impropriety could also result in a mistrial. This is especially true if the attorney who brings up the prejudicial evidence, such as the defendant's prior convictions, is the prosecutor.

1. Physical Evidence

A defendant who believes that the prosecution will seek to introduce physical evidence at trial that was illegally or unconstitutionally obtained should file a motion to suppress.[10] For example, in the *Oceana v. Matthews* hypothetical above, what motions to suppress should a defense attorney file?

---

[6] United States v. Leon, 468 U.S. 897 (1984).

[7] South Dakota v. Opperman, 428 U.S. 364, 375–76 (1976). In some circumstances, courts may allow evidence obtained in violation of the Fourth Amendment to still be admitted if it would have been discovered anyway in an inventory search after the defendant was taken into custody.

[8] FED. R. CRIM. P. 12.

[9] FED. R. CRIM. P. 12(e).

[10] *See* FED. R. CRIM. P. 12.

Unquestionably, defense counsel should file a motion to suppress the gun, arguing that it was improperly seized. The defense should also move to suppress the suspect's statements to the police at the scene as well as his confession at the stationhouse (discussed below). There is no doubt that David Matthews had an expectation of privacy in his home, but what theory should defense counsel argue in her motion to suppress? The Supreme Court has interpreted the Fourth Amendment as presuming a warrant is required and, as such, warrantless searches are presumed unreasonable.[11]

Great news, we won the motion! The judge found your testimony credible that the gun was not yours.

Oh, good! Now can you ask the judge if I can have my gun back?

The Supreme Court has also held that illegally seized evidence can be admitted in order to impeach the defendant.[12] Counsel should thus avoid "opening the door" to what would otherwise be excluded evidence. When a witness or attorney comments on something that otherwise would be inadmissible against the party who raised the issue, then the opposing party may respond with evidence. To avoid a mistrial, counsel should ask to approach the bench and tell the judge, "I believe that opposing counsel's witness just opened the door to this area, and now I believe I should be allowed to inquire for impeachment purposes." For example, during a jury trial in Culver City, California, the prosecutor (co-author Terry Adamson) was able to introduce evidence of a prior conviction that otherwise would have been inadmissible. The defense, in a driving under the influence ("DUI") of alcohol trial, brought a motion to preclude the prosecutor from mentioning the defendant's prior DUI conviction. Since the prejudice substantially outweighs any probative value under Federal Rule of Evidence 403, and since the prior conviction is not a moral turpitude offense (which would go to the defendant's credibility if she were to testify), the court properly ruled that bringing up the prior conviction would not be allowed. The judge's concern was that the jury would conclude that because the defendant drove while intoxicated in the past, she probably did so on this occasion. The contested issue in this case was whether the defendant intentionally refused to submit to a blood alcohol test, thus demonstrating a consciousness of guilt. On direct examination, the defendant testified that she did not really refuse to take a blood alcohol test, such as a breathalyzer. Rather, she simply did not understand what was happening because, as she stated, "I have never been through anything like this before." The prosecutor approached the bench before beginning cross-examination and argued to the judge that the defendant opened the door to the prior incident; to preclude presentation of the earlier conviction would leave the jury with misleading and false testimony. The judge properly agreed. Thus, on cross-examination of the defendant, the prosecutor was able to inquire about the earlier conviction. The jury's deliberation was quick and it returned a "guilty" verdict.

---

[11] Katz v. United States, 389 U.S. 347, 357 (1967). *See also* Johnson v. United States, 333 U.S. 10, 14–15 (1948).

[12] Stone v. Powell, 428 U.S. 465, 485–89 (1976).

2. Confessions or Statements

In addition to suppression of physical evidence, defense counsel can move to suppress statements made by the defendant. In the hypothetical case *Oceana v. Matthews*, for example, David Matthews was questioned and taken into custody for the murder of his wife. At the stationhouse, he confessed to her murder. The prosecutor would like to introduce Matthews's confession and his statements at the scene. Conversely, a defense attorney will most likely move to have the confession or statements suppressed. On what grounds will defense counsel bring a motion to suppress? How will the prosecution respond?

Generally, a defendant can challenge the admissibility of confessions or statements made on three grounds: 1) the confession or statement was obtained in violation of the defendant's right to due process; 2) the confession or statement was obtained in violation of the defendant's Fifth Amendment privilege against self-incrimination; and 3) the confession or statement was obtained in violation of the defendant's Sixth Amendment right to counsel. Moreover, if the defense has proved that the defendant's Fourth Amendment rights were violated due to an illegal search or seizure, or arrest, then any confession that arose from this violation may be suppressed as "fruit of the poisonous tree."[13]

Evidence derived from an illegal detention, arrest, search, or seizure is tainted by the illegality and must thus be suppressed. The Supreme Court does not allow tainted evidence to be admitted at trial.[14] This exclusion applies not only to the primary evidence that was unlawfully seized, but also to the secondary evidence that was gained as a result of the primary evidence. Therefore, "the 'fruit of the poisonous tree,' as well as the tree itself, must be excluded."[15] For example, if the police stop a person without any suspicion, conduct a pat down, and find drugs, those drugs would be inadmissible as evidence against the accused because of the illegality of the search. Furthermore, if the police find a piece of paper in the same pocket as the drugs that has the number of a well-known drug dealer on it, such derivative evidence would also be excluded as fruit of the poisonous tree because its discovery stems from the same tainted search.

Any police conduct eliciting a statement that is not given as a free and rational choice violates due process and renders the confession inadmissible.[16] Likewise, a confession or statement obtained in violation of the defendant's right to due process by means that so subverted the will of the defendant, will render the confession or statement unreliable and, thus, inadmissible.[17] The rationale is that a conviction based upon unreliable information is a violation of due process and, as such, should be void. Defense counsel should ask, looking at the totality of the circumstances under which the confession or statement was obtained, whether the confession or statement was the product of an essentially free and

---

[13] Brown v. Illinois, 422 U.S. 590, 599 (1975).

[14] Wong Sun v. United States, 371 U.S. 471 (1963).

[15] People v. Mayfield, 928 P.2d 485, 538–39 (Cal. 1997).

[16] Blackburn v. Alabama, 361 U.S. 199, 210–11 (1960).

[17] *See* Arizona v. Fulminante, 499 U.S. 279 (1991).

unconstrained choice by the defendant.[18] If the confession or statement was free and not coerced, it may be used against him. If, however, the defendant's capacity for making a free and voluntary statement was impaired, then the use of his confession offends due process and should be excluded at trial.[19] Coerced confessions not only violate due process, but they are also inherently unreliable.

And just what constitutes a coerced confession? The Supreme Court has ruled that confessions obtained by the making of promises are coerced.[20] While the police may rely on pretext in order to obtain a confession, they may not make any promises for a lighter sentence. Instead, the police may promise the accused that they will let the prosecution know of any cooperation, but they may not promise a lighter sentence if a confession is given. It is constitutional, however, for the police to use ruses, such as falsely

telling the accused that his fingerprints were on the murder weapon or that his DNA was found at the murder scene. What is required is that the judge determines that the confession is reliable. The rationale is that an innocent person would not falsely confess when faced with deceit. Police are also not prohibited from falsely telling the accused that his co-arrestee confessed.[21] It is crucial, however, that law enforcement consider ethics when trying to trick defendants into confessing.

I'm sorry, counselor, but the Fourth Amendment does not permit officers to pull out the defendant's hair to get a DNA sample. The evidence is inadmissible.

They must not use methods of deceit that put so much pressure on the suspect that it amounts to coercion or that they offend society's sense of fairness and morality.

Furthermore, confessions or statements obtained in violation of the Fifth Amendment privilege against self-incrimination violate *Miranda*.[22] *Miranda* requires that a suspect in custody and subject to police interrogation be warned prior to questioning that he has a right to remain silent, that any statement he makes may be used as evidence against him in a court of law, and that he has a right to the presence of an attorney, either retained or appointed.[23] The prosecution may not use statements stemming from

---

[18] Factors determining whether a statement or confession was voluntary include: 1) the length of the interrogation or questioning; 2) threats of force; 3) extreme psychological pressure; and 4) age, education, and mental condition of the subject if exploited. *E.g.*, Schneckloth v. Bustamonte, 412 U.S. 218, 226 (1973).

[19] *Arizona*, 499 U.S. at 303–04. Confessions obtained by police brutality violate due process and are also involuntary and unreliable. Psychological coercion can also render a confession inadmissible as violating due process. Brown v. Mississippi, 297 U.S. 278 (1936).

[20] Bram v. United States, 168 U.S. 532, 542–43 (1897).

[21] Frazier v. Cupp, 394 U.S. 731, 739 (1969).

[22] Miranda v. Arizona, 384 U.S. 436, 467 (1968).

[23] *Id.* at 471–72.

custodial interrogation[24] of the accused unless they can demonstrate the use of procedural safeguards designed to secure the privilege against self-incrimination.[25] Additionally, when a defendant invokes his *Miranda* rights, the interrogation must end and any confession obtained thereafter will be suppressed, unless it was a spontaneous statement that was not made in response to police questioning.[26] *Miranda*, however, only applies when the police are interrogating a suspect and the suspect is not free to leave. It is also worth noting, however, that even where there is a *Miranda* violation and a confession is suppressed, any derivative evidence from that confession is not fruit of the poisonous tree and can be admissible.[27] Returning to *Oceana v. Matthews*, how should the *Miranda* requirement be interpreted in regard to the statements Matthews made outside his home?

Finally, defendants are not deemed to have a reasonable expectation of privacy when in jail. As a consequence, statements made from jail are generally admissible; however, certain types of communications, such as wire communications, pose specific legal requirements for admissibility. All motions to suppress the contents of a wire or oral communication must be made before a trial, hearing, or proceeding, unless there was no opportunity to make such motions or the person was not aware of the grounds of the motion.[28]

i. Prosecution

Once the defense has filed a motion to suppress a confession or statement claiming that the defendant did not receive the proper *Miranda* warnings, then the burden is on the prosecution to make one of four arguments to convince the judge that the defendant's Fifth Amendment right was not violated. First, the prosecution can introduce the statement or confession to impeach the defendant's credibility if he takes the stand.[29] The Supreme Court has ruled that defendants may not use *Miranda* as a shield to commit perjury; however, if the confession was obtained through coercion (a due process violation), then it may not be used for any purposes, including impeachment.[30] Second, the prosecution can introduce the statement or confession if it was obtained in an emergency situation (overriding considerations of public safety, for example, justify the officer's failure to provide *Miranda* warnings).[31] Third, if the statement was made at the time of booking, police can ask questions when taking a person into custody, including

---

[24] Custodial interrogation means any questioning initiated by law enforcement officers after a person has been taken into custody or otherwise deprived of freedom of action in any significant way, as where an investigation has focused on the accused.

[25] *Miranda*, 384 U.S. at 478–79.

[26] Edwards v. Arizona, 451 U.S. 477 (1981).

[27] *See, e.g.*, Missouri v. Seibert, 542 U.S. 600 (2004) (holding that even when an initial confession must be suppressed, evidence from a second confession under which *Miranda* was properly given could be admissible if the police acted in good faith to cure the initial tainted confession).

[28] *See* 18 U.S.C. § 2518(10)(a) (2006).

[29] Harris v. New York, 401 U.S. 222, 225–26 (1971).

[30] Mincey v. Arizona, 437 U.S. 385, 386 (1978).

[31] New York v. Quarles, 467 U.S. 649, 655–56 (1984).

inquiring about the arrestee's name, address, date of birth, height, and weight.[32] The booking officer can also ask questions related to prescription medications. Finally, the prosecution can argue that the suspect waived his rights under *Miranda*.[33]

As to the waiver situation, in 2010, the Supreme Court provided prosecutors with a powerful new tool to oppose a motion to suppress a statement or confession. In *Berghuis v. Thompkins*, the Court held that a suspect in custody subjected to interrogation must unequivocally and unambiguously waive his right to remain silent.[34] In that case, the defendant did not invoke his *Miranda* rights, and he also did not respond to the police officer's questions; he was simply silent. Finally, after several questions without any responses, the officer asked the defendant if he felt bad about murdering the girl, and the defendant said, "Yes." The Court held that this was an implied waiver. The *Berghuis* case did not so much change the *Miranda* ruling as much as reinterpret it. Since the defendant did not unambiguously invoke his right to remain silent or his right to have a lawyer present, and instead answered a question, the Court found that he impliedly waived his rights. It is important to note that there was no coercion in this case. If the police had questioned the defendant for hours without him waiving his rights, or subjected him to emotional or physical coercion, then the confession would have been inadmissible as involuntary.

ii. Ethics/Obligations

The prosecution must always be mindful of their ethical obligations, particularly when these obligations are intertwined with the rights granted to suspects under *Miranda*. For example, the prosecution cannot comment at trial on a suspect's silence upon being read his *Miranda* rights. Returning to the *Berghuis* case above, what if the defendant had simply never said anything? Could the prosecution bring up the defendant's silence at trial in an attempt to prove that it was an admission of guilt? Could the prosecution argue that an innocent person would surely protest? The answer, of course, is a firm "no." The prosecution is not entitled to suggest that by invoking his right to remain silent, the defendant had in some way admitted guilt. Analogously, the prosecution is not entitled to suggest that the defendant had admitted guilt by invoking his Fifth Amendment right not to testify at trial. In fact, this type of error would probably result in a mistrial.

Similarly, it would be unethical for the defense to infer that it was improper for the defendant not to be read his *Miranda* rights in a case in which there was no custodial interrogation. Since jurors are familiar with *Miranda* rights due to television and movies, they are sometimes under the mistaken impression that all defendants are entitled to be told their rights by arresting officers. It would be improper for the defense to imply that their client was denied his full rights in a case in which *Miranda* is irrelevant, such as all instances where the prosecution is not attempting to admit a statement made as a result of a custodial interrogation. If the defense uses this type of improper tactic, the prosecutor should move to have the judge admonish the jury that, in the particular case before them, *Miranda* rights did not

---

[32] Pennsylvania v. Munoz, 496 U.S. 582, 601 (1990).

[33] North Carolina v. Butler, 441 U.S. 369, 373 (1979).

[34] Berghuis v. Thompkins, 130 S. Ct. 2250, 2259–60 (2010).

need to be given and should not be a consideration in their deliberations. Seasoned trial attorneys realize that jurors sometimes base their verdicts on irrelevant issues, and prosecutors should be careful to avoid the pitfalls of having jurors sidetracked from the evidence.

3. Identification

Generally, pretrial identifications, such as lineups, are divided into pre-charge identifications and post-charge identifications. At the most basic level, identification procedures used before the initiation of a criminal prosecution do not require the presence of a suspect's attorney. If a witness, for example, is brought to the scene of a crime to identify a suspect just moments after the crime has occurred, then no attorney is necessary. Once a suspect has been charged with a crime, however, the defendant is then entitled to have an attorney present. Such identifications are considered confrontational when they occur after the criminal prosecution process has begun. In practice, this means that physical lineups require the presence of an attorney, while photographic lineups do not because they can be recreated and subjected to cross-examination at trial.[35]

Given the rules above, it is clear that a violation of a suspect's constitutional rights during an identification procedure will most assuredly result in a motion to suppress the lineup and perhaps also any identifications made in court. Notably, the Supreme Court has determined that evidence of an identification obtained in violation of a defendant's Sixth Amendment Rights is *per se* inadmissible at trial.[36] It can then be argued that the procedure so tainted the witness that any subsequent identification would likewise be tainted and, therefore, inadmissible.

Issues regarding the reliability of witnesses' identification of suspects often form the basis for motions to suppress. Sometimes the conduct which taints the identification is minor; for example, studies have shown that an identifying witness who is shown a photograph of an individual in a photographic lineup will later be more likely to identify that individual in a physical lineup. Thus, if a suspect's photograph is in a photographic lineup, and then the suspect is placed in a physical lineup, the identifying witness will be more likely to identify that suspect even if for no other reason than the familiarity of the face. This bias may create solid ground for the court to invalidate the identification from the physical lineup. As such, a defense attorney must always be cognizant of the actions taken by investigating officers during the course of an investigation, because those actions may provide the information necessary to invalidate an identification. A motion to suppress will inevitably require facts to prove that the evidence (in this case, the identification) was improperly garnered. Thus, a diligent defense attorney will pay special attention to the reports and notes of the investigating officers to be on guard for signs of a tainted identification procedure. Examples of tainted identifications would be situations where a police officer hinted that a particular individual is responsible for a crime or pressured a witness to make an identification.

Typically, defense attorneys bring a motion to suppress a witness's identification of the defendant on the grounds that the photographic lineup identification was tainted because the defendant stood out

---

[35] United States v. Ash, 413 U.S. 300, 324–25 (1973).

[36] *See* Gilbert v. California, 388 U.S. 263, 272 (1967).

from the other people placed in the group with the defendant. For example, if the defendant was the only one in a six pack with facial hair, this photo-grouping would be unduly suggestive; and as a result, any identification of the defendant from this six pack would be suppressed. Similarly, if the defendant in a live-lineup is of a different race than the other five individuals in the lineup, the resulting identification would surely be suppressed. Other examples would be if the defendant was the only one with tattoos or if he was significantly taller or shorter than the other individuals in the lineup. On the other hand, if the only difference between the defendant and the other individuals was minor, such as a more serious facial expression or a shorter haircut, then the prosecution should argue that such a slight variance simply goes to the weight and not the admissibility of the identification. The argument that any issues with the identification go to the weight and not to the admissibility is an effective argument because the jurors are the triers of fact. In instances where there was no bad faith and the suggestibility is not egregious, judges often agree with this argument, reasoning that the jurors should be allowed to decide for themselves how much weight to accord the fact that the identification might have been slightly suggestive. If, however, there was a due process violation, then the identification will be suppressed.

The Supreme Court has also made it very difficult to challenge the identification of a suspect on due process grounds.[37] Due process requires that a pretrial lineup be afforded to the defendant when an eyewitness identification proves to be a material issue and a reasonable likelihood of misidentification exists.[38] In *Evans v. Superior Court*, for example, James Liddle was seated at the counter of his restaurant when two robbers entered. One of the robbers held a gun to Liddle's head while demanding his wallet and ring as well as another customer's wallet. The robbers were in the restaurant for approximately five minutes. Police responded to the call reporting the robbery and, while approaching the restaurant in their patrol car, saw two men that fit the description of the robbers. The police apprehended these individuals who were then placed in the back of the police vehicle. Within fifteen minutes, Liddle and other witnesses viewed the suspects through the back window of the vehicle, seeing only the backs of their heads and shoulders. Liddle told the officers that the suspects in the back of the vehicle appeared to have the same physical builds as the robbers. The defendant filed a motion for a lineup prior to his trial, and the court stated that because the People have the opportunity to compel a lineup and use the resulting evidence, it is only fair for the defendant to be given this reciprocal right. To hold otherwise would be a due process violation.[39]

---

[37] *See, e.g.*, Manson v. Brathwaite, 432 U.S. 98 (1977); Neil v. Biggers, 409 U.S. 188 (1972); Simmons v. United States, 390 U.S. 377 (1968).

[38] Evans v. Superior Court, 522 P.2d 681, 686 (Cal. 1974) (in bank).

[39] *Id.* However, the court notes that they are not holding that in every case where there has not been a pretrial lineup one should be afforded. "Rather, as in all due process determinations, the resolution here to be made is one which must be derived after consideration not only of the benefits to be derived from the accused and the reasonableness of his request but also after considering the burden to be imposed on the prosecution, the police, the court and the witnesses." *Id.*

B. MOTIONS TO DISMISS

In addition to attempting to include or suppress evidence, the defense may file a motion to dismiss. Such motions are permitted under Federal Rule of Criminal Procedure 12(b)(2), which allows pretrial motions that raise "any defense, objection, or request that the court can determine without a trial of the general issue."[40] Pretrial motions to dismiss give the criminal defendant the opportunity to avoid trial when the prosecution's legal theory is flawed. Rather than attacking the flaws on the merits of the legal question, defendants can seek dismissal of the indictment by arguing that it is structurally flawed for reasons such as venue, double jeopardy, immunity, or statute of limitations.[41] If the motion to dismiss is granted because of the prosecution's defect in the indictment or information, the prosecutor will not be barred from instituting a new proceeding against the defendant. On the other hand, if the motion to dismiss is denied, it may not be immediately appealable because it is ordinarily not a final decision.[42] A denial of a motion to dismiss on the ground of double jeopardy is, however, immediately appealable.

C. MOTIONS FOR SEVERANCE AND JOINDER

In general, severance is a difficult form of relief to receive; however, counsel may ask the court for a severance of defendants and/or a severance of counts. The trial court may grant such a motion if the joinder of defendants would result in prejudice to either.[43] Even so, courts will not always grant severance *sua sponte* (on their own), so defense counsel should be prepared to move for severance. It is also important to note that a defendant can lose his right to severance if it is not asserted in a timely manner. It is generally within the discretion of the court whether to allow a prosecutor's motion for joinder of defendants or counts. Joinder of defendants or counts is generally proper if the crimes were so closely connected or if the acts were part of a common plan.

HYPO: *Oceana v. Giles*

On the afternoon of July 3rd, a 1975 Oldsmobile station wagon parked in front of the Bank of Oceana. A man wearing a ski mask exited the station wagon and ran into the bank. Susie Laird, a teller at the bank was returning from her lunch break when she noticed the man enter the bank with what appeared to be a handgun. She also noticed that a second man remained in the driver's seat of the station wagon.

Jason O'Halloran, another teller at the bank whose teller window was closest to the entrance, said he got a "real good look" at the man who entered. Although the alleged robber, later identified as Marcus Giles, was wearing a ski mask, Jason said he would "never forget the cold steel-blue eyes staring at him from under the mask." He remembers Giles yelling for everyone to get down and saying, "if everyone keeps cool, no one will get hurt," and that "it will all be over in a minute." Giles then extended his right arm, exposing a tattoo of a heart with the words "Momma's Boy" written inside.

Two and a half weeks after the robbery, Susie and Jason were asked to come down to the station to

---

[40] FED. R. CRIM. P. 12(b)(2).

[41] United States v. Smith, 866 F.2d 1092, 1095–96 (9th Cir. 1989).

[42] *See* Kyle v. United States, 211 F.2d 912, 914 (9th Cir. 1954); FED R. CRIM. P. 12 n.78.

[43] FED. R. CRIM. P. 14.

identify the two bank robbers (the driver and the gunman). Susie, after looking through approximately 150 photographs, finally identified the driver of the vehicle, John O'Reilly. Susie was unable to identify the gunman. Jason, after looking through hundreds of photographs of tattoos, finally identified Marcus Giles's heart tattoo.

In the above hypothetical, the two eyewitnesses are each able to identify separate defendants, but neither can identify both defendants. Would trying the defendants together strengthen the prosecution's case? Would it make sense due to judicial economy to try the defendants together? What if one of the witness's identifications was tainted due to a police officer suggesting whom to pick out, while the other witness's identification was admissible? Would it make a difference if one defendant had a history of bank robbery convictions, and the other defendant had a clean record? Would it make a difference if one defendant made statements that incriminated both defendants, while the other defendant refused to make a statement to the police?

1. Severance and Joinder of Defendants

When considering a motion for severance, co-defendants and defense counsel must consider several factors, including whether the co-defendants' individual defenses conflict and are irreconcilable. Attorneys must ask many questions when deciding how to proceed. For example, must the jury necessarily believe one defendant at the expense of the other? Does the defendant have a stronger legal defense that will be diluted by the co-defendant's weak defense? Will some prejudicial evidence be admissible against the co-defendant but inadmissible against the accused? By the same token, will some exculpatory evidence be excluded if they are tried together? If the answer to any of these questions is "yes," then defense counsel should file a motion to sever. Additionally, defense counsel must consider the fact that, in most cases, different attorneys represent separate co-defendants.[44] What is beneficial for one defendant is often harmful for his co-defendant, and it is common for co-defendants to point the finger at each other in order to try to persuade the jury that the other defendant was the more culpable party. Defense attorneys must keep in mind that while the opposing attorney is the prosecution, attorneys that represent co-defendants are not on the same "team." At the same time, attorneys must vigilantly represent their own client's interests, even if it means requesting the court to admonish the co-defendant's attorney from introducing evidence or making comments that hurt their client. Attorneys should be alert as to when to bring pretrial motions to keep out or redact evidence that unfairly prejudices their client, regardless of whether the party seeking to admit the evidence is a co-defendant or the prosecution.

Nevertheless, courts significantly favor joinder in order to promote judicial economy and efficiency. Judges are encouraged to construe the joinder rules broadly in order to link offenses and parties so as to avoid multiple trials, but the public interest in the efficacious administration of justice must be balanced against the individual's right to a fair trial. Indeed, attorneys can challenge joinder. Attacks on joinder take two forms, and each requires a different showing. The first is grounded on the contention that there has been misjoinder as a matter of law, that is, that the government overreached by

___

[44] If multiple defendants have retained a single attorney, the attorney is obligated to discuss the benefits of independent counsel for each defendant. The possibility for a conflict of interest is significant, which may result in ineffective assistance from counsel. Thus, when defendants are tried together, courts strongly prefer that each defendant have his own counsel.

lumping defendants or offenses together. The second is when there is lack of proof regarding some fact that the joinder rested upon. With respect to the first, under Federal Rule of Criminal Procedure 8(a), for instance, offenses can be joined against a single defendant if they are of the same or similar character, if they stem from the same act or transaction, or if they are connected to each other, as in a common scheme or plan. Such joinder can make a prosecutor's burden to prove each charge much easier, permitting, for example, the trial of a defendant accused of multiple auto thefts on many charges in one case, instead of in multiple separate trials. As a practicality, jurors are more likely to convict a defendant if there are multiple charges against him stemming from separate instances.

In *Bruton v. United States*, the Supreme Court considered whether or not the jury, during deliberations, could consider a statement made by one defendant that implicates the other co-defendant.[45] There, two defendants were tried in one trial as co-conspirators to an armed postal robbery. One defendant, in talking to the postal inspector through the course of the investigation, made an incriminating statement that implicated himself and his co-defendant. That statement was introduced as evidence at trial and was timely objected to by the defense. The court, as a result of the objection, instructed the jury not to consider the statement by the one defendant as evidence against the co-defendant. Nonetheless, both men were convicted.

The case was appealed to the Supreme Court where the justices carved out a new rule. Significantly, the Court ruled that a limiting instruction to the jury would no longer be sufficient to cancel out the harm caused by the introduction of the statement. Rather, the trial court must sever the trials instead of consolidating them. This landmark ruling is based on the Sixth Amendment's Confrontation Clause which allows a defendant to cross-examine witnesses brought forth to testify against him. In these cases of joinder, one defendant is not able to cross-examine the other defendant because both defendants have a Fifth Amendment right not to take the stand, or bear witness against themselves. Because there can be no cross-examination, the introduction of the testimonial statement is inadmissible.

When a defendant makes a statement that incriminates a co-defendant, a court has several options. The court can give the prosecutor a chance to "sanitize" the statement by taking out any portion that incriminates the co-defendant. This redaction is usually ineffective because it is often clear that the statement has a portion left out that would implicate the co-defendant. For example, if Jerome and David are charged with robbing a liquor store and Jerome states, "me and David took the booze," it would violate David's due process rights to allow a statement that was changed to "me and someone else took the booze." The other options would be not to allow the prosecutor to use the statement at all, to have two juries, or to sever the cases. If there were two juries, each jury would hear only the opening statement and closing argument that pertained to their defendant, thus David's jury would be excluded when Jerome testified and when Jerome's admission was introduced into evidence. If the cases were severed entirely, this would mean that each defendant would have a separate trial. This last solution is the most expensive in terms of judicial resources and the most difficult for the prosecutor who would have to

---

[45] Bruton v. United States, 391 U.S. 123 (1968).

present two different trials over the same incident. Judges are allowed wide discretion as to which remedy they choose.

2. Severance and Joinder of Counts

As with severance of defendants, trial judges have wide discretion in ruling on the severance of offenses; however, there is a preference for joining offenses that were committed at the same time and place or that are based on the same act or transaction. Of course, joining related offenses clearly benefits the State because it is simpler to put on the evidence in one trial as opposed to multiple trials. It is also less expensive and more convenient for witnesses; and, of course, jurors are more likely to convict when they hear evidence of additional crimes. Be that as it may, federal and state laws provide for severance if joinder of charges would cause prejudice to either side or where it would serve the interest of justice, but the burden to show prejudice resulting from a joint trial is on the defendant.

3. Criminal Demurrer Motions

Criminal procedure provides for a remedy similar to the civil demurrer. While a civil case may be dismissed for a violation of Federal Rule of Civil Procedure 12(b)(6)—failure to state a claim upon which relief can be granted—a criminal case may be dismissed if the indictment or information fails to invoke the court's jurisdiction or to state an offense.[46] Thus, prosecutors should keep in mind the requirements of the criminal statute when drafting the charging document: a charging document fails to state an offense if the specific facts alleged fall beyond the scope of the relevant criminal statute, as a matter of statutory interpretation.[47] Such motions, moreover, may be made not only

before trial, but also at any time while the case is pending. Upon the defendant's motion or upon the court's own, the court must cease judgment if (1) the indictment or information does not charge an offense, or (2) the court does not have jurisdiction of the charged offense.[48] Importantly, counsel should be mindful of the fact that a guilty plea under a plea agreement, which waives all matters that could have been raised by a pretrial motion, likewise waives any failure of an indictment to state an offense.[49]

However, even if a defense attorney cannot attack the indictment or information, there are several other motions that she can bring that can effectively dismiss the charges. One such motion is an evidence suppression motion under Federal Rules of Criminal Procedure 12(b)(2)(C) or the local state's equivalent. To see how effectively this motion can be used, consider the following example that took place in California. A police officer pulls over the defendant for making a lane change on the highway without

---

[46] FED. R. CRIM. P. 12(b)(3)(B). In California, a defense attorney may file a demurrer alleging that the acusatory pleading fails to constitute a criminal offense under Penal Code section 1004. An example would be that a police officer arrested the defendant for the illegal possession of a billy club, whereas the defendant claims that he is factually innocent of the charge because the stick was merely a walking stick used for his injury, which is perfectly legal.

[47] United States v. Carroll, 320 F. Supp. 2d 748, 752 (S.D. Ill. 2004).

[48] FED. R. CRIM. P. 34(a).

[49] United States v. George, 403 F.3d 470, 472 (7th Cir. 2005).

first signaling in violation of Vehicle Code section 22107. When the officer approaches the car, he smells the odor of an alcoholic beverage, and his subsequent investigation reveals that the defendant is driving under the influence. The defense attorney brings the California equivalent of a suppression motion, codified under Penal Code section 1538.5, challenging the reason for the stop. The motion is submitted in writing to the court, and then there is a hearing where both the prosecution and defense can call witnesses to try to prove that there was or was not probable cause for the arrest; the motion and witnesses are limited to determining probable cause. During the hearing, the defense attorney questions the police officer, who testifies that there were no other vehicles present at the time of the enforcement stop. Realizing that Vehicle Code section 22107 is only violated if a person does not signal when changing lanes *and* the movement affects another vehicle, the defense attorney moves to suppress the evidence. Upon these facts, the motion should be granted, and all evidence arising out of the improper vehicle stop is fruit of the poisonous tree and must be suppressed. Because all the evidence the prosecution has for the DUI charge stems from the stop, they are forced to dismiss the case.[50]

Another motion that the defense can bring in some state courts is for an incarcerated defendant charged with a misdemeanor to establish probable cause that a crime was committed. For instance, in California this motion can be brought under California Penal Code section 991. However, unlike a preliminary hearing or a suppression motion, the misdemeanor lack of probable cause motion is briefly argued orally and the judge decides the matter by reading the police report rather than having the sides call witnesses. The procedure is that the judge reviews the police report and makes a determination of whether the report, if true, establishes that the defendant committed a crime. The judge is not allowed to consider violations of the Fourth Amendment, or other motion to suppress types of violations when ruling on a misdemeanor probable cause motion. Rather, the court is simply to assume that the facts alleged in the police report are accurate, and then assess whether a crime was committed. If after reading the police report, the judge rules that there are no grounds to conclude that a crime has been committed even if the report is accurate, then the remedy is to release the defendant from custody. The purpose of this motion is to ensure that defendants are not capriciously held in custody unless there is probable cause to believe that they committed a crime. The prosecution is then given a chance to further investigate the case or to correct the defect by filing an appropriate charge. In most instances, the prosecution will decline to pursue the case, and the case will simply be dismissed in the interest of justice. An example would be if the police officer was mistaken about the penal code or was simply rousting a defendant, such as charging a homeless person with vagrancy or trespassing just for standing on a street corner in an affluent area.

Other available motions are based on case law interpretations of constitutional rights. One example is a *Serna* motion,[51] which is where the defense argues that the defendant was not brought to trial

---

[50] Another reason that a defense attorney may want to bring a suppression motion is for her client to hear the strength of the case against him. It sometimes happens with even the best defense attorneys that a client stubbornly refuses plea deals because he believes he will win at trial; whereas, the experienced defense attorney knows that there is strong evidence against her client, and the plea deal may be in her client's best interest. By having the client present at a suppression motion (or other motions), he can hear the evidence offered against him and may be more amenable to a negotiated disposition.

[51] Serna v. Superior Court, 707 P.2d 793 (Cal. 1985).

in a speedy manner in violation of his rights under the Sixth and Fourteenth Amendments of the United States Constitution. Usually this issue arises when the defendant has an arrest warrant issued for him, but the police fail to act upon the warrant or arrest the defendant in a timely manner, which is generally interpreted as within a year. The defense can also bring a motion under *Arizona v. Youngblood* arguing that the defendant's due process rights were violated when the prosecution or police, in bad faith or intentionally, lost or destroyed evidence or material evidence was destroyed.[52] The idea behind the motion is that, in being unable to access key evidence, the defendant was denied a full and fair opportunity to build a defense, so it is not fundamentally fair just to hold him to the charges. However, it should be noted that in many cases the police's routine and scheduled destruction of evidence after a lapse of time is not sufficient for the defense to win on such a motion.

Other motions that may lead to a dismissal may be brought as a motion *in limine* prior to trial. For example, a defendant can request a *Frye* hearing where the defendant essentially challenges the foundation of an anticipated witness's testimony based on prevailing scientific standards.[53] As an example, occasionally small, remote police departments may not be trained in the latest Field Sobriety Testing methods or may use alcohol screening equipment that is outdated or not calibrated as frequently as recommended. The prosecution would have to give an offer of proof to show that the officer who is going to testify about the defendant's performance on the field sobriety tests or the officer who administered the screen devices was using the methods and procedures accepted by the scientific community in that field of science. If the defense demonstrates that the officer used scientifically invalid measures, his testimony as it relates to determining alcohol impairment and intoxication may be barred from the trial. In a DUI case, this would likely mean the end of the prosecution's case.

There are many other motions available, particularly as they relate to ensuring that the defendant has access to a fair trial, but the above provides a brief overview of the more common motions that a criminal attorney can expect to encounter.

HYPO: *Oceana v. Burns*

On the night of December 31st, Holden Burns and Maurice Douglas decided to celebrate the New Year by attending a party. Holden and Maurice decided that Maurice would be the designated driver for the evening. Holden had several drinks at the party, while Maurice remained sober.

At 3:00 a.m. on January 1st, when Maurice was driving Holden and himself home from the party, Maurice was pulled over by Officer Stradlater for speeding. Although Maurice was completely sober, Holden was somewhat intoxicated. Officer Stradlater noticed Holden's symptoms of intoxication and subsequently arrested him. Holden did not appear to be unable to care for himself or a danger to himself or others.

What motion should Holden's lawyer make if Holden is in custody? On what grounds?

---

[52] 488 U.S. 51 (1988). *See also* California v. Trombetta, 467 U.S. 479 (1984).

[53] The motion is based off *People v. Kelly*, 549 P.2d 1240 (Cal. 1976), which applied certain federal standards from *Frye v. United States*, 293 F. 1013 (D.C. Cir. 1923) to California. Federally, and highly influential to all states on this issue, is *Daubert v. Merrell Dow Pharm., Inc.*, 509 U.S. 579 (1993). California reconciled the interpretation of all these cases in *People v. Leahy*, 882 P.2d 321 (Cal. 1994).

The *Oceana v. Burns* hypothetical presents an example of when a defense attorney should raise a motion such as California's 991 motion for a misdemeanor probable cause hearing, if that motion is available in the jurisdiction. While it is both a crime to be drunk in public and to be driving a motor vehicle when one's ability to drive is impaired because one is under the influence of alcohol, it is not a crime to be under the influence of alcohol (if not a danger to one's self or others) while being the passenger of a car. Indeed, people who choose to go out and drink are encouraged to have a designated driver, so as not to endanger others. Thus, if a sober person safely drives an intoxicated person home, this is not a crime. If the passenger is arrested for intoxication, an astute defense attorney would bring a probable cause type motion to have the defendant released from custody. It is likely that this motion would be granted. Further, it is likely that, subsequent to the court granting this motion, the prosecutor would move for the case to be dismissed.

4. *Motions for Writ of* Habeas Corpus

Habeas corpus is a writ, or legal action, through which a prisoner can be released from unlawful detention. Writing in 1868, Chief Justice Salmon Chase characterized *habeas* as the "best and only sufficient defence of personal freedom."[54] The writ will issue to test the detention of any person held under custody of the United States.[55] The most important part of the statute today is the provision, first adopted in 1867, which permits a federal court to order the discharge of any person held by a state in violation of the Constitution. The constitutionality of vesting this power in the federal courts is entirely settled;[56] however, an application for *habeas corpus* shall not be entertained until the prisoner has exhausted his state remedies.[57] Further, it may be interesting to note that, in fact, a writ of *habeas corpus* proceeding is not a criminal procedure at all. Instead, it is a civil action taken by a convicted defendant against his captor—in most cases the head of the state or federal prison system. A defendant must also already be in custody in order to challenge the detention, but parole and probation constitute "custody" for purposes of the writ.[58] The writ must contain a claim that some federal constitutional right was violated in the course of the convict's trial, resulting in an unfair or unconstitutional proceeding; however, should the *habeas corpus* proceeding end in favor of the petitioner/defendant, then double jeopardy does *not* apply and the State may retry the petitioner/defendant.

5. Bail Motions

As discussed in Chapter 4, a primary concern of any detained suspect is whether he will be released. Release from jail affects more than the arrestee's freedom—being released from jail means that the client will be better able to assist in the investigation and preparation of his case. The prosecutor, on

---

[54] *Ex parte* Yerger, 75 U.S. (8 Wall.) 95 (1868).

[55] 28 U.S.C. § 2241(c)(1) (2006).

[56] United States *ex rel.* Elliott v. Hendricks, 213 F.2d 922, 925 (3rd Cir. 1954).

[57] Slayton v. Smith, 404 U.S. 53, 53–54 (1971); *Ex parte* Hawk, 321 U.S. 114, 116 (1944); Mooney v. Holohan, 294 U.S. 103, 115 (1935); *Ex parte* Royall, 117 U.S. 241 (1886). Now codified in 28 U.S.C. § 2254(b), (c) (2006).

[58] *See* 28 U.S.C. § 2254(a) (2006).

the other hand, wants to make sure that a violent criminal or defendant, who poses a flight risk, remains in jail throughout the trial; however, it is inappropriate for the prosecutor always to object to the defendant's release from custody. If the defendant does not pose a safety threat and is likely to make all court appearances, then the prosecutor should not object to the release. This furthers justice and also increases the prosecutor's credibility with the judge.

In deciding whether to release or to detain a particular defendant, the Bail Reform Act instructs that the judicial officer may consider four factors: 1) the nature and circumstances of the crime charged; 2) the weight of evidence against the accused; 3) the potential threat to any person or the community posed by release; and 4) the accused's character, physical and mental condition, community and family ties, employment, financial resources, length of residence in the community, past conduct, alcohol and substance abuse history, and track record on past court appearances.[59] Chapter 4 includes a comprehensive discussion of bail issues.

6. Motion to Discover Police Personnel Records

In some jurisdictions, motions can be brought to review limited aspects of a police officer's personnel records. For instance, if Campbell informs his attorney in the above hypothetical, *Oceana v. Campbell*, that he has other friends who have complained about Officer Spade's conduct and claim that he is notorious for "inventing" anonymous tipsters, defense counsel might base their case theory on such information. Perhaps Officer Spade fabricated the anonymous tip and, in order to confirm the theory, defense counsel will want to review Officer Spade's personnel file for any prior complaints made against him. One such jurisdiction that allows parties to make a motion to review police officer's personnel files is California. California codified an exception to the general rule that a police officer's personnel records are confidential.[60] Commonly referred to as a *Pitchess* motion,[61] it is a request made by the defense in a criminal case for the personnel records of the arresting officer if the defendant has filed an affidavit alleging the use of excessive force or if there is reason to believe that the officer has a record of falsifying facts.[62] If granted, the motion will expose the police officer's record of duty and any complaints that may have been made against him or her. Procedurally, a *Pitchess* motion must describe the information sought with sufficient specificity and include affidavits showing good cause, including the materiality and a

---

[59] 18 U.S.C. § 3142(g)(1)–(4) (2006).

[60] California Penal Code section 832.7 states, in relevant part, that a "[p]eace officer['s] . . . personnel records and records maintained by any state or local agency pursuant to Section 832.5, or information obtained from these records, are confidential and shall not be disclosed in any criminal or civil proceeding except by discovery pursuant to Section[] 1043 . . . of the Evidence Code."

[61] Jurisdictions differ on how defendants' request police personnel files when they believe that the officers acted inappropriately and that such information would have exculpatory value. *See, e.g.*, United States v. Newby, 251 F.R.D. 188 (E.D.N.C. 2008) *aff'd*, 403 F. App'x 809 (4th Cir. 2010), *cert. denied*, Newby v. United States, 131 S. Ct. 1804 (2011) (holding that the defendant could not issue subpoenas duces tecum for police personnel files or compel their discovery because Federal Rule of Criminal Procedure 17(c) "is not intended to provide an additional means of pretrial discovery" and such information would already be provided under *Brady*).

[62] Although California codified this motion, defense counsel typically refer to this motion as a "*Pitchess* motion" named after the case which permitted defendants to make a motion to the court to review the contents of a peace officer's personnel file. *See* Pitchess v. Superior Court, 522 P.2d 305 (Cal. 1974); CAL. EVID. CODE §§ 1043–45.

reasonable belief that the governmental agency has the information or records.[63] Due to the privileged nature of personnel records, only documentation of past misconduct that is similar to misconduct allegedly committed by the officer in the pending litigation is relevant and subject to discovery.[64]

Defense counsel making the motion must include: 1) the identification of the proceeding, 2) the identity of the party seeking discovery, 3) the identity of the peace officer, 4) the time and place the motion will be heard, 5) a description of the type of records or information sought, and 6) affidavits showing good cause for the discovery sought.[65] Upon satisfaction of these requirements, the court will examine the peace officer's personnel file *in camera*.[66] If the judge determines that there is relevant material in the file, she will release only that relevant information so as to observe the privacy of the balance of the officer's personnel file.[67]

Counsel should make sure, however, to follow the proper discovery procedure in their respective jurisdiction because, should they file the wrong motion, they may be denied discovery.[68] In federal court, counsel might move to compel examination or production of personnel files of testifying agents where they suspect they can impeach those officers; however, it should be noted that the prosecution has a duty to turn over any *Brady* material for the purposes of impeachment, regardless of whether the defense requests it or not.

HYPO: *Oceana v. Campbell*

Officer Spade received an anonymous tip that Thomas Campbell, a drug dealer, would be leaving his residence at 1212 N. Brookhaven Lane to fly to Miami with a suitcase containing twelve kilograms of cocaine. Police officers staked out Campbell's house. A week after the tip, police observed Campbell and an unidentified man leaving the Brookhaven Lane house with two large suitcases.

Officer Spade followed Campbell's car to the airport where they proceeded to pull the car over. After arresting Campbell and his partner, later identified as Charlie Rocker, Officer Spade opened the trunk to find two suitcases full of cocaine. After transporting Campbell and Rocker to the police station, Officer Spade separated the two and began interrogating Campbell. Eventually, after three hours of questioning, Campbell confessed and implicated Rocker as the head of the drug operation.

What arguments can be made regarding the seizure of the cocaine? What if the defendant had encountered Officer Spade on a prior occasion?

---

[63] Garcia v. Superior Court, 163 P.3d 939, 944 (Cal. 2007).

[64] Cal. Highway Patrol v. Superior Court, 101 Cal. Rptr. 2d 379, 387 (Cal. Ct. App. 2000).

[65] CAL. EVID. CODE § 1043(b).

[66] An *in camera* inspection is conducted within the judge's private chambers. The people present during this in-chambers inspection are the judge, the court reporter, and the deputy attorney general. The defense attorney and prosecutor trying the case are not allowed to be present for this inspection.

[67] *See* Haggerty v. Superior Court, 12 Cal. Rptr. 3d 467, 473 (Cal. Ct. App. 2004).

[68] *See e.g.*, People v. Coleman, 349 N.Y.S.2d 298, 302 (N.Y. Cnty. Ct. 1973). *See also* United States v. Akers, 374 A.2d 874, 876–79 (D.C. 1977) (Court did not allow discovery because the defendants did not have the requisite knowledge of the officer's reputation for violence, and dishonesty; and, false statements were not involved. Additionally, the court did not believe that releasing the documents would further the defense's case.).

SAMPLE MOTIONS

BENJAMIN RAFFITY
District Attorney, # 168346
DARSHINA ABHOOT,
Deputy District Attorney, # 193278
3451 West Richmond Street
Maliwood, Oceana 90120

Attorneys for the Plaintiff

SUPERIOR COURT OF THE STATE OF OCEANA
FOR THE COUNTY OF MALIWOOD

PEOPLE OF THE STATE OF OCEANA,
 	
                              Plaintiff,
 	
    v.
 	
DAVID LILES WILLIAMS,
 	
                          Defendant.
	CASE NO.: 227988
	
	PEOPLE'S OPPOSITION TO DEFENDANT'S MOTION TO EXCLUDE DEFENDANT'S OUT-OF-COURT STATEMENTS PURSUANT TO MIRANDA V. ARIZONA
	
	Date: June 27, C.Y.
	Time: 9:00 a.m.
	Dept: 37

TO THE HONORABLE JUDGE OF THE ABOVE ENTITLED COURT, DEFENDANT, AND DEFENSE COUNSEL:

THE PEOPLE OF THE STATE OF OCEANA, Plaintiff in the above entitled matter, respectfully request that this Court deny Defendant's motion to exclude Defendant's out-of-court statements pursuant to *Miranda v. Arizona*, because Defendant lacks standing to challenge the admissions, which, having been made after Defendant was advised of his rights, did not violate Defendant's *Miranda* rights.

Dated: May 29, C.Y.

Respectfully Submitted,
BENJAMIN RAFFITY
DISTRICT ATTORNEY

By: *Darshina Abhoot*

Darshina Abhoot
Deputy District Attorney

BENJAMIN RAFFITY
District Attorney, # 168346
DARSHINA ABHOOT,
Deputy District Attorney, # 193278
3451 West Richmond Street
Maliwood, Oceana 90120

Attorneys for the Plaintiff

SUPERIOR COURT OF THE STATE OF OCEANA
FOR THE COUNTY OF MALIWOOD

PEOPLE OF THE STATE OF OCEANA,	CASE NO.: 227988
Plaintiff,	**PEOPLE'S OPPOSITION TO DEFENDANT'S MOTION TO EXCLUDE DEFENDANT'S OUT-OF-COURT STATEMENTS PURSUANT TO MIRANDA V. ARIZONA**
v.	
DAVID LILES WILLIAMS,	Date: June 27, C.Y.
Defendant.	Time: 9:00 a.m.
	Dept: 37

I.

EXHIBITS

The following exhibits are attached hereto:

Exhibit 1: Transcripts of statements related to Defendant's *Miranda* Advisement

II.

STATEMENT OF FACTS

On July 14, C.Y.-1, the silent alarm at the First Federal Bank in Universal City, Oceana, was activated. Police and FBI agents responded to the scene of a robbery in progress at 2:15 p.m. By the time police and agents arrived, Defendant had fled the scene. The bank manager, Brenda Corbin, opened the bank doors for the agents.

Agent Ryan was the officer in charge. Agent Ryan gathered witness statements. He first spoke to Thomas Kant, a bank teller. Witness Kant relayed that at approximately 1:50 p.m. Defendant entered the bank. Witness Kant did not have a customer at that time. Witness Kant described the robber as six feet tall and about 190 pounds. Witness Kant stated that Defendant had his hair styled in cornrows and had unusual eyes—large and glassy. Witness Kant relayed that Defendant pulled something out of his jacket and yelled for everyone to get down on the floor. Defendant was holding a gun. Defendant made threats and told everyone to get on the floor. When one customer moved, Defendant yelled that he would "blow her damn head off" if she did not get down. Everyone got down on the floor as instructed.

Witnesses heard Defendant open a drawer. Witness Kant expressed his opinion that the drawer opened was his own cash drawer. Witness Kant heard Defendant open another drawer and attempted to open a third drawer. He then swore and ran out of the bank. The bank manager came out of the back office and informed the witnesses that she had activated the silent alarm, and she then locked the bank doors to ensure that no one left the building.

While waiting for the police to arrive, Witness Kant spoke to Witness Hernandez. They discussed the description of Defendant, both commenting on his unusual eyes.

The FBI arrived at 2:15 p.m. to conduct the investigation. The police officers looked for evidence and dusted for fingerprints. Agent Ryan spoke to the witness individually. Witness Kant showed Agent Ryan the cash drawer that Defendant had opened. Witness Kant noticed that a small plastic card was in the drawer. It had not been there before the robbery. The card was Defendant's driver's license. Witness Kant was able to identify the picture on the license as the same person who robbed the bank.

Agent Ryan ran a background check on Defendant. The search found three prior convictions. One was a ten-year-old misdemeanor for drug possession. The second was a seven-year-old felony for possession with the intent to distribute methamphetamine. The third was a five-year-old conviction for bank robbery. Defendant was recently released from prison and is on parole. Based on this information and the incident at the bank, Agent Ryan obtained an arrest warrant for Defendant.

Williams was arrested at his home on July 17, C.Y.-1. A lineup was conducted. Witnesses Kant, Hernandez, and Nguyen were present. All three recognized Williams as the bank robber.

Agent Ryan interviewed Defendant on July 19, C.Y.-1. At the beginning of the interview, Agent Ryan informed Defendant of his *Miranda* rights; Defendant waived his rights and agreed to speak with Agent Ryan.

On or about October 29, C.Y.-1, in Seaport County, within the Central District of Oceana, Defendant DAVID WILLIAMS was indicted by the Grand Jury on a single charge of bank robbery in violation of title 18 of the United States Code section 2113(d).

III.

MEMORANDUM OF POINTS AND AUTHORITIES

The following discussion of points and authorities addresses issues which the People anticipate the Defense will raise via their motion to suppress Defendant's out-of-court statements.

A.   DEFENDANT WAS ADEQUATELY ADVISED OF HIS RIGHTS PURSUANT TO *MIRANDA v. ARIZONA*

In establishing the principle that defendants should be advised of their rights prior to custodial interrogation, the Supreme Court in *Miranda v. Arizona* created the requirement for an advisement of rights. The Court held that a *Miranda* warning must include a statement of four principles: (1) the right to remain silent; (2) that any statements made can be used against the suspect in court; (3) the right to the presence of an attorney before and during questioning; and (4) counsel will be appointed at no cost if the suspect cannot afford an attorney. The Supreme Court required a formal advisement "unless other fully effective means are devised to inform the accused persons of their right of silence and to assure a continuous opportunity to exercise it . . . ." (*Miranda v. Arizona* (1966) 384 U.S. 436, 444).

In later decisions, the Supreme Court has repeatedly held that no specific warning or "incantation" is required. (*Duckworth v. Eagan* (1989) 492 U.S. 195, 202; *California v. Prysock* (1981) 453 U.S. 355, 359; *Florida v. Powell* (2010) 130 S. Ct. 1195. *See also People v. Kelly* (1990) 51 Cal. 3d

931, 948.) Moreover, courts have held that deviation in the language of the admonition is insufficient to constitute a *Miranda* violation if the warnings reasonably convey to a suspect his or her rights. (*People v. Wash* (1993) 6 Cal. 4th 215, 235–37.)

Here, Defendant was given the following rights advisement by Agent Ryan:

Mr. Williams, you have the right to remain silent and anything you say can be used against you. You have the right to an attorney and if you cannot afford an attorney, one will be provided for you. Do you understand and waive these rights and agree to speak with me?

Under the circumstances in this case, Agent Ryan's advisement, while not directly quoting *Miranda*, nonetheless adequately informed Defendant of his rights.

1.   Any Alleged Defect in the *Miranda* Advisement was Harmless Due to the Defendant's Complete Awareness of His Right to Counsel During Questioning

The People recognize that generally a warning that omits the phrase "before and during questioning" is inadequate, even where the suspect is informed of the right to appointed counsel and the procedure for such appointments in court. (*People v. Lujan* (Ct. App. 2001) 92 Cal. App. 4th 1389.) The Ninth Circuit, however, has held that a defective warning is harmless where it was "abundantly clear" the suspect was "completely aware" of the right to counsel during the interrogation. (*United States v. Pheaster* (9th Cir. 1976) 544 F.2d 353, 365–66.)

In *Pheaster*, the court reasoned that where it was apparent that the defendant was completely aware of his right to have counsel present during the interrogation, the failure of a FBI agent, when giving a *Miranda* warning to the defendant after the arrest, to specifically state that the defendant's right to a government-appointed attorney also included the right to have that attorney present during his interrogation, did not constitute a flaw in the otherwise complete *Miranda* warning. (*Id.*)

Here, Agent Ryan advised Defendant of his *Miranda* rights, but did not specifically state that Defendant had the right to have an attorney present during the interrogation. However, both Agent

Ryan's statement regarding the time it would take for an attorney to be present and Defendant's own statement that he would "give up (his) right to have a lawyer here for this interview" show that Defendant had notice that he was entitled to have an attorney present during the interview.

B.   DEFENDANT'S STATEMENTS WERE VOLUNTARY, NOT THE PRODUCT OF COERCION OR IMPROPER PROMISE OF ASSISTANCE

During the interview, Agent Ryan made two statements that are not at issue for the purposes of this preliminary hearing. They are as follows:

OK, I really want to hear your side. I can help you if I know your story. But, first, I have to know if you understand and waive your rights.

Gosh, David, I'd like to help you out and hear your side, but if you ask for a lawyer now, then I can't talk to you.

Defendant contends that these two statements served as improper promises of assistance to Defendant. The People argue that these statements were not improper promises of assistance, but rather further explanation and advisement of Defendant's *Miranda* rights.

1.   Agent Ryan's Clarifying Questions Asked to Gauge Defendant's Understanding of his Rights Were Proper

The *Miranda* right to counsel is not a right to an immediate consultation with a lawyer, but to the presence and confidential advice of an attorney before and during questioning. (*Miranda*, 384 U.S. at 444.)

It is proper to explain this distinction if a suspect asks for clarification, so long as it is not implied that a refusal to answer questions will have adverse consequences. (*People v. Green* (1987) 189 Cal. App. 3d 685, 692. *See also People v. Williams* (1997) 16 Cal. 4th 635, 657 (where a Los Angeles suspect was arrested in Sacramento; discussion regarding need to postpone the interview until the return to Los Angeles if the suspect wanted counsel was not an invocation; and was not improper to refer to the time before arraignment as suspect's "one shot" to talk to officers)).

Here, Defendant did not ask for a clarification about the presence of an attorney. Instead, Defendant's statements to Agent Ryan show that he understood that he has the right to an attorney during interrogation, and chose to waive the right "to have a lawyer here for this interview" in order to speak to the FBI right away.

Additionally, Agent Ryan's statements were spoken in such a way as to inform Defendant of his right to have counsel present. Agent Ryan mentioned more than once that it could take a long time to have an attorney arrive for the questioning. Any reasonable person could infer this to mean that he had the right to have an attorney present. The People believe that Defendant was properly advised of his rights and that he understood his right to have an attorney present with him during the interrogation.

2. No Impermissible Promises of Assistance or Leniency Were Made to Defendant

The Defense argues that Agent Ryan made an impermissible promise of leniency to Defendant if he agreed to speak to the police without an attorney present. In *United States v. Gamez* (9th Cir. 2002) 301 F.3d 1138, 1144, the court found no coercion in telling a drug and murder suspect that it would "behoove" him to tell what he knew and that the interview was the suspect's "last chance" to come forward. (*See also People v. Carrington* (2009) 47 Cal. 4th 145, 170; *People v. Coffman* (2004) 34 Cal. 4th 1, 61–62 (vague promise to "help" suspect if she "helps" officer is not an impermissible promise of leniency.))

Moreover, the Oceana Supreme Court found no coercion in telling a suspect he would be helping himself by leading officers to the property involved in the case. The Court stated exhortations that a suspect "help himself" by revealing true facts are proper. (*People v. Jackson* (1980) 28 Cal. 3d 264, 299.)

In the current case, Agent Ryan merely told Defendant that he desired to help him, not that Agent Ryan actually could or would help him. Agent Ryan did not offer any incentive or promise of better treatment in exchange for cooperation. He rather stated the simple fact that he would be in a better position to help Defendant if he knew Defendant's side of the story. These statements were not in any way improper, nor did they promise incentives for cooperation.

C.   **DEFENDANT NEVER INVOKED HIS RIGHT TO COUNSEL; AMBIGUOUS STATEMENTS REFERRING TO COUNSEL DO NOT INVOKE THE RIGHT TO COUNSEL**

In the present case, Defendant never invoked his right to counsel. While he discusses calling an attorney, he never said he would not answer questions unless an attorney was present, nor did he tell Agent Ryan that he wanted an attorney.

In *Davis v. United States* (1994) 512 U.S. 452, 461, the Court dealt with a homicide suspect who had waived his rights, but an hour and a half into the interview said, "Maybe I should talk to a lawyer." (*Id.*) The interviewer told the suspect questioning would cease if he wanted counsel, and the suspect twice stated he was not requesting an attorney. (*Id.*) After a break and a reminder about the suspect's rights, the interview continued until the suspect requested counsel. (*Id.*) The Supreme Court held that officers may continue questioning a suspect who waived his or her *Miranda* rights until there is an unambiguous request for an attorney. (*Id.*) The Court added that officers may, but are not required, to ask clarifying questions when such ambiguous invocation occurs. (*Id.*)

Oceana courts have applied *Davis* several times. The statement, "I don't know if I should without an attorney," made shortly after a waiver in response to the officer asking for the suspect's side of the story, was held to be too equivocal to be an invocation. (*People v. Michaels* (2002) 28 Cal. 4th 486, 508.)

In *People v. Simons* (3d Dist. 2007) 155 Cal. App. 4th 948, 958, a suspect who had waived his rights asked how long it would take "for a lawyer to get here" and when a lawyer could be appointed. There was no invocation where officers responded appropriately, offered to stop the interview, and clarified the suspect's willingness to continue talking. In *Clark v. Murphy* (9th Cir. 2003) 317 F.3d 1038, 1046, although the court considered it a "close question," it held that a mid-interview statement, "I think I would like to talk to a lawyer," and a later request for the officer's opinion about whether the suspect should consult a lawyer, were not invocations.

Whether a suspect's response to an admonition is ambiguous is evaluated objectively, from the point of view of the listening officer. (*People v. Williams* (2010) 49 Cal. 4th 405, 428; *United States v. Rodriguez* (9th Cir. 2008) 515 F.3d 1072, 1080.) The Oceana Supreme Court long ago made it clear that unmistakable clarity is not the appropriate standard for invocation of *Miranda* rights. (*People v. Randall* (1970) 1 Cal. 3d 948, 955.)

In the present case, Defendant made several qualifying statements about an attorney. He stated, "Yeah, well, I wanna talk to you, but maybe I should talk to a lawyer first. My lawyers before said I should let them do the talking." But, Defendant did not ask for an attorney at that juncture. Additionally, he said, "Well, um, you know I'd like to explain how it wasn't me, but I think I should talk to a lawyer first. I ain't got no money for a lawyer. How long would it take to get a PD here?" Again, while he referenced speaking to a lawyer, he did not actually ask for one. A third time Defendant mentioned the need for an attorney, saying, "Maybe I need a lawyer. But I don't want to wait here all night. Maybe if I just tell you what happened, I can go. Do you think that it will take so long to get a lawyer?" As is true with his other statements, Defendant did not specifically ask for an attorney to be present. During this exchange, Agent Ryan continued to advise Defendant that he had the right to an attorney. Defendant never invoked his right to counsel, despite mentioning an attorney.

D.   DEFENDANT IMPLICITLY WAIVED MIRANDA BY VOLUNTARILY RESPONDING TO QUESTIONS AFTER HE WAS ADVISED OF HIS RIGHTS

In *Pheaster*, 544 F.2d at 365–66, the Court found that the police officer's failure to tell the defendant that he had a right to government-appointed counsel was not fatal when the officer had otherwise given the defendant a complete Miranda warning and when it was apparent that the defendant knew of his right to counsel. Therefore, regardless of the potential defectiveness of a *Miranda* warning, so long as the defendant understands his rights and his awareness is apparent, the officer may continue with the interrogation. *Pheaster* also requires that a wavier of rights be voluntary, knowing, and intelligent. (*Id.*) As long as this is demonstrated, the officer may proceed.

Here, Defendant demonstrated a voluntary, knowing, and intelligent waiver of his *Miranda* rights. After Defendant was advised of his rights pursuant to *Miranda* and asked if he understood those rights, Defendant immediately began speaking to Agent Ryan, stating, "Well, I want to tell you what happened, 'cause you got the wrong guy. I wasn't near the bank." Agent Ryan replied, "OK, I really want to hear your side. I can help you if I know your story. But, first, I have to know if you understand and waive your rights." Defendant continued to speak with Agent Ryan, even after being advised of his rights.

By continually asking about the presence of an attorney and finally stating, "I'll give up my right to have a lawyer here for this interview," it is apparent that Defendant acknowledged his right to counsel, but waived it in order to explain his side of the story to Agent Ryan.

IV.

CONCLUSION

Based on the foregoing authorities, the People respectfully request the Court to deny Defendant's motion. Defendant's statements should be admitted on the basis that they flowed from a proper, voluntary, knowing, and intelligent waiver of Defendant's *Miranda* rights.

Dated: May 29, C.Y.

Respectfully Submitted,

BENJAMIN RAFFITY

DISTRICT ATTORNEY

By: *Darshina Abhoot*

Darshina Abhoot

Deputy District Attorney

EXHIBIT 1

TRANSCRIPT OF STATEMENTS RELATED TO DEFENDANT'S MIRANDA ADVISEMENT

<u>Agent Ryan</u>: Mr. Williams, you have the right to remain silent and anything you say can be used against you. You have the right to an attorney and if you cannot afford an attorney, one will be provided for you. Do you understand and waive these rights and agree to speak with me?

<u>Williams</u>: Well, I want to tell you what happened, 'cause you got the wrong guy. I wasn't near the bank.

<u>Agent Ryan</u>: OK, I really want to hear your side. I can help you if I know your story. But, first, I have to know if you understand and waive your rights.

<u>Williams</u>: Yeah, well, I wanna talk to you, but maybe I should talk to a lawyer first. My lawyers before said I should let them do the talking.

<u>Agent Ryan</u>: Gosh, David, I'd like to help you out and hear your side, but if you ask for a lawyer now, then I can't talk to you.

<u>Williams</u>: Well, um, you know I'd like to explain how it wasn't me, but I think I should talk to a lawyer first. I ain't got no money for a lawyer. How long would it take to get a PD here?

<u>Agent Ryan</u>: Like I said, you have the right to a lawyer and we will provide one free of charge, but it could take a long time to get one here at this hour of night."

<u>Williams</u>: Hmmmmm. Maybe I need a lawyer. But I don't want to wait here all night. Maybe if I just tell you what happened, I can go. Do you think that it will take so long to get a lawyer?

LINDSEY KEENAN, State Bar No. 190041
LAW OFFICES OF KEENAN AND MILLER
57990 Palm Drive, 11th Floor
Maliwood, Oceana 90120

Attorney for Defendant
ELIZABETH SCHNEIDER

SUPERIOR COURT OF THE STATE OF OCEANA
FOR THE COUNTY OF MALIWOOD

PEOPLE OF THE STATE OF OCEANA, Plaintiff, v. ELIZABETH MAY SCHNEIDER, Defendant.	CASE NO.: 238142 **MOTION PER P.C. § 1538.5 TO EXCLUDE <u>PAS</u> RESULTS BECAUSE <u>CONSENT</u>, IF ANY, TO SAID WARRANTLESS <u>SEARCH</u> WAS EXPRESSLY <u>LIMITED</u> TO HELPING THE OFFICER DETERMINE WHETHER THE DRIVER WAS UNDER THE INFLUENCE; THERE WAS <u>NO</u> KNOWING, VOLUNTARY CONSENT TO SEARCH FOR B.A.C.** Date: Feb. 23, C.Y. Time: 9:00 a.m. Dept: 43

TO THE COURT:

I.

STATEMENT OF FACTS

On October 29, C.Y.-1 at approximately 3:15 a.m., Maliwood Police Department Officer Jordan states in her arrest report that she was "N/B on Castillo at Seacrest Ave, behind a white S.U.V. The vehicle [lawfully] made a west turn [left] onto Seacrest, and I noticed the windows of the vehicle were tinted, a violation of § 26708(a)(1)." The officer also activated her emergency lights and the driver responded appropriately.

Ms. Schneider submitted to a Field Sobriety Test, and the officer contends she did not do them as explained and demonstrated. The officer reported that she gave Ms. Schneider the opportunity to use a

PAS (preliminary alcohol screening) device **and she declined**. The officer then states that she changed her mind and decided to use the PAS device with the result of 0.09% at approximately 3:44 a.m. The officer does not report that she told her words to the effect of "if you do not take this breathalyzer, you will go to jail." It is clear that the officer did not advise her as required by Vehicle Code section 23612(i) that the officer shall advise the person of the "person's right to refuse to take the preliminary alcohol screening test."

The PAS test was a warrantless search of Ms. Schneider's body for the amount of alcohol in her blood. There was no implied consent. The consent, if any, was coerced. There was no knowing, voluntary consent to a search for the amount of alcohol in her blood to be utilized at the time of trial.[69]

The defense has no objection to the preliminary alcohol screening test used for its intended purpose, i.e., to determine the presence of alcohol (as opposed to B.A.C). The prosecution has chemical test results as a result of Vehicle Code section 23612 (the "implied consent" statute). This is **NOT** a refusal case. There is **no consent**, implied or express, to the warrantless search of Ms. Schneider's body for the amount of alcohol in her blood (B.A.C.) by the PAS machine.

The **PAS test results** are the poisonous fruit of a **warrantless search** of Ms. Schneider's body for B.A.C. The **warrantless search** cannot be justified by an exception, e.g., "under arrest," emergency," etc. The warrantless search for the amount of alcohol in Ms. Schneider's blood was **without knowing and voluntary consent**, and violates the **Fourth and Fourteenth Amendments** to the United States Constitution. Further, the warrantless search violates Ms. Schneider's **RIGHT TO PRIVACY**, right to **COUNSEL**, and **RIGHT TO A FAIR TRIAL**.[70]

Regarding advising a driver of a PAS test, many cops say: "Blow into this or you're going to jail" or similar words. Sometimes officers actually advise the driver about "preliminary alcohol screening information" as required by **Vehicle Code section 23612(i)**:

---

[69] Further, the officer only has one result, 0.09%, and the scientific community requires, as a minimum standard, that there are **two breath test results** within 0.02% of each other to ensure accurate and reliable and, therefore, relevant results. There is a foundational problem for the admission of the test results.

[70] This is not a case where the defendant refused a test and is trying to profit from said wrongful conduct. (Based on Ms. Schneider's drinking pattern, she was in the absorptive phase from the time of the stop to the time of the chemical test.)

P.A.S. Admonition: I am requesting that you take a preliminary alcohol screening test to further assist me in determining where you are under the influence of alcohol. You may refuse to take this test; however, this is **not an implied consent** test and if arrested, you **will be required** to give a sample of your blood, breath or urine for the **purpose of determining** the **actual alcoholic** and drug **content of your blood**.

In **either event**, this citizen was **never advised** that the PAS test **would** be used to measure **B.A.C.** This warrantless **search** of Ms. Schneider's body and the **seizure** of her **breath** by way of a PAS test to **determine B.A.C.** was secured without a "**knowing and voluntary consent.**" Consent, **if any**, to the PAS test was **EXPRESSLY LIMITED** to "assist" the officer "in determining" if there was **sufficient probable cause** to arrest for DUI.

The United States Supreme Court has held that "the general rule that a **Non-Consensual Search Is <u>Unconstitutional</u> If Not Authorized by a Valid Warrant**" (*see infra* point III, p. 5), holding that a person **cannot <u>legally</u> give <u>consent</u> unless she is fully informed** about her Constitutional Rights as the standards of "<u>knowing waiver</u>" <u>require</u> (*see infra* point IV, p. 6). **"Full information"** was not provided to this citizen, i.e., that the PAS test **results** could be used as a measure of her B.A.C. In fact, the police advised about implied consent at the time of the search, which reasonably led Ms. Schneider to believe the PAS test would not be used to determine her B.A.C., stating "your **obligation** to **submit** to . . . 'a **chemical test** (implied consent) to **determine**' the alcohol . . . **content** of your **blood** is **not satisfied** by submitting to a preliminary alcohol screening test."

II.

<u>THE UNCONTROVERTED LEGAL PRINCIPLES TO BE APPLIED</u>

The **Fourth Amendment** to the United States Constitution states that "[t]he **right** of the **people** to be **secure** in their **persons**, houses, papers and effects, against unreasonable searches and seizures, **shall not be violated**, and no Warrant shall issue, but upon probable cause, supported by Oath or affirmation, and particularly describing the place to be searched, and the persons or things to be seized."

This is the cornerstone of any inquiry regarding governmental acquisition of evidence from the accused. To determine this matter, certain immutable principles apply.

1.   "For the Fourth Amendment protects people, not places . . . what he seeks to preserve as private, even in an area accessible to the public, may be constitutionally protected." (*Katz v. United States* (1967) 389 U.S. 347, 351–52 (internal citations omitted)).

2.   "**[S]earches** conducted outside the **judicial process**, without prior approval by judge or magistrate, are **per se unreasonable** under the Fourth Amendment—subject only to a few specifically established and well-delineated **exceptions**." (*Katz, supra,* 389 U.S. at 357 (footnotes omitted)).

3.   A Chemical Test Is a Search Under the Fourth Amendment. The Court held that the **taking** of a person's blood, **breath** or urine is a **search and seizure** within the meaning of the **Fourth Amendment** to the U.S. and California Constitutions citing *Schmerber v. California* (1996) 384 U.S. 757 at 767." The "**implied consent**" law of Vehicle Code section 23612(a) is an **exception** to the **Fourth Amendment**. "It is not disputed that the administration of a **breath test** is a **search** within the meaning of the **Fourth Amendment** and therefore subject to the requirements of that amendment." (*Burnett v. Municipality of Anchorage* (9th Cir. 1986) 806 F.2d 1447, 1449 (emphasis added, citations omitted)).

4.   "To pass constitutional muster under the Fourth Amendment a search must be reasonable. Generally, a search must also be supported by probable cause, and must be backed up by a **warrant, or the circumstances must fit within an exception to the warrant requirement**." (*Nelson v. City of Irvine* (1998) 143 F.3d 1196, 1200 (citations omitted)).

5.   "In considering [warrant requirement exceptions], we must not lose sight of the Fourth Amendment's fundamental guarantee as stated by Mr. Justice Bradley's admonition in his opinion for the Court almost a century ago in *Boyd v. United States*, 116 U.S. 616, 635:

> It may well be that it is the obnoxious thing in its mildest and least repulsive form; but illegitimate and unconstitutional practices get their first footing in that war, namely, by silent deviations from legal modes of procedure. This can only be obviated by adhering to the rule that constitutional provisions for the security of person and property should be liberally construed. A close and literal construction deprives them of half their efficacy,

and leads to gradual depreciation of the right, as if it consisted of more in sound than in substance. **It is the duty of courts to be watchful for the constitutional rights of the citizen, and against any stealthy encroachment thereon.**

(*Coolidge v. New Hampshire* (1971) 403 U.S. 443, 453–54(footnote omitted, emphasis added)).

6.   The California legislature has enacted a statutory scheme regarding driving under the influence and chemical testing for blood alcohol content. The legislature passed "**implied <u>consent</u>**" (a legal fiction) in order to be able to lawfully secure the best evidence of blood alcohol content. In balancing the rights of individuals to be free of government searches versus society's right to be protected against drunk driving, the legislature determined that "**consent**" to a chemical test can be **implied** only of persons that drive and are **arrested** for driving under the influence. There is **<u>no</u> implied consent to take a PAS test.** Vehicle Code section 23612(a)(1)(A) provides that "any person who drives a motor vehicle is **deemed to have given** his or her <u>**consent**</u> to **chemical testing** of his or her blood or breath for purposes of **determining the alcohol content of his or her blood <u>if</u> lawfully <u>arrested</u>** . . . ." Vehicle Code section 23612(a)(1)(C) provides in essence that "the **testing** shall be **incident** to a **lawful arrest** . . ." for driving under the influence. Vehicle Code section 23612(a)(1)(A) and Vehicle Code section 23612(a)(1)(C) do **not** apply to the **PAS** test because Ms. Schneider was **not lawfully arrested** when police searched her.

7.   No choice was offered by the officer regarding the PAS test. Vehicle Code section 23612(a)(1)(A) provides that "**if** the person is **lawfully arrested** for driving under the influence of an alcoholic beverage, the person **has the choice** of whether the test shall be of his or her <u>**blood**</u> **or breath** and the **officer shall advise the person that he or she has that choice** . . . ."

There was **no knowing and voluntary consent** by Ms. Schneider to the requested search of her body by the police for the amount of alcohol in her body.

Where there is a lawful arrest for driving under the influence, the legislative requirement to submit to a chemical test is triggered, and there are lawful sanctions (e.g., losing a license, jail, etc.). The police are limited by law to the legislative exception to the Fourth Amendment per the Vehicle Code, i.e., if lawfully arrested, **consent** to the test is **implied**.

III.

THE U.S. SUPREME COURT HAS HELD: "THE GENERAL RULE THAT A <u>NON-CONSENSUAL</u> <u>SEARCH IS UNCONSTITUTIONAL IF NOT AUTHORIZED BY A WARRANT</u>"

In *Ferguson v. Charleston* (2001) 532 U.S. 67, the Court reviewed where a state's hospital performance of a diagnosis test to obtain evidence of a patient's possible criminal conduct for law enforcement purposes constituted an unreasonable search if the patient did not knowingly and voluntarily consent to the procedure. Under the facts of *Ferguson*, patients provided urine samples to a state hospital and the police. Arguably, the **patient was on notice** that the hospital would be using the urine test to determine drug use and would thereafter submit positive results to the police for prosecution. The ultimate goal of the program was laudable: the "immediate objective of the searches were to generate **evidence for law enforcement purposes** in order to reach that goal." (*Id.*) The Court held that **Fourth Amendment's** general **prohibition** against **non-consensual, warrantless searches**" applied. (*Id.*)

In *Ferguson*, the prosecution argued the evidence of drug use was admissible because the search was not done by the police. In our case, the search of Ms. Schneider's body for evidence of her blood alcohol content by the PAS device was done directly by the police. Therefore, this is a stronger case for application of the Fourth Amendment's prohibition against warrantless searches.

IV.

THE U.S. SUPREME COURT RULED THAT A PERSON CANNOT LEGALLY GIVE <u>CONSENT</u> UNLESS HE OR SHE IS FULLY INFORMED ABOUT HIS OR HER CONSTITUTIONAL RIGHTS AS <u>STANDARDS</u> OF "<u>KNOWING WAIVER</u>" REQUIRE

"When citizens undertake to **obtain** such evidence **for the specific purpose of incriminating those patients**, they have a special obligation to make sure that the patients are **fully informed about their constitutional rights**, as <u>standards of knowing waiver require</u>, *cf. Miranda v. Arizona* (1966) 384 U.S. 436." (*Ferguson*, 532 U.S. at 69 (emphasis added)). All the more does this requirement of "knowing waiver" apply when **police** obtain the evidence. Given the misleading advice (not the test for blood alcohol content), the prosecution cannot argue in this case that there was a "knowing waiver" to the search.

V.

THE PROSECUTION HAS THE <u>BURDEN OF PROOF</u> ON THE ISSUE OF CONSENT

The United States Supreme Court held in *Bumper v. North Carolina* (1968) 391 U.S. 543 that the government has the **burden of proving consent** "was, in fact, freely and voluntarily given." If not, the evidence will be suppressed as the result of an illegal search and seizure. In *People v. Shandloff* (1985) 170 Cal. App. 3d 372, the court held that the People's burden is to prove that the consent was the **product** of **free will** and not a mere submission to an express or implied assertion of authority.

VI.

IF THE LANGUAGE OF THE OFFICER WHO SECURED <u>CONSENT</u> FOR THE <u>SEARCH</u> WAS GIVEN, THE PAS TEST WAS TO ASSIST A <u>DETERMINATION</u> OF WHETHER THERE WAS "PROBABLE CAUSE" TO BELIEVE THE DRIVER WAS UNDER THE INFLUENCE; THERE WAS NO CONSENT TO DETERMINE B.A.C.

The admonition in Vehicle Code section 23612, if given by the police officer clearly, informed the driver that the purpose of the test was **only** for establishing **reasonable cause** to arrest for driving under the influence, i.e., Vehicle Code section 23152(a). The driver was told that, **if arrested**, she would then have to submit to the **implied consent test** to <u>determine the alcohol content</u> of her **blood**. The cop advised Ms. Schneider that the chemical test for blood alcohol is different than the PAS test and that she would **have to take a test to determine B.A.C if arrested**.

The *content* of the admonition defines the extent of the consent that was obtained. Ms. Schneider **consented** to the **PAS**, if at all, **only** for the **purpose** of allowing the officer to use the test to assist her in determining whether the driver was under the influence. The driver consented to nothing more; there was only a **limited consent** to the **search** of her body; and there was **no consent** to use the results of the search to determine blood alcohol content.

VII.

THE SEARCH IS LIMITED BY THE EXPRESS TERMS OF THE CONSENT AND CANNOT BE EXPANDED

In *People v. Superior Court (Arketa)* (1970) 10 Cal. App. 3d 122, the police asked the defendant if they could enter the house to search for a suspect seen to enter with a crowbar. Defendant said that there were persons in the house and that the officers could enter. The consent was implicitly limited to **look** for a **suspect**. The police entered and found a crowbar in the closet. The 1538.5 Suppression ruling was affirmed on appeal because the police conduct **exceeded** the **limited expressed consent requested**. The same rule applies to the purpose of the PAS test. The consent is limited to the express purpose of helping the officer determine whether the driver is under the influence and is not to determine B.A.C.

In *People v. Timms* (1986) 179 Cal. App. 3d 86, the defendant made a homicide call to the police and told the officer that intruders shot the victim. The police searched for suspects. The premises were secured. At the police station, the defendant said the gun was in the closet. A .38 gun was found in a jacket in the closet. The court held that the defendant's **non-objection to the search is not consent**. (Citing *Arketa*, 10 Cal. App. 3d at 122).

Another limited consent case analogous to the PAS test scope of consent issue is *People v. Superior Court (Kenner)* (1977) 73 Cal. App. 3d 65, in which consent was given to the police to enter the home to "talk" to Kenner. Even though there was a consent to enter, the limited consent for purposes of having a "talk" did not permit the immediate arrest of Kenner without an arrest warrant. The 1538.5 suppression was affirmed.

To the same force and effect is *In re Johnny V.* (1978) 85 Cal. App. 3d 120, in which the police made an arrest after consent was given for the limited purpose of entering the premises to "talk." The police found blood-stained shoes. A 1538.5 denial was reversed by the Court of Appeal.

VIII.

CONCLUSION

The police, armed and in uniform, searched for evidence of the crime of driving under the influence. **Prior** to an **arrest**, and without the benefit of "consent" **implied** by law, they **searched** for the amount of alcohol in Ms. Schneider's **blood** by way of a PAS test. The police later got a blood test with 0.09% results. Ordinarily, to justify a search the police must have a **warrant**. The prosecution has the **burden** to **justify the warrantless search**. There is no exception for the warrantless search by way of a PAS test in this case, e.g., no arrest, no emergency, no "implied **consent**," etc. The police did **not** advise the citizen of the **scope of the search**. In fact, the police misled the citizen (e.g., this is "**not** a test to **determine your blood alcohol content**"). Ms. Schneider did **not "knowingly" and voluntarily consent** to the **search** of **her body** by way of a PAS test to determine the amount of alcohol in her blood. The PAS test **result** must be suppressed. This court has a duty to enforce the Constitution.

Dated: January 29, C.Y.

Respectfully Submitted,

Lindsey Keenan

LINDSEY KEENAN
Attorney for Defendant

FRANKLIN STEWART, ESQ., SBN 54321
LAW OFFICES OF FRANKLIN STEWART
Maliwood Branch Office
300 W. Mali Blvd.
Maliwood, Oceana 90120
Attorney for Defendant Jimmy McLaughlin

SUPERIOR COURT OF THE STATE OF OCEANA
COUNTY OF MALIWOOD

PEOPLE OF THE STATE OF OCEANA, Plaintiff, v. JIMMY MCLAUGHLIN, Defendant.	Case No. 12345 **IN ORDER TO ADMIT A BREATH RESULT OVER OBJECTION OF FOUNDATION, THE PROSECUTION MUST DEMONSTRATE THAT THE TEST IS ACCURATE (OTHERWISE IT IS NOT RELEVANT). SEE EVID. CODE § 403.**

I.

THE PROPONENT OF THE BREATH TEST RESULT MUST LAY A FOUNDATION (TITLE 17 OR THE THREE ELEMENTS), OR IT IS NOT ADMISSIBLE

People v. Williams (2002) 28 Cal. 4th 408 was a refusal case in which the court did not want the defendant to profit from his wrongful conduct of refusing a chemical test[71] excluding the PAS result. The court held the PAS test results are admissible **IF** there is compliance with Title 17 or the Adams foundation.

The duty of the prosecution is to demonstrate that "**all three foundational elements must be established for the evidence to be admissible; the chain is no stronger than its weakest link**." *Williams*, 28 Cal. 4th at 417 n.5. The **three requirements** are the formulated rules "by which the **reliability** and thus the **relevance of scientific evidence is determined**." *Id*. at 414. The prosecution

---

[71] In our case, the defendant cooperated and submitted to the chemical test -- there is no refusal.

must "demonstrate that **correct scientific procedures** were used in a particular case." *Id.* Admissibility

depends on the **reliability** and the **consequent relevance of the evidence**.

The *Williams* court noted that compliance with Title 17 is one way to demonstrate a standard of

competency. If there is non-compliance with Title 17, the prosecution can obtain admission of the breath

test results but it "**then** must **qualify the personnel** involved in the test, the **accuracy of the equipment**

used, and the reliability of the method followed **before** the **results** can be **admitted**." *Williams,* 28 Cal.

4th at 416. As noted by the California Supreme Court and as the facts per *People v. Adams* (Ct. App.

1976) 59 Cal. App. 3d 559, the **test results** were **admitted** in *Adams* because they were reliable (they met

the foundational requirements not withstanding noncompliance with one technical regulation). In *Adams*,

there was no question raised as to accuracy and reliability, and "noncompliance (a minor violation of

Title 17) goes merely to the weight of the evidence." *Williams,* 28 Cal. 4th at 416. The *Williams* court

found it significant that in *Adams* the defendants **did not "attempt any showing that the**

noncompliance affected the test results in any way, let alone rendered the results inaccurate." *Id.* at

417. The *Williams* court held that breath test results are admissible upon either a showing of compliance

with Title 17 or the foundational elements of: (1) PROPERLY FUNCTIONING EQUIPMENT (2) a

properly administered test; and (3) a qualified operator. All three elements must be proved.

The California Supreme Court concluded with its "concern that laxity in complying with the

regulations may **undermine** the **reliability** of the test . . . Furthermore, compliance (with the regulations)

will ensure that the tests retain their reliability, and their **relevance** and **admissibility** . . . ." *Williams,* 28

Cal. 4th at 418.

Dated: May 21, C.Y.   Respectfully submitted,

                                                          Franklin Stewart
                                                 FRANKLIN STEWART, Attorney for Defendant

JOHN HOLLINGER, ESQ., SBN 54321
LAW OFFICES OF JOHN HOLLINGER
800 E. Mali Blvd.
Maliwood, Oceana 90120

Attorney for Defendant Anthony Miller

SUPERIOR COURT OF THE STATE OF OCEANA
COUNTY OF MALIWOOD

PEOPLE OF THE STATE OF OCEANA,
 	
        Plaintiff,
 	
        v.
 	
ANTHONY MILLER,
 	
        Defendant.
	Case No. 12345
	
	POINTS AND AUTHORITIES TO EXCLUDE EVIDENCE OF THE AMOUNT OF PRESERVATIVE AND ANTI-COAGULANT IN BLOOD VIAL UNLESS "ANALYST" THAT MEASURED AND PREPARED THE CHEMICAL SOLUTIONS TESTIFIES [RIGHT OF CONFRONTATION]

TO THE COURT:

I.

EVIDENCE OF THE AMOUNT OF PRESERVATIVE AND ANTI-COAGULANT SUPPOSEDLY IN THE VIAL OF DEFENDANT'S BLOOD IS NOT ADMISSIBLE IF THE "ANALYST" THAT PREPARED THE CHEMICAL SOLUTIONS IS NOT AVAILABLE FOR CONFRONTATION

The precise amount of preservative and anti-coagulant measured and placed in the vial to store Defendant's blood is a critical piece of evidence. The U.S. Supreme Court and California courts have recently expanded the Sixth Amendment's **Right of Confrontation**. The defense has the right to **confront** the "**analyst**" who prepared the chemical solutions. The analyst may have prepared a "certification" that the vials have a certain amount of preservative and anti-coagulant. If so, the "certificate" prepared by some analyst is "a solemn declaration or affirmation **made for the purpose of**

establishing or proving some fact." *Melendez-Diaz v. Massachusetts* (2009) 129 S. Ct. 2527, 2532

(quoting from *Crawford v. Washington* (2004) 541 U.S. 36, 51). Some person measured and prepared the

precise chemicals. What are that person's qualifications? How did he measure the amount of chemicals?

When did he do it? What procedures were used? What safeguards were utilized? Is he properly trained?

As demonstrated herein below, the defense has the Constitutional right to confront this critical

witness. The defense has the right to confront the witness that prepared the vials and prepares a

"certification" that they contain a precise amount of chemicals.[72]

II.

THIS DEFENDANT IS ENTILTED TO CONFRONT THE WITNESSES AGAINST HIM, A

FUNDAMENTAL AND ESSENTIAL RIGHT TO A FAIR TRIAL, AS PROVIDED BY THE

SIXTH AMENDMENT

In *Crawford v. Washington*, "[w]here testimonial statements are at issue, **the only indicium of**

reliability sufficient to satisfy constitutional demands is the one the Constitution actually

prescribes: confrontation." (2004) 541 U.S. 36, 68–69. The **confrontation clause "commands not**

that evidence be reliable, but that reliability be assessed in a particular manner: by testing in the

crucible of cross-examination." *Id*. at 61. **"Dispensing with confrontation because testimony is**

obviously reliable is akin to dispensing with jury trial because a defendant is obviously guilty. This

is not what the Sixth Amendment prescribes." *Id*. at 62.

Recent case law supports the exclusion of the blood test results. A **blood alcohol test** is within

"the core class of testimonial statements." The blood alcohol report was **prepared in anticipation of**

litigation. *Melendez-Diaz* (2009) 129 S. Ct. 2527. The Supreme Court rejected the argument that a lab

analyst's report is not testimonial because it contains "near-contemporaneous" observations of a scientific

test, rather than statements by lay witnesses of events observed in the past. *Id*. at 2535. The Court also

rejected a related argument that there is a difference between testimony recounting past events, "which is

---

[72] The old adage that "reliable hearsay" can be utilized by an expert has been trumped by the Sixth Amendment of
the Constitution.

'prone to distortion and manipulation," and testimony that is the result of "neutral, scientific testing.'" *Id.* The court explained that **"forensic evidence is not uniquely immune from the risk of manipulation . . .** A forensic analyst responding to a request from a law enforcement official may feel pressure – or have an incentive – to alter the evidence in a manner favorable to the prosecution." *Id.* The Court added, **"Confrontation is designed to weed out not only the fraudulent analyst, but the incompetent one as well."**

In *People v. Lopez* (Ct. App. 2009) 177 Cal. App. 4th 202, 208, the Court of Appeal (after transfer from the California Supreme Court in light of *Melendez-Diaz*) **reversed itself and held that the admission into evidence of a** <u>blood alcohol laboratory report</u> **violated defendant's Constitutional Right of Confrontation by allowing testimony of hearsay evidence prohibited under *Crawford*.** The *Lopez* court noted in *Melendez-Diaz* that "laboratory **reports** of the type presented in *Geier* . . . are **testimonial hearsay** evidence within the meaning of *Crawford* and are inadmissible in a criminal proceeding unless the person **creating the report** is unavailable and the defendant had a prior opportunity to cross-examine the creator." *Lopez*, 177 Cal. App. 4th at 206. In this case, any **testimony about the amount of preservative and anti-coagulant would be testimonial hearsay under *Crawford* because the admissibility of that evidence depends upon proper procedures being followed, testimony that the "analyst" that prepared the chemicals and known standard would have been provided if called as a witness at trial.** *See Melendez-Diaz*, (2009) 129 S. Ct. 2527. The *Lopez* court concluded "it was error under *Crawford* and *Melendez-Diaz* to admit into evidence the . . . lab report." In this case, the defense makes a confrontation objection to a criminalist testifying (without personal knowledge) to some analyst's "certification" (hearsay) that the blood vial has the necessary and proper amount of chemicals. The certificate prepared by the analyst is "a solemn declaration or affirmation **made for the purpose of establishing or proving some fact**." *Crawford*, 541 U.S. at 51. As in *Lopez*, "it cannot be shown that the error of admitting the blood alcohol report . . . was harmless beyond a reasonable doubt . . . ." *Lopez*, 177 Cal. App. 4th 208.

In *People v. Dungo* (2009) 176 Cal. App. 4th 1388, the defendant was entitled to cross-examine a

coroner who prepared an autopsy report where the prosecution expert witness relied on the report to **form**

an opinion. In this case, if allowed over objection, a prosecution witness will form an opinion based in

part, that proper procedures were followed, i.e. that there was a certain amount of preservative and anti-

coagulant. In *Dungo*, the trial court ruled that there was no Sixth Amendment issue of the autopsy report,

which was not introduced, and a prosecution expert was allowed to testify over defendant's Sixth

Amendment objection as to the cause of death, relying on the autopsy report. As the court noted in

Dungo, the "Sixth Amendment issue is whether the autopsy report is 'testimonial,' and if so, where

allowing" an expert, **"who was not present at the autopsy, to testify based on the facts"** in the other

expert's report violated defendant's Right of Confrontation. The court held that the autopsy report is

testimonial and that the person who prepared it is a "witness" for the purposes of the Sixth Amendment.

In our case, there will be no showing that the "expert" who prepared and measured the chemicals for the

vial is unavailable or that Defendant had a prior opportunity to cross-examine this analyst. This

Defendant is entitled to be confronted with the expert that prepared the chemicals, or evidence of known

standard is inadmissible. The *Dungo* court held that the trial court **erred in allowing the non-percipient**

expert witness to testify based upon the contents of a report done by another expert. As in our case,

that error cannot be harmless beyond a reasonable doubt.

Any **"certificate"** that the lot of vials manufactured contains a certain amount of preservative and

anti-coagulant is a **"solemn declaration or affirmation made for the purpose of establishing or**

proving some fact" that would be available for use at a later trial. *See Melendez-Diaz*, (2009) 129 S. Ct.

2527. The **certificate was formally prepared in anticipation of a prosecution**. The opinion of a

criminalist regarding the accuracy of the blood test results in this case is dependant upon the proper

amount of certain measured chemicals **by an analyst who will not testify**. In *Dungo*, 176 Cal. App. 4th

at 1404, the court stated that:

> **"If the [expert's] opinion is only as good as the facts on which it is based, and if**
>
> **those facts consist of testimonial hearsay statements that were not subject to cross-**

examination, then it is difficult to imagine how the defendant is expected to

'demonstrate the underlying information [is] incorrect or unreliable.'"

Substituted cross-examination is not constitutionally adequate. *Crawford's* language simply does not permit cross-examination of a surrogate when the evidence in question is testimonial. As the court observed in *Melendez-Diaz*, the prosecution's **failure to call the lab analyst as a witness prevented the defense from exploring the possibility that the analysts lacked proper training or had poor judgment or from testing their "honesty, proficiency, and methodology."** *Dungo*, 176 Cal. App. 4th at 1404. The same is true here. The defendant never had a prior opportunity to cross-examine the analyst that measured and prepared the anti-coagulant and preservative.

III.

CONCLUSION

The problem for the People is that the crime lab does not manufacture the "known standard," nor do the People verify that the crime lab does not prepare the blood vial. The result is that the defense is denied its Constitutional Right to Confront a critical witness, i.e. the "analyst" who measured and prepared the chemicals for the blood vial. The Constitution requires the exclusion of evidence of the amount of preservative and anti-coagulant unless the "analyst" is presented in court so the defense can cross-examine him.

Dated: June 17, C.Y.

Respectfully submitted,

John Hollinger

JOHN HOLLINGER, Attorney for Defendant

SUMMARY

Pretrial motions are an integral part of a criminal case and can be brought by either the prosecution or defense counsel. Such pretrial motions can include motions to suppress or include evidence, motions to dismiss, motions for severance and joinder, motions for writ of *habeas corpus*, bail motions, motions to discover police personnel records, and criminal demurrers. Competent attorneys should be able to recognize when certain pretrial motions should be brought and when they will be most effective to advancing their case.

Motions to suppress or include physical evidence, confessions, or statements are powerful tools and are governed by Rule 12 of the Federal Rules of Criminal Procedure. Often, defense counsel will bring a motion to suppress alleging that evidence was obtained from an illegal search or seizure, or a defendant's *Miranda* rights were violated, or a confession was coerced, or that a witness's identification of the defendant was tainted. Motions to include should be brought if the attorney wishes to raise something controversial in the opening statement, so as to ensure that this evidence will be admitted, without risking a sustained objection or a mistrial for the impropriety that could result.

Motions to dismiss give the defendant the opportunity to avoid trial by arguing that the legal theory of the prosecution is flawed, such as for reasons of venue, immunity, double jeopardy, or statute of limitations. Even if the motion is granted, however, this does not mean that the prosecution cannot institute a new case against the defendant.

Motions for severance can either take the form of severance of defendants or severance of counts. If joinder will result in some sort of prejudice to the defendant, then the court may grant a severance. The burden is on the defendant to prove the existence of prejudice; however, the court can grant severance on its own. Attacks on joinder include misjoinder as a matter of law or the lack of proof regarding some fact that the joinder rested upon. Motions for joinder are appropriate if the crimes were so closely connected or were part of a common plan, and courts actually favor joinder because it promotes judicial efficiency.

If the defense attorney believes that the complaint or information or indictment is defective, she can bring a criminal demurrer. The two effective arguments to be made by the defense are that (1) the indictment or information does not charge an offense, or (2) the court does not have jurisdiction of the charged offense. The defense can also bring a motion in misdemeanor cases to have an in-custody defendant released from custody on the basis that the police report does not provide probable cause that a crime was committed.

Motions for writ of *habeas corpus* are brought when a defendant has been unlawfully detained as in violation of the Constitution or laws. The defendant must be in-custody for this motion to be brought. Bail motions also seek to release defendants from custody so that the defendant can assist defense counsel with the investigation and preparation of his case; however, the defendant must not pose a safety threat and must be able to make all of his court appearances.

Finally, motions can be brought in order to review the personnel records of the arresting officer, which must either include an affidavit alleging the use of excessive force by the officer or reason to believe that there is a record showing that the officer has fabricated facts. This motion must state, with specificity, the information sought to be obtained by the defendant.

CHECKLIST

✓ Pretrial motions are crucial to effective trial practice. As a prosecutor or defense attorney, one must consider what motions to bring in order to advance one's case theory or the interests of the client. Additionally, one must consider how to anticipate and respond to an opponent's motions and case strategies.

✓ A motion to suppress evidence must be raised before trial or else the issue will likely be waived. Moreover, a motion to *include* evidence should be filed pretrial, so as to ensure that such evidence will not be objected to at trial or result in a mistrial.

✓ Proof of prejudice to the defendant is required for a motion for severance, and it is the burden of the defendant to prove the existence of such prejudice.

✓ Criminal demurrers can be brought anytime while the case is pending. Prosecutors must keep in mind the requirements of the criminal statute when drafting the charging document.

✓ It is important to remember that, to proceed with a Federal Motion for writ of *habeas corpus*, all state remedies must first be exhausted.

✓ Motions to discover police personnel records, such as *Pitchess* motions, must describe the information being sought with great specificity, including affidavits showing good cause for the request.

CHAPTER 12
CASE SETTLEMENT

"All compromise is give and take, but there can be no give and take on fundamentals. Any compromise on mere fundamentals is a surrender. For it is all give and no take."
–Mohandas Gandhi

Although the previous chapters have focused on trial preparation, the vast majority of guilty verdicts are achieved through case settlements, or plea bargains, and not by trial.[1] This was not always the case. "Only recently has plea bargaining become a viable practice accepted as a legitimate component in the administration of criminal justice. For decades it was a *sub rosa* process shrouded in secrecy and deliberately concealed by participating defendants, defense lawyers, prosecutors, and even judges."[2] Now that plea bargaining is commonplace, it is imperative that both the prosecution and defense (and sometimes even the judge) master the requisite skills for successful negotiations. In today's criminal justice system, a successful advocate must be not only a persuasive trial attorney, but also a skilled negotiator.

In order to be a successful negotiator, an attorney must first recognize that the objective of plea bargaining differs from that of trial. Negotiation, importantly, does not mean that the parties necessarily disagree. On the contrary, successful attorneys should realize that their goals might not conflict with those of opposing counsel. Ideally, each side will discern what the other needs, provide it, and thereafter reach a mutually acceptable agreement. When this happens, both parties are content, and a case is settled. Of course, case settlements typically involve compromise whereby each side makes some concession in exchange for arriving at a mutually agreeable disposition. If the prosecution and the defense are unable to come to an agreement, then the alternative is trial.

An attorney, however, should not fear going to trial. Case settlement, while efficient, may not always be in the best interests of the State or the defendant. It should go without saying that attorneys should always place their client's needs over opposing counsel's demands. As the quotation from Gandhi at the start of this chapter suggests, there should not be a compromise of fundamentals. A defense attorney should not simply surrender to the position or demands of the prosecution. If a case cannot be settled without jeopardizing a fundamental need of the defendant, then his counsel should prepare for trial. When the only settlement to which the defendant will agree does not meet society's needs for protection and deterrence, then the prosecutor should insist on moving forward to trial. Moreover, attorneys who have the reputation of being willing and able to try cases are able to obtain more favorable results for their clients. If an attorney senses that her adversary is reluctant to go to trial, then she may take advantage of this vulnerability by making unfair settlement demands. Thus, the critical component

---

[1] In 2010, 96.75% of those convicted in federal court were through guilty or *nolo contendere* pleas. *FY 2010 Offenders Sentenced*, Bureau of Justice Statistics, http://bjs.ojp.usdoj.gov/fjsrc/var.cfm?ttype=one_variable&agency=USSC&db_type=SntcEvnt&saf=OUT (search "2010," "Case disposition," "All values") (last visited Jan. 26, 2013).

[2] Blackledge v. Allison, 431 U.S. 63, 76 (1977).

of being an effective negotiator is to be fully prepared for the possibility of trial. Often, the best negotiating tactic is, in fact, for a lawyer to let the other side know that they are ready and eager for trial, regardless of whether that is, in fact, true.

PLEA BARGAINING

As discussed in Chapter 4, at arraignment the accused typically pleads not guilty. In fact, it is likely that a defendant at the arraignment stage has not yet even retained counsel. While it is unlikely that the prosecution will offer a plea bargain at the arraignment, it is likely that he will do so before the preliminary hearing (or pre-trial hearing, if it is a misdemeanor charge); however, there is no constitutional right to a plea bargain.[3] Nevertheless, the prosecutor will typically offer either a reduction of charges or a lighter sentence in exchange for a guilty plea by the defendant.[4] Of course, sentencing is up to the judge, but it is common for judges to agree to sentence the defendant in accord with the case settlement. Lastly, it is important to remember that no defendant is obligated to settle and enter a guilty plea.[5]

While plea bargaining is generally considered to be an efficient course of action, it was once considered a dubious practice. It was only in the late 1970s that it emerged from the "shadows."[6] Still to this day, there are restrictions in place, such as those limiting judicial involvement, designed to help minimize potential abuses of settling a case with a plea bargain. Acknowledging those restrictions and planning ahead results in more favorable case outcomes. Likewise, understanding why those restrictions are in place will help attorneys achieve their case settlement goals. In other words, advocates who convince opposing counsel that they will benefit from settling the case also increase their chances of successful case settlement. Lawyers who can only view a case from the perspective of their own side are at a disadvantage. The ability to think like the opponent and understand the arguments and needs of the opposing side is pivotal in fashioning a mutually agreeable settlement.

There is a myriad of pros and cons of plea bargaining. Even those who support plea-bargaining sometimes take issue with how it is accomplished. For example, many complain that the prosecution holds all the cards, since it is typically the prosecutor who makes settlement offers.[7] Others point out that, while the result of plea bargaining should ideally replicate what would have been the outcome of a trial verdict, the actual outcome is often distorted or skewed.[8] Instead, there may be more guilty verdicts than

---

[3] Weatherford v. Bursey, 429 U.S. 545, 561 (1977).

[4] This can also be done with a plea of *nolo contendere*, if the jurisdiction allows it.

[5] MODEL RULES OF PROF'L CONDUCT R. 1.2 (2006).

[6] Bordenkircher v. Hayes, 434 U.S. 357, 365 (1978).

[7] *See* ANGELA J. DAVIS, ARBITRARY JUSTICE: THE POWER OF THE AMERICAN PROSECUTOR (2007) (discussing possible unfairness on the part of prosecutors and who they offer plea bargains to, including reasons based on race, class, etc.).

[8] Ronald F. Wright, *Trial Distortion and the End of Innocence in Federal Criminal Justice*, 154 U. PA. L. REV. 79, 83 (2005).

there otherwise would have been. Most critical, perhaps, is the concern over whether plea bargaining chills a defendant's Sixth Amendment rights.[9] While plea bargaining allows the criminal justice system to flow more efficiently, an inherent danger is that a defendant will feel compelled to accept a settlement offer out of fear of serving a longer sentence should he reject the offer and be convicted at trial. The fear is that innocent defendants will plead guilty in order to avoid the risk of being convicted at trial. On the other hand, many find plea bargaining efficient, convenient, fair, and even less risky than trial. Below is a discussion of some of the various important issues affecting case settlements.

A. CONS

HYPO: *Oceana v. Perry*

Imagine that a prosecutor wants to obtain a first-degree murder conviction arising out of the following scenario. Kurt Perry, a retired security guard, walked into a mall and shot Neil Leonard, a transgender teenager, in cold blood. During the shooting, Perry shouted an anti-gay slur at Leonard before pulling the trigger. The shooting was witnessed by a customer in the mall, Robin Keating. Due to Perry's derogatory comment and the lack of any motive other than bias against the transgender community, the prosecution decides to charge Perry with a hate crime in addition to the murder charge. If convicted, Perry would face life in prison without the possibility of parole.

Assume the evidence that Perry shouted an insult referencing Leonard's sexuality is weak, or that the eyewitness, Robin Keating is himself a convicted felon and, thus, of questionable credibility. The prosecutor may be concerned that he might be unable to convince a jury beyond a reasonable doubt that the murder was also a hate crime. Is it within the prosecutor's discretion to charge the hate crime and use it as a bargaining chip in order to persuade the defendant to plead guilty to the murder, in exchange for the dismissal of the hate crime allegation? Although this would be within the bounds of a prosecutor's discretion, this type of overcharging is a major criticism of plea bargaining. A concern of plea bargaining is that some prosecutors purposely overcharge in order to have an advantage at the bargaining table. Indeed, an inexperienced defense attorney may not even recognize this ploy. The defense might settle for the lesser charge thinking she walked away with a bargain, when in effect the agreed upon charge had been the prosecutor's aim all along. It is important to note that, while prosecutors have wide discretion in filing charges, it is unethical to overcharge.[10]

Not only should the defense be on the lookout for prosecutorial overcharging, it should also be concerned about whether the defendant's Sixth Amendment rights might be compromised. The Sixth Amendment to the United States Constitution guarantees the accused the right to such protections as a speedy and public trial, a trial by jury, and the right to counsel.[11] Does plea bargaining chill this right? Does settling a case discourage individuals from going to trial and invoking their right to a trial by jury? Some critics say that it does; however, plea bargaining in and of itself is not unconstitutional. The Supreme Court has, nevertheless, considered circumstances in which constitutional rights are

---

[9] *See, e.g.*, United States v. Jackson, 390 U.S. 570, 581–82 (1968).

[10] H. Mitchell Caldwell, *Coercive Plea Bargaining: The Unrecognized Scourge of the Justice System*, 61 CATH. U. L. REV. 63 (2011).

[11] U.S. CONST. amend. VI.

compromised. For example, in *United States v. Jackson*, the defendants pled guilty in order to avoid the possibility of being sentenced to death, which would only have been possible had they been convicted by a jury under the Federal Kidnaping Act. The Court held that the provision of the statute in question was unconstitutional where it mandated that defendants could only be sentenced to death "if the verdict of the jury shall so recommend."[12] The Court ruled that this encouraged defendants to forego their Sixth Amendment right to trial by jury since they would face the possibility of death only if they invoked their constitutional right to a jury trial.[13]

Another criticism of case settlements focuses on the role of the victims in the process. The family members of a victim might understandably seek retribution and may feel that justice will not be served if the defendant is offered a lighter sentence. Likewise, a victim might perceive the criminal justice system as being more concerned with settling than punishing. Many states, however, allow for victim involvement in the plea bargaining process.[14] But it should be noted that in all criminal proceedings the case is brought by the State or federal government, not by the victim, and can be settled only by agreement between the prosecution and defense. Criminal proceedings are increasingly faced with the challenges of balancing justice for the victim while simultaneously upholding the rights of the accused.

With the passage in 2004 of the Crime Victims' Rights Act (CVRA), victims have become more involved in the negotiating process and have even challenged sentencing. One commentator offered that, "[t]reating the victim's concerns as paramount elevates the private individual above the public—the very opposite of what our criminal justice system seeks to achieve."[15] In some states, such as California, the victim is actively involved in the sentencing process and has the right to be heard, but the sentence is ultimately up to the judge.[16] Meanwhile, in New Jersey, "[t]he views of the victim's family may be taken into consideration when considering a plea agreement, but the family's level of grief or degree of dissatisfaction with the plea cannot be controlling."[17] Indeed, prosecutors and judges alike may take a victim's statement into account, but they are not bound to settle cases or sentence defendants based on the victim's demands.

Ethical concerns also arise in cases involving co-defendants. Turning again to the hypothetical *Oceana v. Perry*, what if Perry carried a gun on him, and told his friend Dylan Cameron to shoot Leonard? Assume Cameron has a criminal record, but Perry does not. Strategically speaking, Perry's attorney would likely benefit if she acts quickly to settle with the State. She might offer to have Perry testify against Cameron, and since Cameron actually pulled the trigger and has a record, the prosecution would likely settle Perry's case in return for his testimony. If not for plea bargaining, the prosecution

---

[12] *Jackson*, 390 U.S. at 571.

[13] *Id.* at 583.

[14] Sarah N. Welling, *Victim Participation in Plea Bargains*, 65 WASH. U. L.Q. 301, 355 (1987).

[15] Danielle Levine, Comment, *Public Wrongs and Private Rights: Limiting the Victim's Role in a System of Public Prosecution*, 104 NW. U. L. REV. 335, 353 (2010).

[16] CAL. PENAL CODE § 1191.1 (Deering 2012).

[17] State v. Madan, 840 A.2d 874, 884 (N.J. Super. Ct. App. Div. 2004).

might not have a strong enough case against Cameron. On the other hand, Cameron might plead guilty knowing Perry will testify against him; and, in this sense, he is discouraged from going to trial. It could be argued that Cameron's constitutional rights would be chilled by Perry's case settlement.

Indeed, the situation could be even more complicated. What if instead of shooting Leonard, Perry and Cameron beat him to death? In this scenario, Cameron has no criminal record. If Perry then settles and agrees to testify against Cameron, is this a fair outcome? What if Perry came from a wealthy suburban Caucasian family, and Cameron came from a poor urban African-American family? Might Perry have been favored in the bargaining process because of his socioeconomic background? Because there is no systematic approach to case settlement, some have called into question its fairness.[18] On the other hand, it is equally important to note that the prosecutor is supposed to act in an unbiased manner.[19] "Prosecutors are also public officials; they too must serve the public interest."[20] Moreover, if the prosecution makes a deal with a co-conspirator or another witness in exchange for his testimony, then he is obligated to disclose that information so that the defense may raise issues regarding witness credibility.[21] In addition, when there are co-defendants, the issue of a "packaged deal" might come into play. Such deals frequently offer more leniency if all suspects plead guilty together under a particular set of charges. Thus, if one goes to trial by refusing the deal, then all accused parties will have to stand trial or plead as charged. Such deals are scrutinized because, it is argued, they may have a coercive effect on a defendant.[22] Moreover, prosecutors often take this position because they are concerned that if one of the defendants accepts a plea bargain and the other does not, then the one who pled guilty could testify falsely on behalf of the co-defendant knowing that his own sentence had already been finalized. One could see this policy as an attempt by an overbearing prosecutor to try to make sure that the truth never surfaces. On the other hand, one could also see this as an attempt to keep a guilty person who accepted a plea agreement from testifying falsely for his co-defendant and accepting all the blame so that his friend who went to trial is found not guilty.

Sometimes the prosecution will insist on obtaining a factual basis for a plea. For instance, when one defendant enters a guilty plea, part of the case settlement might require him to provide a factual statement in court, under oath, setting forth each party's participation in the crime. This prohibits the pleading defendant from later coming to court and testifying to the benefit of the non-pleading defendant if the latter insists on a trial. One option judges have is to accept a defendant's guilty plea, then postpone sentencing to prohibit the pleading defendant from testifying untruthfully on behalf of the co-defendant at trial. It depends on the facts of a particular case, and the strength of the case, whether the prosecution will

---

[18] *See* DAVIS, *supra* note 7, at 50.

[19] MODEL RULES OF PROF'L CONDUCT R. 3.8 cmt. 1 (2006).

[20] Marshall v. Jerrico, Inc., 446 U.S. 238, 249 (1980) (citing Berger v. United States, 295 U.S. 78, 88 (1935)).

[21] Giglio v. United States, 405 U.S. 150, 154–55 (1972).

[22] *See, e.g.,* Bruce A. Green, *"Package" Plea Bargaining and the Prosecutor's Duty of Good Faith*, 25 CRIM. L. BULL. 507 (1989).

only accept this type of deal where one defendant is given a reduction in charge or sentence, even though the co-defendant insists on going to trial.

Lastly, the greatest danger of plea bargaining is that an innocent defendant might be enticed to plead guilty out of fear of going to trial and being convicted. It should be noted, however, that there is a similar risk of being found guilty if a defendant turns down a settlement offer and goes to trial. If the evidence is particularly incriminating, an innocent defendant may ultimately be convicted. In such instances, pleading guilty to a sentence or charge reduction in order to avoid trial may very well be the best option.[23]

B. PROS

Although there are notable drawbacks to case settlement, there are a number of benefits that should be evaluated. Case settlements serve the public and the justice system by reducing caseloads, a reduction that allows the prosecution to focus on the most serious cases and offenders.[24] Consequently, case settlements allow prosecutors to achieve more convictions than otherwise possible, and as a result, justice is served more often than not. Practically speaking, plea bargaining is a cost-effective solution when weighed against the great cost of trial.[25] Trials, especially jury trials, are expensive and time-consuming.

Not only is case settlement more cost-efficient for the public, it is also more cost-effective for private individuals. Case settlements aid the accused as well as their families, who often bear the financial burden. Meanwhile, victims can also reap benefits from case settlements. Although victims want to see justice served, they might get more relief from immediate closure, as the emotional impact of a trial may be too much to handle.[26] Of course, victims, witnesses, the accused, friends, and family are also impacted by the demands of trial, ranging from lost work to the significant emotional toll on all parties. Trial costs are exorbitant, and trials are inconvenient for everyone impacted by the criminal justice system. Case settlements can help remedy those costs significantly. Economic advantages are not the only reason a defendant's friends and family would benefit from case settlement.

The emotional cost of going to trial can be just as significant as the economic cost. The highly publicized Casey Anthony trial illustrates this point well. The defendant, Casey Anthony, was prosecuted for allegedly murdering her young daughter, Caylee. The defense accused George Anthony, father of Casey and grandfather to Caylee, of molesting his daughter and of covering up what the defense claimed was Caylee's accidental drowning. One news reporter said of Casey Anthony's parents: "I've never seen

---

[23] For a detailed history and opposition argument to plea bargaining, see Albert W. Alschuler, *Plea Bargaining and Its History*, 79 COLUM. L. REV. 1 (1979).

[24] Douglas D. Guidorizzi, Comment, *Should We Really "Ban" Plea Bargaining?: The Core Concerns of Plea Bargaining Critics*, 47 EMORY L.J. 753, 765 (1998).

[25] For example, in the Casey Anthony trial, the court estimated that the cost of just twenty jurors would be $361,000. Adam Blank, *Jury Costs in Upcoming Casey Anthony Trial Estimated at $361,000*, CNN JUSTICE (Mar. 17, 2011), http://articles.cnn.com/2011-03-17/justice/florida.casey.jury.costs_1_casey-anthony-trial-jury-selection-murder-trial?_s=PM:CRIME.

[26] *See* Guidorizzi, *supra* note 24, at 767.

people who have to go through so much in any legal case."[27] During the jury trial, George Anthony, who was not a party in the case against Casey Anthony, had to publicly face the serious accusations made against him as part of the defense's strategy. He not only lost his grandchild, but also endured public humiliation. Settling can spare witnesses, friends, and family from the public spectacle and the emotional strain of trial. Indeed, plea discussions remain private unless the exclusionary provisions of plea-statement rules are waived.[28] All the same, many cases, such as the Anthony trial, are difficult to settle because the prosecution does not want to settle for anything less than a murder conviction, and the defendant refuses to plead guilty to murder.

Settling a case without the unpredictability of trial can also aid the prosecution. Prosecutors have an interest in protecting the public and deterring further criminal conduct. By settling a case, the prosecution can guarantee at least some kind of conviction rather than watching the accused go free. For example, in the days leading up to both the O.J. Simpson trial as well as the recent Casey Anthony trial, few predicted that these two defendants would be found not guilty of the crimes charged. To avoid such outcomes, the prosecution could, in some circumstances, settle for a lesser charge or reduced sentence. Even in a case where the prosecution is convinced that a defendant is guilty of first-degree murder, they can achieve their goal of protecting society and punishing the defendant by agreeing not to seek the death penalty should the defendant plead guilty to the murder charge. By settling, the prosecution can maintain their goal of general and specific deterrence of future crimes. The general deterrence factor, when the prosecution makes an example of someone, is fulfilled because the accused is sentenced. The specific deterrence objective, whereby the prosecution punishes the defendant in the hopes of discouraging his future criminal conduct, is likewise fulfilled because he will at least receive some form of punishment for his acts. This opportunity is lost, on the other hand, when there is no case settlement and a jury acquits the defendant. Of course, some cases need to be tried, either because the evidence is particularly strong and, therefore, the prosecution has no incentive to offer a reduction, or because the evidence is weak and the accused wants to fight the charges.

The criminal justice system itself benefits, however, from case settlements because the court dockets are already extremely busy and resources are limited. Given that over ninety percent of criminal cases settle, it is difficult to conceive of how the courts could function if plea bargaining were abolished. If defendants were not offered incentives to plead guilty, it is likely that far more cases would go to trial, putting a huge strain on an already burdened criminal justice system. The Supreme Court has articulated additional benefits of case settlement:

> The defendant avoids extended pretrial incarceration and the anxieties and uncertainties of a trial, he gains a speedy disposition of his case, the chance to acknowledge his guilt, and a prompt start in realizing whatever potential there may be for rehabilitation. Judges and prosecutors conserve vital and scarce resources. The public is protected from the

---

[27] Cindy Adams, *CNN Reporter Describes Emotional Elevator Ride with Casey Anthony's Parents*, EXAMINER.COM (June 15, 2011), http://www.examiner.com/crime-in-national/cnn-reporter-describes-emotional-elevator-ride-with-casey-anthony-s-parent.

[28] United States v. Mezzanatto, 513 U.S. 196, 209 (1995).

risks posed by those charged with criminal offenses who are at large on bail while awaiting completion of criminal proceedings.[29]

In other words, everyone stands to benefit from plea bargaining. Why do the pros and cons involved in plea bargaining matter? In addition to the ethical issues inherent in case settlements, the advantages and disadvantages of this practice affect attorney strategy. When attorneys negotiate cases, it is advantageous to emphasize the pros and deemphasize the cons. Advocates need to convince opposing counsel to accept their proposal, in much the same way ideas are pitched in a business setting. In a similar vein, the defense should emphasize the benefits of plea bargaining to their client if they believe it is in his best interest to plead guilty. Most clients will not understand the legal ramifications of going to trial, as opposed to settling. Many clients become difficult and unrealistic and might demand a trial when, in fact, it is not in their best interests. When appropriate, defense attorneys must emphasize the advantages of settling in order to protect their clients' rights; however, all negotiations must stay within the parameters the court dictates. There are no hard and fast rules for settling a case. There are, however, some legal guidelines that must be observed.

LEGAL PARAMETERS

As stated earlier, there is no automatic right to a plea bargain.[30] The prosecution is in charge of determining whether or not to offer a plea bargain. While the prosecution is usually the one to make the initial offer, defense counsel is not barred from approaching the prosecutor with an offer to compromise. It is the judge, however, who ultimately assigns a sentence. Furthermore, there are no hard and fast rules determining when plea negotiation must begin. While most case settlements occur in lieu of trial, it is possible that midway through trial, or at any point before a verdict is rendered, a plea bargain may be offered and accepted. Thus, while the other events leading up to trial, and the trial itself, are governed by

the procedural rules of the court, plea bargaining is any man's game.[31] Because of this informal structure, a sound strategy is critical, along with adherence to local court rules.

---

[29] Blackledge v. Allison, 431 U.S. 63, 71 (1977).

[30] Weatherford v. Bursey, 429 U.S. 545, 561 (1977).

[31] Not all commentators agree on this last point. *See* DAVIS, *supra* note 7.

A. FEDERAL COURT

First, case settlements are contracts. In *Santobello v. New York*, the Supreme Court held that if one party did not perform under the terms of the agreement, then the plea bargain would be null and void. [32] Both parties would, essentially, return to square one. The court will, in other words, vacate a judgment if the prosecution does not uphold its end of the bargain. If someone from the prosecution's office agrees to make a sentence recommendation, then it must be honored. [33] Conversely, if a defendant agrees to testify against a co-defendant, or against a defendant charged in a different case, as part of the plea bargain, then he must follow through with this promise or the entire plea agreement will be revoked. [34] If a defendant breaches his agreement with the prosecutor, he will likely assert that he was not fully aware of the ramifications of pleading guilty. If this occurs, the defendant will probably point the finger at his counsel for inadequate representation. This is rarely a concern in federal court, however, because in federal court all plea agreements are in writing, with very specific advisements, which state the exact terms of the plea agreement. Thus, a defendant would be unlikely to have a valid argument that he was confused about the ramifications of his decision to plead guilty.

Not surprisingly, the Supreme Court has ruled on several issues concerning defense counsel's role in plea bargaining. First, it is up to counsel for the defense, and not the prosecution or the judge, to make sure that a defendant has all the necessary information to decide whether a guilty plea is the right course of action for her client's individual needs. [35] As discussed below, in order to be valid, a guilty plea must be made knowingly, intelligently, and voluntarily. [36] On the other hand:

> [W]hile most pleas of guilty consist of both a waiver of trial and an express admission of guilt, the latter element is not a constitutional requisite to the imposition of criminal penalty. An individual accused of crime may voluntarily, knowingly, and understandingly consent to the imposition of a prison sentence even if he is unwilling or unable to admit his participation in the acts constituting the crime. [37]

In *North Carolina v. Alford*, for example, Alford was charged with first-degree murder and faced the possibility of the death penalty. In order to avoid capital punishment, he pled guilty to second-degree murder, while still professing his innocence. He received a thirty-year sentence, but appealed and tried to withdraw his plea under a theory that it was involuntary. He was not allowed to withdraw his plea and the Court held that there were no constitutional barriers requiring a judge to reject a guilty plea even when the accused proclaims innocence. [38] This has become known as an *Alford* plea. *Alford* pleas are rare

---

[32] Santobello v. New York, 404 U.S. 257, 262–63 (1971).

[33] *Id.* at 262.

[34] Ricketts v. Adamson, 483 U.S. 1, 9 (1987).

[35] Brady v. United States, 397 U.S. 742, 748 (1970).

[36] *Id.*

[37] North Carolina v. Alford, 400 U.S. 25, 37 (1970).

[38] *Id.*

occurrences however, as federal courts typically require defendants to sign a factual basis written statement admitting guilt.

In federal court, the judge is not a party to plea bargains.[39] After the defendant and his attorney come to a settlement agreement with the prosecutor, the plea is entered in open court.[40] Many of the Supreme Court's holdings in the earliest landmark cases dealing with case settlement have since been incorporated into Rule 11 of the *Federal Rules of Criminal Procedure*. While the judge in federal court will not get involved in plea negotiations, the judge must ask the defendant in open court and on the record under Rule 11(b)(1) if he is aware that with his plea he waives certain constitutional rights.[41] State jurisdictions also follow this rule to ensure that pleas are knowing, voluntary, and intelligent, thus protecting the defendant's constitutional rights.[42]

Although judges do not participate in the plea bargaining process in the federal court system, they still have discretion to reject negotiated pleas. U.S. District Judge Cormac J. Carney, for example, rejected a plea deal prosecutors offered to Broadcom Corporation, co-founder Henry Samueli, that would have allowed Samueli to receive probation for his role in an alleged $2.2 billion stock-option scam. The maximum fine for the conviction that defendant Samueli agreed to plead to was $250,000, but the plea deal provided that Samueli would pay the government $12 million and, in return, he would avoid being sent to prison. The judge rejected the plea deal, finding that justice should not be for sale. To ensure fairness, it is imperative that judges retain the discretion to reject plea negotiations. If the public believes that wealthy defendants can buy their way out of prison, this would not only undermine case settlements, but it could jeopardize society's confidence in the entire justice system.[43]

Finally, it is difficult to withdraw a plea. A defendant may change his mind for any or no reason before a plea has been accepted by the court; however, once the court has accepted the plea, then the defendant must show a "fair and just reason for requesting the withdrawal."[44] If he is successful in withdrawing his plea, then the guilty plea cannot be used as evidence against him in a subsequent trial.[45]

Most recently, however, the Supreme Court has revisited the issue of counsel's impact during the plea bargaining process in the companion cases *Lafler v. Cooper* and *Missouri v. Frye*. In *Lafler*, the accused rejected a plea offer after his counsel had advised him that the prosecution had a weak case because it could not prove an element of the charged crime.[46] He was later convicted at trial. In *Frye*, on

---

[39] FED. R. CRIM. P. 11(c)(1).

[40] FED. R. CRIM. P. 11(c)(2).

[41] Rule 11 codified the Supreme Court decision in *Boykin v. Alabama*, 395 U.S. 238 (1969).

[42] *Boykin*, 395 U.S. at 242.

[43] E. Scott Reckard, *Broadcom Co-Founder Asks Court to Uphold Plea Deal*, L.A. TIMES (Sept. 3, 2009), http://articles.latimes.com/2009/sep/03/business/fi-samueli3.

[44] FED. R. CRIM. P. 11(d)(2)(B). *See also* United States v. Hyde, 520 U.S. 670, 671 (1997).

[45] FED. R. EVID. 410(1).

[46] Lafler v. Cooper, 132 S. Ct. 1376, 1383 (2012).

the other hand, counsel did not advise the accused of a plea offer, and he later pled to a harsher sentence.[47] Because of defendants' Sixth Amendment right to adequate counsel during plea bargaining, the Court held that, if ineffective assistance results in the rejection of a plea and the defendant is later convicted at trial, the State should reoffer the plea agreement, provided that the defendant can show that:

> [B]ut for the ineffective advice of counsel there is a reasonable probability that the plea offer would have been presented to the court (*i.e.*, that the defendant would have accepted the plea and the prosecution would not have withdrawn it in light of intervening circumstances), that the court would have accepted its terms, and that the conviction or sentence, or both, under the offer's terms would have been less severe than under the judgment and sentence that in fact were imposed.[48]

In *Frye*, the Court held that counsel has a duty to communicate to the accused any formal offers that may be favorable to him.[49] The practical effect of these decisions is that it will be easier for defendants to demonstrate the inadequacy of defense counsel's advice during the plea bargaining process and that a court may now provide a remedy by overturning a previous sentence in cases of ineffective assistance.

B. STATE COURTS

Most criminal cases are handled in state courts, and the legal parameters discussed above are similar to what unfolds there. State courts have adopted rules similar to those in federal court that allow *Alford* pleas. In California, for example, per the *People v. West* case, this is known as a *West* plea.[50] In a *West* plea, the defendant pleads *nolo contendere*.[51] There are, however, some significant departures from the federal rules.

One notable difference between the rules of plea bargaining in the federal courts versus the state courts concerns the participation of judges in negotiations. While the judge does not get involved in case settlements under the federal scheme, about half of the states allow the bench officer to participate in negotiations. The presence of a judge can be especially important for determining the settlement strategy.

Those states that allow for judicial involvement express some reservations about the appropriate extent of judicial intervention in the case settlement process.[52] There is a concern that judicial

---

[47] Missouri v. Frye, 132 S. Ct. 1399, 1404 (2012).

[48] *Lafler*, 132 S. Ct. at 1385.

[49] *Frye*, 132 S. Ct. at 1408.

[50] 477 P.2d 409 (Cal. 1970) (in banc).

[51] The consequences of no contest pleas are the same as guilty pleas, except that the conviction cannot be used against the defendant in a civil court. In some states, such as California, a no contest plea can be used in a related civil proceeding if the plea is to a felony, not a misdemanor. Thus, a defendant charged with vehicular manslaughter who pled no contest to the charge might not have to worry about the plea being later used against him in a wrongful death civil trial. It is incumbent on the lawyers to know whether a no contest plea can be used against the defendant in a related civil proceeding in that particular jurisdiction.

[52] In states that do allow for judicial involvement, it is important that the judge remains as neutral as possible, while still trying to find a common meeting ground between the parties. States that allow for judicial involvement include: California, Connecticut, Florida, Illinois, Indiana, Kansas, Louisiana, Michigan, Montana, Nebraska, New York,

involvement can have a coercive effect—thus rendering a guilty plea involuntary. In other words, there is a concern that a defendant might worry that if he does not accept a deal offered by the judge, he might receive a harsher sentence if convicted. It is for precisely this reason that federal courts have restricted judicial involvement. Echoing this concern, section 14-3.3(d) of the *ABA Standards For Criminal Justice* states: "A judge should not ordinarily participate in plea negotiation discussions among the parties. Upon request of the parties, a judge may be presented with a proposed plea agreement negotiated by the parties and may indicate whether the court would accept the terms as proposed."[53]

Lastly, some states impose certain limitations on the availability of plea bargaining. For example, California Penal Code Section 1192.7 provides:

> Plea bargaining in any case in which the indictment or information charges any serious felony, any felony in which it is alleged that a firearm was personally used by the defendant, or any offense of driving while under the influence of alcohol, drugs, narcotics, or any other intoxicating substance, or any combination thereof, is prohibited, unless there is insufficient evidence to prove the people's case, or testimony of a material witness cannot be obtained, or a reduction or dismissal would not result in a substantial change in sentence.[54]

In other words, some jurisdictions limit plea negotiations for the most violent of crimes. For the most serious of sexual offenses, plea bargaining is prohibited entirely unless there is insufficient evidence to prove the People's case.[55] Thus, for certain offenses, plea bargaining can only be employed as a last resort for securing a conviction.

Plea bargaining can be complicated, and some county prosecutor's offices may not even allow it, or may have a policy that dictates or limits the practice. Further adding to the unpredictability of plea bargaining, some prosecutorial supervisors are more opposed to the process of plea bargaining than are other supervisors. This can lead to great disparity in terms of offers, even in the same county. As a result, it is not uncommon for a defense attorney faced with a particularly inflexible prosecutor to continue a pretrial conference, hoping to face a more lenient and understanding prosecutor at the next settlement conference. Clearly, familiarity with the procedure, jurisdiction, and personalities in a particular court will determine a defense lawyer's best negotiating strategy. It should be noted, however, that even in jurisdictions where plea bargaining is limited to cases with insufficient evidence, this rule is often given wide latitude. Individual prosecutors are typically allowed broad discretion to determine whether the case has a factual weakness. Creative attorneys who are skilled negotiators are often able to

---

North Carolina, Ohio, Oklahoma, Oregon, South Carolina, Utah, and Vermont. In Alaska, for example, judicial involvement is strictly prohibited. Other states with a similar disposition, either totally prohibiting or highly limiting judicial involvement, include: Colorado, the District of Columbia, Georgia, Maine, Maryland, Minnesota, Mississippi, Nevada, New Mexico, New Jersey, North Dakota, Pennsylvania, South Dakota, Tennessee, Texas, Virginia, Washington, West Virginia, Wisconsin, and Wyoming.

[53] STANDARDS FOR CRIM. JUSTICE § 14-3.3(d) (1999).

[54] CAL. PENAL CODE § 1192.7(a)(2) (Deering 2012).

[55] *Id.*

arrive at case settlements in most cases—including when the charges brought against their clients are violent or particularly serious. A thorough understanding of the sentencing laws is critical.

Should a prosecutor settle a case where the crime is violent but the evidence is weak, he would be wise to write a memo to put in the case file explaining the disposition. Prosecutors' offices often have forms for their attorneys to fill out to memorialize the weaknesses of a case that led to a plea bargain. Prosecutors need to protect themselves by putting factual weaknesses of a case in writing and orally on the record at the time of the plea. In serious cases, prosecutors often have to have their supervisor authorize a case settlement. Most prosecutors' offices have case settlement guidelines and require prosecutors to obtain permission from a supervisor before deviating from the settlement policy. For example, prosecutors typically need approval before striking an allegation of a serious prior conviction or of a weapon enhancement. Conversely, prosecutors are allowed more settlement authority in misdemeanor cases. One exception to this policy typically occurs in driving under the influence cases because these offenses impact public safety. For instance, in jurisdictions where it is illegal to drive with .08 or greater blood alcohol, the prosecutorial guidelines may limit plea reduction offers to cases with .10 or lower blood alcohol levels unless there are significant factual weaknesses.[56]

The crucial lesson is that if a prosecutor wishes to deviate from what is clearly allowed by his office's guidelines, or if the case is particularly serious, sensitive, or a high-publicity case, the prosecutor should be sure to write a memo in the file clearly delineating the reasons for the negotiated plea. These justifications might include problems of proof, the defendant's lack of a criminal record, or sincere efforts at rehabilitation. If the prosecutor's supervisor approves the settlement, this should also be memorialized in the file. It is not uncommon for an irate victim to complain to the head of the prosecutor's office after a negotiated plea. Particularly in cases involving crimes of violence, maintaining a clear record of the plea negotiations is vital. The prosecutor who enters into a negotiated plea should always protect himself by explaining the reasons for the settlement in the case file.

AT THE BARGAINING TABLE

Once an attorney is familiar with the law of her state, or the federal rules if she is in federal court, then she is ready to strategize. A strategic plan should center around one basic idea: plea bargaining is a process of compromise. The chances of successfully negotiating a case settlement increase when opposing counsel are not acrimonious. As legal experts in the highly regarded book, *Getting To Yes: Negotiating Agreement Without Giving In* explain:

> It is easy to forget sometimes that a negotiation is not a debate. Nor is it a trial. You are not trying to persuade some third party. The person you are trying to persuade is seated at the table with you. If a negotiation is to be compared with a legal proceeding, the situation resembles that of two judges trying to reach agreement on how to decide a case.

---

[56] Such problems of proof could include: the police did not comply with proper procedures; the machine used to test the blood alcohol level was not properly calibrated; or there is a valid rising blood alcohol defense. These factors could justify a reduction to an alcohol related reckless driving, even if the blood alcohol level tested at over .10.

Try putting yourself in that role, treating your opposite number as a fellow judge with whom are you attempting to work out a joint opinion.[57]

Perhaps the early skepticism regarding plea bargaining arose from a basic misunderstanding of the goals and dynamic of the process. In Chapter 2, it was noted that many attorneys invoke a metaphor of war when talking about going to trial. While this might be true of preparing for trial, the idea of peaceful compromise is likely an appropriate description of the case settlement process. Indeed, many negative connotations associated with plea bargaining arise from the misconception that the process inevitably involves one side surrendering to the other; however, in practice that should never happen. The authors of *Getting To Yes* correctly emphasize that successful negotiations focus on mutual gain and should be "hard on the merits, soft on the people."[58] In other words, it is counter-productive to alienate opposing counsel when trying to settle a case. Skilled negotiators focus on the merits or weaknesses of the case and on the defendant's background and future potential to become either a law-abiding citizen or a criminal recidivist. It is not productive to personally attack opposing counsel, and angry outbursts can fatally jeopardize plea negotiations. Swearing, and other types of name calling, should be avoided at all costs—even when an attorney believes that opposing counsel is completely unreasonable. The best approach when tempers flare is to take a deep breath and limit discussion to the case.

A. A DIRECT APPROACH

One of the most common jokes about lawyers asks: "How do you know a lawyer is lying?" The answer: "His lips are moving." That is not the reputation an attorney wants if he is planning on being an effective advocate. If an attorney is known for lying, or "hiding the ball," then opposing counsel will not trust him during the bargaining process. Perhaps more than in any other scenario, having a reputation for being trustworthy can be the greatest tool an attorney can possess in order to have leverage during a case settlement. For example, in the earlier hypothetical case of the murder of Neil Leonard, the State brought charges against Kurt Perry. Perry retained defense counsel renowned for being forthright and direct. The prosecutor, on the other hand, has a reputation for overcharging. When the prosecutor approaches Perry's counsel, he offers to drop the hate crime enhancement. Perry's counsel, however, is aware of this prosecutor's reputation. She might not take the deal, and instead insist on going to trial. She might even get Perry acquitted; however, if the prosecution had been more reasonable and agreed to accept a plea to second-degree murder instead, Perry's lawyer might have been amenable to taking the deal. In fact, if the prosecution has a respectable reputation, Perry would be more likely to conclude that the offer presented is a legitimate one.

---

[57] ROGER FISHER & WILLIAM URY, GETTING TO YES: NEGOTIATING AGREEMENT WITHOUT GIVING IN 35 (2d ed. 1991).

[58] *Id.* at xviii.

A direct approach is also the best approach. Depending on where an attorney practices, the community might be small. Even in large metropolitan areas, public defenders and prosecutors regularly deal with each other at the same courthouses. Reputations are earned early on in an attorney's career, and stories spread quickly throughout courthouses, especially if an attorney is unethical or unreasonable. It is wise to earn a reputation for being forthright. The straightforward approach saves time and energy, as opposing counsel will understand that certain attorneys take a direct approach and are honest about what they believe a case is worth. Playing games, such as not being honest about a case's true value, only hampers fair case settlements. Effective negotiators, on the other hand, can put their egos aside and strive to reach a just resolution. Perhaps there is common ground, but how can that be discovered if one party is trying to trick the other? Moreover, attorneys who develop a reputation for not being candid about what a case is worth end up haggling unnecessarily with opposing counsel. If an attorney has a reputation for being frank about the worth of a case, opposing counsel is much more likely to offer a fair settlement. Negotiating a criminal case is not analogous to bargaining for a car, where one is expected to haggle.

It is never wise to jeopardize future cases for the sake of a current case. A reputation for being dishonest or unethical can have long-term detrimental consequences. By telling each other what they really want to walk away with, both sides are in a better position to negotiate. Indeed, only by being straightforward can the prosecution and defense obtain a favorable case settlement. Attorneys should never lose sight of the fact that they represent someone else. Personally disliking the prosecutor should not interfere with the defense's ability to represent her client; and conversely, not liking the defense attorney is no reason for the prosecution to forego a chance to protect the public and save taxpayer dollars with a reasonable, albeit lesser, charge or sentence. Of course, the defense attorney is in the precarious position of not revealing the client's defense, in the event the case goes to trial; however, this should not preclude defense counsel from letting the prosecutor know what she thinks is a fair settlement.

As part of a direct approach, once discussions have begun with opposing counsel, an attorney should look for mutual gains.[59] The defense should start by considering her client's needs. Indeed, before meeting with the prosecutor, the defense attorney should ask her client exactly what he wants. Does he want to avoid jail time at all costs? Does he need to keep his driver's license in order to work? If jail time cannot be avoided, how much is he willing to accept? It might be useful for the defense to brainstorm with her client. In some cases, settling is going to be impossible. For example, some cultures would find an admission of guilt more shameful than a conviction resulting from a jury verdict.[60] Defense counsel should, therefore, consider each client's needs on an individual basis. In cases where a settlement is possible, defense counsel can come up with various solutions in the hopes that the prosecution and judge will be accepting of at least one of them. It is often helpful for attorneys to think

---

[59] *Id.* at 56.

[60] *See* Sue Bryant & Jean Koh Peters, *Five Habits for Cross Cultural Lawyering, in* RACE, CULTURE, PSYCHOLOGY, AND LAW 50 (Kimberly Barrett & William George eds., 2004) (discussing, as an example, a Chinese woman who felt that serving twenty-five years in prison was less offensive than the shame her ancestors and descendants would bear if she admitted guilt).

outside the box in order to achieve a case settlement. Sometimes, creative thinking can help to break a settlement impasse.

To facilitate the process, defense counsel could make a chart. In the first column, she can list non-negotiable terms (e.g., no jail time). In the middle column, she can write in negotiable terms (e.g., suspension of a license). In the final column, she can write in whatever the defense is willing to sacrifice in order to appease the prosecution (e.g., a felony charge). By having several options, it is more likely that one will be accepted. On her own, the defense should consider what benefits the prosecution will get from the deal. If she has carefully thought through her client's needs, in addition to evaluating the pros for the prosecution, then the defense counsel will be more convincing and in a position to better negotiate the terms of the settlement.

Similarly, the prosecutor should also begin by making a chart. He should start out by considering what charges he needs the defendant to admit in order to obtain a just result and what he would be willing to drop in order to obtain a guilty plea. He should also consider ahead of time how ardently he must protect society in each particular case. While a defendant might be willing to plead guilty for a lesser sentence, he might be a dangerous criminal that the prosecution wants to put behind bars for many years. The prosecution should, before sitting down at the bargaining table, consider all the possibilities and then rank them. He should first consider which elements are most important for the State and then which would be most likely to satisfy the accused. The ethical considerations involved with making fair offers are even more applicable to prosecutors, since they have the duty of seeking justice.

If both sides make their charts before case settlement talks begin, then upon meeting, they might find that they do not disagree at all. Their interests might even overlap. Often, the prosecutor's primary concern is the actual charge or charges to which the defendant agrees to plead guilty, whereas the defendant's main concern is the actual consequences of the conviction. In other words, the prosecution is typically concerned with obtaining convictions, whereas the defendant is generally worried about the specific punishment, such as the length of incarceration and other ramifications, such as the loss of a license. Sometimes a major factor for both sides is whether the defendant pleads to a charge that is "priorable," meaning that a future conviction would entail a more severe sentence because of the conviction of the case at bar. In California, for example, the "Three Strikes Law" requires that the defendant serve a longer prison term with each strike allegation that is proved, and after three strikes he may end up in prison for life. Often, the biggest sticking point in resolving serious felonies in California is whether the prosecutor or court will "strike a strike" or require the defendant either to plead to the strike or to go to trial.

While it is obvious to look for mutual gains, what might be less obvious is the power of looking for mutual loss. If the talks get difficult, counsel should make a list of all that they have to lose should the case settle. It might be that one side feels it is giving up more than the other. If presented with such a list, the prosecutor, for example, might realize that he is getting what he wants most. After all, something lost by one side is a gain for the other. By emphasizing one side's loss, the defense or the prosecution is simultaneously suggesting the other side's victory. While it is possible to have a win-win situation, more often than not a given situation requires both give and take.

Having a respectable reputation can also be a major advantage in jurisdictions where the judge is involved in plea negotiations. The last thing an attorney wants is to be disliked by a particular judge. Counsel's past conduct in the courtroom, or during plea negotiations, can affect any or all future situations. If the prosecution regularly overcharges, then the judge may see this behavior as habitual. The judge, after all, ultimately decides the sentence. She might be more inclined to reduce a sentence because she suspects that the prosecution is unethical. The same holds true for the defense. If the defense counsel has a reputation for trickery, then the judge might be more inclined to support the prosecution's sentencing recommendation.

Whether or not judges participate, case negotiations can significantly impact settlements. As previously discussed, the federal court system does not allow judges to become involved in plea negotiations, whereas about half the states do allow such involvement. When allowed to participate, the judge is restricted to a specific role. At all times, the judge must remain neutral; however, in some states she acts more as a mediator, and in others, more like a referee. The presence of a judge makes a difference: professional behavior is especially necessary when a judge is present during the negotiations. A judge will appreciate the attorney that comes into negotiations with an honest, carefully considered, and sincere offer.

Although a judge's participation in plea bargaining has been criticized because it has the potential to create a coercive environment, it has some benefits. First, defense counsel will quickly recognize if the judge favors a particular sentence, and the judge's acceptance of a negotiated settlement insures that the accused will not show up to sentencing only to be blind-sided by a higher sentence. This will also decrease the likelihood of a successful appeal. If the defendant is aware of the sentence the judge will assign, then he will be unlikely to try to withdraw his plea at a later date. As discussed above, withdrawing a plea can be an uphill battle; therefore, a judge's presence can benefit the defendant as well.

B. A CREATIVE APPROACH

Whether or not a judge is present for plea negotiations, however, counsel should be creative, in addition to being direct. There is no rule that requires that a plea bargain consist of a sentence or charge reduction. Instead, it may be that the best course of action is to ask for different allowances. For example, a defense attorney might represent a medical practitioner whose main concern is to continue his career. The following hypothetical illustrates how a client's career can dictate his settlement concerns.

HYPO: *Oceana v. Nuñez*

Alfred Nuñez, a psychologist residing in Sandy Beach, Oceana, had a teenage daughter who went through a rebellious stage. The two got into a verbal argument at a restaurant one day. She cursed at him and threatened to run away. Nuñez grabbed her, lost his temper, and pushed her against the wall. Another customer called the police. As a result, Nuñez was charged with assault. Nuñez expressed to his counsel that his biggest fear was not about going to jail or being on probation, but of losing his license to practice. In *Oceana v. Nuñez*, it should be clear that a charge reduction or sentence reduction is not always the defendant's primary goal. Instead, the case settlement should be tailored for each defendant's particular needs.

COLLATERAL CONSEQUENCES

As over ninety percent of criminal cases are resolved with a plea bargain and not a trial, a defense attorney's guidance during a case settlement is perhaps the most important assistance she provides her client.[61] The decision to plead guilty requires care and thought. As discussed above, the plea must be made knowingly and intelligently however, a defendant, for the most part, need only be made aware of the direct consequences of the plea. The defendant is entitled to be informed of consequences including: length of incarceration and probation, priorability, limitations on Fourth Amendment search and seizure rights, and other consequences depending on the jurisdiction. Although the Sixth Amendment guarantees the right to adequate counsel,[62] the Supreme Court held in *Brady* that adequate counsel does not mean that the accused must be notified of "every relevant factor."[63] There are indirect consequences to pleading guilty, known as collateral consequences. Even if the defendant is not informed of such collateral consequences at the time he enters his plea, this is not necessarily grounds for him to withdraw the plea later. Collateral consequences, however, can often have a greater impact on the defendant than the direct consequences. Collateral consequences could involve a wide variety of possibilities, including a loss of financial aid, ineligibility to serve on a jury, ineligibility to serve in the military, loss of a medical license, loss of a driver's license, loss of the right to bear arms, or court orders requiring the defendant to stay away from particular locations or certain people.

Often, the collateral consequences will affect a defendant as significantly as incarceration. For example, a guilty plea might affect one's immigration status. Jose Padilla, a legal resident of the United States for over 40 years, was a native of Honduras. In October 2002, final judgment was entered on

charges against him for several crimes related to the trafficking and possession of large amounts of marijuana. His plea agreement provided that he would serve five years of a ten-year sentence, and afterwards he would be placed on probation for the remaining five years.[64] His defense counsel told him not "to worry about immigration status since he had been in the country so long."[65] Under Title 8 of the United States Code § 1227(a)(2)(B)(i), however, it was clear that Padilla's guilty plea would subject him to automatic deportation.[66] Nevertheless, Padilla's counsel failed to properly advise him of this consequence, and Padilla pled guilty. Padilla sought post-conviction relief and said that, but for his counsel's incorrect advice, he would have gone to trial.[67] The Kentucky Supreme Court denied him relief, and supported its

---

[61] Gabriel J. Chin & Richard W. Holmes, Jr., *Effective Assistance of Counsel and the Consequences of Guilty Pleas*, 87 CORNELL L. REV. 697, 698 (2002).

[62] U.S. CONST. amend. VI.

[63] Brady v. United States, 397 U.S. 742, 757 (1970).

[64] Commonwealth v. Padilla, 253 S.W.3d 482, 483 (Ky. 2008).

[65] *Id.*

[66] Padilla v. Kentucky, 130 S. Ct. 1473, 1477 (2010).

[67] *Id.* at 1476.

decision based on the fact that it considered deportation to be a collateral consequence.[68] The Supreme Court of the United States, in this landmark decision, disagreed. On March 31, 2010, the Court handed down one of the most significant decisions to affect plea bargaining to date. In this decision, the Court held: "[w]e agree with Padilla that constitutionally competent counsel would have advised him that his conviction for drug distribution made him subject to automatic deportation."[69]

Padilla, however, did not overturn the law regarding direct and collateral consequences. Instead of defining deportation as a direct consequence, the court refused to place it in either category. They explained:

> Deportation as a consequence of a criminal conviction is, because of its close connection to the criminal process, uniquely difficult to classify as either a direct or a collateral consequence. The collateral versus direct distinction is thus ill-suited to evaluating a *Strickland* claim concerning the specific risk of deportation. We conclude that advice regarding deportation is not categorically removed from the ambit of the Sixth Amendment right to counsel. *Strickland* applies to Padilla's claim.[70]

Here, the Court held that, as a constitutional matter, effective assistance of counsel required that the accused be informed of the possibility of deportation. Under *Padilla*, when it is reasonably clear that a client may face deportation, the failure to disclose that information is constitutionally deficient.[71] The practical consequence of this ruling is that the prosecutor or judge should inform the defendant, on the record, of any possible deportation consequences of a conviction.

To support its decision, the Court instead relied on *Strickland* in order to determine whether the defense counsel's incompetency would allow for the withdrawal of a guilty plea. In *Strickland*, a two-prong test was defined in order to determine whether a defendant has had adequate representation. The first prong of the test examines whether representation falls "below an objective standard of reasonableness."[72] The next prong considers whether, "but for counsel's unprofessional errors, the result of the proceeding would have been different."[73]

While this new rule affects only one specific possible consequence of pleading guilty, and therefore counsel is not technically incompetent for failing to warn about the other consequences, that is simply the minimum required of effective counsel. Constitutional rights aside, ethical defense counsel will make sure their clients are fully informed.

Moreover, by knowing the potential collateral consequences involved in a conviction, defense counsel will be in a better bargaining position. It is possible that the prosecution is more concerned with a direct consequence (such as a conviction that is priorable), whereas defense counsel primarily wants to preserve a privilege that would be jeopardized as a collateral consequence (such as her client's ability to

---

[68] *Padilla*, 253 S.W.3d at 485.

[69] *Padilla*, 130 S. Ct. at 1478.

[70] *Id.* at 1482.

[71] *Id.* at 1483.

[72] Strickland v. Washington, 466 U.S. 668, 687 (1984).

[73] *Id.*

practice medicine). If this is the case, then defense counsel can give the prosecutor what he wants in exchange for what she wants. For example, in a reckless driving case the prosecution may achieve its goal of having the defendant placed on probation with a fine and two points against his driving record, and the defendant can achieve his goal of not losing his driver's license. Further, in some jurisdictions, such as California, certain offenses, such as possession of marijuana or other narcotics by a person under the age of twenty-one, can result in a one-year license revocation, even if the offense did not involve a car. Additionally, possession of any amount of alcohol by someone under twenty-one can also result in a one-year license suspension, as could a conviction of vandalism. With these minor types of offenses, prosecutors and judges are often willing to consider alternative charges, such as sentences including community service and Alcoholics or Narcotics Anonymous meetings, so as not to have an otherwise law-abiding person lose his privilege to drive for one year. Other offenses, such as driving under the influence of alcohol or narcotics, or reckless driving, typically result in license revocations or suspensions.

Alternatively, in a case involving driving under the influence, perhaps the defendant's goal is to end up with only a restricted license, allowing him to drive to and from work, as opposed to a license suspension or revocation. In some cities that do not have adequate public transportation, it is extremely difficult to commute to and from work without a valid driver's license. In such a situation, maintaining the privilege to drive can be a defendant's paramount concern. Generally, the prosecution's main concern in a first offense driving under the influence case is that of public safety. The prosecution can achieve its goal by having the defendant on probation with terms that typically include paying a fine, attending alcohol education classes, not driving with any alcohol in the blood system, a restricted license, and priorability. If it is the defendant's first offense and there is no accident involved, it is unlikely that the prosecution will require the defendant to lose his privilege to drive. In fact, society will not benefit in any way from an unemployed defendant with a prior record and no form of transportation to look for work. Thus, if the defendant's primary goal is to maintain the privilege to drive to work, he and the prosecutor do not have conflicting goals.

Collateral consequences can also affect a student's ability to receive financial aid. Federal law suspends federal student aid eligibility for any student who has been convicted of the possession or sale of illegal drugs, if the offense occurred while the student was enrolled in school and receiving federal student aid. Thus, it is important to discuss any licenses or benefits that a client has that might be in peril because of a criminal conviction.

Another significant consequence of a conviction can be the defendant's loss of a professional license, which could render him unable to continue his career. For example, medical doctors, nurses, lawyers, teachers, and psychologists all face the possibility of losing their professional licenses and their ability to make a living, if they are convicted of certain serious offenses or repeat offenses. If the defendant does not have a serious criminal record, and if the case is not egregious, the judge and prosecutor may likely allow the defendant to plead to a charge that does not lead to loss of a professional license. Of course, such a reduction is less likely if the defendant's conduct threatened public safety, particularly if the conduct involved abuse within the defendant's profession, as when a medical doctor endangers his patients, or a teacher abuses a student. Collateral consequences and alternative charges and sentences must be analyzed on a case-by-case basis.

A particularly serious consequence of certain offenses is the requirement that defendants register as sex offenders for life. Sometimes, a similar offense will not have this severe consequence, or it may be within the judge's discretion at sentencing to modify such a serious consequence. Clearly, the lawyer must know whether she is pleading her client to an offense for which he will be burdened for the rest of his life. If an alternative is available, it is the defense attorney's obligation to explore these possibilities.

Another serious consequence of certain offenses is priorability. In California, under the "Three Strikes Law," certain second felonies will result in a long mandatory prison sentence, with a third serious felony having the potential sentence of life in prison. The defense attorney must be intimately familiar with enhancements and strikes and any consequences of priors, to avoid accepting a deal without realizing that, if the defendant sustains a future conviction, the defendant will be facing a long (or lifetime) prison term.

Additionally, certain narcotics offenses require that the defendant register as a narcotics offender. It is the defense attorney's responsibility to become aware of which offenses require this type of registration. Clearly, a case is not just a simple narcotics offense if it would result in the client having to register as a narcotics offender.

The key to dealing effectively with collateral consequences of a criminal conviction is awareness, knowledge, and preparation. The lawyer must first be aware of the potential collateral consequences for the charged offenses, and she has to be knowledgeable enough to seek alternative dispositions and be persuasive enough to convince the judge and prosecutor that the collateral consequences for the charged offense are not justified based on the defendant's background and conduct. The defense lawyer must be prepared to present reasonable alternatives that will convince the judge and prosecutor that the proposed alternative charge and sentence will result in a fair settlement and sentence for both sides and that society will be protected.

Finally, there are numerous state and federal statutes that prohibit the possession of firearms for people convicted of certain crimes. The list of these crimes is long and includes many misdemeanors as well as most felonies. Although a lawyer may have little or no leverage if the client is charged with a serious felony, the lawyer may be able to work out an alternative sentence when the client is charged with a low-grade misdemeanor. This is especially important if the client has a job, such as that of a peace officer or security guard, which necessitates possession of a firearm. For example, in many jurisdictions, a simple battery can result in a firearm prohibition, but an alternative charge such as disturbing the peace or trespassing will not have this impact. Other examples of misdemeanor offenses that result in weapons prohibitions include domestic violence, brandishing a weapon, and stalking. Sometimes judges and prosecutors will agree to an alternative charge in exchange for more community service, additional counseling, or some other penalty.

By fully considering collateral consequences, even when not required to do so, both the defense and prosecution are in a better position to bargain creatively and directly. Indeed, if the punishment at issue would bring about a collateral consequence, a creative approach would often be the most effective way to resolve the issue truly concerning the accused. It is imperative to recognize that collateral consequences of a criminal conviction often impact a client more than the actual conviction. For some defendants, collateral consequences, such as losing the privilege to drive or one's ability to possess firearms, facing deportation proceedings, or registering as a sex offender, are far more crucial to the client than having a conviction or having to pay a fine, or even having to serve time in custody. A competent lawyer must be aware of all the potential collateral consequences of a particular case before considering any type of settlement. Some areas of the law, such as immigration, are so complicated that it often behooves the lawyer or client to consult with an immigration lawyer before agreeing to a settlement.

Often, the slightest change in the charge to which the client pleads guilty can bring about an enormous change in the client's life. Many judges and prosecutors are willing to work out alternative resolutions that will not detrimentally affect the defendant in unintended ways. For example, most branches of the military will not enlist someone who is on probation. An effective defense attorney may be able to persuade the prosecutor and judge that it would be in the best interest of society to allow the defendant to serve in the military, and thus the attorney may work out a settlement that does not require probation. In some circumstances, criminal convictions may bar military service, and a persuasive defense attorney may be able to have the charge reduced to an infraction in order to allow the defendant's enlistment in the armed forces.

It is crucial for defense attorneys to discuss collateral consequences with their clients, since defense counsel may come to realize that a plea bargain is not ultimately in the defendant's best interests. While there are many advantages to case settlement, the fact remains that there are situations in which going to trial is the better choice for one or both sides. To return to the above hypo, *Oceana v. Nuñez*, assume that, after the altercation Nuñez had with his daughter in public, he drove away and was then pulled over by a police officer after someone in the restaurant reported the incident. When the police officer approached the car, Nuñez acted strangely and quickly threw something out of the car window. The police officer, now with probable cause, searched the vehicle, and found one kilogram of cocaine. Nuñez claimed that he only flicked a cigarette out of the window and was unaware of the drugs. He was prosecuted for both assault and possession, and his counsel encouraged him to plead guilty. Nuñez, however, was born in Mexico but legally resided and practiced in the United States. Prior to *Padilla*, if his counsel had failed to warn him of the possibility of deportation, Nuñez would find it difficult to withdraw his plea. After *Padilla*, Nuñez will have an easier time withdrawing his plea. Nuñez might prefer to go to trial, even if the evidence is against him, rather than face automatic deportation.

To put it bluntly, "lawyers who ignore collateral consequences of legal actions are, to that extent, bad lawyers."[74] This also applies to more than just defense counsel. If the defense counsel is incompetent, then the plea will be withdrawn. If that happens, then the prosecution incurs the loss of the conviction. All those involved in plea negotiations have something to lose when the accused is inadequately informed.

---

[74] Chin & Holmes, *supra* note 61, at 718.

ENHANCEMENTS

Prosecutors and defense lawyers alike should keep in mind that enhancements can be instrumental to arriving at case settlements. Enhancements are allegations that add to the seriousness of an offense, and often, if found to be true, can add significant custody time to a sentence. Examples of enhancements include consideration of whether there was use of a firearm or other weapon, whether there have been prior serious convictions, whether there was infliction of great bodily injury during the course of the crime, whether it was a hate crime, whether the victim was either elderly or a minor, whether the defendant's alcohol level was at .20 or above, or whether the defendant drove over 100 miles an hour.

Enhancements can add to the stigma of an offense, as well as adding time to any potential incarceration. If the prosecutor's primary settlement goal is to obtain a conviction, and the defendant's primary goal is to avoid the added sentence that would be imposed if an enhancement were proved true, then an amicable settlement could be for the defendant to plead guilty to the charge in exchange for the prosecutor's dropping the enhancement allegation. Of course, this would only be appropriate if the case was not egregious. For example, if the defendant with a .21% blood alcohol level had been charged with driving under the influence of alcohol, with a .20 enhancement, it might be appropriate to drop the enhancement in exchange for a plea to the driving under the influence count. Likewise, it might be appropriate for a prosecutor to drop a great bodily injury allegation in exchange for a plea to battery if the victim completely recovered, with no permanent injuries, and the defendant had no prior record of violent conduct. Of course, settlement negotiations should be evaluated on a case-by-case basis, and enhancements should only be dismissed if that action would produce a just result.

While being creative may be a more effective form of advocacy, an attorney should not become overzealous. Because plea bargaining is not confined to sentence and charge reductions, attorneys and judges should take care not to abuse the practice with absurd forms of "*ad hoc* bargaining." As Joseph A. Colquitt, professor of law and retired Sixth Circuit judge, explains:

> Ad hoc bargaining, however, may involve neither a plea nor a sentence. For example, if a defendant charged with public intoxication seeks to avoid a statutorily mandated minimum sentence of ten days in the county jail, the prosecutor might agree to dismiss the charges if the defendant agrees to make a monetary contribution to a local driver's education program. An ad hoc settlement may also result in the case being dismissed before or after a plea. Even if a plea is forthcoming, a nonsanctioned alternative to the statutorily established punishment may be imposed by the court.[75]

Sometimes the court is used for improper reasons. One commentator notes that coerced contributions, "scarlet letter" punishments, banishment, and forced military participation are just some examples of sentences that have been handed down as a result of plea bargains that push the limits. This is unethical; it is an abuse of the criminal justice system. For example, Colquitt cites many examples of strange punishments, including: a wholesale bakery sentenced to donate baked goods to nine charitable

---

[75] Joseph A. Colquitt, *Ad Hoc Plea Bargaining*, 75 TUL. L. REV. 695, 711 (2001).

organizations;[76] a man who forfeited his automobile;[77] and one defendant who was required to place a bumper sticker on his car reading "CONVICTED D.U.I. RESTRICTED LICENSE."[78] It is also illegal to banish a defendant from a jurisdiction, so even if a recidivist defendant is a nuisance to a particular county, judges are not allowed to order a defendant to stay away from an entire county as part of the plea bargain or sentence. The issue of ethics, in other words, is at the center of plea bargaining. While walking away from a case settlement and only having to donate freshly baked goods might sound like a defense victory, this type of unethical settlement would call into question the integrity of the judge, prosecutor, and defense attorney.

A. ETHICAL CONCERNS APPLICABLE TO THE DEFENSE

One of the most difficult challenges defense counsel faces is how much pressure to place on the accused in order to convince him to agree to a plea bargain. The defense attorney, by virtue of training, experience, and objectivity, is in a much better position than the defendant to ascertain whether a plea offer is a good offer. If a defendant turns down a reasonable plea offer, only to be convicted and receive a much longer sentence than what was offered in a plea deal, this can present the most difficult aspect of a criminal defense attorney's job. Those charged with crimes may be distraught and not thinking clearly, or they may not have a realistic perspective on the strength of the prosecution's case. Additionally, many defendants suffer from substance abuse addiction, which can, of course, cloud their judgment. Some defendants are unrealistically convinced that they can beat the charges, or they may simply not want to face the possibility of serving jail time. It is the defense attorney's responsibility to "talk some sense into the client," if this is what is necessary, and to explain the pros and cons of the plea bargain. Her job is to protect her client, and sometimes that means protecting him even from himself. This is particularly true in cases where a defendant is facing a long prison term or, in the most extreme case, the death penalty. A defense attorney should remind her client that, as a lawyer, she has the training and experience to advise the client about whether to settle a case. It is appropriate for defense counsel to be persuasive if she truly believes it is in her client's best interest to accept a plea offer, but she cannot force him to plead guilty. It is imperative to respect the client's wishes and understand that the client is the one who will be serving the time. Ultimately, it is the client's decision whether to accept a plea offer.

There is a fine line between strongly advocating for accepting a plea offer and insisting that a client take a deal. Even if an attorney is not demanding, a defendant who wants to withdraw a plea may later claim he was forced. For example, a twenty-three-year-old man in Utah, accused of murdering a Brigham Young University professor, claimed that his attorneys had forced him to plead guilty.[79] Similarly, a twenty-five-year-old man in Cedar Rapids, who was accused of throwing a Molotov cocktail

---

[76] United States v. Danilow Pastry Co., 563 F. Supp. 1159, 1164–65 (S.D.N.Y. 1983).

[77] State v. Gladden, 620 N.E.2d 947, 948 (Ohio Ct. App. 1993).

[78] Goldschmitt v. State, 490 So. 2d 123, 124–26 (Fla. Dist. Ct. App. 1986).

[79] Jennifer Dobner, *Utah Man Says Guilty Plea to Murder Was Forced*, FOX13NOW (July 21, 2011, 8:42 AM), http://provo.fox13now.com/news/crime/utah-man-says-guilty-plea-murder-was-forced/58408.

into an occupied apartment, tried to withdraw his guilty plea on the grounds that had been coerced into pleading guilty to second-degree arson because of statements his public defender made to him. He stated that he felt he "didn't have a choice and had to take [the plea bargain]."[80] Of his public defender, he said that, "she told me if we went to trial we wouldn't win, so I didn't have any confidence in her and I didn't know if she was prepared. She didn't want to call any of the witnesses. She felt it would be damaging to the case."[81] These examples are common. A defendant who has regrets will reframe the issue as one of coercion and defense counsel's incompetency. Whether the attorneys actually coerced the defendant to plead guilty is for a judge to decide.

While it is of course unethical to force a client to plead guilty, it may also be incompetent not to explain the benefits of settling a case. The best a defense counsel can do is to keep a detailed and accurate record of all communications with the client. If defense counsel has established an effective and open relationship with her client, she will have a better chance of convincing her client when to accept a plea offer.

Defense attorneys also have a duty to be ethical towards the court. The relationship with the client aside, it is inappropriate for defense counsel to use delay tactics in an attempt to pressure prosecutors to offer reduced charges. Prosecutors are encouraged to settle cases, especially in metropolitan areas where the caseloads are enormous. It is possible for a defense attorney to request multiple continuances with time waivers, in an attempt to age a case either to weaken it or to pressure the prosecutor with a backlog of cases. Sometimes prosecutors reduce offers in old cases because the evidence is not as strong (due to unavailable witnesses or witnesses with faded memories) or because there are too many cases set for trial. While it is not illegal for the defense counsel to use delay tactics, it is not advisable. Continuances may be necessary to properly prepare a defense; however, delaying a case in an attempt to pressure the prosecutor to reduce the charge may cause prosecutors and judges to form a negative opinion about the defense attorney. Unethical defense tactics may incite the prosecution to overcharge as a way to compensate and balance the power. Further, if an attorney acquires a negative reputation, then opposing counsel will gain the advantage of the court's favor. Thus, unethical approaches lose sight of the real issue: Settling a case should be for the benefit of the criminal justice system, society, the defendant, and witnesses. It should not, therefore, dissolve into a battle of egos. In fact, delay tactics are counter-productive to case settlement.

B. ETHICAL ISSUES APPLICABLE TO THE PROSECUTION

The prosecution faces inherent ethical issues while engaged in plea bargaining. There are certain standards prosecutors must maintain. As emphasized, overcharging is a problem that plagues plea negotiations because prosecutors sometimes unfairly use this mechanism to gain the upper hand. However tempting it might be to prosecutors, overcharging is an unethical abuse of power. As explained in Chapter 3, the discretion to file criminal charges is a weighty power that must be used judiciously.

---

[80] Trish Mehaffey, *CR Man Claims He Was Forced to Take a Guilty Plea*, EASTERN IOWA NEWS NOW (Mar. 15, 2011, 3:34 PM), http://easterniowanewsnow.com/2011/03/15/cr-man-claims-he-was-forced-to-take-a-guilty-plea/.

[81] *Id.*

Indeed, regardless of how rampant the problem, "whenever a prosecutorial agency files charges that are disproportionate or misrepresentative of the defendant's actions, that agency runs afoul of the ethical guidelines governing prosecutors, abuses its prosecutorial power, and compromises the justice system as a whole."[82] Moreover, there are few checks in place to deter prosecutors from overcharging, for prosecutors have no "political incentive to refrain from overcharging because most communities want the State to be tough on crime."[83]

While some ethical issues like overcharging are not a violation of the accused's rights *per se*, others are. "A prosecutor's discretion is 'subject to constitutional constraints.'"[84] Thus, a prosecutor must not discriminate during plea negotiations. Equal protection standards, in other words, apply to plea negotiations. For example, the Ninth Circuit heard a case in which the male defendants (who were drug mules) argued that they were treated more harshly than the female mules; however, the court ultimately found that there was no such discrimination.[85] If there had been discrimination, this might have violated equal protection.

In her article, *Prosecution and Race: The Power and Privilege of Discretion*, Angela J. Davis argues that prosecutorial discretion is "a major cause of racial inequality in the criminal justice system."[86] She contends that she regularly observed racial discrimination while working as a public defender in the District of Columbia.[87] She witnessed prosecutors give more favorable case settlements to Caucasian defendants and harsher treatments when the victim was not Caucasian.[88] It is important to understand that the "decision whether to prosecute may not be based on 'an unjustifiable standard such as race, religion, or other arbitrary classification.'"[89]

There are still other examples of prosecutorial misconduct that must be avoided. For example, a guilty plea will become invalid if induced by false promises.[90] In some states, such as Pennsylvania, if a guilty plea is entered primarily to shield a family member from prosecution, then the plea will be withdrawn.[91] Finally, prosecutorial vindictiveness is unethical. Although the Court held in *Bordenkircher v. Hayes* that the prosecution was not barred from charging a higher offense when the

---

[82] Caldwell, *supra* note 10, at 66.

[83] *Id.* at 84.

[84] United States v. Armstrong, 517 U.S. 456, 464 (1996) (citing United States v. Batchelder, 442 U.S. 114, 125 (1979)).

[85] United States v. Redondo-Lemos, 27 F.3d 439 (9th Cir. 1994).

[86] Angela J. Davis, *Prosecution and Race: The Power and Privilege of Discretion*, 67 FORDHAM L. REV. 13, 17 (1998).

[87] *Id.* at 15.

[88] *Id.* at 15–16.

[89] United States v. Armstrong, 517 U.S. 456, 464 (1996) (citing Oyler v. Boles, 368 U.S. 448, 456 (1962)).

[90] Blackledge v. Allison, 431 U.S. 63, 77–78 (1977).

[91] Commonwealth v. Dupree, 275 A.2d 326, 326 (Pa. 1971).

defendant was warned of the consequences when choosing not to accept a plea bargain;[92] the Court held in *Blackledge v. Perry* that the State cannot retaliate against a defendant who asserts his constitutional and statutory rights with a charge more serious than the original one.[93] Importantly, the reach of *Perry* has since been limited. For pretrial matters, the Court declines to presume vindictiveness.[94] Regardless, prosecutors should not act vindictively towards defendants, or even give the slightest appearance that they are doing so. In *Perry*, for example, the Court found that a due process violation occurred even though there was no actual evidence of the prosecutor's bad faith.[95] The prosecution should act in accordance with the ethical standards of the profession, which serve a very real purpose. If prosecutorial misconduct or vindictiveness is found, then a conviction will be overturned. The prosecutor who walks away from a plea negotiation thinking he has won, but who has used unethical means to obtain that success, not only jeopardizes the case settlement but also violates his ethical duty to seek justice.

Another category of prosecutorial abuse of discretion is to refuse to accept a reasonable defense settlement offer for inappropriate personal reasons. Some examples of this type of unethical conduct would be to insist on going to trial for political reasons, or for the purpose of gaining publicity, obtaining a promotion, or beating a particular adversary. High publicity cases, such as those involving celebrity defendants or high profile defense attorneys, or hot political cases, might tempt a prosecutor to try a case rather than accept a fair defense settlement offer. Prosecutors would be wise to take their egos and their own personal gains out of the equation and remember that the prosecution's role is to seek justice.

---

[92] Bordenkircher v. Hayes, 434 U.S. 357, 365 (1978).

[93] Blackledge v. Perry, 417 U.S. 21, 28 (1974).

[94] United States v. Goodwin, 457 U.S. 368 (1982). *See also* Note, *Breathing New Life into Prosecutorial Vindictiveness Doctrine*, 114 HARV. L. REV. 2074 (2001).

[95] *Blackledge*, 417 U.S. at 28.

SAMPLE MOTION

COLIN STEVENS
District Attorney
By: SAM LEVINE
State Bar No. 54321
Deputy District Attorney
Sex Crimes Division
500 E. Mali Blvd.
Maliwood, Oceana 90120
Telephone: (555) 555-1234
Fax: (555) 555-1235

Attorney for Plaintiff

SUPERIOR COURT OF THE STATE OF OCEANA
FOR THE COUNTY OF MALIWOOD

PEOPLE OF THE STATE OF OCEANA, Plaintiff, v. HARRY HENDERSON, Defendant.	Case No. 12345 **RESPONSE TO MOTION TO WITHDRAW PLEA PURSUANT TO PENAL CODE § 1016.5** **DATE:** July 1st, 2012 **TIME:** 8:30 a.m. **DEPT:** 1

TO THE HONORABLE JAMES MUIR, JUDGE OF THE SUPERIOR COURT, IN AND FOR THE COUNTY OF MALIWOOD, RON PARKER, ATTORNEY FOR DEFENDANT, AND HARRY HENDERSON, DEFENDANT:

The Plaintiff, through its attorney, Deputy District Attorney Sam Levine, moves that this court deny Defendant's Motion to Withdraw Plea, based upon the attached points and authorities, court pleadings, records, and files pertaining to this case, and any argument or evidence presented in court at the hearing on the motion.

Dated: June 1, 2012

Respectfully submitted,

COLIN STEVENS

District Attorney

By SAM LEVINE

Deputy District Attorney

MEMORANDUM OF POINTS AND AUTHORITIES

I. INTRODUCTION

Defendant seeks to withdraw his no contest plea for the following reasons:

(1)   He was not notified by the court, pursuant to Penal Code section 1016.5, that one of the consequences of his no contest plea was the possibility of exclusion from naturalization in the United States, and deportation from the United States.

(2)   His lawyer did not properly advise him of the possible immigration consequences of his no contest plea.

(3)   He was not advised, nor did he know, that the duty to register as a sex offender was a lifetime requirement.

II. PENAL CODE SECTION 1016.5 NOTIFICATION

The Reporter's Transcript of Misdemeanor Plea (hereinafter "R.T." [attached as Exhibit A]), case number 12345, Tuesday, May 7, 2012, clearly reflects that the court met its statutory notification requirement.

If you are not now a citizen of the United States, this conviction could result in your being deported, excluded admission or denied naturalization as a citizen.

(R.T., p. 8, lines 20-22).

If you are not a citizen, you are hereby advised that conviction of the offense for which you have been charged may have the consequences of deportation, exclusion from admission to the United States, or denial of naturalization pursuant to the laws of the United States.

(Pen. Code, § 1016.5, subd. (a)).

There are minor differences in the wording, and the notification was read by the deputy district attorney, not the judge, but these details are insignificant. "[S]ubstantial, not literal, compliance with section 1016.5 is sufficient." *People v. Gutierrez*, 106 Cal. App. 4th 169, 174 (2003).

Immediately afterwards, the sex-offender registration and the restitution requirements were stated, and then the deputy district attorney asked, "Mr. Henderson, do you understand all the consequences I just explained to you?" Defendant replied, "Yes." DDA then asked, "Yes?" Defendant again replied, "Yes." (R.T., p. 9, lines 10-14).

Defendant's declaration that he was not advised of the immigration consequences of his plea would be unconvincing in light of the reporter's transcript, but he does not even make this claim (see DECLARATION OF HARRY HENDERSON). He merely states that he was not properly advised by his attorney. The issue of ineffective assistance of counsel is addressed in Section II of this response.

III. INEFFECTIVE ASSISTANCE OF COUNSEL

Defendant cites *In re Resendiz*, 25 Cal. 4th 230 (2001) to support his claim of ineffective assistance of counsel. *Resendiz* dealt with a Petition for Writ of Habeas Corpus. Penal Code section 1016.5 does not authorize a plea withdrawal because of ineffective assistance of counsel.

In *People v. Miranda*, 123 Cal. App. 4th 1124 (2004), defendant was placed on probation in 1997 pursuant to a guilty plea. Defendant then fled the jurisdiction. In 2003, the Los Angeles County Superior Court granted his motion to withdraw his plea pursuant to Penal Code section 1018, but the Court of Appeal reversed the order setting aside the judgment and vacating the guilty plea.

The trial court lacked jurisdiction to consider and grant respondent's motion to vacate his guilty plea. The ruling setting aside the judgment and vacating the guilty plea must be reversed, and the matter must be remanded to the trial court for appropriate proceedings on the probation violation allegation. The issue of ineffective assistance of counsel may be raised, in accordance with established rules, by petition for writ of habeas corpus in the trial court (*People v. Gallardo*, 77 Cal. App. 4th 971, 983 (2000); *see In re Resendiz*, 25 Cal. 4th 230, 248 (2001); *see also Miranda*, 123 Cal. App. 4th at 1134).

Defendant must seek relief with a Petition for Writ of Habeas Corpus, not a Motion to Withdraw Plea Pursuant to Penal Code Section 1016.5.

IV. CONCLUSION

Plaintiff has shown that defendant's motion lacks merit, and respectfully requests that this Honorable court deny defendant's motion to withdraw his plea.

Dated: June 1, 2012   Respectfully submitted,

                                                   COLIN STEVENS
                                                   District Attorney
                                                   By SAM LEVINE
                                                   Deputy District Attorney
                                                   Sex Crimes Division

SUMMARY

Since the majority of guilty verdicts are achieved through plea bargaining, attorneys are expected to possess the requisite skills to negotiate pre-trial settlements effectively. Successful negotiators must also learn to recognize the goals of the opposing side, and be prepared to compromise in order to reach mutually agreeable settlements. As with any negotiation, plea bargaining demands solid preparation, assessment of risks, and prioritization of the needs and willing concessions of both the prosecution and the defense. Equally important to the process is the understanding that the parties involved acknowledge the limits and terms of the contract that has been created. Poorly negotiated pleas will only result in missed opportunities and a variety of disappointing outcomes. It is a remarkable process when one considers that such criminal adjudication is, at least in part, in the hands and subject to the very will of the target of the criminal charges. This is high-stakes negotiation, arguably the highest form. It seems the remaining work to be done is instilling public confidence in this now commonplace process, underscoring the advantages of avoiding placing the victim and his family under further duress. Plea bargains, as a system of negotiation, encourage formulating the most principled bargaining system imaginable, one allowing everyone involved to move forward with their lives—a win-win situation, indeed.

CHECKLIST

✓ The defense attorney must always act in the best interest of her client, just as prosecutors must focus upon the interests of the State—neither side compromising on matters of principle nor fearing trial if it becomes necessary.

✓ Concerns, such as prosecutorial overcharging, chilling of Sixth Amendment rights, or the unfair treatment of victims or co-defendants, must always be carefully evaluated.

✓ Effective case settlement can result in greater efficiency and cost-effectiveness for the court system, much-needed closure for victims and their families, and reduced financial and emotional costs for all parties involved.

✓ Although case settlement negotiations are less formally structured than trial proceedings, it is important to understand and adhere to the local rules of court, as well as to take into account the ethical concerns that arise during the course of the bargaining process.

✓ There is no automatic right to a plea bargain, and while the defense may always approach the prosecutor with a suggested compromise, the decision to commence plea negotiations ultimately rests with the prosecution.

✓ Case settlements are contracts. If a party fails to perform under the terms of the settlement, the agreement as a whole becomes void.

✓ In federal court, a guilty plea must be made knowingly, intelligently, and voluntarily to be valid. Defense counsel is responsible for ensuring the client is properly informed of both settlement and trial consequences, but deciding whether to plead guilty is ultimately up to the defendant.

✓ In federal court, as well as many state courts, the judge is not a party to the case settlement process, although she has the discretion to reject a negotiated plea.

✓ Negotiators should always engage with the opposing side in a frank, honest, and ethical manner, while taking into account what each values most highly, beyond just the reduction of charges or sentence term.

✓ Defense counsel should always consider collateral consequences and discuss them with her client. Collateral consequences can include such ramifications as the loss of a professional license or financial aid, a loss of the right to bear arms, or ineligibility to serve in the military.

✓ When fashioned successfully, plea bargains can result in a win-win situation for all parties concerned, and the process should, correspondingly, be ardently pursued towards a fruitful end.

CHAPTER 13
SPECIAL PRETRIAL
CONSIDERATIONS

"By failing to prepare, you are preparing to fail."
–Benjamin Franklin

While the principal phases of pretrial advocacy are the focus of this book, there are also many other miscellanies that, if prepared for and advanced, can have a decisive impact on a case. Taking these more minor components into account, the options for moving forward in a criminal jury trial are potentially endless. Jury selection, for example, can determine the outcome of a case. Counsel must consider which jurors they want to include, and even more importantly, those that they hope to exclude. In order to make that decision, counsel might want to hire experts, or jury consultants to aid in the selection. Furthermore, attorneys have wide latitude in deciding *how* to present their cases, and because of this, they can and should make use of visual aids, stipulations, judicial notice, and trial notebooks in order to gain an advantage and put forth the best case theory they can.

Methods that aid in the organization and presentation of the case are an essential part of thorough and successful trial preparation. After all, following counsels' selection of jurors, attorneys will also have to consider which methods of presentation, what rhetorical devices, and what visuals will persuade that particular segment of the population. On this matter, jury consultants can also offer an expert perspective on the overall trial presentation and suggest which visuals might sway a specific jury. Visual aids are, of course, essential in large part because modern juries expect them. People tend to be stimulated by visual presentations as well as retain better what they see than what they hear. Consequently, the importance of visual exhibits cannot be overstated, and understanding the applicable law and local rules is crucial to gaining permission to use such cutting edge or even controversial visual aids. Furthermore, litigators need to be prepared to counter the visual presentations of opposing counsel and object to them when their prejudicial effect substantially outweighs their probative value.[1]

After counsel has selected a jury and decided which visuals will appeal to them, organization is the next requisite to assuring a persuasive presentation. In order to keep organized, attorneys should put together a trial notebook. A trial notebook is typically made up of a binder that contains separate sections that pertain to various aspects of the trial. Trial notebooks also aid litigators when they have to locate a crucial document quickly in the midst of trial, such as a witness statement. This chapter will examine all of these previously mentioned components of trial preparation and offer tips on how to prepare them in order to maximize their effective use at trial.

---

[1] FED. R. EVID. 403.

JURY CONSULTANTS

The use of jury consultants is becoming increasingly popular in high publicity cases as well as in cases that are particularly serious or complex. Some trial lawyers believe that jury selection is the most important aspect of the trial. Since the prosecution must convince the jurors beyond a reasonable doubt in order to obtain a conviction, prosecutors have a huge incentive to avoid a hung jury. This is particularly important in jurisdictions where the prosecution bears this burden of proof to twelve unanimous jurors.[2] Clearly, not all jurors are forthcoming in jury selection; sometimes jurors have an agenda or strong biases that they refuse to reveal. Typically, lawyers are not trained in psychology and their ability to ferret out an irrational or hostile juror is quite limited. When the case warrants the expense (or, in the case of a private defense attorney, when the client can afford the fee), trial lawyers sometimes turn to jury consultants to aid them in both jury selection and in testing out case theories and witness testimony through the use of mock jurors. In a federal prosecution, counsel may request investigative or expert services, including jury consultants, for an indigent defendant under the Criminal Justice Act of 1964;[3] however, indigent defendants are not, under the Act, entitled to a jury consultant at the public's expense.[4]

Jury consultants are used in civil and criminal cases. In the highly publicized civil case *Texas Beef Group v. Winfrey*,[5] for example, the celebrity talk show host Oprah Winfrey was sued by Texas cattlemen for defamation, among other claims. On April 16, 1996, the Oprah Winfrey Show aired their "Dangerous Foods" program in which they discussed Mad Cow disease. One segment of the show questioned whether American beef could be affected as British beef had been. One guest on the show said that American beef was at risk, but neither Texas nor any of the plaintiffs in the case were specifically mentioned.[6] When the

---

[2] Not all states require a unanimous jury to convict a defendant. In capital cases, however, the federal government and thirty-four of the thirty-five states which still impose the death penalty require unanimity; Florida is the only state which requires a simple majority for capital cases. For a survey of state and federal requirements regarding unanimity, see Raoul G. Cantero & Robert M. Kline, *Death is Different: The Need for Jury Unanimity in Death Penalty Cases*, 22 ST. THOMAS L. REV. 4, 10–12 (2009). In general, the requirement of unanimity depends on the size of the jury. In *Williams v. Florida*, 399 U.S. 78, 86 (1970), the Supreme Court held that "the 12-man panel is not a necessary ingredient of 'trial by jury,'" and a court's decision to impanel six jurors does not violate a defendant's Sixth Amendment right. However, while the Supreme Court left it to each state to choose under what circumstances it would impanel six or twelve jurors in *Johnson v. Louisiana*, 406 U.S. 356, 364 (1972), it further held that "conviction for a nonpetty offense by only five members of a six-person jury presents a . . . threat to preservation of the substance of the jury trial guarantee and justifies our requiring verdicts rendered by six-person juries to be unanimous." Burch v. Louisiana, 441 U.S. 130, 137 (1978). For a survey of state requirements regarding jury size, see Robert H. Miller, *Six of One is Not a Dozen of the Other: A Reexamination of* Williams v. Florida *and the Size of State Criminal Juries*, 146 U. PA. L. REV. 621, 645–50 (1998). While the Supreme Court has interpreted the Sixth Amendment as not requiring unanimous verdicts, federal courts require unanimous verdicts in criminal cases. Apodaca v. Oregon, 406 U.S. 404 (1972).

[3] 18 U.S.C. § 3006A(e)(1) (2006).

[4] United States v. Rivera, 292 F. Supp. 2d 823 (E.D. Va. 2003). *See also* United States v. Caro, 442 F. Supp. 2d 296 (W.D. Va. 2006).

[5] 11 F. Supp. 2d 858 (N.D. Tex. 1998).

[6] *Id.* at 861.

case went to trial, psychologist Phil McGraw, later to become the host of *The Dr. Phil Show* with Winfrey's support, was a jury consultant on the case and was faced with a predicament. Nearly everyone in the jury pool had ties to the beef industry. One cattle rancher was even included in the jury, but was noted for being a "strong free-speech guy." McGraw's consultations paid off, and Winfrey was found not liable.[7] At times, keeping jurors with close ties to the case, either from work, residence, or personal beliefs, may be impossible. But consultants can look to other aspects of their personalities in order to determine if they can be a good fit.

Jury consulting services can be quite expensive, however, so their use in criminal cases is typically reserved for high publicity cases, as in the cases against Kobe Bryant, Heidi Fleiss, Michael Jackson, Scott Peterson, Jerry Sandusky, O.J. Simpson, Phil Spector, and Martha Stewart. Those with unusual significance, or when serious charges are filed against wealthy defendants, might also warrant the high cost of jury consultation services.

Depending on the case at issue, the charges, the client, and the alleged conduct, jury consultants will have to consider many different issues when tailoring their questions for prospective jurors. One consultant, Paul D. Tieger, has remarked that the selection process is not so much about selecting your ideal jury, but more about dismissing "people with strong bias."[8] In fact, Tieger served as the consultant in the criminal case against Jack Kevorkian for assisted suicide in which Kevorkian was acquitted. In that case, Tieger subjected prospective jurors to a twelve-page questionnaire and wanted to avoid jurors who were pro-life, finding them also to be anti-Kevorkian. Tieger relied on psychoanalysis to aid him in trying to assess the biases of potential jurors, and jury consultants do regularly turn to a myriad of social sciences in order to help them understand the predilections of potential jurors.[9]

Consultants will focus on topics pertinent to the circumstances surrounding their clients, so their questionnaires will of course vary for each trial. When Scott Peterson, for example, was charged with murdering his pregnant wife, the defense's jury consultants, who had also served as consultants in the OJ Simpson and Martha Stewart trials, subjected potential jurors to a twenty-three page questionnaire that focused on extracting the jurors' attitudes towards the death penalty, infidelity, and law enforcement.[10] Sometimes, however, jury consultants take risks, as did the consultants in the case against Phil Spector. Spector, a record producer and songwriter, was accused of murdering actress, Lana Clarkson, in 2003. In the case against him, a TV producer was, surprisingly, left on the jury; however, Spector was convicted, so the risk may have been a significant one. Questions asked of that jury included: "Over the past several years, what publicized court cases have you followed or paid attention to (e.g. O.J. Simpson, Robert

---

[7] Susan Snyderand & Jeremy Roebuck, *Sandusky Jury has Strong Penn State Ties*, THE PHILADELPHIA INQUIRER (June 9, 2012), http://articles.philly.com/2012-06-09/news/32125098_1_judge-john-m-cleland-jury-room-sandusky-jury/3.

[8] Lynne Tuohy, *Consultant Helps Defense Team By Getting Inside Jurors' Heads*, HARTFORD COURANT (May 3, 1994), http://articles.courant.com/1994-05-03/news/9405030215_1_jury-selection-fieger-and-kevorkian-kevorkian-s-lawyer.

[9] *Id.*

[10] Donna Horowitz, *Jury Questioning to Resume in Peterson Trial*, LA TIMES (Apr. 5, 2004), http://articles.latimes.com/2004/apr/05/local/me-jury5.

Blake, Michael Jackson, etc.)?" They were also asked whether they agreed with the following statement: "Celebrities and high-profile people in Los Angeles are treated the same way by the police as anyone else."[11]

There are, however, many types of jury consultant services that go beyond selection: the most common are focus groups, mock trials, and shadow juries. The differences among focus groups, mock trials, and shadow juries lie in their design, scope, and purpose. Focus groups and mock trials are used to prepare for upcoming trials, while shadow juries are used during trial.

CHART 13.1
Types of Jury Consultant Services

• Jury Research	• Pre-trial
o Focus groups	o Witness preparation
o Mock trials	o Case analysis
o Shadow juries	o Theme development
o Juror profiling study	o Venue analysis
o Change of venue research	o Graphics consulting
o Damages analysis studies	o Drafting/Analyzing opening and
o Mock arbitrations	closing statements
o Venue overviews	o Attorney communication training
o Verdict searches	• Post-trial
• Jury Selection	o Interviewing jurors post-verdict (unless
o Assisting with jury selection in-court	prohibited by local rules or laws)
o Drafting juror questionnaires	
o Drafting *voir dire*	
o Juror Profiling	

A. FOCUS GROUPS

A focus group is primarily a qualitative research project in which a small group of people, whose demographics have been matched to those of the actual jury pool, are asked about their perceptions and opinions of the case. Typically, research assistants at jury consultant firms input detailed amounts of data into computers in order to come up with a random group of individuals who will be somewhat representative of potential jurors in the jurisdiction. The members of the focus group are paid for their time, and they are generally not psychologists or people with any expertise in law or in the field of jury selection. The focus group is also not told which side hired them, as extensive efforts are made not to reveal which side the jury consultants work for in order to ensure that this would not influence their conclusions. In some instances, the attorneys who hired the jury consulting team present their case to the focus group. When that is done, the presentations typically resemble a combination of an opening

---

[11] Peter Y. Hong, *TV Producer on Spector Jury*, LA TIMES (Apr. 21, 2007), http://articles.latimes.com/2007/apr/21/local/me-spector21.

statement and a closing argument. Consequently, these hybrid opening/closing presentations are sometimes referred to as "clopenings." In other instances, the jury consultant presents the case to the focus group respondents by reading or providing a neutral summary of the case.

After the case is presented, the respondents engage in a focused/structured discussion led by a moderator (a jury trial consultant or experienced research associate) about the case. Throughout the discussion, the moderator may present additional information or evidence and assess the focus group respondents' reactions to the new information. Focus groups provide the trial team a substantial amount of data on the respondents' opinions regarding both general and specific pre-determined issues pertinent to the case. Focus groups are, on the one hand, designed to provide a broad overview of an actual case to the respondents, and on the other, examine specific issues that are of utmost interest to the trial team. For instance, in a murder case, in which the defendant was under the influence of narcotics, the issue for the focus group might be whether the defendant was too incapacitated to form the malice aforethought element of murder. In a domestic violence case, in which the defendant is a woman, the issue might be whether the focus group thinks it is reasonable that an unarmed woman could batter her much larger husband. Focus groups, however, rarely examine all of the issues in a case. In fact, they are typically conducted early in the litigation process to help develop preliminary themes and to help the trial team focus and organize their efforts during the discovery and trial preparation processes. In particular, focus groups are useful in aiding litigators as they shape their case theories for complicated cases.

B. MOCK TRIALS

A mock trial is an extensive type of jury research project that allows the trial consultant to obtain both qualitative and quantitative data. The consulting team recruits mock jurors from the community in which the case will be tried. Consultants closely match the sample of mock jurors to the demographics of the actual jury pool. Mock trials are essentially mini-trials that can include fairly detailed, argumentative opening statements (i.e., "clopenings"). They can also include witnesses' testimony (live or on video) and final closing arguments. The mock trial participants complete questionnaires throughout the day that measure the participants' reactions to the presentations and evidence. Upon conclusion of the trial presentation, the jury (or juries) deliberate and reach a verdict, just as the actual jury would. They then provide feedback about the key issues in the case, which in turn helps the trial consultants provide useful strategic recommendations for the trial team. A mock trial also helps trial attorneys formulate or refine trial theories and themes, prepare witnesses to testify for trial, and aid in the process of selecting the actual jury for the real trial. In other words, the results obtained from mock trials are essential to the trial team in evaluating their approach and in preparing for the trial.

Mock trials can be particularly helpful in settling a case as well. Since the proceeding is a mini-trial, or a realistic preview of the way a jury would view the evidence, if a defendant is reluctant to accept an offer that his attorney thinks he should take, then the results of the mock trial might provide a dose of reality to the defendant. If the defendant learns that the mock jury would have convicted him, this might convince him to accept a negotiated plea. Alternatively, if a mock jury thinks that the prosecution's case is weak, this could provide incentive for the State to offer a more generous plea bargain, or in extreme cases, to reduce the charges or dismiss the case altogether. Just as criminal defense attorneys have to convince their clients to accept a plea deal, prosecutors usually need the approval of their supervisor to settle a serious case.

Mock trials are especially beneficial to attorneys trying to test out their case theories, their exhibits, and other courtroom visual aids. These mini-trials also give the attorneys a chance to see the impact their witnesses have on a mock jury, allowing them to make informed decisions about which witnesses to call (when there is a choice between witnesses) and also to counsel witnesses to adjust their demeanor when necessary. For instance, in a case where an attorney plans to hire an expert witness to testify, the reactions of the mock jurors can assist the lawyer in determining which expert to call in the actual trial. Additionally, if an expert witness came across as arrogant, abrasive, or condescending, she can modify her attitude and testimony in the actual trial. A mock trial is an exceptionally useful tool for litigators; however, the process is expensive and time consuming, so it is used sparingly.

C. SHADOW JURIES

A shadow jury consists of individuals who are "matched" both by attitudes and demographics to the actual people that comprise the jury. They are utilized to observe ongoing trials and provide immediate feedback to the trial team on a daily basis. At various intervals throughout each trial day, the shadow jurors complete questionnaires or answer interview questions designed to measure the shadow jurors' "leaning" in favor of, or against, each party in the trial and their opinions on the evidence and arguments presented in court. Consultants and their team of research assistants and associates typically interview the shadow jurors on specific, focused topics at least once per trial day and then provide daily feedback to trial counsel, but the shadow jurors are not informed which party hired them in order to maintain as much impartiality as possible. Shadow juries provide the trial team valuable insight on "what's working and what's not working" as the trial progresses: in response to this feedback, the trial team can then modify its approach and present additional evidence as needed. Perhaps if the shadow jurors think that an attorney is being too aggressive, the consultants might advise the lawyer to tone it down.

D. DISCLOSURE RULES

Permission from opposing counsel or a judge to utilize a trial consultant is not required, and parties do not need formal permission from a judge to conduct a shadow jury. Although the use of a jury consultant does not *need* to be disclosed to the judge or opposing counsel, it is often good practice for a party that wishes to use a jury consultant to make such disclosures to the judge and to opposing counsel to prevent objections by opposing counsel or any interference from the judge or court staff. Judges cannot prevent a party from using a trial consultant, but they can limit the effectiveness of trial consultants in a courtroom in several ways. For example, judges can bar the consultant from sidebars or discussions in chambers, or they can order the consultant to sit in the galley of the courtroom instead of at counsel table, where the consultant can be most effective. It is imperative that shadow jurors be instructed not to make facial expressions or comments during the trial that could be disruptive or that could influence the jurors. Jury trials in America are public forums, so available seats in the galley may be used by anyone who is not disruptive, but the judge controls allowable conduct and exercises the right to have the bailiff remove individuals who do not abide by the judge's rules.

E. ETHICAL ISSUES

Jury consultants can be ethically and legally used in both criminal and civil cases. In criminal cases, trial consultants are often used when the case has been highly publicized. Many individuals and

entities involved in lawsuits, including small businesses in civil cases and individual defendants in criminal cases, cannot afford the costs associated with utilizing a consultant; however, some trial consultants offer *pro bono* work in those situations. The American Society of Trial Consultants has an ethical code for its members; however unlike attorneys, at this point, there are no legally binding ethical rules for trial consultants. That said, because trial consultants work closely with attorneys, consultants generally must adhere to applicable ethical codes for attorneys, such as the one provided by the American Bar Association. It is also possible that, if a case has high significance to a particular group, such as the American Civil Liberties Union or Mothers Against Drunk Drivers, the cost of hiring a jury consultant firm could be paid by an organization. The prosecution is much more likely to use the services of jury consultants in high publicity cases, or those where the prosecution is aware that the privately hired defense counsel are using a jury consultant. Likewise, if a government lawyer represents an indigent defendant, then it might be appropriate for the defense to hire a consultant at tax-payer expense if the prosecution hired one. In this regard, hiring jury consultants is similar to hiring any expert witness— when deemed to be appropriate by the judge, it is paid for by taxpayers.

The question of a trial court's role in providing an indigent defendant with a jury consultant has been raised by numerous authorities and in various cases. Often, the prosecution has the funds to provide for jury consultants in order to bolster the possibility of getting a conviction, while an indigent defendant does not. The Supreme Court addressed the issue of providing indigent defendants with necessary experts at the public's expense in *Ake v. Oklahoma*.[12] In *Ake*, an indigent defendant was convicted of murder in a capital case.[13] Though the defendant raised an insanity defense, he was denied access to a psychiatric evaluation regarding his mental state at the time the crime was committed.[14] The defendant was then convicted of murder and sentenced to death.[15] Upon reviewing the case, the Supreme Court held that based on "the Fourteenth Amendment's due process guarantee of fundamental fairness . . . justice cannot be equal where, simply as a result of his poverty, a defendant is denied the opportunity to participate meaningfully in a judicial proceeding in which his liberty is at stake."[16] A court must adhere to the principles of "fundamental fairness" and provide a defendant the basic tools necessary to sufficiently defend his case.[17]

The Court in *Ake* determined that in order to establish whether or not the state must provide an indigent defendant with expert assistance, it must balance three factors: (1) "the private interest that will be affected by the action of the State"; (2) "the governmental interest that will be affected if the safeguard is to be provided"; and (3)

---

[12] 470 U.S. 68 (1985).

[13] *Id.* at 70.

[14] *Id.* at 72.

[15] *Id.* at 73.

[16] *Id.* at 76.

[17] *Id.* at 77.

"the probable value of the additional or substitute procedural safeguards that are sought, and the risk of an erroneous deprivation of the affected interest if those safeguards are not provided."[18] In applying this test, the Court in *Ake* held that the defendant was in fact entitled to the assistance of a psychiatric expert because he demonstrated that his mental state was a "significant factor at trial."[19]

Although the *Ake* standard was established specifically in regards to psychiatric experts, subsequent cases have extended the application of this "significant factor" standard to experts in other fields, including hypnosis, DNA, fingerprinting, and dentistry, among others.[20] The application of this standard to jury consultants specifically, however, is still tentative. While various courts have addressed the question, there has yet to develop a standard interpretation of the Supreme Court's intent in creating the "significant factor" test.[21] Different courts have applied the standard with different levels of flexibility: while some courts require a "particularized" or "substantial need," others require a "defendant to show both a reasonable probability that the consultant would assist the defense and that the denial of the consultant would result in an unfair trial."[22] Additionally, "other courts applied *Ake* but concluded that a jury consultant does not constitute a 'basic tool' to an adequate defense."[23] Regardless of the approach taken by the court, however, the results are quite often the same: lower courts in general deny indigent defendants access to jury consultants.[24] A few courts have relied on a more flexible interpretation of the "significant factor" standard established in *Ake*.[25] For instance, Justice Johnson's concurring opinion in *Moore v. Kemp* argued that "*Ake* requires flexible jurisprudence," and that a "rigid application of *Ake* undermines the Court's vision for expert assistance for defendants."[26] Furthermore, in one case, the California Supreme Court relied on a more flexible interpretation of the *Ake* standard and "granted a defendant a jury consultant because of excessive pre-trial publicity."[27]

Of particular importance are the conclusions of the Fifth and Eleventh Circuits regarding funding of jury consultants for indigent defendants. In *Moore v. Johnson*, the Fifth Circuit Court held that "a defendant cannot expect the state to provide him a most-sophisticated defense."[28] Rather,

---

[18] *Id.*

[19] *Id.* at 74.

[20] Kate Early, Comment, *The Impact of Pretrial Publicity on an Indigent Capital Defendant's Due Process Right to a Jury Consultant*, 16 ROGER WILLIAMS U. L. REV. 687, 712 (2011) (citing Little v. Armontrout, 835 F.2d 1240 (8th Cir. 1987); *Ex parte* Dubose, 662 So. 2d 1189 (Ala. 1995); State v. Bridges, 385 S.E.2d 337 (N.C. 1989); Thornton v. State, 339 S.E.2d 240 (Ga. 1986)).

[21] Steven C. Serio, Comment, *A Process Right Due? Examining Whether a Capital Defendant Has A Due Process Right to a Jury Selection Expert*, 53 AM. U. L. REV. 1143, 1178 (2004).

[22] *Id.*

[23] *Id.*

[24] *Id.*

[25] *Id.* at 1179.

[26] *Id.* (citing Moore v. Kemp, 809 F.2d 702, 741 (11th Cir. 1987)).

[27] *Id.* at 1180 (citing Corenevsky v. Superior Court, 682 P.2d 360, 368–69 (1984)).

[28] Moore v. Johnson, 225 F.3d 495, 503 (5th Cir. 2000).

"[c]ommunicating with the jury is a quintessential responsibility of counsel."[29] Therefore, "indigent defendants are not privileged to force the state to expend its funds on" providing jury consultants, as that is merely "an exercise in bolstering an attorney's fundamental skills."[30] Additionally, the Eleventh Circuit held in *Moore v. Kemp* that as long as a defendant is provided with the opportunity to present his case, "[t]he state need not provide indigent defendants *all* the assistance their wealthier counterparts might buy."[31]

Despite the discrepancy in interpretations, however, the need of providing indigent defendants with jury consultants may present a due process issue, in cases where taxpayers are paying for the prosecution to use a jury consultant. Moreover, jury consultant services, especially the use of shadow jurors, might strike some people as unethical. Of course, whenever exorbitant sums are spent defending a case, there is a danger that a wealthy defendant might "buy" his way out of a conviction; however, the United States is a free society, and people accused of crimes have the option of paying for expensive lawyers, private investigators, expert witnesses, and jury consultants if they can afford to. In this regard, hiring jury consultants is no different than hiring expert witnesses, or investigators. Indeed, especially in subjective matters, such as psychology, there is much criticism that many experts are "hired guns" who will render any requested opinion, no matter how absurd, if the fee is high enough. Moreover, often the most effective, experienced defense lawyers in the courtroom are the deputy public defenders. The government lawyers who represent indigent defendants typically have more experience than attorneys in private practice. They tend to be highly passionate about their jobs, and they know what a case is worth in a particular courthouse.

Nevertheless, there are legitimate ethical concerns with the propriety of jury consulting services, and it is crucial that lawyers conduct themselves within the ethical standards directed by the Model Rules to avoid these pitfalls. For example, trial attorneys must avoid the temptation to coach witnesses to tailor their testimony to meet the desires of the mock jurors. In other words, it is appropriate, as discussed in Chapter 5, to counsel witnesses as to their courtroom demeanor and appearance (including attire and grooming), but it is never ethical to coach a witness as to what to testify.[32] For example, if in a mock trial, the mock jurors do not believe the defendant's testimony about the incident that is the basis for the charge, it would violate ethical standards to have the defendant change his story for the real jury and testify to a version that the lawyer believes to be false.[33] Likewise, if the victim's version of the crime is not credible to the mock jury, then it would be extremely unethical for the prosecution to advise the victim to change her story. This would not only be a fraud on the court and suborning perjury, but would also violate the prosecutor's primary duty of seeking justice. On the other hand, if a witness does not come across as credible because the witness hesitates too long before answering, mumbles, fidgets, sits

[29] *Id.*

[30] *Id.*

[31] Moore v. Kemp, 809 F.2d 702, 709 (11th Cir. 1987).

[32] MODEL RULES OF PROF'L CONDUCT R. 3.4(b).

[33] *Id.* at 3.3(a)(3).

back with his arms crossed, looks away from the attorney and jury, comes across as hostile or arrogant, or a myriad of other ways of not being believable, these are aspects of testifying that the lawyers ethically can, and should, advise the witness to change. Similarly, it is proper for attorneys to modify their case theories as long as doing so does not involve a fraud on the court. It would be unethical for a prosecutor to argue a theory contrary to the evidence or one that the prosecutor thinks is patently false or exaggerated, just because this theory is more persuasive to the mock jury; however, if alternative theories could ethically be consistent with the evidence, then it is permissible to alter a case theory based on the impact it has on the mock jury. Additionally, mock juries might be particularly helpful to the defense in the decision of whether the defendant should testify.

HYPO: *Oceana v. Baron*

Charles Braun, jury consultant of the Shulz Corporation, was hired by Linus Wood, an attorney representing Manfred Baron, charged with murder in the first degree and possession of a firearm. Braun assembled a mock jury to see if they were sympathetic towards Baron. Lucy, a 30-year-old woman on the jury, remarked that she did not like Baron's red shirt, facial expressions, or the twitch in his left eye. She thought this made Baron appear untrustworthy. Can Wood instruct Baron not to twitch, alter his attire, and smile more often?

Another juror, Frank, a 25-year-old man, remarked that he did not believe Baron's story. Baron claimed that he heard a knock on his door, opened it, became startled, and shot the man at the door. Frank said that he did not believe the story because the man's body was found five feet from the door, and so he doubts that Baron heard a knock. Wood instructs Baron to change his story. Wood tells Baron to claim that he was opening the door to check his mail when he was confronted by a strange man and shot him. Is this unethical?

Lastly, Sally, a 19-year-old woman on the mock jury, said that she would have been more sympathetic towards Baron if he said he had a motive for shooting the man at the door. She told jury consultant Braun that, had the man at the door been a criminal, she would be less inclined to distrust Baron and his story. Baron then decided that he would tell the jury he thought the man at the door was a registered sex offender living in the neighborhood. The attorney, Wood, decides to change his case theory accordingly. Is this ethical? Is Wood subject to discipline? Would it make a difference, if Baron tells Wood, that this actually was his motive for shooting the man, and he simply did not disclose the motive earlier, because he did not realize that his intent was relevant?

While potentially beneficial to trial preparation and presentation, jury consultant services should be reserved for cases that merit this type of expensive service. Other issues of trial preparation, such as visual aids and trial notebooks, should be utilized in all trials because even if the jury trial is not high profile or is conducted without jury consulting services, the attorneys will still have to persuade the jury. As mentioned earlier, visual aids can have an immense impact on jurors. Thus, an understanding of these tools, as well as common issues such as stipulations and judicial notice, is essential for effective trial preparation.

VISUALS

In an age of smartphones and social networking, much of society expects instant access to stimulating information. Because many have come to rely on the most up to date technology when communicating and accessing information, attention spans have tended to decrease while expectations have increased, and in truth, a compelling visual background to a case may mean the difference between conviction and acquittal. It is, for the most part, against this backdrop that attorneys must vie for the attention of the modern American jury. Luckily, attorneys have wide access to modern technology with which to create effective visuals. Visuals should be informed by the case theory, and attorneys should try to make them as simple and easy to understand as possible. Nevertheless, it is imperative to understand that while visuals may be interesting and effective, they do not replace connecting with the jury. Attorneys need to be mindful that there is still no replacement for looking the jury in the eyes, believing in one's case, and being persuasive. Visual aids enhance an attorney's presentation, but should not be used in place of the successful litigation techniques, such as building a persuasive case theory, discussed throughout this book.

A. ADMISSIBILITY OF VISUALS

Because illustrative exhibits are generally considered to be "demonstrative evidence," counsel should make sure that they will be admissible. Admissibility of demonstrative evidence is generally governed by judicial discretion. The Federal Rules of Evidence allow the court "reasonable control over the mode and order of interrogating witnesses and presenting evidence so as to: (1) make those procedures effective for determining the truth; (2) avoid wasting time; and (3) protect witnesses from harassment or undue embarrassment."[34] As is the case with all proffered evidence, the visual must be relevant or related to relevant evidence in order to be admissible. Additionally, the visual aid must fairly and accurately depict what it purports to represent.[35] The trial court also has discretion on the admissibility of exhibits such as diagrams, charts, and other visual aids.[36] Generally, it is the responsibility of the attorney offering the visual aid to demonstrate to the court that the exhibit will aid the trier of fact in understanding or evaluating the evidence.

Counsel should keep in mind that the probative value of the visual evidence has to be greater than the prejudicial effect. Federal Rule of Evidence 403 requires this balancing test in order to make sure, among other things, that visuals are not used solely to stir emotions in the jury.[37] For example, if counsel presents crime scene photographs that depict horrific violent images that would tend to elicit an emotional reaction from the jury, without convincing the judge that the photographs are relevant to an issue in the case, then the judge is unlikely to allow the evidence. On the other hand, if the crime scene photographs depict a specific *modus operandi* or other forensic quality despite gruesome imagery, the court will likely allow the evidence to be admitted. Generally, crime scene photographs will be allowed because, although prejudicial, typically the prejudice does not substantially outweigh the probative value. For example, the position of the victim's body when it was found is always relevant, even if the photo is bloody and upsetting to view. Likewise, the location of the victim's body, in relation to the surroundings in which it was found, is typically highly relevant. Attorneys do not need to accept a stipulation of a fact in lieu of showing photographs; indeed, it would generally be unwise for the prosecutor to accept such a stipulation, as it will make his case less powerful. For example, in a murder trial, it would be unwise for the prosecution to accept a stipulation of fact with regard to the position of the victim's body or the location of bullet holes. The court, however, has broad discretion to limit the number and size of photographs, and may order, for instance, that only black and white photographs of gruesome crime scenes be admitted, in an effort to lessen the inflammatory impact of gory photographs.

Demonstrations, and in fact all demonstratives in addition to photographs, are subject to the same rules. In *Ellis v. State*, for example, the prosecution displayed the trousers and shoes of a deceased victim over a chair positioned directly in front of the jury. The shoes were placed on the floor directly below the trousers, making it appear as if the victim were seated in the chair. The trial judge explicitly admonished the prosecutor to rearrange the clothing so as to not face the jury in such a fashion.[38] The category which a visual aid falls under does not have bearing on its admissibility. In *Lillie v. United States*, the court held

---

[34] FED. R. EVID. 611.

[35] Scheble v. Missouri Clean Water Comm'n, 734 S.W.2d 541, 555 (Mo. Ct. App. 1987).

[36] United States v. Crockett, 49 F.3d 1357, 1360 (8th Cir. 1995).

[37] FED. R. EVID. 611. *See* People v. Chavez, 329 P.2d 907, 916 (Cal. 1958) (holding that gruesome photographs "should be excluded where their principal effect would be to inflame the jurors . . . [but] if they have a probative value . . . that outweighs the danger of prejudice to the defendant, they are admissible, and the resolution of this question is primarily for the trial court in the exercise of its discretion"); State v. Farley, 290 P.2d 987, 992 (Wash. 1955) (holding that "[p]ictures that accurately represent the true state or condition of the thing depicted, are admissible if they have probative value upon some element of the crime charged").

[38] Ellis v. State, 651 P.2d 1057, 1063 (Okla. Crim. App. 1982).

that the distinction between types of visual aids is semantic and anything that "helps the fact finder determine what the truth is and assimilate evidence" can be considered admissible evidence.[39] Indeed, visual aids are an area of trial preparation where it behooves litigators to be creative. Generally, limitations regarding the use of visual aids are an area in which trial judges are given wide discretion.

B. Types of Visuals

1. Physical evidence

Physical evidence is a highly effective visual aid that can have a great impact on the jury. For example, producing a murder weapon in court can connect the jury to the reality of the crime. Caution must be used, however, when weapons are brought into the court. The attorneys should seek permission from the judge and bailiff if handing a weapon to a witness (especially the defendant), and it is unlikely that a judge would permit an attorney to allow a defendant charged with a serious or violent offense to handle a weapon in the courtroom. Additionally, it is imperative, if bringing a gun into the courtroom, to make sure that the court bailiff has checked the gun to ensure that it is unloaded, and this fact should be brought to the attention of the judge and put on the record. One of the surest ways to anger a judge is to handle a gun in court without first notifying the judge that the bailiff has determined that the gun is unloaded.

Physical evidence can also be used as exculpatory evidence. For example, if shoe-prints were left at the scene of a crime, counsel may use the shoe-print casts to show that the defendant's feet are too large to have created the prints. One well known example of such evidence is the glove recovered from the crime scene of the Nicole Brown Simpson and Ronald Goldman murders. In court, OJ Simpson tried on the glove, which famously, did not fit.

2. Images

Images can be used to portray victims, defendants, or illustrate crime scenes and any other details that would be beneficial to depict for a jury. A picture can impart insight into a detail or moment that counsel wishes to convey. For example, photographs of a crime scene might show the jury pertinent details of a location better than a description could. As such, images are particularly versatile, and counsel can use diagrams, photographs, illustrations, or any other pertinent imagery to support the case theme. Typically, the image will be enlarged and placed on an easel, so witnesses and attorneys can point to aspects of the visual, or mark on it. Sometimes transparencies are placed over the image, allowing each witness to mark the exhibit separately as part of their testimony. These images are not only helpful in terms of holding the jurors' attention, but also for clarifying aspects of witnesses' testimony.

While this book examines pretrial advocacy, as opposed to trial techniques to be used during trial, it is crucial for attorneys to be aware of the fact that carefully preparing exhibits and going over them with witnesses before the trial is a fundamental aspect of trial preparation. Some images are so persuasive that they may even be useful tools when trying to negotiate a case settlement. For instance, a photograph showing that the location and position of a gun relative to the decedent's body, along with a suicide note,

---

[39] Lillie v. United States, 953 F.2d 1188, 1190 (10th Cir. 1992).

and a statement from a forensic expert that it is likely that the death was a suicide, might persuade a prosecutor to drop or to reduce murder charges. Or perhaps, a diagram drawn by a witness, accompanied by crime scene photographs, will convince the prosecution or defense that they would be better off settling instead of risking a trial. The point is that visuals are an essential aspect of trial preparation, and their usefulness is not limited to the actual trial.

3. Re-creations and Reenactments

While planning for trial, an attorney will have to consider what kinds of visuals will better suit her needs. Because an attorney can convey more information with a re-creation than with a static image, she may elect to create a re-creation even though it will likely require more preparation. A re-creation depicts a scene and may demonstrate the manner in which counsel believes a crime occurred. This is typically accomplished through the aid of computer software. For example, in a hit and run case, the prosecution may present a 3D animation of a truck colliding with a parked car and then speeding off. Re-creations have been held admissible, given that the re-creation is authenticated, relevant, and not unduly prejudicial.[40] Counsel can use re-creations when mere images are not enough to convey a dynamic scenario in a crime. This may involve motion or a complicated sequence of events that is better portrayed in video.

Like re-creations, reenactments can also depict a scene and may demonstrate how an alleged crime occurred. As the case moves closer to trial, the preparation of visual aids will and should begin to crystallize. Both sides will have to consider admissibility issues and how far they can ethically push those limitations. For example, the prosecution especially may be keen to present a reenactment of an alleged crime. In *People v. Rodrigues*, the police made a videotape the day after a murder occurred. The neighbor of the victim aided the taping, and ultimately the reenactment depicted a man standing in for the defendant and showed him running off in the same direction that the assailant had run.[41] Although counsel did not make the videotape, they strategically relied on it as a reenactment. When counsel seeks to admit such demonstrative aids, they will need to lay a foundation showing the accuracy of the scenes as what was witnessed.[42] Matters that would be appropriate for the court to consider include lighting, soundtrack, suggestive figures, and vantage points. Thus, the court must determine if the reenactment is a reasonable representation of what it alleges to portray without misleading jurors.[43]

Reenactments can also be useful in efforts to settle a case. The Los Angeles County Sheriff's department created a reenactment video in its investigation of a vehicular manslaughter case that was being prosecuted in Malibu, California in 2006. In that case, it was undisputed that the defendant had accidentally run over the victim with his car while the victim was crossing the street in a cross walk. Vehicular manslaughter, however, requires the prosecution to prove that the defendant violated a law. Upon filing

---

[40] Harris v. State, 13 P.3d 489, 495 (Okla. Crim. App. 2000).

[41] People v. Rodrigues, 885 P.2d 1, 25 (Cal. 1995).

[42] *Id.* (citing People v. Boyd, 271 Cal. Rptr. 738 (Cal. Ct. App. 1990)).

[43] *Id.* at 26.

the case, the prosecution theorized that the defendant violated the vehicle code by failing to yield to the pedestrian using a crosswalk. Upon investigating the case further, the diligent detective began to question whether the victim, who was wearing beige-colored clothing, would have been visible against the background of beige mountains at sunset (the time of the fatal accident). In this particular case, the defendant was not drinking alcohol, speeding, texting, or otherwise distracted. To his credit, the detective made a video of a police officer dressed in beige clothing crossing the same street at sunset and it was apparent from the video reenactment that it was not reasonable to have expected the driver to have observed the pedestrian given the circumstances. After viewing the video, the prosecution moved to dismiss the case and co-author Terry Adamson, who was the judicial officer presiding over the case, granted that motion and dismissed the case. This is an example of the impact that reenactment visuals can have on a case, and also provides an example of the prosecution recognizing that its duty is to seek justice, as opposed to obtain convictions, regardless of the circumstances of a particular case.

4. Summary Slides

In general, counsel uses visual aids that summarize information for the jury during the opening or closing statements, and the trial court has discretion on the admissibility of such visuals. As such, summary visuals are limited only by admissibility and counsel's imagination; however, attorneys should never use summary visuals unless it serves a specific function, and counsel should keep in mind the utility of any visuals. For example, in a case with numerous defendants, counsel may present a photograph of each defendant, the charges they are facing, and how they contributed to the specific crimes that were committed. This type of visual can be useful to clarify what might otherwise be confusing to the jury and judge. Further, if jury instructions for a particular case present nuanced issues, then counsel may list the elements of the jury instructions during their closing arguments so as to reiterate and clarify the issues for the jury.

C. EFFECTIVE VISUALS

It should go without saying that visuals should be simple and easy to understand because jurors are faced with a barrage of information in the courtroom. They must listen to the attorneys and the witnesses, all the while keeping track of their own thoughts and notes. Visuals should serve to clarify or to explain points being made in the courtroom. Attorneys should avoid pitfalls like a wall of text, which forces jurors to read intently as well as listen to the court proceedings. Of course, different types of visuals require various levels of detail. A summary slide at the opening will impart far less information than a scene re-creation during direct examination. Litigators must always be mindful of not only what information they are trying to convey, but also how a juror will receive that information. Visuals need to be made large enough so that all of the jurors and alternates can see them. Part of trial preparation also encompasses planning how to position the visuals in a manner in which the jury will easily be able to see them. When possible, counsel should view the courtroom before the trial to understand its layout. They might want to make note of the location of the witness stand in relation to the jury box as well as the availability of easels and whiteboards. Part of trial preparation includes bringing necessary materials to court, such as markers and an easel if they are not provided.

1. Visuals and the Case Theory

Visuals should reinforce the case theory, and each piece of visual information presented to the jury should reflect the case theme. If the theory revolves around self-defense, then visuals that focus on this aspect of the trial will be the most effective. For instance, if the defendant, in an attempted murder case, is much smaller than the alleged victim, photographs or other demonstrative evidence showing the size disparity can aid a self-defense theory. It might be effective to have the victim stand and have the defendant stand so that the jurors can see their relative height difference. Since such demonstrations do not involve testimonial evidence, defendants do not have a Fifth Amendment right to refuse to cooperate.[44]

2. Tools

There is a plethora of tools to aid in the creation of visuals. While an analog approach of whiteboards and markers is certainly acceptable, visuals that have been created in advance present the jury with an air of preparation and conviction. Also, one must be mindful of the technology present in the courtroom. Nearly all courtrooms will have a projector that can connect to a computer or tablet. In the event that counsel chooses to use slides of any length, they should invest in either a remote control application for a smartphone, a tablet, or a pointer remote. This will allow movement about the courtroom and engagement with the jury without being tied to the computer. For slides, the platform will largely determine which software to use. For Windows computers, Microsoft PowerPoint is a staple. For Apple computers, Keynote provides the same features.

3. Resources

http://office.microsoft.com/en-us/powerpoint/
http://www.apple.com/iwork/keynote/
http://finereader.abbyy.com/

---

[44] *See* Schmerber v. California, 384 U.S. 757, 765 (1966) (holding that, if the evidence in question does not involve a defendant's testimony or "evidence relating to some communicative act or writing by the" defendant, the defendant cannot invoke his Fifth Amendment right against self-incrimination).

Examples of Visuals

A. Opening

XYZ

Alias: X

Shooter

XYZ

Alias: Y

Driver

XYZ

Alias: Z

Lookout

B. Closing

Felony False Imprisonment

The defendant **intentionally** and unlawfully **restrained** someone by **violence** or **menace**

AND

the defendant **made** the other person **stay against** that person's **will.**

Violence: physical force that is greater than the force reasonably necessary to restrain someone.

Against a person's will: if that person does not consent to the act freely and voluntarily.

C. TIMELINES

Counsel should use a timeline if the temporal details are especially important. For example, a litigator may need to place a suspect at the scene of the crime or prove that a defendant could not have been at a particular location. Counsel should present an overview of the timeline before delving into the details. The timeline should be grounded within the framework of the rest of the case. After the backdrop to the timeline has been set, counsel should go through each point and emphasize its importance. The importance of any timestamp might be relative to another. For example, the point at which the crime was committed should be prominently highlighted. After the detailed run-through, counsel should present one more overview to solidify the timeline.

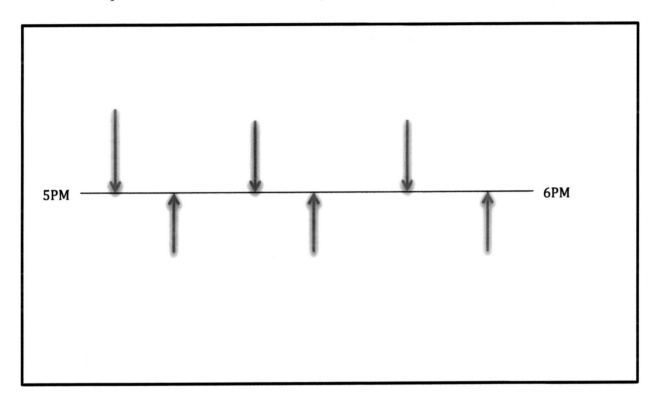

D. DIAGRAMS

Diagrams can help counsel explain complicated issues and reinforce testimony. Often times, witness testimony that describes visual events can be greatly clarified through the use of visual aids. For this reason, diagrams can be helpful during witness testimony as well as during the closing argument. Once the relevant diagram has been introduced into evidence, counsel can have the witness make notes on the diagram directly from the stand. For example, as a coroner is testifying to the location of gunshot wounds, an attorney may have the coroner annotate a human body diagram. Also, counsel may publish the diagram that was used in the coroner's report that the jury can use to follow along.

FRONT/BACK   LEFT/RIGHT

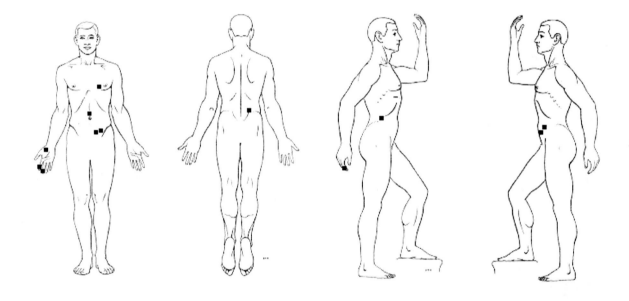

E. MAPS

Maps are important visuals for accident re-creations and logistical or geographic issues. Effective maps and accident re-creations should depict enough detail to convey relevant information but be simple enough so as not to present the jury with unnecessary information. Counsel should keep in mind that when using a map, attorneys should not add information directly onto the map, for the witness must testify and add the relevant information to the map. For example, an attorney should ask the witness to place an arrow on the map where the accident occurred, then orally recount what the witness included for the record. Once the witness has contributed testimony and marked the map, then counsel can present the exhibit as evidence during closing argument or present a re-creation that represents the same facts.

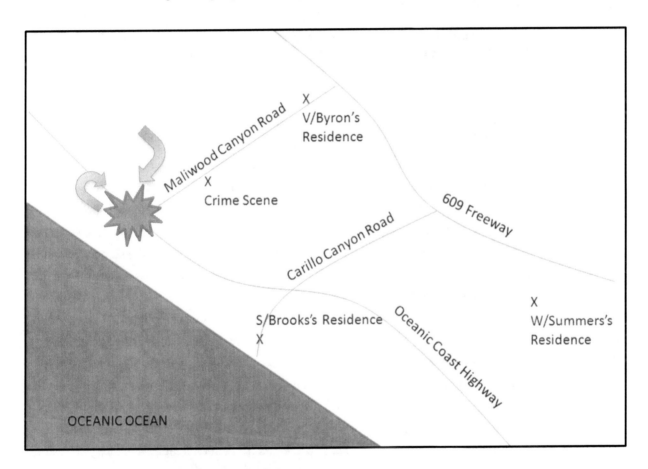

COMMON PRETRIAL CONSIDERATIONS

As important as jury consulting and the production and presentation of visuals can be for persuading the jury, so too are other common pretrial considerations that can help alleviate the complexities of trial. For example, agreements and other undisputed facts can be settled before trial; and, therefore, the judge's time and court resources can be maximized to focus on the issues in dispute. Additionally, narrowing the matters that are in dispute will allow the jurors to resume their regular lives sooner. Likewise, where visuals can aid the jury in understanding the circumstances of a given case, there are other methods of proof, such as crime scene visits, which can also impact the outcome of a case. These miscellaneous aspects of trial advocacy should be contemplated and prepared before trial.

A. STIPULATIONS

Stipulations are agreements between the lawyers. If opposing counsel stipulate to a fact, then that fact is deemed proven to the jury. Counsel can also stipulate to the admissibility of exhibits or to jury instructions, and it is common for defense attorneys to stipulate to the testimony of certain witnesses for the purposes of a preliminary hearing. For instance, instead of requiring a chemist to leave the lab and come to court, defense counsel will often stipulate to what the chemist would have testified to for the preliminary hearing stage. For example:

> Prosecutor: "Counsel, will you stipulate for the purpose of the preliminary hearing only that if called to the stand Mr. Gregory would testify that he is a chemist with the Oceana crime lab and he analyzed People's One for identification and determined it to contain cocaine?"

> Defense Counsel: "So stipulated for the purpose of the preliminary hearing only."

Generally, stipulations are worked out before they are put on the record in open court. It is worth noting that it is unethical for an attorney to indicate that she will stipulate to a fact or witness, and then renege on the stipulation. Once a stipulation has been entered into, in other words, the fact stipulated to is no longer a contested issue in the trial. Generally, it is up to the attorneys whether they want to enter into an agreement that becomes a stipulation. Likewise, in most instances, the court has the authority whether to accept an offer of a stipulation and thus find that a fact has been proven. When this happens, there is no reason for opposing counsel to offer any evidence to prove that fact. There are some circumstances, however, when it is considered an abuse of discretion not to accept a proposed stipulation. For example, if an element of proof of an offense or allegation is that the defendant has a particular prior conviction, this is a simple fact that is either true or not true. If the defense offers to stipulate that it is true, then it may be an abuse of discretion if the court refuses to accept this stipulation and allows the prosecution the authority to admit the full record of the conviction.[45] It is often the case, however, that an attorney has the choice of whether to enter into a stipulation. It is often wiser to prove each aspect of one's case, rather than lessen the impact of evidence by agreeing to a stipulation. For example, it is rarely wise at the trial stage to accept a stipulation that a witness is an expert in their field. While such stipulations are common at preliminary hearings, they should rarely be entered into in a jury trial. Generally, it is the better strategy to have the expert testify as to all of his credentials and background as to a particular subject and impress the jury with his knowledge. Likewise, it rarely behooves the prosecutor to stipulate to an element of proof when they can show photographs that will have a substantial emotional impact on the jurors. Proving one's case is largely a matter of persuading the jury, and it is rarely accomplished by entering into a dry recitation of uncontested aspects of a case.

---

[45] Old Chief v. United States, 519 U.S. 172 (1997).

HYPO: *Oceana v. Baritone*

Tony Baritone is accused of murdering rival organized crime figure Joey "the Bulldozer" Lugano. The prosecution's case theory is that Baritone crushed Joey's head with a sledgehammer, then took photographs of the smashed head and sent it to the rival gang with a note that read, "Now who is the Bulldozer?" The prosecution's theory is that Baritone wanted to intimidate Lugano's gang into leaving the area, and that the photograph proves Baritone's motive for murder. The defense argues that per FRE 403, the prejudice of the gruesome photograph of Lugano's pulverized and bloody head substantially outweighs any probative value of the image. The defense offers to stipulate that the cause of death was homicide due to the victim's head being smashed. The defendant does not dispute that Lugano was murdered, but denies that he is the one who committed the crime. Defense counsel argues to the judge that the cause of death is not in dispute and that the prosecution only wants to inflame the jurors by showing them the graphic photograph.

Should the prosecutor accept the defense stipulation to the cause of death in lieu of using the photograph as an exhibit? If not, what should the prosecution argue in order to show the jury the photograph and admit it into evidence as an exhibit? How should the judge rule?

What if the photograph depicted knife wounds to a murder victim and the defense offers to stipulate to the cause of death, location of, and number of knife wounds? Would it generally be wise for the prosecutor to accept this stipulation? For what reasons would a photograph of knife wounds on a decedent be relevant? Should photographs of homicide victims generally be allowed into evidence over defense objections? What can the court do to limit the inflammatory impact of these types of images? Does the court have discretion to limit the size and number of these types of photographs? Does the court have authority to limit the prosecution to showing graphic photographs in black and white?

B. CRIME SCENE VIEWS

In unusual cases, when warranted, judges may allow a jury to view a crime scene as part of an attorney's case presentation. When this viewing occurs, the entire jury (including alternates), the judge, the prosecutor, the defense attorney, the defendant, court reporter, bailiff, clerk, and other security personnel, all view the scene together. There is statutory authority for crime scene views in many states, but such field trips are uncommon. Because such views are expensive and time consuming, the burden is on the proponent of the view to show the judge why the viewing is necessary. In addition to being expensive and time consuming, crime scene views also present significant security issues. In unusual cases, such as the OJ Simpson case, the judge may grant such a request. If an attorney desires to have the jurors visit the crime scene, this is something that should be worked out well before the trial begins. Any crime scene viewing involves logistics, such as security personnel provided for the judge, jurors, attorneys, and others who attend the viewing. Often, transportation such as a court bus must also be arranged. Additionally, it is likely that the judge will want to view the scene with the attorneys before the jurors have a chance to visit the scene in order to make sure that it is relevant and not too prejudicial. All of this requires time and careful planning, which is why it is a matter that should be addressed pretrial. Typically, these requests are denied because there are other methods of demonstration, such as models and photographs.

In fact, a model was used in the high-publicity multiple murder trial, *People v. Chinh & Chan* (known as the "Chinatown" case) tried in downtown Los Angeles, California in 1988.[46] In that case, a large model of the jewelry store that was the scene of the robbery was built to scale with intricate details. It was brought into the courtroom and included dollhouse-like furniture and figurines, which witnesses could use to describe the confusing ballistic events that resulted in multiple gun battles, numerous deaths and injuries, and even the death of a police officer. Since the Chinatown case involved multiple robbers and victims who were armed and engaged in a violent gun battle, it was crucial for the prosecution to prove who was shooting whom and from what location within the store. Thus, the model was helpful for witnesses to demonstrate their testimony. The Chinatown case also made use of life size "dummies" with stick type devises protruding from body parts to aid in the expert witnesses' explanations of the trajectory of bullets. Attorneys for both the prosecution and the defense should be creative about using demonstrative exhibits, and judges are given wide latitude regarding the admission of such exhibits.

C. JUDICIAL NOTICE

If an attorney needs to prove a point that is an undisputed fact, she can request the court to take judicial notice of it. Federal Rule of Evidence 201 allows this when facts are "generally known" in the community or "capable of accurate and ready determination by resort to sources whose accuracy cannot reasonably be questioned." For example, an attorney can ask the court to take judicial notice that a certain date fell on a particular day of the week. Thus, if a crime occurred on December 28, 2011, the attorney might ask, "Your honor, would the court take judicial notice that December 28, 2011 fell on a Wednesday?" Alternatively, other undisputed issues, such as the general time that the sun sets in a certain geographic area on a particular day, or the fact that sixteen ounces is the same measurement as one pound, might be matters where the court will take judicial notice. Typically attorneys will request a court to take judicial notice of a fact once the trial is already underway; however, as with other aspects of trial preparation, attorneys should be thinking of issues, such as matters that they might request a court to take judicial notice of, well in advance of trial. An important method of keeping track of the myriad issues that arise in a jury trial, such as requesting stipulations, the use of visual aids, and judicial notice, is to prepare a trial notebook.

TRIAL NOTEBOOK

In addition to the previously discussed miscellany of pretrial advocacy, the production of trial notebooks can also be a constructive use of an attorney's preparation time. In complex cases, a trial notebook is practically essential for organization purposes, and it is advantageous to make one for most cases. The trial notebook needs to have separate sections for each witness, and the pages should be numbered for quick reference. They are especially helpful in preparing for direct and cross-examination.

---

[46] Co-author Terry Adamson prosecuted this case. While this case is not published, for the sake of clarity, it will be referred to as *California v. Chinh & Chan* throughout the text.

For example, during cross-examination, in order to impeach a witness who testified contrary to a prior statement, a trial notebook allows an attorney to quickly reference the witness's prior statement. While complex cases require more elaborate trial notebooks, the basics for a trial notebook include:

A. An Index

Counsel should use an index to organize their binder and allow easy access to relevant information.

B. Witness Statements Separated by Tabs

Witness statements are key tools for a case. These statements can influence everything about a trial, from the case theory to closing arguments. Having each witness statement separated by tabs allows a litigator to cross reference facts and testimony.

C. Preliminary Hearing Transcript

The preliminary hearing transcript should be used to solidify an attorney's case as well as discern opposing counsel's weaknesses. As a prosecutor, often times the attorney that proceeds to trial is different from the one that conducted the preliminary hearing. Because of this, a firm grasp on the preliminary hearing transcript is essential. A prosecutor should refer back to the preliminary hearing transcript often to make sure everything on the record is consistent with the current case framework. Familiarity with the transcript will allow litigators to attack the credibility of witnesses when they stray from the record. The preliminary hearing transcript is often an effective source of impeaching witnesses on cross-examination.

D. Police Reports and Supplemental Reports

Police reports and supplemental reports are the backbone to most criminal proceedings. Case theory will largely be developed from the investigation that the police conducted. The prosecution should bolster and support the police report with its own research and findings. The defense should find as many holes and weaknesses in the police report as possible to cast doubt on the charges. Witness statements from police reports are frequently used to impeach witnesses on cross-examination.

E. Lab Results

Lab data is often introduced as evidence in cases. Counsel should keep all the lab reports in one place in order to scrutinize or to reconcile the conclusions with the case theory.

F. Exhibits

Counsel should be well aware of all the exhibits that will be used in a case. It is important to remain flexible and yet plan out a string of compelling exhibits that support the case theory. This includes any exhibits an attorney intends to use in her opening or closing argument, as well as any digital presentations planned.

G. <u>Evidentiary Issues</u>

This section should include motions, such as a Motion to Suppress, and the relevant points and authorities. Furthermore, it is important to keep track of planned evidence and anticipate the objections the other side will have. Counsel should include the relevant legal foundation for evidence so as not to be caught off guard.

H. <u>Case Theory & Theme</u>

Attorneys should spend a significant portion of their time developing the case theory and theme. Counsel should use this section to brainstorm the direction of the entire trial, which will help the attorney, who must develop a theme that can carry over throughout the entire trial.

I. <u>Witness List</u>

It is important for counsel to maintain a witness list not only to keep track of planned witnesses, but also to consolidate contact information that will allow an attorney to get in touch with witnesses.

J. <u>To-Do List</u>

A trial is a constant juggling act. Counsel should keep a to-do list in order to remain organized. An attorney cannot forget anything with the stakes as high as they are in a criminal proceeding.

K. <u>Complaint, Information, or Indictment</u>

The complaint is the starting point of a case. Litigators should keep this archived for charging issues as well as to aid in finding the relevant jury instructions.

L. <u>Motions *in Limine*</u>

Motions *in limine* should be archived in this section.

M. <u>Opening Statement</u>

In preparing for the opening statement, attorneys should keep all relevant information in this section. It will help attorneys collect their thoughts and serve as an archive during the composition of the closing argument.

N. <u>Closing Argument</u>

When crafting a closing argument, counsel should flip through the entire notebook to get a recap of the case. This process will allow a litigator to detail the big picture, as well as include pertinent details. Since the closing argument acts as a summary, a well-organized trial notebook goes a long way in clarifying the guideposts of the trial.

O. Jury Profiling Notes

Well before trial starts, trial lawyers should be strategizing the types of jurors that they want on the case and the types of jurors that they do not want to be selected for the case. While some individuals are generally more pro-prosecution or pro-defense, jury profiling entails determining what type of juror would be best suited for a particular type of case given the charges, defendant, victim, and/or other witnesses. Attorneys can create charts or lists delineating factors in a potential jury that are ideal or harmful to their case theory. Attorneys are allowed wide discretion in their peremptory challenges to excuse jurors, as long as they do not try to exclude a class of people based on race, gender, or other types of ethnic discrimination.[47]

P. Jury Selection Notes

Detailed notes on the jury will allow an attorney to argue a case better to specific jurors. If counsel keeps track of the answers of individual jurors during *voir dire*, then those insights will prove invaluable for any adjustments that need to be made to the case theory or theme.

Q. Jury Selection Chart

Litigators should use this section to organize the jury selection chart. Typically, this chart is made with a piece of paper and Post-its delineating potential and selected jurors. Tablet computers, however, such as the iPad, have applications that allow the process to be streamlined through software.

R. Jury Instructions

The jury instructions should inform the entire case. Counsel should make sure to get a copy of the sample jury instructions for the client's charges. Also, this section should be used when researching and presenting a set of jury instructions for the judge to decide upon.

DIGITAL TRIAL NOTEBOOK

Attorneys should consider using a digital trial notebook. Documents can be scanned using OCR (optical character recognition), and instead of organizing by tabs, relevant documents can be put into computer folders. This will allow counsel to have an indexed, searchable archive of all the documents. For example, if counsel wants to search for instances where Mary is mentioned in the preliminary hearing, a search highlighting all the instances of "Mary" can be conducted within the preliminary hearing transcript. Furthermore, if counsel would like to turn to the eighth page of the preliminary hearing, it is much faster to open a computer file than to open a physical binder and turn to the page. Attorneys should experiment with various technologies and methods of organizing a case and adopt the methods that suit

---

[47] *See* Batson v. Kentucky, 476 U.S. 79, 89–95 (1986) (holding that "the Equal Protection Clause forbids the prosecutor to challenge potential jurors solely on account of their race," and that "a defendant may make a prima facie showing of purposeful racial discrimination in selection of the venire by relying solely on the facts concerning its selection *in his case*").

their skills and style the best. Lastly, a trial notebook is an attorney's work product. A trial notebook is not subject to discovery, rather it is a tool that a litigator uses to organize a case.

The crucial aspect of all of these pretrial considerations is that they are tools to aid attorneys in their quest to be fully prepared for litigation. In our adversarial criminal justice system, the attorney who is the most prepared has a distinct advantage. As basketball coach Bobby Knight put it, "the will to succeed is important, but what's more important is the will to prepare." Thorough preparation enhances a trial lawyer's confidence and vastly improves her chances of obtaining a positive case outcome.

SUMMARY

Jury consultants have become more prevalent as the importance of jury selection has become more apparent. There are a variety of services provided by jury consulting firms, and these include focus groups, mock trials, and shadow juries. A focus group consists of a group of people who closely match the jury pool. A part of the case is presented to the group in order to garner feedback and precipitate changes in strategy. A more extensive tool is a mock trial. Mock trials are mini-trials, which allow attorneys to see the key issues within a case. While focus groups and mock trials take place pretrial, shadow juries are used during the actual trial and provide ongoing feedback to the trial team. The use of jury consultants does not need to be disclosed to the judge or opposing counsel, but with the additional information garnered through jury consultants, it is paramount that attorneys do not run afoul of the ethical rules. Jury consultant services can help attorneys formulate cases theories, decide which witnesses to call, modify opening statements and closing arguments, and decide whether it would be more advantageous to settle the case.

While selecting the right jury is important, it is equally vital to know what presentation will best appeal to that specific group. Counsel should prepare visuals that will be appealing to their jury and present this case in a simple and persuasive manner. At the same time, visuals should reinforce the case theory and reflect the case theme. Visuals should compliment the presentation, however, and should not be relied upon in the absence of a compelling case.

In order to spare court resources and the jury's time, there are some common pretrial considerations that counsel should take into consideration. For example, stipulations, crime scene views, and judicial notice can be determined before trial. Stipulations are agreements between the two sides that are generally worked out before they are put on the record. Crime scene views are based upon a judge's discretion and are fairly rare. At times, a judge may take judicial notice of generally known facts. Together, these considerations can reduce delays by settling issues that are not necessarily contested.

Finally, an attorney can organize her case and thoughts by putting together a trial notebook. The use of a trial notebook allows all the information in a trial to be readily accessible. In it, counsel should include, among other things, an index, the preliminary hearing transcript, exhibits, a to-do list, the opening statement, the closing argument, and the jury instructions. Although these miscellaneous issues of pretrial advocacy do not on their own comprise the major phases of pretrial preparation, they can nonetheless be determining factors in the outcome of a case.

CHECKLIST

✓ In addition to the principal phases of pretrial advocacy, there are many other ways that an attorney can prepare for a case. For example, the use of jury consultants, visual aids, stipulations, judicial notice, and trial notebooks can also have a decisive impact on a case.

✓ Jury consultants are growing in popularity and can be used in both civil and criminal trials. Usually, however, they are used in particularly complex, high-profile, or particularly significant trials.

✓ In a federal prosecution, counsel may make a request for jury consultants when representing an indigent defendant under the Criminal Justice Act of 1964; however, indigent defendants are not necessarily entitled to a jury consultant at the public's expense.

✓ Ideally, a jury consultant will evaluate prospective jurors and help eliminate those that would be unlikely to be persuaded by counsel. They might handout questionnaires to jurors or research their backgrounds, but generally consultants will rely on sciences, like psychology, in order to determine if a juror is suitable.

✓ In addition to jury selection, jury consultants offer a variety of other services, which include the use of focus groups, mock trials, and shadow juries. Before trial, a consultant might put together a focus group or a mock trial. A shadow jury, on the other hand, is used during trial.

✓ A focus group consists of a small group of people, whose demographics have been matched to the jury pool. They are asked about their perceptions and opinions of the case. Mock trials, on the other hand, are basically mini-trials. After the case is presented, the mock trial deliberates and provides feedback on the issues presented in the case.

✓ A shadow jury consists of individuals who are "matched" to the actual people that comprise the jury. They observe ongoing trials and provide immediate feedback to the trial team on a daily basis.

✓ Attorneys do not need permission from opposing counsel or a judge to utilize a jury consultant or their services.

✓ While jury consultant services are expensive and not used in all trials, visual aids, stipulations, judicial notice, and trial notebooks should be utilized in all trials.

✓ Attorneys can and should use the most up to date technology when making visuals to present before the jury, but such visual aids should also be easy to understand, persuasive, and informed by the case theory. Moreover, counsel should make sure that any demonstrative evidence is admissible and that their probative value will outweigh any undue prejudice.

✓ There are many different kinds of visuals that an attorney could prepare for trial. Presenting physical evidence, images, re-creations, reenactments, and summary slides can aid in presenting the case in a persuasive fashion. Timelines, diagrams, and maps can also be particularly effective visuals. Visual aids are not a substitute for connecting with the jury.

✓ If possible, counsel should view the courtroom before the trial to note its layout, the location of the witness stand, and the jury box. Counsel should also check on the availability of easels and whiteboards. If such necessary materials are not provided, then counsel should bring them to court themselves. Most courtrooms, however, will have a projector that can connect to a computer or tablet.

✓ Common pretrial considerations, such as stipulations and judicial notice, can help alleviate the complexities of trial and maximize the court's resources. When certain matters can be settled before trial, they should be. Attorneys will have less to worry about, and the jury, already subject to information overload, can be spared.

✓ A trial notebook can help attorneys stay organized. The notebook should be tabbed and the pages numbered, and it should include the following sections: an index, witness statements (each witness should be separately tabbed), preliminary hearing transcript, police and supplemental reports, lab results, exhibits, evidentiary issues, case theory and theme, witness list, to-do list, complaint/indictment, motions *in limine*, opening statement, closing argument, jury profiling notes, jury selection notes, jury selection chart, and jury instructions.

✓ Trial notebooks are particularly useful in preparing for direct and cross-examination. During cross-examination, should an attorney wish to impeach a witness, then she can quickly reference a prior statement in the notebook.

CPSIA information can be obtained
at www.ICGtesting.com
Printed in the USA
LVOW09s0053120118
562804LV00006B/61/P

9 781600 421884